The Four Talent Giants

Studies of the Walter H. Shorenstein Asia-Pacific Research Center

Andrew G. Walder, Series Editor

The Walter H. Shorenstein Asia-Pacific Research Center (APARC) in the Freeman Spogli Institute for International Studies at Stanford University sponsors interdisciplinary research on the politics, economies, and societies of contemporary Asia. This monograph series features academic and policy-oriented research by Stanford faculty and other scholars associated with the Center.

The Four Talent Giants

NATIONAL STRATEGIES FOR

HUMAN RESOURCE DEVELOPMENT

ACROSS JAPAN, AUSTRALIA, CHINA, AND INDIA

Gi-Wook Shin

Stanford University Press

Stanford, California

Stanford University Press
Stanford, California

Library of Congress Cataloging-in-Publication Data
Names: Shin, Gi-Wook, author.
Title: The four talent giants : national strategies for human resource development across Japan, Australia, China, and India / Gi-Wook Shin.
Other titles: Studies of the Walter H. Shorenstein Asia-Pacific Research Center.
Description: Stanford, California : Stanford University Press, 2025. | Series: Studies of the Walter H. Shorenstein Asia-Pacific Research Center | Includes bibliographical references and index.
Identifiers: LCCN 2024048812 (print) | LCCN 2024048813 (ebook) | ISBN 9781503642669 (cloth) | ISBN 9781503643024 (paperback) | ISBN 9781503643031 (ebook)
Subjects: LCSH: Human capital—Government policy—Case studies. | Skilled labor—Government policy—Case studies. | Manpower policy—Case studies. | Transnationalism—Economic aspects—Case studies.
Classification: LCC HD4904.7 .S439 2025 (print) | LCC HD4904.7 (ebook) | DDC 331.11—dc23/eng/20250118

LC record available at https://lccn.loc.gov/2024048812
LC ebook record available at https://lccn.loc.gov/2024048813

Cover design: Archie Ferguson

The authorized representative in the EU for product safety and compliance is: Mare Nostrum Group B.V. | Mauritskade 21D | 1091 GC Amsterdam | The Netherlands | Email address: gpsr@mare-nostrum.co.uk | KVK chamber of commerce number: 96249943

Contents

Tables and Figures

FIGURES

Preface

In the summer of 1983, I left my home country of South Korea (hereafter Korea) to attend graduate school at the University of Washington in Seattle. It was a temporary relocation, at least in my mind at that time, because I was certain that I would return to Korea upon graduation. I had never visited a foreign country before coming to the United States—in fact, it was my first time flying in an airplane. Life in the United States, not to mention the highly demanding PhD program, was new, strange, and challenging, though not without some excitement. I kept reminding myself that it would only be a temporary adjustment since I would be back on the plane to return to life in Korea after receiving my doctoral degree.

Most of my fellow Korean friends and other international students whom I had studied with went back to their home countries one by one. But despite my initial plan, I wanted to test the US job market alongside my cohort of American classmates. I was lucky enough to land a job at the University of Iowa as an assistant professor in 1991, which I could not resist, at least for the experience. Even a few years of professorship at a decent US university would promise me better job prospects in Korea when I returned.

More than three decades later, I am still in the United States, teaching at Stanford after spending three years at Iowa and then seven years at University of California, Los Angeles (UCLA), with no plans to permanently relocate to Korea. The decision to remain in a "foreign" country was not an easy one to make and took years of contemplation. Like other expats, numerous factors—including personal, professional, and institutional factors—all came into consideration.

My story is hardly unique. There are so many foreign-born professors on US campuses and immigrant professionals in industries who came to the United States for education and remained. In the School of Engineering at Stanford, for instance, about 13 percent of the faculty are from India or China. There are far more cases of this kind in Silicon Valley: Elon Musk of Tesla (South African), Sundar Pichai of Google (Indian), Eduardo Luiz Saverin of Facebook (Brazilian), and Garett Camp of Uber (Canadian), just to name a few. In 2017, 60 percent of college-educated science, technology, engineering, and mathematics (STEM) workers in Silicon Valley were reportedly foreign-born. A study by the National Foundation for American Policy finds that as of October 2018, fifty of ninety-one billion-dollar start-ups in the United States had at least one immigrant founder, and 23 percent of them had come to the United States as a student.

While going abroad, staying overseas, or returning home is ultimately an individual choice based on a number of considerations, the decision is in large part shaped by the broader social, cultural, economic, and even geopolitical contexts. That means that individual choices are not isolated, and there must be some sociological patterns that we can identify. Otherwise, it would be difficult to explain why few Japanese leave their country for study or work, whereas a large number of Chinese students study overseas and then return.

These patterns raise several complex—scholarly, practical, and policy—questions for both the home and host countries of this mobile talent. For example, am I a case of brain drain for Korea? That is a central question for many developing countries who lose their top talent to more advanced nations. Relatedly, why are some countries more attractive to foreign talent than others? Is it primarily due to job markets / economies, language, cultures, or something else? How do nations train and retrain their talent or bring them back from overseas while simultaneously inviting talent from the outside? Does transnational competition for talent have to be a zero-sum game, or are there ways to make it a win-win game for all the countries involved? That is, can I still contribute to Korea while staying in the United States?

This study seeks to address these questions regarding transnational talent flows from historical and comparative perspectives by looking at four leading Asia-Pacific nations—Japan, Australia, China, and India—from the period of their economic rise to the present. As human capital has become more transnational with increased mobility, this study has contemporary relevance and policy implications beyond scholarly merit.

This book is truly a product of collective efforts with my students (current and former, undergraduate and graduate) and colleagues at Stanford and elsewhere. First, there are so many students who tirelessly worked as research assistants for the book project over the last several years. They are Fedelle Austria, Matias Benitez, Brook Beyer, Sean Chen, Vineet Gupta, Margaret Hong, Zhenqi Hu, Elise Jiang, Dylan Junkin, Elisa Kim, Yoojung Lee, Sievlan Len, Jorge Nam, Jeongeun Park, Emily Yu Wan, Maleah Webster, Mengmeng Xiao, and Yiguo Zheng. Dexter Simpson, an undergraduate student majoring in film, suggested making a documentary, titled *Brain Bridges*, based on our research on global talent and transnational bridging and did a wonderful job.

I express special appreciation to the three people who devoted their time and energy so that I could complete this project: Joyce Lee, Kelsi Caywood, and Haley Gordon. Kelsi and Haley also coauthored papers with me and are in doctoral programs in sociology at Michigan and Stanford, respectively. Kerstin Norris, also a student of mine in the master's program of East Asian Studies at Stanford, helped finalize the manuscript.

Many others read various chapters of the book, offering highly valuable comments and suggestions. They are Joon Nak Choi, Eve Dill, Rafiq Dossani, Rie Hiraoka, Irene Kyoung, Jenny Lee, Xinru Ma, Rennie Moon, Junki Nakahara, Kazunobu Sakuma, Makoto Shishido, Nirvikar Singh, Jitukrushna Swain, and Sana Sugita. Their expertise and experiences in a particular country or subjects greatly improved the quality of the book.

I am also very grateful to the leading scholars of higher education and migration who attended a virtual book workshop in 2022: Akiyoshi Yonezawa, a top expert on higher education in Japan; Lesleyanne Hawthorne, a leading expert on migration and active advisor for the Australian government on migration policies; Ha Wei, a leader of international higher education in China and a consultant for development agencies; David Zweig, a top expert on the talent programs of China; and Anthony D'Costa, an expert on talent development in India and Japan. Jenny Gavacs, a developmental editor, helped with the organization of the book. I would also like to thank those who agreed to be interviewed for this project, some of whom completed their interviews virtually during the pandemic. Dinsha Mistree helped introduce potential interviewees for the chapter on India.

I had an opportunity to serve as an consultant for the Asia Development Bank dealing with brain drain issues for less developed countries in Asia. I greatly benefitted from that experience of engaging development assistance and policy communities and thank Sungsup Ra, who supported the consulting project. In the summer of 2023, I had the privilege of giving a week-long lecture based on this book at the National Taiwan University in Taipei and am very grateful to my host, Pei-Chia Lan.

Parts of the chapters of this book were published in a separate article in *World Development* 184 (2024): "Toward a Portfolio Theory of Talent Development: Insights from Financial Theory, Illustrations from the Asia-Pacific" (with Haley Gordon). I am also working with current and former students to apply the framework of this study (talent portfolio theory) to other countries, such as Korea, the Philippines, Argentina, and more. I hope this book can be useful for understanding talent strategies of countries beyond the four cases.

I can't express enough of my gratitude to Changwon Chey, chairman of the Foundation Academia Platonica, who understands the value of academic research. His generous support of the New Asia Project at the Asia-Pacific Research Center (APARC) not only was instrumental to producing this research outcome but also led to an exciting new endeavor, the Stanford Next Asia Policy Lab, that I launched in the summer of 2023. All these exciting projects could not have happened without his friendship, trust, and support for over a decade. I would also like to acknowledge the Korea Foundation for an intermediary role in supporting this book project.

Finally, Dan LoPreto, my editor at Stanford University Press (SUP), and my colleague Andy Walder, the APARC series editor with SUP, greatly helped facilitate the review and publication process. Likewise, constructive comments from the two readers for this manuscript that they secured helped clarify many parts of the book. My team at APARC, especially Heather Ahn, George Krompacky, Kristen Lee, and Noa Ronkin, all supported this project. Laura J. Vollmer's meticulous copyediting has polished and brought this book to life.

Last but not least, I would like to acknowledge my lifelong "debt" to Mee-Sun. Like myself, she never imagined staying for this long in the United States when we married in 1987. She gave me unwavering support and trust throughout my life—never complaining while I kept moving from Seattle to Iowa City to LA to Palo Alto—and raised three wonderful children: Kelley, Ashley, and William. When I was struggling to decide on whether to return to Korea or stay in the United States, she said, "Honey, make up your mind. I will support whatever you decide to do." Without the unconditional support of my family, I wouldn't be here today. Thank you all!

The Four Talent Giants

ONE

Talent in the Asia-Pacific Century

The rise of Asia-Pacific nations as economic powerhouses since the second half of the twentieth century has been truly phenomenal. Led by Japan, followed by the "Four Little Dragons"— Korea, Taiwan, Hong Kong, and Singapore—and now China and India, the region's economic power is ever growing. The more remote Asia-Pacific nations of Australia and New Zealand have also been integrated into the region through economic, educational, cultural, and social exchanges and interactions. According to the International Monetary Fund (IMF), the gross domestic product (GDP) of Asia and the Pacific (USD 38,870 billion) far exceeds that of North America (30,730 billion) and Europe (24,880 billion) as of 2023.[1]

Today, China, Japan, and India are among the top-five economies in the world, and Korea, Australia, and Indonesia belong to the top twenty in terms of GDP.[2] Despite a relatively small population size, Australia is third in terms of wealth per adult, and Singapore is a top-ten nation in GDP per capita in the world. Led by China and Japan, Asia accounts for two-thirds of the total exports in the world. China and India have become two of the world's main suppliers of talent—in the forms of skilled workers and international students. Once stricken with colonialism, war, national division, and poverty, the Asia-Pacific has become a global center of economic dynamism, and the twenty-first century is lauded as the Asia-Pacific century.[3]

While the ascendance of these Asia-Pacific nations has received a great deal of scholarly research and policy attention,[4] less studied are their divergent paths to success. Routes to development among those Asia-Pacific

powers were not uniform but significantly varied, reflecting their historical, cultural, and geopolitical differences. For example, Australia and Japan
were incorporated into the capitalist world system much earlier than India
and China. Japan was a colonial power that occupied Korea and Taiwan,
while India, Singapore, and Australia were all distinctively influenced by
the legacy of British colonization. Northeast Asian countries have homogeneous populations with developmentalist states, while Australia and India
have more diverse populations with regulatory states. There are differences
even in Northeast Asia, where domestic (or "homegrown") talent was crucial to Japan's rise, while foreign-educated talent played a key role in the
development of Korea, Taiwan, and China. Given the diversity in the history, culture, and institutions of these countries, we should expect their
developmental success to have occurred through divergent routes.

In addition, some countries have been able to sustain their development
better than others. For example, whereas Japan entered the "lost decades"
of stagnation in the 1990s after becoming the second-largest economy in the
world, Australia continued its growth free of a major recession for twenty-
seven years until COVID-19 hit the world economy. Similarly, among the
Four Little Dragons, Singapore was able to sustain its economy better than
Korea or Taiwan.[5] In fact, experts and pundits in Korea—as the country faces a demographic crisis, high household debt, and a low economic-
growth rate—have begun to ask if Korea's rise and national power have
peaked, reminiscent of a similar question that was asked about Japan thirty
years ago.[6] It remains to be seen if more recently emerging powers like
China and India can continue their economic ascendance through various
challenges—internal and external. Such variation in the long-term sustainability of development requires close research attention too.

Nonetheless, the current literature tends to overlook such variation in
developmental paths and sustainability, instead seeking to find common
"recipes" of success among Asia-Pacific powers. We need a new lens, or
framework, to explain their successes while also accounting for cross-
national variation in development and sustainability. This study takes
human resources, or "talent," as a key variable in the new framework, as its
contribution to economic growth has been well recognized but with varying degrees of success. This is because all countries must mobilize human
resources for development, but their strategies for doing so—that is, their
"talent strategies"—diverge, reflecting historical, cultural, and institutional

differences.[7] While development is a complex, long-term process that takes many different steps and iterations involving multiple actors and institutions at local, national, and global levels, this study focuses on national talent strategy in proposing the new lens.

More specifically, this study presents a new framework called talent portfolio theory (TPT) in order to explain cross-national variation in the ways and the extent to which various forms of human resources were utilized to achieve and sustain development. TPT views a nation's talent development, like financial investment, as constructing a "talent portfolio" that mixes multiple forms of talent—domestic, foreign, and diasporic—adjusting its portfolio over time to meet new risks and challenges. The new theory is applied to explaining not only the emergence of Asia-Pacific powers but also their evolution over time from a comparative perspective. This study has both scholarly merits and policy relevance as its framework can be generalized beyond the four cases examined here and its findings have policy implications for other countries—in particular, for less developed countries.

Human Resources and the Rise of the Asia-Pacific Nations

Several theories have been posited to explain the rise of Asia-Pacific nations, but they tend to focus on identifying common formulas of success. Such focus inherently limits analytical power to account for cross-national variation in development and sustainability.

Advocates of "Asian values," for example, claim that the successful development of many East Asian economies in the post–World War II period was due to the shared culture or value of their societies, especially their Confucian heritage. These include collectivism over individualism and concentrating decision-making power in the hands of appointed officials,[8] even to the extent of soft authoritarianism. The Asian-values argument gained prevalence in the 1990s as scholars in the West and policymakers in East Asia, such as the Singaporean leader Lee Kuan Yew, advocated a set of values that were viewed as distinctively "Asian," in contrast to Western liberal ones, as critical to development. However, this argument lacks clarity on what constitutes "Asian" values as the countries to which it is often applied—Japan and the Four Little Dragons—also differ greatly from one another, let alone from other countries in the region, such as Australia, India, and Indonesia. Moreover, Asian values are alleged to have become an obstacle for the new knowledge economy, which requires a more creative and flexible labor force in a globalized world unable to sustain development.[9]

Another line of research presents a more historical explanation by focusing on how colonial legacies stimulated development in the region. Some scholars argue that Japan's colonial rule, for example, enabled industrial development in Korea and Taiwan after 1945,[10] while others note that British colonial rule left a lasting impact on the economic practices of places like Hong Kong, Australia, and New Zealand.[11] However, many former colonies in the region—such as Cambodia and Myanmar—remain underdeveloped, suggesting a negligible or even adverse impact of colonialism in some cases. The track record of colonialism in leading to development thus remains mixed at best.

It is also posited that nationalism or national identity played a key role in economic development. As P. Duara points out, nationalism has been used as the rationale for development in many parts of Asia,[12] and Japan's defensive modernization and Korea's modernization of the fatherland well capture the nationalist tone of development. However, nationalism also hurt development in such cases as North Korea and China under Mao. In addition, Asia-Pacific nations have greatly different conceptions of national identity, and not all are geared toward development in the same way as the ethnic nationalisms of Japan and Korea.[13] In India and Indonesia, for instance, religion plays an important role in the formation of national identity—a far cry from a nationalism entwined with developmentalism. On the other hand, Australia and Singapore have embraced multiculturalism, which has been instrumental to their developmental success. Multiculturalism also has been more effective in sustaining development than ethnic nationalism during the fourth industrial revolution, which requires diversity and innovation.

In a similar vein, the developmental state has been viewed as instrumental to economic growth in several Asian nations.[14] In his seminal book *MITI and the Japanese Miracle*, Chalmers Johnson defines the "developmental state" as a state that is focused on economic development and takes necessary policy measures to accomplish that objective. He stresses that Japan's industrial development had much to do with farsighted intervention by bureaucrats. Japan first developed this model, which has been adopted by other countries, such as Korea, Taiwan, Singapore, and even China.[15] However, not all economic success in the region has been led by developmental states—a fact that is illustrated by the regulatory states of Australia and New Zealand, as well as the lack of a developmental role of the Indian state. Furthermore, it is noted that such an interventionist developmental model could be a liability in a globalizing world.[16]

Accordingly, these factors—cultural, historical, and institutional—have limited analytical power in explaining divergent developmental paths and sustainability across the region. In some cases, they have made a positive impact on development, but in others, they have had no impact or even a negative one. Some factors are even considered to have become an obstacle after making some initial contribution to development. Unlike these factors, however, human resources have been crucial to the rise of *all* nations but in *different* ways. That is, cultivating and maintaining a force of robust human resources empowered leading Asia-Pacific nations to catch up and even surpass the early developers of the West.[17] Yet strategies in nurturing, attracting, and utilizing talent were not uniform but varied considerably among these nations, reflecting cultural, historical, and institutional differences. Thus, this study presents a new framework based on human resources, or talent, strategies to explain cross-national variation in development and sustainability.[18]

In particular, the framework focuses on the two mechanisms of education and migration that are key to talent development. As J. F. Kirkegaard argues, "The long-term economic growth of an advanced country . . . is with certainty highly correlated with the skill level of its residents. . . . The skill level in turn depends heavily on both the education and immigration policies of the country. The combined outcome of these policies is a ready supply of high-skilled workers, which is critical for globally competing businesses."[19]

The importance of education—particularly, higher education—in developing human resources is undeniable.[20] Japan and the Four Little Dragons all built strong national educational systems that supplied the workforce needed for industrialization. In Australia and Singapore, higher education has been crucial not only for training domestic manpower but also for attracting foreign talent, who provide both financial and human capital to the country. Even India, still underdeveloped overall in education, is known for producing top-notch engineers and scientists. The renowned Indian Institutes of Technology (IITs), for example, have become a major supplier of leading software engineers to not only India but also the world.

Migration has been crucial to developmental success as well. Foreign talent constitutes a core element of the labor force in Australia and Singapore and is becoming important for Japan and Korea too. In Taiwan, Korea, and China, diasporic talent who migrated overseas for education and work experiences and then returned home played instrumental roles in advancing science and technology. The Filipino and Indian diasporas, while not returning home, contributed to the development of their home countries through remittances and knowledge partnerships. Healthy mobility of talent—whether immigration, emigration, or temporary migration—has been important.

Thus, an array of rich human resources—domestic, foreign, and diasporic—that were developed through education and migration made an indispensable contribution to the rise of Asia-Pacific powers and will continue to shape their trajectories. Yet, once again, the ways in which various forms of talent have been utilized varies among the nations, which merits careful analysis to delineate divergent paths to development. Furthermore, to sustain development, talent strategies must evolve in response to various challenges and risks—both new and recurring—and some have done better than others. This cross-national variation in sustaining development over a prolonged period of time warrants explanation too.

New Demands, Risks, and Challenges

A full analysis of divergent paths to development among Asia-Pacific powers thus should include not only their emergence but also evolution over time. It needs to be both comparative and historical, exploring how talent strategies have prolonged over time to address various demands, risks, and challenges. These challenges are outlined below.

COMPETITION FOR TALENT

The emergence of a new knowledge economy demands a more creative and flexible labor force than the standardized, disciplined labor required by industrialization. This means that countries need to nurture new, different types of talent, upgrade their existing workforces, and/or import talent from outside. It is for this reason that nations around the world have been expanding their expenditures on higher education and research and development (R&D). Between 2005 and 2016, spending on higher education grew an average of 28 percent for Organization for Economic Cooperation and Development (OECD) countries,[21] and the number of higher education students in the world more than doubled over the last two decades (from eighty-nine million in 1998 to two hundred million in 2017).[22] Likewise, global R&D expenditures tripled in current dollars, from USD 676 billion in 2000 to USD 2 trillion in 2018.[23] Such trends can be seen most clearly in Asia-Pacific nations, which boast some of the highest ratios of college attendance and R&D spending. As of 2021, Korea ranked first, and Japan and Australia, third and eleventh, respectively, in tertiary education–attainment rate among the population aged twenty-five to thirty-four years old.[24] Korea, Taiwan, and Japan are ranked second, third, and sixth, respectively, in their R&D spending in terms of percentage of GDP.[25]

The world has also seen significant expansion in internationalization of higher education, aimed at improving the quality of domestic human capital and facilitating talent flows, particularly inbound. In 1975, there were fewer than one million international students in the world. This number reached more than four million by 2010 and is expected to double by 2025, led by Chinese and Indian students.[26] Whereas "traditional internationalization" consists of campus-based initiatives that help "enhance the competitiveness, prestige, and strategic alliance of the college,"[27] current internationalization has been propelled by the profitability motives of higher education institutions and the private sector in response to insufficient domestic capacity to address the needs of the changing labor market. Singapore, Hong Kong, Australia, Japan, Korea, and Malaysia all actively pursue the internationalization of higher education to nurture a new breed of talent and attract foreign talent.

This new industrial demand and increased transnational mobility have intensified global competition for talent, especially in the science, technology, engineering, and mathematics (STEM) fields as talent in these fields is highly pursued but in scarce supply. For example, artificial intelligence (AI) is becoming critical to diverse sectors of the new industry, or what is called "industry 4.0." While countries establish new programs to train AI experts, most are unable to produce a sufficient supply of talent quickly enough to meet the new demand. A recent study estimated that out of 22,400 AI experts who have published at one or more of the top machine-learning conferences in 2018, almost half (46 percent) worked for employers in the United States, followed by China (more than 11 percent) and the United

Kingdom (7 percent). Asian nations are far behind: Japan boasts only 4 percent of these AI experts, and Korea, less than 2 percent. Given these trailing numbers, it is hardly surprising to see growing competition for AI experts among these countries and increased transnational mobility of these experts. In fact, about one-third of the AI experts in the study worked for an employer based in a country that is different from the country where they received their PhD.[28] While more Chinese and Indian AI experts tend to stay home in recent years,[29] the high demand and mobility of such global talent will continue, suggesting the need for a twofold strategy: produce new domestic talent and attract/compete for overseas talent.

DEMOGRAPHIC CRISES

Demographic crises amplify the urgency of sustaining an adequate level of the talent pool. Most advanced countries, from Europe to North America to Asia, face pressing demographic challenges due to low birthrates and aging populations, particularly with the decline in the working-age population. None of the European Union (EU) member states have a fertility rate at or above the replacement level of 2.1, and North America is experiencing a similar trend. Yet, declining birthrates are the most acute in Northeast Asian countries—Japan, Korea, and Taiwan are all sitting on ticking demographic bombs, facing futures without enough workers to fuel their economies, and China will soon face one too.

During industrialization, Asian nations vigorously pursued birth control policies, which worked quite well in containing population growth. Population control known as "family planning" was credited as one of the contributing factors to development in Korea and China.[30] Now, the situation has changed so dramatically that countries like Japan and Korea have world-record low birthrates, and their populations are aging very rapidly. Japan was the first advanced nation to undergo a demographic crisis, with its working-age population declining since the 1990s (see figure 1.1). Its struggle to deal with the resulting problems contributed to the country's decade-long economic stagnation in the 1990s and 2000s,[31] often referred to as the "lost decades."[32] Korea faces similar problems—in 2021, the country's total fertility rate dropped to below 1 percent (.81), the lowest among OECD nations, and individuals aged sixty-five and over constituted 16.6 percent of the country's population—a figure projected to increase to 40.1 percent by 2050 (in comparison to the projected OECD average of 27.1

percent).[33] As figure 1.1 shows below, the working-age population in Korea, as well as other East Asian nations, including China, has been in decline since the 2010s.

Some Asia-Pacific countries, such as Australia and Singapore, were able to better handle such demographic risks thanks to their steady influx of foreign talent, and there is growing pressure for Japan and Korea to open their doors to immigration as well. However, importing skilled foreign labor, let alone allowing mass migration, is largely unknown territory for the many Asia-Pacific nations that are marked by relatively homogeneous populations and a lack of cultural diversity. Their overall record in foreign-talent attraction has been very poor due to both cultural and institutional barriers. According to the 2022 Global Talent Competitiveness Index by Institut européen d'administration des affaires (INSEAD), these countries lack "tolerance of immigrants"—with rankings of sixty-fifth for Korea and China and seventy-first for Japan out of 133 countries.[34] Despite public discourse and official rhetoric on the value of foreign talent and migration, these countries lack cultural diversity, tolerance, and effective immigration policies and are far from becoming favored destinations for skilled migrants. Even when the governments have stepped in to promote mul-

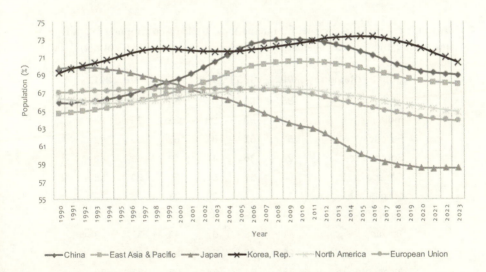

FIGURE 1.1. Age fifteen to sixty-four as percentage of total population.
Source: World Bank (n.d.b).

ticulturalism to support foreign residents, as in the cases of Japan and Korea, their multicultural policies have tended to fall short. Rather than appreciating cultural differences of the new members through pluralism, the so-called multicultural policies tend to be assimilationist in nature by aiming to integrate a minority group into the dominant culture—a potential turnoff to would-be migrants.

BRAIN DRAIN

Brain drain—a longstanding policy issue for Asia-Pacific countries like China, Korea, Malaysia, and Taiwan—has now taken on more urgency given the looming demographic crisis. These nations face the triple challenges of retaining top talent, bringing back their own talent from overseas, and attracting foreign talent to compensate for the declining working-age population. As shown in table 1.1, a very high percentage of Asian international students in the United States have stayed to work after graduation—even in STEM fields, which are high in demand in their home countries. While this figure declined from 2001 to 2011 for Chinese and Indians, the two largest groups, it still remained very high, at above 80 percent for each. This trend persists: recent statistics from the report *2020 Science and Engineering Indicators* by the National Science Board show that well over 80

TABLE 1.1. Five-year-stay rates for international students on temporary visas receiving science and engineering doctorates in selected countries, 2001–2011 (%)

Country/Region	2001	2003	2005	2007	2009	2011
China	98	93	95	94	89	85
India	89	90	89	83	79	82
Europe	53	63	67	67	60	62
South Korea	22	36	44	42	42	42
Canada	66	63	60	56	53	55
Mexico	31	22	32	33	35	39
Japan	24	39	41	33	40	38
Taiwan	41	48	52	43	37	38
Brazil	26	26	31	32	33	37
All countries	58	64	67	63	62	66

Source: Finn & Pennington (2018).

percent of Chinese and Indian STEM-PhD holders remain in the United States after graduation.[35] The stay rate has even increased for STEM talents from other countries—for Koreans, for instance, it jumped from 22 percent in 2001 to 42 percent in 2011.

This trend is likely to continue in the foreseeable future. Among all doctoral recipients with temporary visas in the United States between 2012 and 2022, 71.7 percent reported their intention to stay, with particularly high rates among Indians (86.5 percent), Chinese (80.1 percent), and Taiwanese (73.5. percent), which are higher than their European and Latin American peers (see table 1.2).[36]

While brain drain has not yet become a major concern for countries like India, which has a young population with a large labor surplus, or Australia, with its steady stream of foreign talent to the country, the issue has become more serious for countries that also face demographic crises, like Korea, Taiwan, and China, as loss of talent through brain drain compounds their already flagging working populations. According to the 2022 report *IMD World Talent Ranking*, the brain drain index (on a scale of first best to sixty-third worst) is high for these Asian countries: Korea ranks thirty-third, China thirty-fourth, and Taiwan fortieth out of sixty-three countries.[37]

GEOPOLITICS

Geopolitics pose other risks and challenges for transnational talent mobility.[38] Ongoing conflict between China and the United States has discouraged Chinese students from coming to study—for 2022–2023, the number of Chinese international students was 289,526, the lowest since 2013–2014[39]—and tensions over technology and investment have increased the political risks of China's strategy of bringing overseas talent back home. Recent disputes with China have also affected Australia, causing the number of Chinese students and workers coming to the country to similarly decline. Such aggravating geopolitical situations may redirect Chinese talent to other destinations or turn China inward to invest more resources in nurturing its own talent at home. On the other hand, China's Belt and Road Initiative will increase the influx of international students from developing countries, including African countries, into Chinese universities, and Australia's Indo-Pacific strategy seeks to attract more international students from India and Southeast Asian countries. The newly emerging geopolitical

TABLE 1.2. Doctorate recipients with temporary visas intending to stay in the United States after (not just STEM) doctorate receipt by country of citizenship, 2012–2022 (%)

Country	Avg. 2012–22	2012	2013	2014	2015	2016	2017	2018	2019	2020	2021	2022
China	80.1	82.6	82.0	81.3	81.1	81.0	83.3	79.4	79.2	80.1	73.9	76.7
India	86.5	85.7	84.3	86.2	84.6	87.2	88.5	87.1	85.9	88	85.8	88.2
Europe	64.5	65.3	62.3	63.4	61.4	62.7	67.4	63.3	64.4	67.2	63.7	68.7
Canada	57.9	58.4	55.5	55.1	56.6	56.6	59.2	62.2	62.3	57.8	54.5	59.1
Japan	49.6	45.0	47.5	48.6	39.6	53.6	58.1	50.0	51.6	50	49.6	52.1
Taiwan	73.5	65.2	67.4	68.6	70.4	77.9	76.7	78.0	73.4	76.9	73.9	80.3
Mexico	64.2	59.2	61.6	54.9	53.1	61.1	69.4	71.4	64.2	64	71.6	76.1
Brazil	58.4	46.6	46.5	50.4	50.3	56.4	61.3	61.2	63.6	60.7	72.3	73.5

Sources: National Science Foundation (2019); National Science Foundation (2022).

environment will undoubtedly complicate the future of talent movement and policy in the Asia-Pacific region.

Relatedly, the recent politicization of migration issues in North America and Western Europe can affect the talent flows of Asia-Pacific nations too. The impact will be felt mostly by India and China—the two largest sources of international students and skilled workers to those places. On the other hand, this trend might offer a new opportunity for Asia-Pacific nations that were not previously favored destinations for skilled-migrant labor to become hosts to such talent. Besides Australia and Singapore, which have long appealed to foreign talent, other advanced economies—particularly those that face demographic crises, such as Japan, Korea, and Taiwan—are actively courting international students and skilled workers. It is important to consider how the recent politicization of migration in major talent-receiving countries in the West will affect talent flow into the Asia-Pacific region.

THE PANDEMIC

Finally, the COVID-19 pandemic served as a shock to the global talent market. The closure of schools and educational institutions and the resulting learning losses set back human capital development in many countries.[40] COVID-19 also increased volatility in the global labor market, limiting talent mobility in both inbound and outbound countries. Decline in talent outflow during the pandemic may have helped to reduce brain drain, but it also may have negatively affected the formation of human capital and social capital in many nations. If skilled individuals never leave their home country, they lose the opportunity to upgrade their skills, gain new experiences, or forge valuable ties between their home and destination countries. In the postpandemic era, talent mobility has resumed, but institutions and cultures have had to adapt to the "new normal," in which remote work and education are more common.

The Emergence and Evolution of Talent Giants

Against this backdrop, this study seeks to explain the emergence and evolution of Asia-Pacific powers through the lens of talent development. It analyzes not only countries' talent strategies during their rises but also how they have addressed new demands, risks, and challenges in more recent years to sustain development, with some informed discussions about their future trajectories. Accordingly, this study not only is historical but also has contemporary relevance and implications for future development.

More specifically, this study focuses on four leading countries in the region—Japan, Australia, China, and India—which I call "talent giants" because of the instrumental role of talent in their respective achievement of economic power.[41] Historically, Japan was the first Asia-Pacific nation to rise to economic prominence in the modern era, challenging US dominance by the late 1980s, and Australia, despite its relatively small population, was a top-ten nation in GDP in 1960 and has since maintained its place as a top-twenty nation. China followed Japan's footsteps and became the second-largest economy in the world by the early 2010s. India is moving up fast and has become a top-five nation in terms of total GDP in the twenty-first century, surpassing its former colonial power, the United Kingdom. Their talent strategies were instrumental to their economic rise and closely inter-connected with each other, as China and India have been top providers of talent to the region, while Australia and, to a lesser extent, Japan, have been talent destinations.

While the effective use of talent was crucial to their rise, as this study shows, the four talent giants adopted different strategies for talent development. Japan and Australia joined the capitalist world system much earlier than China and India and were therefore both inbound oriented in talent flows, with more coming in than going out. Still, Japan and Australia diverged in their talent strategies as Japan has heavily relied on homegrown talent in achieving its prominence, while Australia's success owes much to the contributions of foreign talent. In contrast, China and India were late developers, joining the capitalist world system only in the 1980s, and both were outbound oriented in talent flows. They still supply the largest number of international students and skilled laborers to the world and have the two largest diaspora communities. Unlike Australia or Japan, however, they also have an abundance of domestic labor and therefore do not have an urgent need to attract foreign talent (at least for the time being) except in a few specific areas. Nonetheless, they differed in how they utilized and engaged with overseas nationals. China sought to bring overseas Chinese talents back home, while India focused on connecting with its international networks of overseas Indians, who remained abroad.

Furthermore, the four talent giants have encountered different risks and challenges, which they have attempted to address by adjusting or modifying their talent strategies. For example, Japan has faced a crisis of demographic change, while geopolitical tensions pose a serious challenge for China. As a result, Japan has been seeking to tap into foreign talent, whereas China has become more inward-looking. China and India continue to have to deal with brain drain, whereas Australia and Japan are competing over foreign talent, especially from the Asia-Pacific region. All four countries faced a serious challenge from the pandemic, but its impact was uneven as their respective COVID policies had diverse effects on talent flows—inward and outward. As this study shows, some countries were more successful than others at surmounting such risks and challenges. When they succeeded, they were able to sustain development. When they failed to make timely adjustments in talent strategies in response to new challenges, however, they struggled to sustain earlier successes.

This study explicitly takes a comparative approach in explaining such diverse paths and evolutions. Looking at the role of talent or human resources in development is not new, and country-specific stories about talent strategy and development are well documented.[42] Indeed, my own previous work on talent and development includes *Global Talent: Skilled Labor as Social Capital in Korea*, coauthored with Joon Nak Choi, which delves deeply into Korea's contemporary talent-development efforts with a focus on transnational social capital. Still, there is a lacuna in the current scholarship to explain cross-national variation in the ways and the extent to which various forms of human resources were utilized to achieve developmental success. Country-specific studies cannot capture the complexity in the talent-development nexus, as they miss important analytical and policy insights that can be gained from a comparative analysis. A comparative approach is especially important in offering policy suggestions for developing countries, both in and outside of the region, that may seek to emulate the developmental achievements of the Asia-Pacific talent giants.

To explain the formation and evolution of various talent strategies among the four talent giants, I propose the talent portfolio theory as a new framework for studying human resource, or talent, development at the national level, as elaborated in the next chapter. Recognizing that much like financial investment, countries invest in and compete for talent on a global labor "market,"[43] TPT views a country's talent development as formulating a national "talent portfolio," capitalizing on the capabilities of their human and social capital. It also explains the evolution of a country's talent strategy by looking at how its talent portfolio, like a financial portfolio, is diversified and rebalanced over time. Thus, TPT can provide a holistic picture of a country's talent portfolio, capture changes over time through rebalancing, and offer a framework for cross-national comparison in talent-development strategies via comparison of talent portfolios, as chapters 3–6 will demonstrate.

In applying TPT to this study, I will closely consider multiple forces that affect the trajectory of talent mobility and shape talent strategy in the Asia-Pacific region. These forces are economic (market demand and globalization), social (demographic changes), cultural (ethnic and cultural homogeneity and diversity), and geopolitical (the rise of populist nationalism and protectionism). The decision to move abroad or return home is ultimately an individual one and can be attributed to a multitude of push-and-pull factors relating to one's family, career, personal finances, corporate culture, or lifestyle choices as previous studies have documented well.[44] However, this book deals with macrolevel forces affecting national and transnational talent mobility and strategy.

In analyzing talent strategies, I focus on two main areas—the practices of higher education institutions and the policies of central governments—though the role of industry will be examined where appropriate. Higher education is the most important and common venue for talent development, and national governments play a key role in designing and implementing talent strategies. This is particularly the case in Northeast Asian countries, like Japan and China, which still hold the tradition of the developmental state, but it is also true in Australia and India, where the government's role is less direct and considered more regulatory than developmental. As D. G. Papademetriou, W. Somerville, and H. Tanaka point out, "Governments' role in mediating the decisions of both firms and individuals by shaping the conditions under which firms can broadly access global talent (and vice versa) has grown in importance."[45]

My main objective in this study is not simply to describe historical details of each of the talent giants but, more importantly, to use TPT to analyze their respective strategies, comparing the diverse ways in which talent can be utilized to spur and sustain development. I will rely on various sources of data, ranging from national-policy reports to cross-national statistics to interviews with experts and practitioners. Based on evidence and analysis, I will delineate distinctive features of each country's talent model, or "portfolio," identify the conditions required for each portfolio as well as its shortcomings, and investigate its evolution over time. As such, my historical-comparative approach can offer new analytical insights into not only the dynamics of this important region but also talent-development theory in general, showing the applicability of TPT to other cases beyond the four. In addition, I plan to draw on the rich and diverse experiences of the four talent giants to offer valuable lessons for developing countries that are trying to emulate their success. I also seek to illuminate policy implications for the United States, as it is closely connected with these countries not only via talent flows but also in geopolitical, social, and cultural ways.

In the next chapter, I present a new conceptual framework to guide this study.

TWO

A New Framework
Talent Portfolio Theory

The value of human resources in contributing to economic development has been well established and largely accepted in academic and policy communities.[1] The original idea of human capital can be traced back to at least Adam Smith in the eighteenth century, and it has been popularized by Nobel laureate Gary Becker and other economists since the 1960s.[2] According to Becker, "Expenditures on education, training, medical care, etc." are investments in human capital, which is different from physical or financial capital "because you cannot separate a person from his or her knowledge, skills, health, or values the way it is possible to move financial and physical assets while the owner stays put."[3] Labor economists F. H. Harbison and C. A. Myers stress that a country's prosperity relies on its ability to cultivate and efficiently harness the natural talents of its citizens. Without developing its human resources, a country cannot achieve other significant milestones, such as establishing a modern political system, fostering national unity, or achieving economic success.[4] More recently, in the new global knowledge economy, skilled and highly skilled labor, or what I call "talent," has taken center stage—particularly in STEM fields.

From a policy standpoint, close attention has long been paid to the role that human capital can play in driving growth in developing countries and what, if any, lessons they can derive from the human resources practices of advanced nations, which harnessed the power of human capital to achieve economic prominence.[5] A related concern that has been the subject of much academic and policy inquiry is that of brain drain, or the outward migration of talent, in particular from less developed countries to more advanced ones.[6] A study that uses counterfactual simulations to estimate the net effect of brain drain in 127 countries finds that there are slightly more "losers" than "winners" from the drain and that the losers tend to lose relatively more than the winners gain.[7] Developing nations thus have sought to find prescriptions to prevent a large-scale brain drain while training their talents.[8]

Without doubt, the development of human resources is a highly complex, challenging, long-term process involving multiple agents and institutions. There is no simple recipe or quick fix, and nations adopt different human resources strategies with consideration of their cultural, historical, and institutional situations. In addition, as noted in the previous chapter, talent strategies evolve over time, addressing new demands and risks with varying degrees of success. In order to capture such complexity, evolution, and cross-national variation of talent development, I present talent portfolio theory, a new analytical framework that looks at talent development as a collection, or portfolio, of investments in four Bs: brain train, brain gain, brain circulation, and brain linkage.[9]

This theoretical framework is a novel approach to looking at talent that allows us to take a more *holistic* view than current literature, which is narrow in focus. Examining talent development via talent portfolio theory also enables us to explain *shifts* in talent strategies over time—that is, why and how a country may change (or "rebalance") its talent portfolio. Furthermore, TPT offers an analytical framework to explain cross-national *variation* in talent-development strategies, as I demonstrate in the chapters to follow.

Talent as a Multidimensional Concept

In this study, I use a broad definition of "talent" to encompass the skilled occupations that a country most needs for its industries. This enables us to account for the fact that different nations require different types of talent in national development, despite an increasing global focus on highly skilled laborers—largely STEM talent. For example, while India is famous for information technology (IT) and software talent, Australia has a wider need for talents in sectors related to its tourism industry. I focus on skilled labor because the skilled workforce contributes most to a country's economic growth,[10] as opposed to unskilled or semiskilled workers, who have limited economic value. Skilled labor is labor that "has specialized know-how, training, and experience to carry out more complex physical or mental tasks than routine job functions."[11] Skilled laborers generally have achieved post-secondary education. In addition to the scope of skill level, there are other aspects of talent (i.e., social capital) that must be understood, as talent is a multidimensional concept.

First, we have to consider multiple layers of talent. Every nation seeks to grow the talent capacity of its own people through education and other training programs. However, it is practically impossible for any nation to produce sufficient labor of its own to adequately fuel its economy, nor can it prevent some of its best talent from leaving the country for various reasons, whether personal or professional. Countries need to compensate for areas of labor shortage or address brain drain by importing foreign talent or utilizing their diasporas.[12] Talent can thus be domestic, foreign, or diasporic.

Second, we need to appreciate the aspects of talent as regards both human and social capital. Human capital is represented by an individual's knowledge, skills, and experiences, whereas social capital refers to the capacity embodied in the ties and networks linking individuals and organizations. The total capacity of human resources is therefore the sum of its domestic, foreign, and diasporic talent in terms of the human and social capital these talents contribute. In studying talent, we tend to focus on its human capital value—and rightly so, as this is the main source for development. Yet, as I have argued elsewhere,[13] we must look further, as social capital can add a different kind of value, especially in the increasingly interconnected world.

When skilled workers move from one place to another, they bring not only their knowledge and experiences but also their social and professional ties and networks, thereby serving as connectors to other pools of knowledge and talent. Social capital can provide less tangible but important benefits, such as enhanced trust, information sharing, and cooperation.[14] In addition, unlike human capital, the use of social capital does not necessarily require a physical presence at a particular place—social capital can be used to connect different places regardless of where the person resides. In this sense, while diaspora members may not contribute human capital to their country of origin, they can still contribute social capital. Such connection, or "bridging," can be local, national, or transnational, but transnational bridging has particularly growing value, as it facilitates the movement of social capital across borders in this era of globalization.

Finally, we need to pay close attention to the flow of talent, as opposed to just stock. Stock is important for the present, but flow determines the future. For example, wealth is a stock, while income is a flow. Likewise, the population of a country is a stock, while birthrates, death rates, and migration rates are flows. Without a steady flow of income, wealth decreases, and without certain levels of fertility and immigration, population declines. The same can be said for talent. Brain drain occurs when a nation loses its talent to other countries without flowing it back home. R. E. Ployhart et al. define talent stock as the "quality and quantity of talent at any given point in time," whereas "talent flow is the change in the quality and quantity over time."[15] What really matters is not just the current stockpile of talent but also a constant healthy flow of human and social capital that will continue to fill and improve the talent pool and its capacity. As far as talent keeps flowing in and out of the country, even brain drain does not have to be a permanent loss; rather, it can be converted into a developmental asset through circulation or linkage. In today's world, a flow that is transnational in nature is a particularly keen way for a country to ensure a robust talent pool as talent is exposed to new knowledge and ideas overseas.[16]

It is, therefore, imperative to consider multiple layers of talent available for use—domestic, diasporic, and foreign—each with a different capacity and potential of human and social capital, and as both stock and flow. Based on such understanding of talent, I identify four main methods by which a country can harness talent across these various dimensions: brain train, brain gain, brain circulation, and brain linkage (the four Bs).

Four Bs: The Ingredients of Talent Development

I define "brain train" as efforts to produce and grow domestic talent or human resources. This is a primary way of increasing the stock of talent for most countries, which occurs through formal education and other training programs. "Brain gain" is the import of talent from outside to supplement a domestic workforce by increasing the existing stock of human capital. "Brain circulation" involves returning brains that have flowed overseas, or bringing back national talent residing abroad for education, employment, or immigration. "Brain linkage" is the utilization of the social capital of overseas talent who do *not* reside in a country in the form of transnational cooperation. All four Bs involve increasing the quantity or raising the quality of talent in terms of either human or social capital or both.

BRAIN TRAIN

Countries rely upon a variety of educational and training institutions and programs, both formal and informal, to develop domestic human capital. Brain train is seen as the most foundational of the four Bs as it has to do with a country's domestic population, and countries therefore tend to place paramount emphasis on attaining a strong brain train system. Key examples of brain train include school education (private and public), study-abroad opportunities, and on-the-job-training programs (within an industry or company). In particular, national education has been most important in creating the standardized, homogeneous, disciplined labor necessary for industrialization.[17]

While K–12 education has been the backbone of brain train through national education and different countries have different priorities and objectives, higher education has been considered most important in creating the talent or skilled labor needed for development. An important body of literature highlights the value created by higher education, which includes job creation, innovation, enhanced entrepreneurship, and research—a core higher education activity—for countries' economies.[18] On-the-job training is also important for improving a workforce needed for a particular industry or company.

In this study, I define "brain train" as training that is undergone while a talent remains embedded in the domestic labor market. As such, short-term study or training abroad, such as exchange and corporate-affiliate programs, can also be an important means of brain train insofar as talents are still employed by their country of origin while undertaking such training overseas. Even longer-term scholarships for overseas study can be seen as a brain train strategy when talents are sent abroad on the condition that they return home after education to work for an agreed-upon number of years. Conventionally, such overseas experiences have been lumped into the rubric of brain circulation. However, this is a theoretical oversight to be corrected because brain circulation involves an initial brain drain of human capital, yet these talents are not a drain as they remain affiliated with domestic institutions during their overseas stays and are expected to return.

BRAIN GAIN

While the stock of human capital can be increased by brain train, it is very difficult for any country to rely exclusively on its domestic talent. Every nation has certain areas of labor shortage that must be supplemented by labor imported from outside, and "brain gain" is the import of foreign talent to supplement a domestic workforce, thereby expanding the overall human capital capacity. In particular, skilled foreign labor is essential to the economies of immigrant countries, such as the United States, Canada, and Australia.[19] Even nonimmigrant countries, such as Germany, Japan, and Korea, have a growing need for foreign talent due to the demographic crisis with the declining size of the working-age population. For this reason, these nations not only train their own citizens but also recruit skilled labor from outside that possesses desired expertise in fields as diverse as medicine, finance, information technology, and software engineering.

In addition to increasing the *quantity* of a nation's human capital by filling areas of labor shortage, foreign talent can also improve the *quality* of domestic human capital by enhancing cultural diversity in a society.[20] Besides specific knowledge and skills, foreign talents bring a variety of backgrounds and experiences that can help hatch new ideas, novel thinking, and innovative technologies. The best examples of the contributions of foreign talent (and, by extension, cultural diversity) to technological innovation are Silicon Valley and Israel, which are known as the "startup nations." Both opened their doors to a wide range of foreign talent, which played a critical role in spurring technological innovation. It is no accident that Silicon Valley and Israel have become global high-tech centers.[21]

Countries use a range of pathways for brain gain. They may import foreign talent directly into the workforce (the "work-migration path") or choose to first educate talent at their educational institutions before employing them (the "study-work path").[22] The study-work path is most likely to be found in the popular destinations of international students, such as the United States, the United Kingdom, Australia, and Canada. In fact, the availability of poststudy work opportunities is a major factor in attracting international students to these countries.[23] This path is becoming important and popular even for places like Japan, Korea, and Germany, which were not previously regarded as favored destinations for international students. In these places, the internationalization of higher education plays an instrumental role in attracting international students, who are encouraged to stay to work after graduation.[24]

The work-migration path is a common route in migrant countries around the world. The United States offers the H-1B visa for foreign skilled labor, and Canada and Australia have elaborate point-based systems for skilled temporary migrants. According to the World Economic Forum, two-thirds of OECD countries have implemented or are in the process of implementing policies to attract skilled labor from abroad.[25] The study-work path can also evolve into a "study-work-migration path," which is common among international students in places like Australia and Canada. After working for a few years, foreign talent can obtain permanent residency or even naturalize; about half of skilled temporary workers in Australia become permanent residents after four years,[26] and 60 percent of international students in Canada are interested in becoming permanent residents.[27]

On the other hand, the study-work path may lead to only temporary rather than permanent migration. This is common in countries like Japan, the United Kingdom, and New Zealand, where international students remain in the host country for short-term work experience and then leave. Very few international students who stay to work in Japan or Korea become permanent residents, let alone naturalized citizens. In the United Kingdom, most non-EU citizens who receive work visas leave within five years, and this share has increased over the past decade.[28] In New Zealand, where international students are encouraged to stay after their studies, only a small portion remain in the country long-term. The reasons for this are varied, with one study of Chinese students in New Zealand pointing to difficulty in getting jobs, concerns over immigration-policy changes, or language barriers.[29] Nonetheless, such temporary migration and permanent migration as well still remain major sources for supplementing a domestic-talent stock in many countries around the world.

BRAIN CIRCULATION

Talent flow is not a one-way stream, however. It can be circulatory as talent often departs and then reenters the domestic labor market. As a recent report by the Asian Development Bank and Migration Policy Institute examining labor mobility across Association of Southeast Asian Nations (ASEAN) countries shows, outward flow does not necessarily result in permanent brain drain if the flow becomes circulatory. The report stresses that "in a globally connected world, the departure of skilled nationals is neither necessarily permanent nor a net drain, at least in the long run. Many return with new skills, financial and social capital, and access to valuable business and educational networks."[30] In this study, I define such return migration as "brain circulation."[31] Unlike study abroad taken as part of brain train, brain circulation involves an initial brain drain of human capital—that is, talents' exit or departure from the domestic labor market and then reentry after migration.[32]

Brain circulation can be market driven, or it can be initiated by the government. Studies have shown that financial incentives or professional opportunities are most important for returnees but not always sufficient; social, cultural, educational, political, and environmental factors can also be significant.[33] While return migration, like initial emigration, is ultimately individuals' decision, national-level policies and challenges can play a role. For example, a home country's talent-recruitment programs, anti-immigrant sentiments in the host country, or geopolitical tensions between home and host countries can all affect brain circulation. China's well-known Thousand Talents Program is a representative example of a government policy aimed at promoting brain circulation. Malaysia serves as another case: its Talent Corporation, a national agency that heads the country's talent strategy, established the Returning Expert Programme aimed at circulating back Malaysian talents who have been employed overseas for three years or more.[34] The impact of host-country attitudes toward immigrants is well illustrated by the fact that in the wake of the September 11 attacks in the United States, a large number of expatriates returned home amid anti-immigrant sentiments.[35] The role of geopolitical tensions in brain circulation has recently become more salient, as the rise of anti-Chinese sentiments in the United States have encouraged Chinese talents to return home.

Brain circulation played a key role in development, especially in ethnically homogeneous nations that were not receptive to embracing foreign talent. In Taiwan, over three million students went abroad to study, and one-fifth returned between 1950 and 1998, comprising about 30 percent of master's- and doctorate-degree holders in the country during this period.[36] In Korea, there was a dramatic reversal between the 1960s and 1980s. Over 80 percent of Koreans who received their PhDs in science and engineering in the United States in the 1960s chose to stay; by 1987, more than two-thirds of those who had received PhDs in the 1980s chose to return.[37] In China too, while the return rate of overseas students was low until the early 2000s, it has increased sharply since 2008.[38] F. Tian estimates that over 2.2 million, or 79.9 percent, of Chinese students who had completed their tertiary or postgraduate degrees overseas returned to China by the end of 2015.[39] Taiwan, Korea, and China all prioritized brain circulation (the diaspora) over brain gain (foreigners), and their governments were deeply involved in the circulation process. As they have not been so open to foreigners historically and culturally, brain circulation targeting the diaspora has proven more effective than brain gain of foreign talent.

BRAIN LINKAGE

The current literature tends to focus on countries' objective of achieving permanent return of diasporic talents, reflecting the long-held perspective in scholarship and practice that "retaining, engaging and recruiting skilled professionals from their diaspora" is an optimal response to brain drain.[40] While this is often the case, such a view fails to capture the fact that brain drain can be converted into a developmental asset *without* permanent return. Those who gain footing in the host country may engage with their home country through transnational collaboration or even short-term stays, despite not returning permanently. Such ties ("bridging") between two places can create a win-win, positive-sum situation for both sides,[41] which I define as "brain linkage." This concept is not limited to the interactions between a diaspora and its home country but can also apply to other types of transnational collaborations, such as when, for example, international students return to their home country after graduation but continue to engage with their former host country. That is, brain linkage highlights the use of social rather than human capital.

A. Saxenian's widely used framework does not distinguish between brain circulation and brain linkage and includes the two under the rubric of brain circulation.[42] Certainly, overlaps exist between brain circulation and linkage, as returnees can engage in brain linkage with the former host country. Still this conceptual distinction is imperative because it enables us to show how countries can make use of talents that remain overseas permanently—that is, brain linkage without circulation. It also enables a clear distinction between the contribution of returnee talent via brain circulation (largely human capital) and that of brain linkage (social capital).

Indeed, many diasporas engage with their homelands using their financial and social capital without reentering the domestic labor market that they left. Remittance is one important form of financial capital, but such engagement often goes beyond this to encompass business and research collaboration, or "knowledge transfer," through brain linkage.[43] Unlike ties linking members of a local group (bonding social capital) or ties linking members of diverse social groups in the same geographic area (local bridging social capital), "transnational social capital" refers to ties or networks connecting members and communities of different countries (see figure 2.1).[44] It makes possible transnational bridging over geographic and cultural distances, offering benefits for both home and host countries. In a global labor market, such capital is increasingly valuable.[45]

Israel is a good case of brain linkage through active diaspora engagement. The Jewish diaspora has impacted the Israeli economy by linking Israel with economies in Europe and North America, notably Silicon Valley. Recognizing the benefits of this linkage, the Israeli government created Birthright Israel in 1999, a program that brings more than fifty thousand young adults annually from overseas to Israel for short sojourns. The program strengthens Jewish identity among the members of its diaspora and fosters connection between them and resident Israelis. Notably, the program seeks to build a Jewish identity and foster transnational social capital rather than recruit them to relocate to Israel. Similarly to Israel, India also regards its diaspora as a "brain bank" based on the premise that even if they don't return home, they can still contribute to home development from abroad through financial investments, knowledge transfer, and transnational connections. Even China, a paradigm of brain circulation, has turned to the concept of "serving the country" over "returning to serve the country," implying that as far as one can support the homeland, physical residency matters less. Over half a dozen countries in Europe, as well as

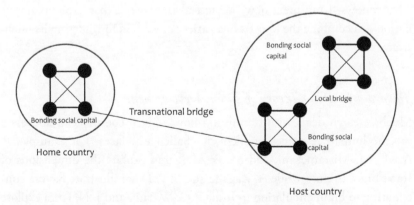

FIGURE 2.1. Transnational social capital. Source: Shin & Choi (2015), p. 12.

TABLE 2.1. Summary of the four Bs

B strategy	Talent layer involved	Primary change in capital
Train	Domestic	Human enhanced or increased
Gain	Foreign	Human gained
Circulation	Diaspora	Human lost and then gained
Linkage	Domestic with diaspora or domestic with foreign	Human (sometimes) lost; transnational social gained

Note: This chart simplifies and separates the four Bs conceptually, but it is worth noting that social capital often may accompany a human capital change. For example, domestic brain train efforts can also increase bonding social capital among domestic talents, and there may be a social-capital gain in brain gain and brain circulation, as there can be an element of linkage with a former home or host country that follows from these.

Australia, have sought to engage in brain linkage with former international students who had lived in these countries only temporarily while obtaining their education. These countries have initiated nationally led global alumni networks to make use of their now-overseas alumni's accumulated social capital.[46]

Taken together, the four-B framework enables a comprehensive and holistic view of a country's available talent resources, encompassing domestic, diasporic, and foreign talent from a perspective of both human and social capital (see table 2.1). While existing scholarship has used the language of the four Bs to study talent, few studies take all the Bs into account. In what follows, I outline a new theoretical framework that explains how a nation can combine the four Bs in a variety of ways in formulating its talent strategy.

Toward a Portfolio Theory of Talent Development

Much research deals with examining how a given country can address a specific human resources problem or challenge it faces. For example, P. Azadi, M. Mirramezani, and M. B. Mesgaran explore the dimensions of Iran's brain drain,[47] while A. Zagade and S. P. Desai illustrate factors contributing to brain circulation in India.[48] G.-W. Shin and J. N. Choi explore how Korea can harness transnational social capital of both its diaspora and international students via brain linkage.[49] Cross-national studies also tend to focus on one particular human resource issue. R. A. Adeyemi et al. explore the dimensions of brain drain in select African countries,[50] whereas Saxenian looks at the brain circulation of Silicon Valley's Indian and Chinese talent.[51] A special issue of the *Journal of Ethnic and Migration Studies* offers cross-national comparison of brain linkage of transnational entrepreneurs,[52] and a comparative issue of the journal *Advances in Developing Human Resources* looks at the brain train policies of eleven countries and regions.[53]

Such studies are valuable but inherently limited as they do not present a holistic picture of a country's various talent-development efforts and practices, missing the ways in which they may interact and supplement each other. For example, studies that focus on a country's brain train efforts do not consider the possibility of including other components in talent development, like brain gain or brain circulation, to address the country's human resource challenges or goals. A study that focuses on a country's brain circulation may miss the valuable potential outcomes of brain linkage with diaspora members. Accordingly, M. Heitor, H. Horta, and J. Mendonça note the importance of taking a broader view, one that considers "the co-evolution of brain gain, brain drain and brain circulation over time and space."[54]

Temporally, research to date also tends not to meaningfully address the historical evolution in the composition of a given country's talent pool over time or why and how a talent pool evolves in a particular way aside from outlining how current policies and practices shape strategy.[55] For example, Saxenian's seminal work *The New Argonauts: Regional Advantage in a Global Economy* addresses the brain circulation of Silicon Valley's Chinese and Indian immigrants but does not capture the crucial differences in the way they engage with home countries and how their respective engagement has evolved over time. As this study shows, overseas Indians first engaged in brain linkage with India before beginning to circulate back, whereas brain circulation largely came first among the Chinese diaspora, followed by brain linkage.[56] The difference is important because a country's history of talent development can yield clues as to constraining and facilitating factors for its potential future paths, as well as offer insights for other countries that may seek to emulate its strategy.

Finally, there is no comprehensive framework in current scholarship for analysis and comparison of talent strategies at the national level. As noted before, a talent's decision to move abroad or return home is ultimately an individual one and can be attributed to push-and-pull factors relating to one's family, career, personal finances, corporate culture, or lifestyle choices. Many studies have explored these and other factors that impact the migration decisions of skilled workers and international students in diverse countries.[57] Other studies have gone further to point out the importance of looking at the interaction between these individual-level decisions and in-stitution- and national-level policies.[58] However, it is important to establish a better framework for illustrating and comparing different experiences and impacts of talent development at the national level, which is key in offering policy prescriptions for human resource strategies.

To address the urgent need for a more complete understanding of dif-ferent nations' experiences of talent development—past and present—from a historical and comparative perspective, this study presents talent portfo-lio theory (TPT). TPT draws insights for human resources development from modern portfolio theory, a well-established theoretical framework in financial-investment literature. Financial theory's applicability to talent theory rests on the notion that countries do, in fact, make an investment in human resources that is akin to financial investment, competing for talent in the domestic and global markets and adjusting their portfolios over time. Modern portfolio theory, crafted by Nobel Prize–winning economist Harry Markowitz, prescribes how an investor can create a financial portfolio that yields maximum returns at low risk.[59] Similarly, TPT outlines how a nation can create a talent portfolio that will offer high returns at minimal risk.[60] While a financial portfolio consists of a collection of different financial investments allocated across asset classes, such as stocks, bonds, and cash, I conceive of a nation's talent portfolio as a collection of different types of investments in talent—that is, the four Bs outlined above.

In this book, I utilize TPT as an analytical framework to examine how each of the four talent giants has distinctively combined the four Bs to con-struct its own national talent portfolio and how this portfolio has evolved over time. I outline the core concepts of TPT below, derived from modern portfolio theory: diversification, risk, and rebalancing.

DIVERSIFICATION

According to modern portfolio theory, a given investment (and its risk and return qualities) should not be evaluated in isolation but rather by how it impacts the portfolio's overall performance. Thus, in building a portfolio of multiple types of assets, an investor can achieve greater returns while minimizing risk "by investing in different assets that would each react differently to the same event(s)."[61] Therefore the "core concept" that undergirds modern portfolio theory is *diversification*, which is a "common and reasonable investment practice . . . to reduce uncertainty" that "directly relies on the conventional wisdom of 'never putting all your eggs in one basket.'"[62] The same can be said of talent development: a nation seeks to minimize risks, both systematic and unsystematic (see below for details), and maximize returns by diversifying its talent portfolio. To do so, every nation constructs a portfolio with a certain mixture of the four Bs, like how a financial portfolio consists of investments in different asset classes.

A financial investor can diversify in two ways: first, by investing in different asset classes (like stocks, bonds, and cash, e.g.) and, second, by investing in different types within each class (growth vs. value stocks or corporate vs. municipal bonds, e.g.). Likewise, diversification can occur not only across the four Bs, but also within each B in a talent portfolio. For example, brain train can be diversified by investing in different forms of training (secondary, tertiary, or vocational education), training of different segments of the population (those of working age, the female labor force, and rural populations), and training at domestic or overseas institutions. Likewise, brain gain can be diversified by targeting talents from different industries or geographic countries of origin. In this book, I examine how each talent giant has sought to maintain a diversified talent portfolio not only across the four Bs but also within each B, paying close attention to how its overall talent portfolio has mitigated risks by diversifying in these two ways.

RISKS: SYSTEMATIC VERSUS UNSYSTEMATIC

Financial-investment theory distinguishes between systematic and unsystematic risks, where the former are tied to the market as a whole, and the latter are specific to each individual investment. In talent investment, too, there exist systematic risks that are caused by external factors that impact the overall global talent market, such as wars, pandemics, recessions, or natural disasters. As these risks tend to affect the market as a whole, they are difficult to completely avoid, and, therefore, a nation cannot entirely mitigate them via diversification. However, investing in multiple Bs will, to an extent, help cushion against systematic risk, as each B—just like each financial-asset class—will be affected differently by a major systemic event.[63] For example, war or pandemic (as shown recently) can interrupt talent flows, impeding brain gain, circulation, and linkage to differing extents. And this demonstrates that it is important to also develop a strong domestic brain train system, which would be less vulnerable to this systematic risk.

On the other hand, unsystematic—or specific—risks relate to one particular investment and can be better mitigated via diversification.[64] Generally speaking, there is a primary risk associated with each B (see table 2.2), and it can be mitigated by investing in other Bs. In the case of brain circulation and brain linkage, the B-specific risk is clear: the potential for brain drain as talents leave the domestic labor market to move overseas if they do not ultimately circulate back or otherwise link to their home country. While brain train may seem like a comparatively less risky strategy, it, too, has its own risk: talent that is trained domestically could become isolated from global trends and pools of knowledge, stifling innovation or transnational collaboration. The risk associated with brain gain, meanwhile, is that the influx of foreign talent can provoke anti-immigrant sentiments among the domestic population—a challenge that even the most multicultural and immigrant-friendly nations still encounter.[65] This can in turn limit the effectiveness of brain gain, causing immigrant talents to become isolated or unhappy or even to depart the country with resentment.[66] Unsystematic

TABLE 2.2. Primary risks of each B

B	Primary risk
Train	"Inward-lookingness": talents detach from global trends, markets, and research collaboration
Gain	Resentment and anti-immigrant sentiments among domestic population
Circulation	Potential for permanent brain drain of talents
Linkage	Potential for permanent brain drain of talents

risk can be specific to investments within a B as well. For example, geo-political tensions between sending (China) and host countries (the United States) may impede the flow of talent from the former, but they would only be specific to brain gain from that particular country.

REBALANCING

A diversified portfolio is key to countering risks and maintaining a sound investment strategy, but the composition of a portfolio may need to be adjusted periodically. This is because a portfolio can become skewed as investments perform differently, earning different returns over time.[67] Such adjustment is called "rebalancing," and in financial portfolios, this is done by buying or selling off assets to achieve the target portfolio composition. In talent portfolios, it represents a shift in strategic focus. Because it is important to maintain diversification both *across* the four Bs and *within* each B, rebalancing can be done by shifting emphasis in both of these ways.

Rebalancing is generally done for one of two reasons. First, if a particular B or talent investment becomes successful, then the portfolio can become less diversified and increasingly tied to the performance of that B or investment, thereby making it vulnerable to systematic and unsystematic risks. These risks can be mitigated through rebalancing both across Bs and within a B. Secondly, rebalancing may be necessary if a country's desired portfolio composition has changed as its talent needs and goals evolve. It can therefore rebalance its talent portfolio to meet its new circumstances. In this way, rebalancing ensures that diversification is maintained, and it is therefore an essential part of managing a talent portfolio.

TPT, thereby, provides a framework that looks at the overall picture of a country's talent pool and strategy and offers a lens through which to understand changes over time by exploring how and why a country may alter—or "rebalance"—its talent portfolio. Rather than taking a narrow binary view of the usefulness of converting brain drain into circulation or of how to harness the power of a diaspora via linkage, TPT allows for a holistic outlook of the many layers of talent a country invests in via all four Bs. It also offers a framework for examining cross-national variation—a main focus of this book—by comparing different talent-development strategies among nations as talent portfolios.

Talent Portfolio Theory and the Talent Giants

I use TPT as an analytical framework to study the four talent giants in the Asia-Pacific region. As the following chapters show, there is no one-size-fits-all model for a talent portfolio. Theoretically, just like with financial investments, a talent portfolio could take almost indefinite forms, mixing the four Bs to varying degrees. However, this study analyzes and compares the four distinctive portfolios because each of the four talent giants—Japan, Australia, China, and India—has developed a talent portfolio that heavily emphasizes one B in particular. Thus, they serve as illustrative cases, or "ideal types," for how each B can function within a talent portfolio, not only revealing theoretical merits of TPT but also offering lessons for other countries, as discussed in the policy chapter (chapter 8).

It is important to note the difficulty of quantifying the four Bs or measuring the exact contribution of each B given the nature and scope of talent-development efforts. Many different entities can contribute to a country's talent portfolio, ranging from national and local governments to educational institutions, businesses and the private sector, individual decisions, and more. The often-informal factors that contribute to social-capital formation are even more elusive to measurement. Furthermore, different individuals may derive different amounts of human or social capital from the same train or linkage experience. It therefore would not be feasible to quantify the exact contributions of the four Bs by, for example, the number of brains trained or gained or the amount of money invested into each B. TPT conceptualizes investment in talent as a strategic emphasis that encompasses not only financial expenditure but also policy focus, private-sector efforts, and the time, energy, and expenditures of institutions like universities or diaspora organizations.

Accordingly, this study will take a qualitative and analytical approach by highlighting distinctive features that stand out in each of the four portfolios. In doing so, I pay close attention to areas that are most critical to constructing each portfolio: higher education and brain train for Japan, migration and brain gain for Australia, talent recruitment and brain circulation for China, and diaspora organizations and brain linkage for India. I then examine the risks of each strategy before showing how each country has rebalanced its talent portfolio over time, playing up additional Bs to compensate for risks and addressing new and recurring challenges. Along the way, this study identifies the historical, cultural, and institutional conditions that give rise to each country's portfolio before exploring its contributions to the country's development. It is hoped that this book can provide theoretical guidance for studying talent development beyond the four Asia-Pacific talent giants.

THREE

Japan

Of Ours, by Ours, for Ours

"I am sorry. I cannot speak English," Maskawa Toshihide, a native of Nagoya, said with a shy smile as he assumed the podium for his Nobel lecture at Stockholm University in 2008. A homegrown Japanese physicist, Maskawa had never left the country before. The first thing he had to do to accept his Nobel Prize in Sweden, reportedly, was to apply for a passport, at the age of sixty-eight. Described as "allergic to English," he said that he had always sent colleagues in his place when he had been invited to give a speech or receive an award abroad.[1] Maskawa is an extraordinary example of a scholar who dedicated his career to thinking about the mysteries of the universe but who never expanded his education or work opportunities beyond his native country.

He is by no means unique in the Japanese context, however. Of the twenty-five Japanese Nobel Prize winners in the natural sciences (including the three who later became US citizens), only three received their highest degree from a university outside of Japan.[2] In the computer science department of Japan's most prestigious higher education institution, the University of Tokyo, all twenty-five faculty members received their PhDs from Japanese universities.[3] In 2003, it was estimated that in research universities, most faculty members had earned their PhDs in Japan—only 6.2 percent had done so internationally.[4] Among the CEOs of the top-thirty Japanese public companies,[5] only seven received any education overseas—

fewer than half as many as those from the top-thirty public companies in Korea and Taiwan.[6]

These examples nicely capture the quintessentially Japanese approach to talent development that sought to preserve a homogeneous workforce during industrial development.[7] Even in other Asian neighbors—including China and the Four Little Dragons, which are considered to have followed the Japanese developmental model—advanced degrees from prestigious Western universities and proficiency in English as well are often of higher value.[8] However, in Japan, companies and academia have favored graduates of domestic universities. While Japanese who speak English may be considered unique or cool, as former dean of the School of Education at the University of Tokyo Ryoko Tsuneyoshi points out, in Japan, "English is not linked to elitism as it is in most other parts of Asia."[9] Even in academia, the importance of school networks in faculty recruitment and promotion offered little incentive for students seeking academic careers to study abroad. This explains why most Japanese scholars, including the majority of the Japanese Nobel laureates, have obtained advanced degrees from domestic universities. Even so, Japan was able to produce world-class scholars, such as Maskawa. What, then, has made the country pursue the "Japanese way" of talent development that has been so successful?

Japan displayed unique cultural and structural features that emphasized doing things the Japanese way. *Nihonjinron* (日本人論), an ethnocentric belief that the Japanese are a homogeneous people (*tan'itsu minzoku*; 単一民族) who constitute a racially unified nation (*tan'itsu minzoku kokka*; 単一民族国家), provided a social and cultural basis for such efforts. And with established, high-quality systems of higher education and in-house training, as well as plentiful domestic opportunities, Japan was able to retain talent at home. Even when Japanese talent went abroad for training, they remained in the domestic labor market. As a result, Japan placed greater value on *its* people, *its* education, *its* culture, and *its* system—in other words, on potential employees who shared *Japanese* social and cultural norms. Foreign-born or foreign-educated talent was not important to Japan during its rise; its cultural homogeneity made Japan inhospitable to foreign talent, and the Japanese diaspora was highly assimilated into the host country (e.g., the United States) or largely unskilled (e.g., Latin America). The Japanese way of talent development incentivized Japanese talents to stay home, thereby preventing a serious brain drain, but it also diminished the chance for brain circulation or linkage. The Japanese talent portfolio was heavily skewed toward brain train.

Japan indeed did its brain train very well, diversifying its types of training through higher education and industrial training. Yet those were not confined to domestic training, and short-term overseas training also became a valuable element of Japan's talent development. Still, Japanese who went abroad for education or work experiences, unlike Chinese or Indians, tended to remain embedded in the domestic labor market, thereby representing a form of brain train that did not create any serious brain drain.[10] Therefore, the high-quality human capital that led to the Japanese economic miracle was largely the product of Japanese education and employment systems, with short-term overseas experiences enabling the country and its talents to connect with global centers of knowledge.

However, in the face of the industrial changes and demographic crises of the 1990s and 2000s, Japan's talent portfolio that relied on brain train had to transform, but the country struggled to do so. While Japan was able to increase female labor participation, efforts to rebalance its overall talent portfolio by adding other Bs, such as brain gain, have so far been very limited. The country was not able to overcome the cultural and institutional inertia that took deep roots during the so-called miracle era. There is, therefore, an irony in Japan's success, as its brain train system that worked so well for many decades blinded the country to the need to diversify and rebalance its talent portfolio when it began falling behind in the 1990s.

I begin this comparative study of talent giants with Japan not only because it became the first Asia-Pacific power in the postwar period but also because of its extraordinary emphasis on brain train, which is the bedrock of any nation's talent development. While the initial success and subsequent struggle of Japanese talent development are well recognized, the current literature does not offer a fuller historical picture of Japan's talent development and its evolution over time. In this chapter, I use talent portfolio theory to explain Japan's ups and downs in the postwar period by illuminating where the country succeeded or failed to adjust its talent portfolio. The case of Japan clearly illustrates the importance of continuing to rebalance a talent portfolio to counter potential risks, even after initial success.

Brain Train in the Miracle Era (1950s–1980s)

Post–World War II Japan caught the world's attention, as it achieved re-markable economic reconstruction and expansion in the aftermath of dev-astating wars and demoralizing defeat. Japan's GDP per capita dropped to less than half of its prewar level in 1945—a mere 19 percent of UK and 11 percent of US figures. However, Japan soon embarked on its four-decade "economic miracle." Japanese gross national income grew at an average rate of 9.1 percent a year in the late 1950s, and by the 1960s, the annual growth averaged over 10 percent. Although such high rates of growth have since become commonplace in later industrializing nations like Korea and China, the speed and duration of Japan's economic growth in the postwar era was unprecedented at the time. Japan ascended to become the world's second-largest economic power by the late 1960s and challenged US dominance in the world economy by the mid-1980s. America's trade deficit with Japan had reached USD 40 billion in 1985. There was talk that, in the words of the late Harvard scholar Ezra Vogel, Japan would soon become "number one."[11]

There exist plenty of works to explain Japan's rise, and many have pointed to a successful "catching-up" strategy through technology borrowing from more advanced Western nations. Unlike its US and European counterparts, which emphasized basic research and "disruptive innovation," Japan pursued "incremental" innovation with a focus on engineering and commercialization, importing advanced technology available abroad. According to Akio Morita, a cofounder of Sony, "Too much basic research could prevent companies from being competitive." He was referring in particular to Sony's Walkman, a device that was globally popular in the 1970s and 1980s yet contained little new technology.[12] He believed the most important task for his researchers was to come up with products that would sell well in the market.[13] The automobile industry was another example. Embracing a philosophy of continuous improvement and refinement of existing technology, Toyota was able to refine imported equipment, production techniques, and procedures to achieve much greater efficiency, higher productivity, and better quality.[14] From 1950 to 1980, Japanese enterprises entered into more than thirty thousand licensing and technology-importation agreements, for which they paid an estimated USD 10 billion.[15] To borrow the language of the German scholar Alexander Gerschenkron, Japan was a classic case of mastering the "advantage of backwardness."[16]

What, then, explains the success of Japan's catch-up strategy from a talent-development perspective? An important body of literature points to the contributions of Japan's human resources with its cooperative, dedicated, and well-educated workforce.[17] Japan's strategy required two specific types of human capital: (1) high-level scientists and engineers who could adopt and translate foreign technologies for domestic use and (2) a mass supply of decently educated workers who could understand the basics of the translated technologies and perform the actual manufacturing processes.[18] Japan successfully developed the two workforces based on cultivating homegrown talent for its industrial development, employing diverse methods of brain train: domestic education, in-house training of employees, and short-term overseas training. In other words, Japan developed a talent portfolio hinged on the brain train, which was well diversified.

NURTURING HOMEGROWN TALENT

The foundation of Japan's brain train was its well-developed and rounded education system. Japan established a robust national system of education dating back to the prewar period, with the Ministry of Education directing the entire curriculum of primary and secondary education. Japan was one of the few countries in Asia that was not colonized by a Western power and thus was never forced to adopt a foreign educational system, even under American occupation after 1945.[19] The educational catch-up, in terms of school-enrollment ratio and average years of schooling, progressed rapidly in the postwar period. The duration of compulsory education was extended from six to nine years in 1947. A remarkable literacy rate of 97.5 percent was achieved by 1950, and the enrollment ratio in upper-secondary education reached over 80 percent by the early 1970s (see figure 3.1).

Japan's education system, both primary and secondary, excelled in preparing students to perform standardized tasks so that they would be well suited to provide able labor for industrialization under the factory system and hierarchical management. Large group activities, morning assemblies, standardized exams, and school uniforms accustomed students to collective action and conformity. Such a system worked well for preparing students for a hierarchical corporate system and a highly group-minded work culture in Japan. The famous Japanese proverb "The nail that sticks out shall be hammered down" (*deru kui wa utareru*; 出る杭は打たれる) reveals how conformity and harmony are considered core values in Japanese society. In

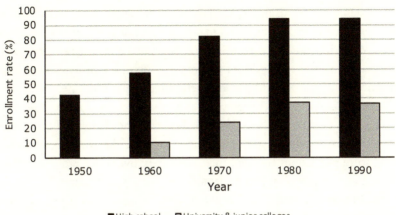

FIGURE 3.1. School-enrollment rate in Japan.
Source: Japan Ministry of Education, Culture, Sports, Science and Technology (n.d.b).

a culture where deviation is frowned upon, it is only natural for employers to favor employees with standardized qualifications who bear the hallmarks of Japanese education, culture, and values.

Japan's talent development through robust brain train was also characterized by notable diversification into different types of education and training. One important educational institution was vocational and technical training within the secondary and postsecondary education systems. Such courses as manufacturing, machinery, electricity, and civil engineering were introduced in secondary schools to meet the needs of the rapidly industrializing Japanese economy in the 1950s and 1960s and became required subjects in all lower-secondary schools by 1958. Designated vocational high schools, such as industrial, commercial, and agricultural schools, provided special training, along with basic academic education, for those who would enter the labor force right after graduation. Employed by a wide range of industries, these graduates, equipped with experiential learning and practical skills, formed the industrial-factory workforce to support the country's economic march.

As Japan saw a further need for an enhanced pool of highly skilled technical personnel to accelerate its success in the 1960s and 1970s, it continued to expand its composition of brain train by improving higher-level technology education, both in quantity and quality. As a response to the labor market demands, for example, "colleges of technology" were established in 1962 by the Ministry of Education to offer a dual track to higher science and technology education. Two-year junior colleges had already been established in 1950 on a provisional basis but became a permanent feature of the higher education system in 1965.[20] Five-year technical colleges combined three years of high school with two college years as a means for producing more mid-level technical workers with well-rounded general knowledge and a thorough specialized knowledge in technology and to foster the students' ability in their future profession. By 1976, there were sixty-five colleges of technology and at least one school in each of Japan's forty-seven prefectures.[21]

In addition to colleges of technology, Japan's brain train relied on junior colleges, which offered students opportunities for both academic studies and vocational credentials with practical applicability to midlevel technicians in civil-, mechanical-, electrical-, and systems-engineering sectors. They also trained women to become professionals in early-childhood education, such as kindergarten teachers and nursery school teachers. The number of junior colleges grew from 280 to 513 between 1960 and 1975, and the number of students attending junior colleges increased to over 350,000 (4.3 times the 1960 figure—see table 3.1).

At the apex of the higher education system, four-year universities provided both undergraduate and graduate training for those aspiring to

TABLE 3.1. Student enrollment at higher education institutions in Japan, 1955–1985

Year	Colleges of technology	Junior colleges	Universities
1955	-	77,885	523,355
1960	-	83,457	626,421
1965	22,208	147,563	937,556
1970	44,314	263,219	1,406,521
1975	47,955	353,782	1,734,082
1980	46,348	371,124	1,835,312
1985	48,288	371,095	1,848,698

Source: Japan Ministry of Education, Science and Culture (1995), as cited in Teichler (1997).

Note: This includes enrollment for all students, including part-time students, graduate students, etc.

become elite scientists and engineers. Whereas junior and technical colleges were designed to produce intermediate-level human resources essential for the operation of an industrial economy, the universities were to nurture higher-level human capital to lead scientific research and development (R&D).[22] The number of four-year universities rapidly grew from 245 to 420 between 1960 and 1975, and the number of students attending universities (including graduate schools) increased to over 1.7 million by 1975 (2.8 times the 1960 figure—see table 3.1). Whereas in 1955, the majority (72 percent) of new entrants to the workforce in manufacturing were middle school graduates (and only 4 percent university graduates), by 1985, 23 percent were university graduates, and 65 percent, high school graduates. Workers who had graduated only from middle school had almost disappeared from the labor market by then thanks to Japan's well-developed and expanded brain train system.

It was the Japanese developmental state that played a key role in nurturing the human capital needed in its key industries. Preemployment vocational education, provided by three major types of institutions—vocational high schools, technical colleges, and engineering courses at junior colleges and universities—all came under the control of the Ministry of Education, the Ministry of Labor, and other ministries, such as the Ministry of Health and Welfare. In particular, the government successfully pushed forward two large-scale plans to increase high-level science and technology manpower—namely, the Eight Thousand Students Plan (1957–1960) and the Twenty Thousand Students Plan (1961–1964). The Eight Thousand Students Plan was aimed at boosting tertiary-level science and technology student capacity by eight thousand over four years, and the Twenty Thousand Students Plan at cultivating twenty thousand more science and technology personnel over the next four years. Thanks to massive financial support from the government, the former succeeded in meeting 99.5 percent of its target, and the latter brought the cumulative number of graduates in the fields of science and technology to approximately one hundred thousand by 1963.[23] Because the promotion of science and technology education met the industrial demands during the time of growth, the job-placement rate for graduates of undergraduate engineering programs (including junior colleges) as well as those of technical colleges approached 100 percent in the 1960s.[24] These programs became a model later for Korea and Taiwan, which sought to emulate Japan's economic success.

Where Japan succeeded at having strong and well-rounded education at other levels, however, it did not pay as much attention to graduate-level advanced education in science and engineering. Education beyond the bachelor's level was commonly viewed as preparation for an academic career, as "historically, the graduate school in Japan was primarily a system to train university professors."[25] There were only a handful of jobs outside of academia for which an advanced degree or training was useful. Employers preferred to hire employees right out of high school or college and provide the equivalent of graduate training within the confines of the firm.[26] Even as late as 1997, the number of graduate students per 1,000 Japanese was only 0.8, compared to 7.1 for the United States.[27] Given the narrow purpose of graduate education and the lack of associated employment opportunities, advanced education was undervalued and underdeveloped in Japan during this growth period. In fact, this issue persists even today: as one former Rakuten employee who started in 2017 told me in an email correspondence on February 17, 2023, "There is very little difference in base salary for 'new grad' employees with [a] bachelor's degree [or a] master's degree," meaning that there is "little incentive for students to apply for further education after bachelor's."[28] Still, Japan's well-diversified system of brain train—encompassing high enrollments, vocational training, colleges of technology, junior colleges, and higher education—helped propel the country through its economic miracle.

THE JAPANESE WAY OF HUMAN RESOURCES MANAGEMENT

Japan's brain train was further expanded from school education into the employment system. The latter not only improved brain train via on-the-job training but also utilized social customs and practices—such as lifetime employment, seniority-based wages, and tightly knit social and professional networks—to make the most of Japanese talent. Two leading Japanese business experts, Ikujiro Nonaka and Hirotaka Takeuchi, point out that the key to Japan's success during the miracle era was its focus on tacit, experience-based knowledge and the ability of Japanese firms to transform that to explicit, object-oriented knowledge.[29] Educational institutions played instrumental roles in providing cooperative, disciplined, committed, and homogeneous manpower to industries, and the industries in turn effectively utilized and further developed the manpower to meet the specific needs of the Japanese economy. The most distinctive features of Japanese human resources management, which made experience-based learning and continuous training indispensable, were lifetime employment and the seniority-based wage system. These institutions served as the essence of Japan's *uchiwa* (内輪), or "all-in-the-family," economic system and helped Japan accomplish high-speed growth. Yoshihisa Ojimi, the former vice-minister of the Ministry of International Trade and Industry, claims that these institutions enabled Japan to have greater labor commitment, lose fewer days to strikes, innovate with greater ease, ensure quality control, and make products more quickly than its global competitors.[30]

While lifetime employment and seniority wages had prewar roots, they became an integrated system in the postwar development period.[31] After World War II, the Japanese government tried to reduce the high employee-turnover rate by strictly regulating "hiring, firing, and voluntary termination."[32] The developmental state again played a significant role in guiding, regulating, and constraining the labor market in the name of improving efficiency and stability during the postwar high-growth period. Large firms had good economic reasons to offer skilled employees job security and seniority-based wages to incentivize them to stay and develop firm-specific skills that could not be easily transferred elsewhere. This also allowed firms to receive a decent return on investment in training. Although there was no written contract guaranteeing lifetime employment, both employer and employee naturally understood their mutual obligations and commitments under this system. Strong labor laws, such as the doctrine of the Abuse of the Right to Dismiss, also restricted employers from dismissing their employees and reinforced long-term or lifetime employment.[33] Lifetime employment and seniority-based promotion and wages meant that firms trained and promoted their own employees to fill higher managerial positions rather than hiring specialists or senior managers from outside, as was a common practice in the West. These institutional arrangements worked especially well during the period of postwar economic growth with a young, energetic, and devoted workforce.

As lifetime employment and seniority systems were institutionalized as human resources practices, an annual mass hiring of new graduates for entry-level roles became common across industries. New employees were chosen based on their general potential, not any specialized skills or previous knowledge of the job, to be nurtured simultaneously and incrementally through new-hire training and constant on-the-job training and retraining throughout their career-long employment. It was in this context that college education was largely seen as workforce preparation, and advanced education or foreign experience prior to employment was viewed largely as irrelevant to one's career prospects. Such on-the-job training represented an essential part of Japan's brain train–heavy talent portfolio.

Training in Japanese companies was thorough, lengthy, and ongoing.[34] A 1989 survey revealed that the average number of hours spent on in-house training in the Japanese car industry was 370 per year, compared to forty-six hours and 173 hours per year in American and European car factories, respectively.[35] Relocation and redistribution of employees within Japanese organizations were common human resources practices. This rotation system exposed employees to different sectors of the company, enabling them to perform tasks in different divisions and to learn a variety of skills through experience and retraining. The extensive range of work experience through on-the-job training, job rotation and internal promotion within the firm, and lifetime employment were essential to the Japanese way of improving worker skills and performance in firms.[36] Most Japanese top managers were employed by only one firm during their entire professional career.[37] They worked their way up within the firm until they were assigned to take a leadership role in the company, which they knew very well by then.

R. Domingo even asserts that as part of *uchiwa*, "Japanese loyalty to their company is so strong that it transcends family ties."[38] With lifetime employment, it was claimed, the employees tended to identify with the organization they worked for. Companies provided employees with a basis for collective identity and security that guaranteed a stable life and promotion path. In return, employees felt a strong sense of collective mission and loyalty, much like a family. Colleagues were seen as part of one's inner circle, and informal ties and social networks were considered essential to one's future career.[39] This helped cement the primacy of brain train in Japan's talent portfolio, as overseas networks or transnational social capital were not so useful in the Japanese employment system.

The importance of social and professional networks in one's career advancement was even more pronounced in academia.[40] The concentration of national talent and resources in a limited number of universities (e.g., former imperial universities) allowed the formation of strong alumni networks in the process of establishing a new national academic system. Universities relied heavily on "academic inbreeding," a practice in which universities hire their own doctoral students who then stay at the institution for the du-ration of their careers and favor those within their own academic networks in the recruitment and promotion of the faculty.[41] According to H. Horta et al., the underlying factors for inbreeding in Japanese universities have been (1) closed recruitment processes for faculty roles, (2) the "one university learning experience," in which students complete their undergraduate and postgraduate degrees at the same university, and (3) the role of students' doctoral supervisors in hiring.[42]

In this reality, an advanced degree from a foreign university had little value for those who hoped to become academics at Japanese universities. Joining specific scholarly networks during graduate studies was far more useful than a degree from a prestigious foreign university for a doctoral student to increase the chance of being hired at a Japanese university. In the two leading universities, Kyoto and Tokyo, over 70 percent of the faculty in engineering and over 80 percent of the faculty in law received their final degrees there as recently as 2012. It is precisely in this context that, as noted above, most Japanese Nobel laureates in the natural sciences as well as all faculty members in the computer science department at the University of Tokyo received their PhDs in Japan. The practice of academic inbreeding led academics to stay largely within the Japanese system and also permit-ted a quick buildup of research and teaching capacity through solidarity, loyalty, and teamwork—a practice which dominated the academic labor market during this period and beyond.

GLOBALIZED LOCALIZATION

While Japan heavily relied on homegrown talent, this did not mean iso-lation from the global talent market at all. Instead, the country was well integrated into the capitalist world system when it embarked on its postwar economic march and was able to nurture globally connected talent through study abroad as a key component of brain train. Unlike many Chinese or Indians (see chapters 5 and 6), who went abroad for advanced degrees or employment and stayed, however, Japanese rarely left the domestic labor market, instead returning to their previous positions after overseas train-ing.[43] As *Open Doors*, an annual report by the Institute of International Ed-ucation, points out, prior to the early 1990s, "few of these Japanese graduate students [in natural sciences and engineering] remain long enough to com-plete a lengthy doctoral program of science or engineering in U.S. universities."[44] Even when they pursued PhDs to completion, most Japanese tended to return home with their advanced degrees.[45] As table 3.2 shows, Japanese had the lowest stay rate among foreign science and engineering doctoral students who were working on their PhDs in the 1980s—only about one out of ten stayed to work in the United States, in sharp contrast to Indians and Chinese. Still such overseas experiences were a crucial part of Japan's talent development, playing a key role in translation of foreign technology for domestic use during the miracle era. Overseas brain train enabled the country to stay globally connected despite the fact that its talent portfolio had limited flows through brain gain, circulation, or linkage.

The temporary nature of the overseas training is well documented by the relatively large number of Japanese, compared to individuals from other countries, on short-term visas, such as the exchange visitor visa (J) or in-

TABLE 3.2. Stay rate of foreign doctoral students in science and engineering

Country	Engineering	Physical sciences	Life sciences
India	77	71	66
People's Republic of China	66	67	65
Iran	72	64	47
Other Asia/Pacific	45	49	25
Greece	47	48	34
Taiwan	53	46	42
Mexico	51	46	13
Other Central/South America	41	44	26
Egypt	20	44	28
Other Africa	45	43	32
Other Europe	38	37	13
Canada	47	32	22
Korea	20	15	20
Brazil	15	12	13
Japan	12	8	8

Source: Finn (1996).

Note: This includes temporary residents receiving science and engineering PhDs in 1987–1988 who were working in the United States in 1992, sorted by field of doctorate.

tracompany transferee visa (L). From the mid-1960s through the 1980s, for instance, Japanese were one of the largest nonimmigrant (i.e., temporary) groups in the United States.[46] These visas represented Japanese from universities, companies, and government agencies who were sent overseas as exchange students, visiting scholars, and intracompany employees while remaining in the domestic labor market. Those who were interested in studying abroad, particularly for masters of arts or masters of business administration, could be described by the phrase "studying abroad using the company's money" (*kaisha no okane de ryūgaku suru*; 会社のお金で留学する)—a saying that is still in use today, as one University of Tokyo graduate told me in 2023. Such short-term training, like corporate-affiliate programs in foreign universities to which Japan dispatched outstanding employees for advanced research or education, was a well-utilized method of human resources development. The practice was able to prevent brain drain as the talents remained tethered to the domestic labor market, though they also diminished the chance for brain circulation and linkage, which may bring enhanced benefits through longer-term stays overseas.

Statistics indeed show that in the 1960s and 1970s, Japanese visiting scholars made up one of the largest groups in the United States, accounting for over 10 percent of the total foreign-scholar population at US universities (see figure 3.2).[47] Some of them were part of the industrial-liaison programs between American universities and Japanese firms. Japanese firms sent relatively large numbers of individuals abroad for further training: in terms of industrial trainees, in 1960, Japan was the country with the second-highest number (453) in the United States, following the United Kingdom, which had 554.[48] Industrial trainees visited for experiences encompassing technical, managerial, or manufacturing engineering and advertising sales.[49] As late as 1992, Japanese firms sent 329 of their R&D personnel to US universities "for advanced course work and cooperative research."[50] Such short-term training could involve brain linkage in the form of research collaboration, though it was often too short to accumulate transnational social capital.[51]

A good example of an industrial-liaison program is Toshiba's career development program, which started in the early 1960s and sent researchers to leading US universities, such as Stanford, University of California (UC), Berkeley, and MIT for a period of one to two years as visiting researchers or graduate students. Japan's Toray Industries has sent pharma-

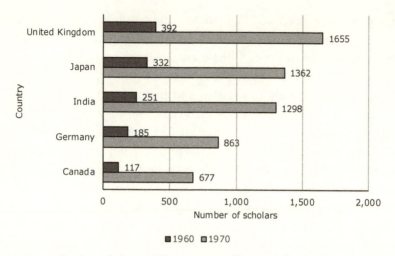

FIGURE 3.2. Foreign scholars at US universities (from top-five sending countries).
Sources: Institute of International Education (1960); Institute of International Education (1970).

ceutical researchers to US universities such as MIT, Harvard, Stanford, and UC Berkeley.[52] Stanford University's Global Affiliates Program (GAP)—formerly known as the Corporate Affiliate Visiting Fellows Program, established at the Shorenstein Asia-Pacific Research Center (APARC) in 1983—hosted personnel from affiliated Japanese institutions (both governmental and private) as visiting fellows for one or two years of research, education, and enrichment (through mentorship, global peer networking, a curated experience in Silicon Valley, and more).[53] More than four hundred personnel from over fifty Japanese organizations—such as the Ministry of Economy, Trade and Industry, the Development Bank of Japan, Sumitomo Corporation, and Mitsubishi Electric—have participated in this program over the last four decades.

Intergovernmental agreements such as the Japan-US Science and Technology Cooperation Program, instituted in 1979, also allowed Japan to dispatch researchers and technicians with expertise and knowledge for training and research in the partner country. This particular program began in the field of high-energy physics but later expanded to other areas, such as nuclear physics, high-performance computing, and brain science. As *Open Doors* reports, the relationship between high-technology firms in Japan and leading research universities in the United States has been important, as researchers in Japanese companies wanted to study with their field's top research professors, who tended to be in the United States. Such overseas programs thus enabled Japan to remain well connected to global centers of knowledge that featured the latest advanced technologies and practices, which they could bring back upon their return.

Japanese companies extensively invested in research labs overseas as well. By 1993, there were over 150 Japanese R&D labs in the United States, accounting for 60 percent of the total foreign facilities. They included Sony Electronics (est. 1960), Toshiba America (est. 1965), Canon (est. 1955), and Toyota Motors (est. 1960s). These facilities conducted research in areas where Japanese industry was behind that of the United States, including parallel computing, software development, and artificial intelligence. They tended to be located near major research universities, which allowed Japanese corporations to "access the available pool of multinational or multicultural R&D scientists in the United States, which is largely unavailable in Japan, and to create an environment capable of attracting these scientists." They were "designed to generate and harness new sources of knowledge which leverage existing corporate technological capabilities" and employed US scientists and engineers, aimed at not only keeping up to date with technology but also "localiz[ing] R&D."[54] Thus, these facilities were used to train Japanese talent and also as a platform to utilize foreign talent (brain gain) on the ground (rather than importing to Japan) and facilitate brain linkage. This way, Japan was able to diversify its train-heavy talent portfolio into brain gain and linkage without disrupting the harmony of the domestic labor market.

This pool of globalized local talent supplied highly competitive human capital to the Japanese economy. Another look at the case of Japanese Nobel laureates well illustrates such a Japanese model of brain train. In the twenty-first century, Japan boasted the second-most (behind the United States) Nobel Prize winners in the natural sciences at twenty-five, and fifteen of them (60 percent) were homegrown (never leaving the Japanese labor market before their Nobel Prize–winning work). Still, six of these laureates acquired some degree of brain train experience abroad prior to developing their Nobel-winning work. For example, Shuji Nakamura, a 2014 recipient of the Nobel Prize in Physics, worked for the Japanese chemical firm Nichia, where he proposed a project to develop the first bright-blue LED light in the world. In order for him to learn a necessary technique for grow-ing crystal, the company sent him overseas in 1988 for a year of training at the University of Florida. Like 2008 Nobel winner Toshihide Maskawa, mentioned at the opening of this chapter, Nakamura had never before been outside of Japan—or even on an airplane. He returned to Nichia in 1989, and four years later, his overseas training bore fruits as he developed the first bright-blue LED.[55] As such, Japan was able to achieve globalization of its local talent during the miracle era without the consequences of brain drain and while preserving its labor homogeneity.

Skewed Portfolio in the Lost Decades (1990s–2000s)

A well-rounded brain train system was an effective means of catching up with the West during Japan's miracle era. Significantly, while the country did not engage in much brain gain, circulation, or linkage, it was still able to stay globally connected via overseas brain train experiences. However, its lack of diversification into other Bs became problematic when its brain train proved to be insufficient in the face of intensifying globalization and a de-mographic crisis. Hallmarks of Japan's brain train, such as lifetime employ-ment and seniority-based wages and promotions, also came under fire as obstacles to innovation and globalization. The lifetime-employment system provided stability but created an inflexible labor market at the same time. Seniority-based, rather than merit-based, advancement reduced turnover but did not motivate job performance and sometimes instilled complacency among workers.[56] Company training tended to produce generalists, while the new knowledge economy required more specialists. Ironically, Japan's human resource–management model, which had been praised as central to the success of Japanese companies in the miracle era, was now blamed as a cause for Japan's economic woes and a barrier to efficiency.

Y. Godo and Y. Hayami argue forcefully that "the very success of the miracle growth mechanism, which relied on the translation of foreign tech-nology for domestic use by a small number of scientists and engineers . . . then effectively utilized by high-quality laborers with mid-level education at relatively low costs, had blinded the eyes of communities of Japanese entrepreneurs and policy makers to the need for the higher-level human capital at the end of the catch-up process." They regard this as "one of the major factors underlying the descent of the Japanese economy into stagnation."[57] In other words, Japan failed to rebalance its talent portfolio in a timely manner in the face of the new global knowledge economy—the country now saw a huge mismatch between the demand for, and supply of, the type of human capital it needed to sustain economic competitiveness. Mikitani Hiroshi, CEO of the e-commerce company Rakuten, regarded the exclusive use of local talent with inward-looking attitudes as hurting the global competitiveness of Japanese corporations.[58]

Similarly, Japan was struggling to meet the new demand for postindustrial talent via higher education. As noted above, the prioritization of undergraduate over graduate education and generalists over specialists may have been good enough in providing human capital needed for industrial development in the postwar catch-up period. However, the underinvestment in advanced education and the lack of emphasis on research in Japanese academia constrained Japan's ability to nurture a new breed of talent that was necessary in the post-catch-up era. Changing economic conditions since the 1990s demanded the higher education system produce graduates with specialized skills, creative thinking, and research minds and experience.[59] Japan sought to address this new demand by emphasizing graduate education in the 1990s, but, as Godo and Hayami lamented, that came far too late.[60]

Compounding the skill-mismatch problems in the corporate and academic worlds was the demographic crisis—an unsystematic risk that Japan was ill equipped to address given its highly skewed talent portfolio toward brain train. Low fertility, an aging population, and a shrinking workforce posed serious challenges to Japan's talent model anchored on domestic labor. When the country was hit with a record low rate of 1.57 births per woman (known as the "1.57 shock") in 1990, it felt the real threat of demographic changes. While the total population continued to grow until 2009, though at a very low rate, the working-age population already began to decline as of 1994 (see figure 3.3), and the dependency ratio jumped from 43.6 in 1990 to fifty-six in 2010.[61] The Japanese talent model necessitated a robust supply of domestic manpower, but that became increasingly difficult to sustain due to the demographic crisis in the post–miracle era.[62]

Japan urgently needed to rebalance its talent portfolio in order to tap into new pools of talent—in particular to mitigate the risk posed by the demographic crisis—but its options were limited. It could seek to (re)diversify its brain train or add additional Bs to its portfolio. The government

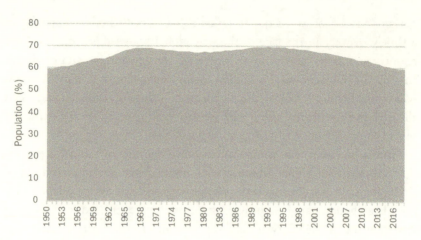

FIGURE 3.3. Japan's working-age population (aged fifteen to sixty-four).
Source: OECD (n.d.).

opted initially to stick with brain train and sought to grow the domestic population. It established various programs to encourage young adults to have more children—by reducing the costs of childcare, forcing companies to adopt more parent-friendly policies, etc. These plans did not work, however. Japan's fertility rate continued to decline to a record low of 1.26 in 2005,[63] and Japan became a "super-aged" nation in 2006, with more than 20 percent of its population over sixty-five years old.[64] The intensifying demographic challenges forced Japan to officially recognize that it could no longer provide sufficient labor for the economy with its domestic-talent pool as it had before. Its train-anchored talent portfolio had to be modified to solve the crisis. Japan had utilized some foreign and ethnic Japanese workers from China, Southeast Asia, and Latin America, but they were mostly unskilled and employed in the so-called 3D (dangerous, difficult, and dirty) industries. Many then left the country after the 2008 financial crisis.[65]

Another problem was the increasing inwardness of Japanese society and business and their detachment from global trends, another unsystematic risk of brain train. While adapting Western technologies, as discussed above, Japan chose to develop unique Japanese technology standards. Heading into the "lost decades," Japanese companies successfully localized foreign technologies and developed products that fit the domestic market but were often incompatible with the rest of the world. In some cases, Japanese technologies and products, such as cell phones, were more sophisticated and advanced than those of the West, but they could only be used in Japan. Their incompatibility with global markets gave Japanese companies a competitive edge in their home market, but they failed to capture global value and made Japan a technological leader without followers.[66]

It was in this context that "Galápagos" became a popular metaphor—originally coined to describe Japan's technologically advanced cell phones[67]—for Japan's inward focus and self-imposed isolation from the broader currents of global business. The term is borrowed from Charles Darwin's observations that species in the isolated Galápagos Islands had evolved separately from those on the mainland to adapt to the unique local environment on the islands, just like Japan's technology. "Galápagos effects" were visible in various sectors, particularly in corporate culture, research, and education, as well as in societal pillars, such as English proficiency, gender equality, and immigration policy. Like its technology and products, Japanese talent was also primarily nurtured to serve the domestic market, becoming less competitive in the global labor market. A study based on interviews with humanities and social sciences majors in 2013–2014 at the University of Tokyo confirms that "the market the students are hoping to break into is largely domestic and 'Japanese.' There is no need to speak English except if one is in a specific position that deals with the outside."[68] Japanese workers became less willing to work overseas. According to a study by the Sanno Institute of Management, the percentage of newly employed workers (eighteen to twenty-six years old) who did not want to work abroad increased from 28.7 percent in 2004 to 58.7 percent in 2013. The Japanese had little reason to trade the comfort and safety of home for a study or work experience abroad that could be challenging with little incentive. Naturally, young Japanese became risk averse, with little in the way of transnational ambition.

It is quite clear that fewer Japanese went abroad to study in the post–miracle era.[69] This is in part because, due to the declining birthrate, there were simply fewer Japanese students overall: after an initial peak in the 1960s, the number of eighteen-year-olds in Japan has been on the decline since a second peak in the early 1990s.[70] At the same time, the decrease in the Japanese youth population, as Akiyoshi Yonezawa, a professor specializing in higher education policy at Tohoku University, points out, meant that there was high demand for workers at home, making studying or working overseas unnecessary. The overall number of Japanese going overseas for study or work stagnated in the 1990s and precipitously declined in the new century. For example, figure 3.4 shows the abrupt and rapid decline in the number of student visas (category F) issued to Japanese nationals in the last two decades, which is corroborated by the overall number of outbound tertiary students from Japan. After peaking in 1997 (over thirty-five thousand), the number dropped to only around fifteen thousand in 2010, and further declined to just over five thousand by 2020. There were declines in other visa categories (such as the J visa and the L visa) too, though they were more subtle and modest.

Japan saw a notable decline in international research collaboration as well. A study by N. Shirakawa et al. shows how Japanese researchers used to work independently in parallel to international research trends and publish the results in the Japanese language only, diminishing their productivity and impact in the global science community.[71] Between 1990 and 2010, Japan's scientific papers in the Web of Science research database grew only 1.7 times, compared to an eighteenfold increase by China and twenty-seven-fold increase by Korea. Such rapid growth in research productivity by the two neighbors has been made through active regional and transnational collaboration, whereas Japanese academia is significantly isolated/disconnected from the international community.[72] The emergence of the global university-ranking system in the 2000s increased the importance of English publications, which in turn spurred international collaboration. Yet Japan lagged behind. From 2003 to 2013, the number of Japanese universities in the top five hundred as ranked by the Academic Ranking of World Universities dropped from thirty-six to twenty, whereas the corresponding number of Chinese and Korean universities increased from nine to twenty-eight and from eight to eleven, respectively.[73] "Galápagosization" has clearly become visible in Japan. With its population inward-looking and aging, Japan was left stuck with a talent-development model that rendered it globally uncompetitive and was not suited to its new economic needs.

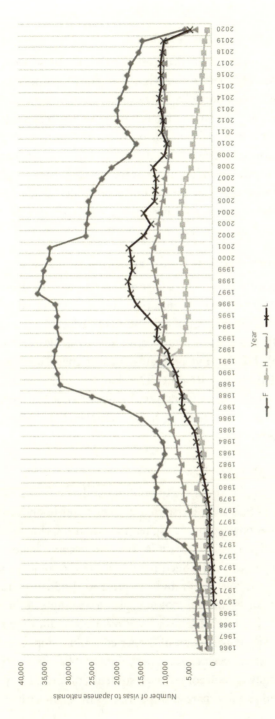

FIGURE 3.4. The United States' F, H, J, and L visas (annual issuance) to Japanese nationals. *Source:* US Bureau of Consular Affairs (1966–2020).

Rebalancing, but Too Late (2010–present)?

Leaders across government, higher education, and industry sectors have recognized the urgency of fostering a new breed of globally minded talent and rebalancing Japan's talent portfolio to revive the country's competitiveness in the global economy.[74] So far, the focus has been on two areas: (1) within brain train, by upskilling and globalizing domestic talent and (2) across Bs, by importing foreign talent for brain gain. In other words, while Japan has maintained the primacy of brain train, brain gain, if not circulation or linkage, has become more salient in its talent portfolio, which is expected to increase diversification. It was in this context that Japan sought to reform higher education and to introduce new measures of migration.

DIVERSIFICATION THROUGH EDUCATIONAL REFORM

Growing concern over Japan's Galápagosization as well as demographic crisis has put pressure on higher education policy and spurred a series of major reforms. The primary goal of reforms was to educate domestic talent to be more globally competitive (brain train) and attract international students (brain gain). Policies and programs such as the Global 30 Project (2009–2013), Global Human Resource Development (since 2012), and the Top Global University Project (2014–2023) have all aimed to internationalize higher education institutions with the interrelated objectives of brain train and brain gain in mind.

TRAIN OF "GLOBAL JINZAI"

While such factors as global university rankings and a need to attract international students to bolster university enrollments and financial revenues have driven internationalization of higher education, a primary objective of internationalization was to educate Japanese to become "global human resources" (global *jinzai*; 人材). Such refocused brain train seeks to foster Japanese talent that is tolerant of and receptive to different cultures and who can, rather than be inward-looking, play a leading role in international society. The Top Global University Project nicely illustrates Japan's new approach toward globalization of higher education. Supported by the government, selected universities are expected to establish new curricula to enhance the intercultural skills of Japanese students, promote study abroad, build academic and research partnerships with leading universities around the world, increase the number of courses taught in English, and recruit international students.[75] The program also supports hiring foreign faculty and Japanese nationals with foreign degrees.

Keio University, a top private Japanese university and participant in the Top Global University Project, for example, launched the Global Interdisciplinary Courses Program (GIC) in 2016. The GIC offers courses delivered in English to mixed classrooms of Japanese and international students, focusing on learning strategies and academic development in the humanities and sciences.[76] At Keio, undergraduates are expected to write research papers in foreign languages (especially in English) and learn skills for presenting at international conferences. The University of Tokyo, another Top Global University school, has not only sought to increase foreign language proficiency and intercultural skills among its student population but also forged strategic partnerships with schools such as Cambridge, Princeton, and Australia National University.[77] They host student exchanges, hold joint workshops and colloquia, and offer summer programs as well as research collaborations.[78] Rikkyo University, meanwhile, has joined the Asian Consortium for Excellence in Liberal Arts and Interdisciplinary Education, alongside Peking University in China, Seoul National University in Korea, and the National University of Singapore. The consortium enables Rikkyo students to study abroad in the consortium schools and to participate in two-week intensive courses on various topics along with other Asian students at the foreign campuses. As a Rikkyo participant in one such two-week course in Korea told me in 2023, "It was a great opportunity for me to network with the top students from other Asian countries" because she enjoyed being able to "discuss economic and political issues surrounding the Asian regions."[79] Whereas in the past, internationalizing meant promoting Japanese culture and education internationally, now it means embracing the forces of globalization through curricular reform and interacting with international students at Japanese campuses.

Study abroad has received renewed attention as part of educational reform. As noted above, it was a key element of the Japanese model of brain train during the miracle era but lost its salience in the lost decades. More recently, it reemerged as an important part of then prime minister Abe Shinzo's economic-revitalization plans, known as Abenomics. In a May 2013 speech at a meeting hosted by Japan Akademeia, Abe pledged to subsidize "all motivated and able Japanese youth who wish to study abroad."

Less than a year later, the Ministry of Education, Culture, Sports, Science and Technology (MEXT) launched a new public-private initiative, Tobitate! (Take off!), seeking to double the number of Japanese students abroad by 2020—which would send a total of 180,000 students abroad (120,000 at the university level and sixty thousand at the high school level).[80] Some universities made study abroad mandatory. At Chiba University, for example, students are required to study abroad for between one week and two months at least once during their degree program, with tuition covered by the university. In 2016, it introduced a six-semester system to facilitate access to overseas programs, and study abroad became compulsory for students enrolling in the newly established College of Liberal Arts and Sciences. This new system divides the traditional two-semester academic year into six two-month terms. While long-term study abroad is still an option to fulfill the requirement, the division of terms allows for ample opportunities for short-term exchanges, such as language camps, research, and social/cultural experiences. The university has been active in developing partnerships with overseas institutions and now has student exchange agreements with three hundred institutions around the world. By 2023, ten thousand undergraduate and 3,500 postgraduate students were expected to gain overseas experience.[81]

Thanks to such efforts, the number of Japanese students going abroad has steadily increased since 2011, reaching over one hundred thousand in 2017.[82] Including junior high school students and working adults who attend overseas language programs, the number exceeded two hundred thousand studying around the world in 2016.[83] Study destinations have also become more diverse. According to a survey of 80,566 students abroad by the Japanese Association of Overseas Studies, while the United States still leads with 22 percent of Japanese students overseas, it is closely followed by Australia (20 percent), Canada (17 percent), the Philippines (10 percent), the United Kingdom (8 percent), and New Zealand (7 percent).[84] Demand for study abroad has been accelerated as English proficiency has become more valuable for new hires and management-level positions in Japanese companies aim to now expand to the global market. It is no coincidence that the top-six destinations for Japanese students abroad are all English-speaking countries. This indicates increased globalization of Japanese higher education, although these experiences tend to be short-term brain train and thus not sufficient to build transnational social capital or promote brain circulation.[85]

Government and academic communities have also worked together to promote international research collaboration. The Japanese government has initiated various programs to support early career researchers and doctoral students to go overseas for further training. While such programs still aim to enhance brain train, they can also foster transnational research collaboration. For example, the Strategic Young Researcher Overseas Visits Program for Accelerating Brain Circulation, funded through the Japan Society for the Promotion of Science (JSPS), seeks to build international research networks by supporting Japanese universities and research institutions with programs to dispatch young researchers to counterpart countries for long stays and to invite researchers from those countries to Japan.[86] Another JSPS scheme for international collaboration, named Open Partnership Joint Research Projects/Seminars, has, since 2013, provided Japanese researchers with opportunities to conduct joint research or seminars with researchers from a country that has diplomatic relations with Japan.[87] The Japan Science and Technology Agency's Strategic International Collaborative Research Program has also supported international research exchanges and joint research in specific fields of cooperation designated by MEXT on the basis of intergovernmental agreements since 2009.[88] All these transnational collaborations are efforts to combat Japan's Galápagosization in the academic and research communities.

Reducing the notorious academic inbreeding was another objective of higher education reform. The practice of inbreeding is typically observed during the early stages of higher education development and is gradually deterred by more open hiring processes over time.[89] But this transition has not happened in Japan, impeding both brain circulation and gain. It not only discouraged Japanese students who sought an academic career from pursuing advanced study abroad but also became a strong barrier to the recruitment of foreign scholars. As noted above, most faculty received their advanced degrees within Japan, fewer than 0.6 percent of all full-time faculty in Japan were foreign, and the forty-five national universities had no foreign faculty at all as of 1992.[90] Even among the foreign faculty working in Japanese universities, more than half had earned their PhDs in Japan.[91] Still, they found it difficult to break into the closed and exclusive networks of Japanese academia and often were relegated to secondary status, given only short-term contracts, and barred from applying for key administrative posts.[92]

Japan has sought to weaken inbreeding through increased transparency in faculty recruitment and evaluation as well as cross-border mobility. Whereas in the past, faculty search committees sought out candidates for vacancies within their own networks and controlled who applied, now Japanese universities advertise vacancies nationally and internationally.[93] Such efforts appear to have had some success. At the computer science department of the University of Tokyo, for example, all but one of eight professors appointed between 2001 and 2010 were the department's own PhD graduates. In comparison, a decade later, between 2011 and 2020—during which time fifteen new professors were appointed—only seven were its own alumni. The schools of engineering at top universities in Japan show clear declining trends of inbreeding in the new century: between 1994 and 2010 at the University of Tokyo and Kyoto University, the percentage of inbred faculty declined from, respectively, around 95 and 90 percent to close to 70 percent each. At the private Keio University, the decline was from about 85 percent to just over 50.[94] While internal hiring is still prevalent with little brain circulation and gain, recent reforms are expected to increase openness of Japanese academia.

GAIN THROUGH *KOKUSAIKA*

Another dimension of *kokusaika* (国際化), or internationalization, is to bring international students to Japanese campuses, which can help Japan with its dual-fold rebalancing efforts in brain train and brain gain. In 2008, the government announced plans to host three hundred thousand international students by 2020 with half of them working in the country after graduation. Under the Top Global University Project, the University of Tokyo has established an exhaustive international-outreach model, including the creation of an online course on studying at Japanese universities, and even sought to change its academic calendar so that international students can enter in September, as opposed to the traditional Japanese intake in April.[95] These students can be invaluable to brain train by bringing diverse perspectives to Japanese campuses, exposing Japanese students to global norms and values. Such exposure is particularly important to Japanese who are accustomed to cultural and ethnic homogeneity. While the levels of interaction between Japanese and international students have reportedly been low due to language, cultural, and institutional barriers,[96] increased emphasis and opportunities for intercultural interaction are expected to enhance sociolinguistic and intercultural competence of Japanese students, an important aspect of *kokusaika*.

More importantly, international students have been recognized as an important new source of human capital, increasing the value of brain gain in Japan's talent portfolio.[97] The University of Tokyo's Programs in English at Komaba (PEAK) is an example of an internationalizing effort that has achieved some success in the realm of brain gain. PEAK was launched in 2012 as the university's first undergraduate degree offered entirely in a language other than Japanese, and it has admitted around thirty-five to seventy applicants annually. Its students come mainly from East Asia (including Japan), but there are also others from different parts of the world, including Europe, North America, and Southeast Asia.[98] PEAK's graduate outcomes reveal that the program has successfully gained brain for Japan: 48 percent of its graduates move on to employment, and 46 percent go on to graduate school. Of those in employment, a whopping 85 percent work in Japan after graduation.[99] While the overall number of participants in this program is rather small, as students at a top Japanese university, they exemplify new efforts in Japan's approach toward brain gain of skilled labor.

To promote the study-work path, the government has encouraged international students to work part-time while in school and has relaxed employment rules for international graduates. Working part-time can help these students improve Japanese language and cultural skills and enhance chances for employment after graduation, as most Japanese companies require a certain level of Japanese proficiency. At Ritsumeikan Asia-Pacific University (APU), for example, more than half of the students and faculty members are now foreign, representing over ninety-one countries. APU offers dedicated on-campus housing, closer to US-style dormitories, and provides resources and materials in English, which has traditionally not been common in Japanese universities. Thanks to such efforts, the job-placement rate of international graduates of APU is incredibly high, at 85.6 percent.[100]

As such, the number of international students who found a job in Japan after graduation has significantly increased from 5,878 in 2005 to 25,942 in 2018.[101] As recently as 2019, about 75 percent remained in Japan after graduation—31 percent for employment, another 31 percent for further study, and the rest for other reasons (see figure 3.5 below).[102] While the percentage of international students following a study-work path falls short of the government's target of 50 percent, it is nevertheless a remarkable achievement for a society that values cultural homogeneity.[103] Brain gain has now become an important element in diversifying Japan's talent portfolio. The prospect of employment at a Japanese company after graduation entices international students, especially those from Asia, to choose Japan.[104] Most students come from Asia (93.6 percent)—in large part from China (39.9 percent)—and only a small portion (4.4 percent) from Europe and North America.[105]

Nonetheless, Japan's efforts to facilitate its study-work path cannot be considered a resolute success of brain gain. Japan Student Services Organization surveys show that while 60 percent of international students expressed interest to stay in Japan to work, only 31.1 percent actually did after graduation (figure 3.5). A study of South and Southeast Asian students in

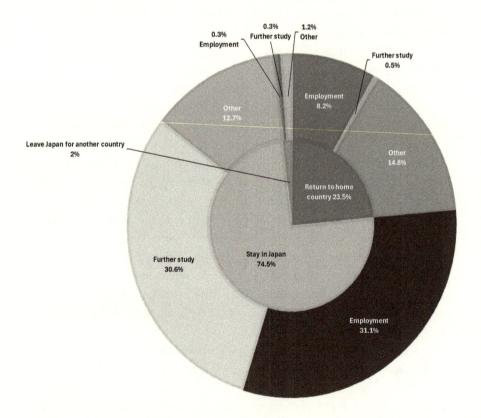

FIGURE 3.5. What international students do after completing study in Japan. *Source:* Nippon.com (2018).

Japan finds that among those who stayed in Japan, many ended up working in low-skilled jobs or in industries with worker shortages due to relatively unfavorable working conditions. Proficiency in Japanese, not in English as in other places, is still important to a student's success in finding work— while 43 percent of Northeast Asian students hold the highest-level certificate (N1) in the Japanese-language proficiency test, for other students (mostly South and Southeast Asian), only 3 percent hold an N1 certificate.[106]

Japan's efforts to diversify its talent portfolio were then hit hard by the COVID-19 pandemic—a systematic risk—as the numbers of international students coming to Japan and Japanese students going overseas significantly declined. Before the pandemic, foreign student enrollments reached 312,214 in 2019, surpassing the government's goal of three hundred thousand in 2020.[107] However, the pandemic caused Japan to close its borders to foreigners. This made international students wait for Japan's border to reopen, with some choosing more open countries, like Korea. In May of 2021, the number of international students had declined by about 22 percent to 242,444. Moreover, the number of Japanese students studying overseas dropped precipitously during the pandemic: while 115,146 Japanese students went overseas in fiscal year 2019, only a mere 1,487 were abroad in 2021. In March of 2022, Japan reopened the country, but the damage to Japan's efforts of brain gain and overseas train would be long lasting. MEXT does not expect to restore both the number of international students in Japan and Japanese students studying overseas to prepandemic levels until 2027.[108]

FURTHER DIVERSIFICATION THROUGH
LABOR MARKET REFORMS

Foreign workers have long been visible in Japan, often as students, trainees, or low-skilled laborers but not so much as skilled workers. Similarly, the work-migration path was much less developed in Japan than the study-work path described above. The government recognized that the country had the urgency and capacity to take on more foreign talent beyond unskilled workers, though, in response to demographic changes as well as new demands from industry for global talent. The Japanese government has introduced various policy measures to increase brain gain in its talent portfolio. As a result, the number of foreign workers more than tripled over a decade from 0.48 million in 2008 to 1.46 million in 2018.[109] The number hit a record 1.6 million in 2019, of which 19.8 percent were in specialist and technical fields.[110] While the brain train of domestic labor still dominates Japan's talent portfolio, brain gain of foreign talent has become more salient.

Of particular importance in facilitating brain gain was the introduction of a points-based system (PBS) in 2012 that provided highly skilled foreign professionals with preferential immigration treatment. They were defined as "unsubstitutable human resources who have a complementary relationship with domestic capital and labor" and "who are expected to bring innovation to the Japanese industries, to promote development of specialized/technical labor markets through friendly competition with Japanese people, and to increase efficiency of the Japanese labor markets." Eligible candidates are those from outside Japan who are in "advanced academic research activities," "advanced specialized/technical activities," or "advanced business management activities."[111] The conventional trainee visa did not allow the holders to stay in Japan longer than five years or move to jobs other than those stipulated in the visa. In contrast, the PBS allows the flexibility for skilled workers to extend stays indefinitely and engage in activities that fall under different visa categories.

Immigration reform was an important part of Abenomics. In his speech at a Diet session in 2018, then prime minister Abe Shinzo acknowledged, "We accept foreign human resources who have a certain level of expertise and skills and are ready to use them. We will revise the Immigration Control Act and establish a new status of residence for the purpose of working. We will establish a new Immigration Bureau to ensure supervision of the host companies."[112] The following year in April 2019, Japan indeed embarked on a new era of immigration policy, aiming to bring in 345,000 new foreign workers over the course of five years. The new immigration law expanded visa programs to allow foreign workers with specialized skills to stay in Japan indefinitely, along with their family members, and to change employers, if necessary—a major change from previous policies. In this regard, the 2019 reform can be seen as a milestone in embracing skilled foreign workers as crucial for the economy—the first time after World War II that Japan had officially welcomed blue-collar workers.[113]

However, the outcomes were disappointing. By December 2019, only 1,621 foreign talents were accepted for the new skilled worker visa—just over 3 percent of the government's quota for the fiscal year.[114] By April 2020, 4,496 individuals with specialized skills were registered under the new system.[115] Japan still faces social and cultural barriers to actualizing its goal. In the wake of immigration reforms, only 26 percent of Japanese companies planned to hire foreign skilled workers, as opposed to 34 percent who did not plan on hiring many and some 41 percent not considering hiring foreigners at all, citing language barriers and culture gaps as the main deterrents.[116] Yo-yo immigration policies have been all the more common due to COVID-19 and under the prime ministership of Kishida Fumio. His stances—that foreigners were barred from entering Japan, while Japanese citizens were unable to exit the country—were lauded by voters: 89 percent of Japanese favored Kishida's foreigner ban in a December 2021 poll by the Fuji television network.[117] To some, these changes recall *sakoku* (鎖国); translated as "locked country," *sakoku* was the prevailing isolationist foreign policy for over two hundred years during the Japanese Tokugawa shogunate, the hereditary military dictatorship, before opening to the West in the nineteenth century.

Besides importing foreign talent, Japan has turned to female labor, rebalancing to achieve a better return on this investment of its brain train by ensuring that this population remains in the labor market. Through the twentieth century, Japan was notable for having a lower female labor force participation when compared to other advanced nations. This was because of a strong "M-shaped pattern" in the participation rate, where many women would participate in the workforce until early-childhood-rearing years and rebound later. Women were also considered "temporary" rather than "permanent" employees and were exempted from the benefits of social institutions such as the lifetime-employment system.

In the face of the declining working-age population, however, Japan sought to increase women's participation in the labor market through overhauls of the laws on childcare and women's labor. For example, in 1999, there was an amendment to the "women's protection provisions," which limited women's working hours, overtime, and ability to work in "dangerous" occupations. More recently, a pillar of Abenomics was "womenomics," policies like lower taxes for married women, child-care enhancement, and increase in women in business leadership. Government support consisted primarily of generous funding packages for education and childcare, making it easier and more socially acceptable for women to balance their family life with their career. Corporations were also required to increase the appointment of women to management positions. Thanks to such efforts, the participation rate for women aged fifteen and older has risen in the past decade (see figure 3.6).[118]

Business communities have also faced the urgent need to adapt to

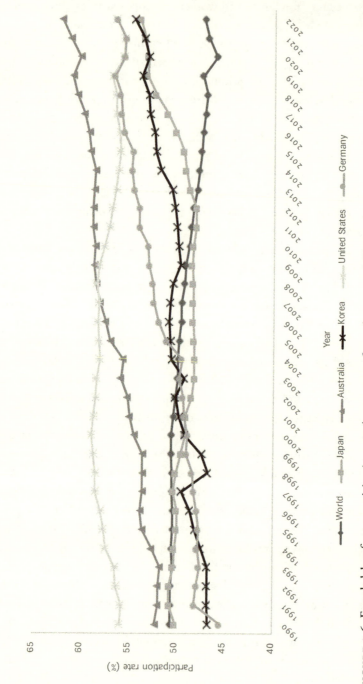

FIGURE 3.6. Female labor force–participation rate (percentage of population, aged fifteen plus).
Source: World Bank (2023a).

new realities of global demand and competition for talent. Revisions in organizational structure, corporate culture, and policy were required to upgrade human resources and better utilize them. Accordingly, companies have increasingly emphasized merit rather than seniority by adapting performance-based schemes and shifted focus from embracing homogeneity and collectivism to appreciating diversity and individualism. Some firms have allowed employees to determine their professional tracks without being subject to the mandatory job rotation that human resources departments have traditionally controlled. Employment of atypical workers—such as part-timers, dispatched workers, and contractors, which enables the company to cut labor costs and gain more flexibility—has become much more common as well.[119] Japanese firms have also begun to change their employment policies to hire university graduates year-round, a significant shift from the long-standing practice of mass recruitment only during designated times.[120]

Like higher education, Japanese corporations sought to upgrade human resource development practices through globalization. Of particular importance was overseas training of corporate leaders through executive programs. Historically, as noted above, company-sponsored overseas education involved early to midcareer employees, who would return with new ideas and experiences but who were often frustrated by the constraints of the rigid seniority system. The newer executive programs, on the other hand, were designed for senior managers who could readily put what they have learned overseas into practice and yield a more immediate impact on the business. Since 2010, for example, Sumitomo Corporation has trained approximately thirty department managers annually through a customized overseas-training program with IMD, a renowned business school based in Switzerland, for a period of ten months.[121] Mitsui launched a Global Management Academy Program in 2011 to annually send thirty elite managers in their forties to Harvard Business School for a four-week program. Mitsui's Executive Education Program also sends between twenty and thirty additional senior staff every year to top business schools in the United States and Europe.[122] The diversification into such overseas brain train of individuals at the executive level represents an important means of seeking to globalize Japanese corporations from the top.

Globalization of a company also entails an influx of foreign personnel with a better understanding of the company's culture. Japanese companies

have turned to international students as "global talents," who would undergo traditional Japanese human resources management, such as seniority pay and lifetime employment.[123] Daikin's Global Training Program for
Overseas Personnel, which began in 2015, has been training employees from
Daikin's overseas bases to deepen their understanding of the company so
that they can lead Daikin's worldwide efforts at their respective locations.[124]
Nonetheless, while there have been corporate reforms since the 1990s, the
human resources practices of large Japanese firms have not changed well
enough to accommodate foreigners.[125] Instead, the Japanese firms still tend
to prize conformity in their workers and personalities that "fit" in an organization, which leads to low job satisfaction among highly skilled foreign
workers.[126]

In sum, due to the industrial and demographic pressures of the lost decades, Japan has leaned into new sources to bolster its talent pool, thereby
trying to adjust its portfolio. Japanese universities have sought to globalize
their domestic students and stamp out academic inbreeding (brain train)
and increase their international-student population (brain gain). Japanese companies have similarly reformed labor practices to globalize their
local workforce (brain train) and have turned to untapped-talent sources
(women) as well as hiring more foreign labor (brain gain). Table 3.3 summarizes the evolution of Japan's talent portfolio from the miracle era to the
present. Yet these efforts to rebalance within and between the Bs have faced
mixed success so far. Despite Japan's attempts to attract foreign talent and
diversify its workforce, these measures have been implemented too sparsely
and too late to counteract the longstanding economic and demographic
challenges. The changes have not been substantial enough to significantly
rejuvenate Japan's economy or effectively address the shrinking labor pool
and aging population.

The Pitfalls of a Skewed Talent Portfolio

Talent portfolio theory enables us to capture a holistic picture of the tri-
umphs and tribulations of Japan's talent strategy after World War II to the
present. We see that a robust and well-rounded brain train system empowered the country to succeed during its miracle era. Japan's prioritization
of homogeneous, homegrown human resources was founded on a healthy
stream of manpower and a strong education and training system, which

TABLE 3.3. Japan's talent portfolio: Past and present

B/Period	Miracle era	Present: The new knowledge economy
Train	**Strong, well diversified** Domestic education → National education system → Vocational schools → Colleges of technology → Junior colleges → Higher education (small in terms of graduate education) Domestic employment practices → On-the-job training: flexible workforce with rotation system Short-term, overseas training → Industrial liaison programs → Visiting scholars → Corporate-affiliate programs	**Rebalancing; expanding** Increasing female-labor-force participation Internationalization of higher education → Study abroad → Fostering intercultural skills Overseas training for company employees, particularly at the executive level
Gain	Little to none	**Rebalancing; adding** International students and foreign faculty Efforts to attract skilled foreigners
Circulation	Little to none	Little to none
Linkage	Little to none	**Rebalancing; adding** Partnerships with overseas universities International research collaboration among scholars

connected the country globally without causing brain drain, making up for the lack of circulation or linkage in Japan's talent portfolio. Japan's brain train–based portfolio was also less vulnerable to outside risks, such as geopolitical tensions or global labor market fluctuations.

On the other hand, Japan's overreliance on brain train and its failure to diversify in a timely manner into other Bs caused its talent portfolio to succumb to risks such as "inward-lookingness" and the demographic crisis, contributing to economic woes during the lost decades. Despite its success during the miracle era, the Japanese model has made the country increasingly detached from global trends and isolated in the global labor market, making it difficult for Japan to meet the new demands of the changing global economy. Japanese education, which was designed to develop standardized team players who were modest, respectful, perseverant, risk averse, and inconspicuous, failed to produce a generation of globally competitive scientists and engineers to lead "disruptive" innovation after Japan's catch-up was complete. *Nihonjinron* may have been useful for promoting internal solidarity and social cohesion during the miracle era, but it has become a barrier to cultivating intercultural skills and a global mindset. The distinctive features of Japanese culture and institutions, which were well designed to deliver high growth and did so admirably during the miracle era, proved inflexible and unable to meet new challenges.

Japan's talent portfolio fell prey to another risk—a demographic crisis—stemming from its overreliance on domestic talent. With the decline of the working-age population, the country had little choice but to rebalance its talent portfolio by increasing the value of foreign talent (brain gain). Yet brain gain policy has been constrained by the same cultural and institutional arrangements that supported Japan's successful brain train. While Japan is becoming more appreciative of foreign talent, a high priority is still placed on developing a robust workforce of homegrown local talent. Brain gain is supplementary at best and at times used to bolster brain train via helping domestic Japanese talents gain intercultural skills. Neither brain circulation nor linkage have had a chance to gain any salience in the Japanese talent portfolio, as most talented Japanese still stay home or go abroad rather briefly. Japanese diasporas are either highly assimilated into the host country (e.g., Japanese Americans) or unskilled (e.g., Japanese Brazilians), limiting transnational linkage.

I recognize Japan's recent attention to brain gain as an important step toward rebalancing the country's talent portfolio. Yet that may have come too late with limited impact due to cultural and institutional inertia of Japan's education and employment systems. It is such an irony that the success of Japan's brain train strategy blinded the country to the danger of a highly skewed talent portfolio, hindering its timely rebalancing in tandem with changing circumstances. Japan understands the importance and urgency of catching up with the new reality, but the adjustment process is likely to remain protracted, incremental, and even superficial for the foreseeable future.

FOUR

Australia

A Land of Expats

"After [international students'] graduation, Australia wants to use all the human resources to help develop Australia. That's why I wanted to come here," says Sopheak Tum. Sopheak is originally from Cambodia and currently works as a food technician in Melbourne. He did his undergraduate studies in Cambodia and moved to Australia in 2018 to pursue a master's degree in biotechnology food science at the Royal Melbourne Institute of Technology. In his words, "Australia has a system that motivates immigrants to come here to pursue their education or build their skills in jobs that Australia needs."[1] Australia did not fall short of his expectations: Sopheak felt supported in the country from day one. He feels he has received an adequate orientation, help navigating immigration paperwork, assistance with job placement from his university, and much more. He has made some good Australian friends too.

Sopheak and his family, including an older sister who also resides in Melbourne, chose Australia because it provides quality education at a comparatively low cost and, more importantly, a pathway to employment and permanent residency. When asked if he plans to live in Australia permanently, Sopheak said yes without any hesitation. In his eyes, Australia is the total package—a welcoming, multicultural society with a prestigious education system and robust opportunities to grow—and he is far from alone. Sopheak is only one of many migrant talents who now account for 30 percent of Australia's population.

Australia is a place of expansive land (the sixth-largest country in the world) and abundant natural resources (mining is its top industry) but with a relatively small population of twenty-five million (ranked fifty-fifth globally). It is an island that faces "the tyranny of distance,"[2] as its geographical remoteness has profoundly shaped its history, economy, and identity. Yet, unlike Japan, another island nation, Australia is hardly an isolated Galápagos in a sea of talent flows. In sharp contrast to Japan's heavy reliance on homegrown talent, it is foreign talent that has been instrumental to shaping what Australia is today. Foreign talent has been an indispensable source of human capital in key sectors from IT to accounting to the food industry, and migration has made the Australian population continue to grow, avoiding a demographic crisis as in Japan. Multiculturalism also defines Australia's identity today.

Like Japan, brain drain is not a major concern for Australia as the country has abundant domestic opportunities to retain talent.[3] Even though some talented Australians leave home for education or employment and stay overseas, the number is relatively small, and Australia has more than offset this brain flight through brain gain. This lack of outward migration also means that Australia has a small diaspora, estimated at approximately one million,[4] so that brain circulation and linkage have been rather marginal in the country's talent portfolio.

Australia has diversified its brain gain–heavy portfolio with constant rebalancing. Its immigration policies, high quality of educational and vocational institutions, multicultural environment, and other social infrastructures have all worked well to attract talent from abroad. Its policy has gradually shifted from family to skilled migration and from permanent to temporary migration in response to newly emerging market demands. Recently, international students have become increasingly important as financial and human capital, and they have been key to sustaining Australian development. Presently, Australia continues to bolster the resilience of its talent policy, rebalancing its talent portfolio to pay more attention to the transnational social-capital value of its vast network of global alumni. Australia is unique in that it engages its international alumni more actively than its diaspora, which makes sense given that the former is more than twice as large, at 2.5 million. This recent focus on brain linkage with foreign alumni can further strengthen Australia's brain gain strategy and support its vision of leading the emerging Indo-Pacific region.

While Australia's success story of brain gain is well recognized, it needs to be understood in the larger context of talent strategies that have been so crucial to spur and sustain development over time. Talent portfolio theory enables us to capture such historical evolution by showing how Australia has been able to build and maintain a well-diversified talent portfolio over time. As shown in this chapter, Australia's success had much to do with its constant rebalancing of its portfolio, especially in order to preserve the diversification of its brain gain, through the expansion of migration to diverse ethnic groups and categories. In this regard, Australia is a good contrast to Japan, which struggled to rebalance its brain train portfolio after its initial success during the miracle era.

From White Australia to a Multicultural Nation

As part of the larger British sphere, Australia was able to develop early on and rise from a peripheral colony to an independent, semiperipheral country by the mid-twentieth century. It was ranked ninth in terms of total GDP and seventh in GDP per capita in 1960, becoming a key player in the capitalist world system that was then led by the United Kingdom and United States. The country has sustained its development for long without major setbacks, although its global rankings fluctuated over the following decades due to the faster growth of some rising economies, such as Korea and China. As of 2021, it is ranked thirteenth in total GDP and eighteenth in GDP per capita.[5] In 2022, the nation ranked fifth out of 189 countries on the United Nations' Human Development Index, a composite measure capturing achievements in major dimensions of human development, such as life expectancy, education, and national income per capita.[6]

The rise of Australia as such an Asia-Pacific power in the second half of the twentieth century was largely due to the influx of foreign talent to the country. Australia is one of the world's major immigration nations, together with New Zealand, Canada, and the United States. Its foreign-born-resident population grew from 10 percent in 1945 to 30 percent in 2020 (see figure 4.1), which is over double the OECD average of 14 percent.[7] Australia's 2016 census finds that nearly half (49 percent) of all residents were either born overseas or have at least one migrant parent.[8] Net migration accounted for an average of 55 percent of population growth from 2001 to 2015,[9] far surpassing the natural population increase every single year.

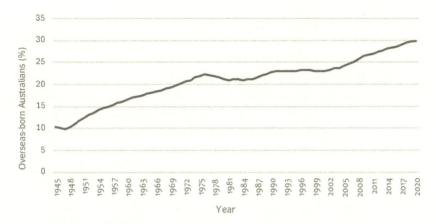

FIGURE 4.1. Percentage of overseas-born Australians to 2020. Source: Australian Bureau of Statistics (2021a).

Note: Population estimates for 2020 are preliminary.

In terms of labor implications, migrants and their descendants have accounted for almost 60 percent of postwar growth in the Australian workforce.[10] In particular, they provided critical manpower for high-priority skilled sectors with labor shortages, and this extends into more recent decades. For example, in 2001, 46 percent of general practitioners, 37 percent of specialist medical practitioners, and 25 percent of nurses in Australia were foreign-born, and the figures increased to 56 percent, 47 percent, and 33 percent, respectively, in 2011. Likewise, in 2006, 48.4 percent of engineers in the country were foreign-born, and this number increased to 53.9 percent in 2011.[11] Across the board, the labor force–participation rate is even higher for migrants with Australian citizenship (79 percent) than for Australian-born citizens (68 percent).[12]

Migrants are well represented in business leadership too. A 2019 study reveals that almost half of Australia's top CEOs were born overseas, coming from diverse ethnic and national backgrounds.[13] This figure is much higher than that of the United States, where just 3 percent of CEOs at the top-five-hundred publicly listed companies were foreign-born. The report concluded that "equality of opportunity for people from different ethnic backgrounds is alive and well in Australia, compared to the world's largest economy."[14] Another 2019 study based on census data reveals that foreign-born workers are more likely to reach the top of companies than people born in Australia.[15] In this regard, Australia is the opposite of Japan, in which it is almost impossible for foreigners to reach the top spots in corporations.[16]

Furthermore, thanks to the steady stream of migration, Australia has been able to avoid the demographic time bomb looming across the Asia-Pacific region. The life expectancy of Australians rose to 83.2 years in 2020, just shy of Japan's 84.7 years, but its population is relatively young with the elderly accounting for less than 16 percent—well below OECD peers, such as Japan (28 percent) and Italy (23 percent), which are saddled with limited working-age populations and an aging workforce.[17] Migrants are typically younger than residents, with around 84 percent of those arriving in 2016 under forty years old, compared to 54 percent of the resident population, largely thanks to the Australian migration point system that favors the young. Far from facing a crisis, Australia stands to reap a demographic bonus. The Migration Council of Australia's latest report points out that Australia's projected population will be thirty-eight million by 2050, and migration will contribute USD 1.6 trillion to its GDP and add 15.7 percent to the workforce-participation rate.[18] This is in sharp contrast to Japan, which expects a 21 percent population decline by 2050.[19] Brain gain is the most important component of the country's talent portfolio and central to Australia's present and future.

However, Australia has not always been a place that welcomes diverse groups of migrants. On the contrary, it pursued a racially exclusive so-called White Australia Policy since it became a nation in 1901 up until the early 1970s. While immigration has remained important, the country's policies evolved significantly over time to address new demands and risks.

WHITE AUSTRALIA

The original Australian expats were the European colonizers who settled on the continent in the eighteenth century, displacing Indigenous Australian populations that, with a history spanning more than fifty thousand years, represent one of the oldest living cultures in the world. With abundant natural resources, colonial Australia soon became an integral part of the international division of labor in the emerging, UK-led capitalist world system. England began sending convicts in 1788 to live in "penal colonies," and more settlers arrived of their own volition from all over the world, especially after the gold rush touched off in 1851. In particular, thousands of Chinese migrated to Australia; many were successful in the gold field. Concurrently, the mid to late 1800s to early 1900s saw significant pushback against the logistics of indentured servitude, in which Chinese laborers sought to stay after their contracts ended, leading to stricter repatriation and settlement measures, such as tight contract terms, mandatory repatriation clauses, and increased enforcement to prevent these laborers from staying. These measures ensured that indentured laborers would return to their countries of origin rather than integrating into Australian society and contributing to the growing non-European population in the colonies. The tensions with an influx of "Asiatic" laborers provoked strong anti-Chinese sentiments and legislation in the colony.[20]

Once Australia obtained independence in 1901, it unified the anti-Chinese legislations of the colonial era through passing the Immigration Restriction Act, known as the White Australia Policy. The policy was a set of measures that aimed to bar people of non-European ethnic origin, especially Asians (primarily Chinese) and Pacific Islanders, from migrating to Australia. Under the act, migrants seeking citizenship were required to take a dictation test that few "undesirable" non-White migrants could pass.[21] As a result, the majority of immigrants remained "White," with the United Kingdom as the main source. The White Australia Policy was essentially a racist policy mechanism to keep Australia "British" after independence.[22]

However, the limitations of the White Australia Policy—which rendered the country's brain gain relatively undiversified—became apparent in the postwar period, as the Land Down Under faced an unsystematic risk of waning demographics. While Australia's manufacturing industry was operating below capacity due to labor shortages,[23] no Western European country, except the Netherlands, was promoting emigration, given their own increased demand for labor at home.[24] In response, the Australian government introduced an assisted-passage scheme to attract more immigrants from Scandinavia and the United States. Moreover, while their inflow decreased, more European settlers were leaving Australia for Europe due to the economic-recovery boom there in the postwar period. Settler loss, the percentage of migrants who returned to their home countries, dramatically increased from 6 percent in 1959–1960 to 22 percent by 1974–1975.[25] This loss was largely European migrants—above 20 percent for British, German, Dutch, Italian, and Greek migrants. Clearly, the White Australia Policy was increasingly out of step with the postwar realities. Australia faced a labor shortage, concerns over the security risks of underpopulation, and growing criticism from Asia over its discriminatory immigration policies, which collectively pushed the country to reconsider its approach to immigration. Australia urgently needed to diversify its brain gain, expanding to include migrants from other countries.

The Australian government incrementally rolled back its exclusionary measures, gradually allowing migration of displaced people from southern and Eastern Europe, as part of migration campaigns with the slogan "Populate or perish."[26] Then, in 1966, the government under Prime Minister Harold Holt conducted a major migration-law review, which was a milestone in the abolition of the White Australia Policy. Under the new laws, "migrants to Australia were to be selected for their skills and ability to contribute to Australian society, rather than race or national affiliation." The White Australia Policy was officially denounced and replaced with multiculturalism in 1973.[27] Australia was set to rebalance its brain gain portfolio, expanding into migrants from diversified countries of origin.

THE TURN TO MULTICULTURALISM

Multiculturalism as a public policy generally encompasses legal and governmental tools and means to ensure inclusion of a diverse group of people. In Australia, multiculturalism sought to overcome the limitations of previous racist approaches toward assimilation and integration under the White Australia Policy and secure broader brain gain. The concept of Australia as a "multicultural society" was first mentioned in Al Grassby's 1973 speech titled "A Multicultural Society for the Future." Then minister of immigration Grassby proclaimed, "The social and cultural rights of migrant Australians are just as compelling as the rights of other Australians. The full realization of these rights would lead to reduced conflicts and tensions between the groups which are weaving an ever more complex fabric for Australian society as we hurry towards the turn of the century." He concluded with his "personal ambition" that "Australians of all backgrounds will always be proud before the world to say in whatever accents, 'I am an Australian.'"[28] With the introduction of multiculturalism, all migrants, regardless of race, ethnicity, or national origin, became eligible for Australian citizenship after three years of residence.

Multiculturalism has since then quickly been adopted across areas of public life. School curricula emphasized cross-cultural understanding and language acquisition. Public schools trained teachers on cultural diversity and sensitivity, how to link lessons to different cultural contexts, and, most importantly, how to support multilingual learners. They also provided prayer rooms for religious students, and hijabs were allowed. Multicultural-ism was introduced in the public media as well. The Australian Broadcast-ing Corporation Act of 1983 stipulated that the broadcasting system provide "programs that contribute to a sense of national identity and inform and entertain, and reflect the cultural diversity of, the Australian community."[29] The Special Broadcasting Station (SBS), one of two public stations, broad-casts the news in multiple languages, with a mandate to do 90 percent foreign and non-English broadcasting. The government also established the Australian Multicultural Council, which is responsible for creating in-tergroup collaboration and supporting cultural expression through sport events, festival grants, and other initiatives.[30]

As more Asians began to come (particularly as temporary skilled mi-grants, discussed below), the ethnic composition of the migrant population significantly changed over time. In 1961, all the top-ten countries of birth for the foreign-born population were European, except New Zealand.[31] In contrast, only the United Kingdom, Italy, and New Zealand remained in the top ten by 2016, while six Asian countries, led by China and India, rose to the top of the list (see table 4.1). After 2001, new immigrant streams emerged from the Middle East and Southeast Asia, supplementing the cus-tomary countries of origin and increasing the number of countries repre-sented outside of the top ten. Such ethnic diversification of Australia's brain gain was largely owed to the introduction of multicultural policies since the mid-1970s.

From a talent-development perspective, Australia's shift from White Australia to a land of expats was the most significant change for the nation in the second half of the twentieth century. While brain gain remained the most prominent B in its talent portfolio, Australia has continued to diver-sify its brain gain in terms of ethnicity/nationality. Despite some lingering concerns over social problems associated with migration, there exists a gen-eral consensus among the leaders and public alike that migration plays a vital role in Australia's economy and society. As Arzan Tarapore, an Indian Australian political scientist, puts it, "Australia would not be a G20 econ-omy if it weren't for immigration."[32]

TABLE 4.1. Top-ten countries of birth for overseas-born population, 1961, 2001, and 2016

Rank	1961 census		2001 census		2016 census	
	Country	Share (%)	Country	Share (%)	Country	Share (%)
1	United Kingdom	39.7%	United Kingdom	25.5%	United Kingdom	17.7%
2	Italy	12.8%	New Zealand	8.8%	New Zealand	8.4%
3	Germany	6.1%	Italy	5.4%	China	8.3%
4	Netherlands	5.7%	Vietnam	3.8%	India	7.4%
5	Greece	4.3%	China	3.5%	Philippines	3.8%
6	Poland	3.4%	Greece	2.9%	Vietnam	3.6%
7	Ireland	2.8%	Germany	2.7%	Italy	2.8%
8	Yugoslavia	2.8%	Philippines	2.6%	South Africa	2.6%
9	New Zealand	2.6%	India	2.3%	Malaysia	2.2%
10	Malta	2.2%	Netherlands	2.1%	Sri Lanka	1.8%
Other		17.4%		40.6%		41.3%
Total overseas born		100%		100%		100%

Sources: Australian Bureau of Statistics (1961); Australian Bureau of Statistics (2001); Australian Bureau of Statistics (2016).

Note: In 2001, "other" included about 219 countries, of which 114 have one thousand or less migrants, and forty-five have over twenty thousand (many countries with only a handful but also many with significant populations). The next six major countries of origin were South Africa (1.9%), Malaysia (1.9%), Lebanon (1.7%), Poland (1.5%), the United States (1.4%), and Sri Lanka (1.4%). The ten next most represented countries for 2016 were Germany, Korea, Greece, United States, Lebanon, Ireland, Indonesia, the Netherlands, Iraq, and Thailand.

Diversifying Brain Gain

Another measure that has further diversified Australia's makeup of brain gain is a policy shift from family to skilled migration. Historically, the migration program set annual quotas for family and skilled migrants, who were granted permanent visas upon arrival, under strict government control. Until the late 1990s, the majority of permanent visas were granted to family migrants. However, the situation began to change as the Australian government increased the number of skilled visas to alleviate the prevailing labor shortage. Since 1998, the skilled stream has overtaken the family stream every single year, shifting the balance in its favor (see figure 4.2). By 2008, two-thirds of all permanent visas granted were to skilled migrants. Through rebalancing the brain gain composition, if not its overall talent portfolio, Australia was able to better attract and retain its pool of skilled expertise and contributions, thereby filling labor shortages and fostering economic growth.

Australia went one step further in diversifying its brain gain makeup by introducing a "temporary" track within the skilled stream in the 1990s.[33] This was a necessary measure as the nation still faced a serious labor shortage, but permanent migration was too "inflexible" to compete in the globalizing labor market.[34] The new visa scheme was not subject to quotas or caps, unlike permanent migration or the equivalent scheme offered in the United States (H-1B visa), and allowed temporary skilled migrants to later apply for permanent residency. From 2009–2019, two-thirds of these temporary workers were highly skilled.[35]

In addition, Australia gradually shifted away from supply-driven, independent skilled migration (without employment arranged prior to migration) toward demand-driven skilled migration (with employment arranged prior to arrival), aimed at better ensuring that skilled migrants are employed in the industries of highest demand.[36] In 2012, Australia introduced a new two-stage system called SkillSelect, which invited potential permanent skilled migrants to join a pool of applicants, whom the Australian government and employers could nominate for their required skills, giving the Australian government a way to rank potential migrants. Thanks to these changes, by 2016, the nomination stream accounted for more visas than the points-based stream in skilled worker visa processing.[37] This system honed the success of Australia's brain gain strategy.[38] Table 4.2 summarizes the

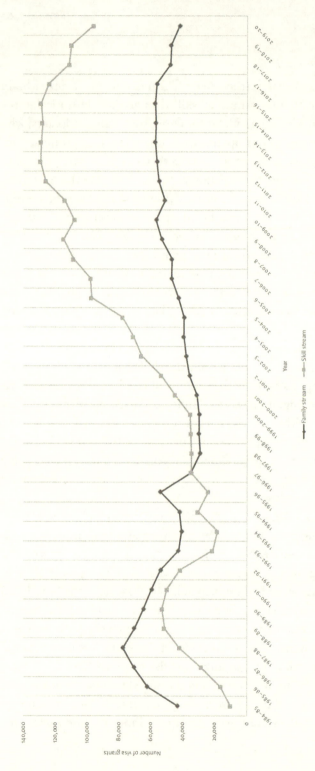

FIGURE 4.2. Australia's permanent migration outcome by stream, 1984–1985 to 2022–2023. Source: Australian Government Department of Home Affairs (2023).

Note: The family stream excludes child visas for comparative purposes. Information from 1983–1984 to 1994–1995 is rounded and reflects changes in reporting. Program outcomes exclude New Zealand citizens (prior to 2017–2018) and certain humanitarian visas. Numbers represent net outcomes, excluding provisional visa holders.

TABLE 4.2. Summary of Australia's migration policies

Migration type	Change
Permanent migration	Family to skilled
Skilled migration	Permanent to temporary
Temporary skilled migration	Supply driven to demand driven
Sources of temporary skilled migration	Temporary workers to international students

evolution of Australia's migration policies that contributed to the diversification of brain gain.

The ethnic and occupational composition of skilled migrants (both permanent and temporary) has changed over time, further diversifying Australia's brain gain. While the United Kingdom was historically the leading source of migrants, it is now second to India. Asia accounts for seven out of the ten top source countries of permanent skilled visas and four out of the ten for temporary skilled visas. It is interesting to observe the breakdown of main occupations, which reflects their countries' respective strengths. Indians concentrate in software and application programming and nursing (see chapter 6 for more on India's strength in software engineering). On the other hand, the British are largely advertising and marketing professionals and human resource experts.[39] The Philippines, which has a long history of sending nurses overseas, sends about the same number of nurses as India.[40]

In looking at Indians, the largest migrant group in permanent and temporary skilled visas today, we see the characteristics that make this group successful. The India-born population in Australia is fast growing, increasing by 48 percent from 455,385 in the 2016 census to 673,352 in the 2021 census.[41] As of 2016, they have a higher median income than native born Australians, making 14 percent more per week.[42] This success is seen in the percentage of Indian migrants employed in their fields of expertise when compared to the Chinese, another large migrant population. In medicine, for example, 46 percent of Indian migrants are employed in the field within five years, as opposed to 3 percent of Chinese migrants. In nursing, the numbers are 62 percent and 28 percent, respectively.[43] While there are multiple reasons that explain Indians' success, according to Lesleyanne Hawthorne, professor at the University of Melbourne and a leading scholar of migration in Australia, one key component is their English proficiency when compared to Chinese and other migrant groups. Taking into consideration the youth of Indian migrants (their median age is thirty-three years old as opposed to thirty-eight for the whole of Australia), they are expected to continue to benefit Australia greatly.[44] Indian migrants' thriving could also lead to brain linkage with their homeland in the years to come, as their fellows in Silicon Valley have done so well (see chapter 6).

The work-migration path has worked very well as most immigration to Australia results in a permanent residency and citizenship. About half of skilled temporary workers become permanent residents after four years, and, in 2020, 80 percent of approved skilled permanent residencies were already in Australia as skilled temporary visa holders or as former international students.[45] In 2006, Australia's adjusted citizenship rate was 80 percent, which is 20 percent higher than the OECD average and higher than other immigrant countries, like Canada (75 percent) and the United States (48 percent),[46] let alone Japan and Korea, where most foreign talents leave the country after a few years. The higher rate of naturalization attests to the effectiveness of brain gain in Australia's talent portfolio.[47]

The overall success of Australia's brain gain is largely thanks to the government's proactive monitoring and continual rebalancing of its foreign talent portfolio through adjustments in its migration system. While its government is not developmentalist, as in Japan or China, its role has not been passive at all. On the contrary, the government constantly monitors the employment outcomes of temporary and permanent skilled workers, with studies like the Longitudinal Studies of Immigrants to Australia, Continuous Survey of Australia's Migrants, and the national census. As Lesleyanne Hawthorne, whose skilled-migration studies have impacted Australia's migration policy, told me in July 2022, Australia's systematic refinement immigration system has made the country a "brain gain exemplar."[48]

International Education in Talent Strategy

Skilled migration is not unique to Australia but quite common for advanced nations in North America, Europe, and Asia. Even Japan, a nation that was not historically receptive to migration, seeks skilled migrants in the face of a demographic crisis, as discussed in the previous chapter. What sets Australia apart from not only its Asian neighbors but also its peer immigrant nations in the West is its use of international students both extensively and effectively as financial, human, and social capital. Since 2015, Australia has been a top-five most popular destination for international students in the world, attracting 8 percent of tertiary students that studied outside of their home countries in 2020.[49] Australia tops the world in its percentage of international students to total student population, and this percentage grew faster than that of other popular destinations of international students: from 2015–2019, as figure 4.3 shows, it increased significantly in Australia (from 15.5 percent to 28.37 percent), faster than that of the United States (4.6 percent to 5.2 percent) or the United Kingdom (18.5 percent to 18.7 percent).

It is no surprise that international education had become Australia's fourth-largest export by 2005 and the largest non-resource-export industry in 2018, generating around USD 35.2 billion for the national economy. Major Australian college campuses are filled with international students who pay much higher tuition than domestic students (typically more than double)[50] and are overwhelmingly self-funded.[51] International education is estimated to contribute around 250,000 full-time-equivalent jobs to the Australian economy.[52] As discussed below, Australia's vast global alumni network offers the opportunity for brain linkage, which can help further

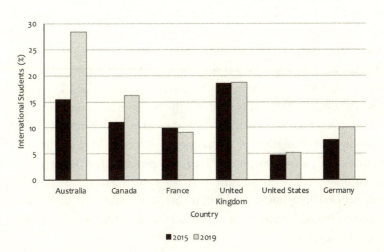

FIGURE 4.3. International students as percentage of tertiary students enrolled in top-destination countries.

Source: UNESCO Institute for Statistics (n.d.).

diversify the country's talent portfolio. In short, international students offer a key source of financial, human, and social capital to Australia.

THE RISE OF AUSTRALIA'S INTERNATIONALIZED
HIGHER EDUCATION

Before 1985, like Japan, Australia's involvement in internationalized education was limited to the provision of foreign aid as part of public diplomacy, and almost all foreign students studying in Australia were either fully or partially funded by government programs.[53] Two government-commissioned reports in 1984—by G. Jackson and J. Goldring—were instrumental in reorienting Australia's international education. The Jackson report recommended that education be regarded as "an export industry in which institutions are encouraged to compete for students and funds."[54] It further contended that charging international students would allow Australia to create more spaces for them without incurring costs for Australian taxpayers or depleting opportunities for domestic students. This would not only mitigate anti-foreign-student sentiments among Australians but also bring Australia earnings and better education for its citizens.[55] The Goldring report recommended that the extra funds earned from international students be used to improve the education system, enhancing Australian brain train so that Australia could better compete with the United States and United Kingdom in higher education.[56] The financial capital that came along with international students was seen as supporting brain train by offering resources to improve higher education.

Meanwhile, Australia was trying to expand the narrow resources-based export industry to include specialized services, and education was a key target. As a result, from 1985 through the 1990s, education policy focused almost entirely on the commercial export of higher education services, with the result of an explosion of international students.[57] From 2001 to 2019, domestic-student enrollment averaged 2.62 percent growth per year, while international-student enrollment grew an annual average of 7.01 percent. While still trailing domestic enrollments in total numbers, international students are steadily growing as a percentage of all higher education enrollments (see figure 4.3).

To attract international students, Australia has provided a very friendly institutional and cultural environment. Institutionally, the Australian Qualification Network (AQF) is found to be particularly useful to international students. It was established in 1995 to ensure that qualification titles across the country were consistent and to "represent the same high standards of education" in all Australian educational institutions.[58] The government also provides supportive regulations to ensure quality education for international students. For example, the 2000 Education Services for Overseas Students (ESOS) Act sets out the standards that Australian education providers must meet in offering education and training services to international students, outlines the institutions' as well as the students' responsibilities, and, most importantly, protects the rights of foreign students, including the right to tuition-protection service (TPS).[59] Thanks to such measures, the four-year-graduation rate for international students in Australia remains very high (70.8 percent, compared to 45 percent for their domestic peers).[60]

Australia's strategy to attract international students has worked well. Andrew Norton—the higher education program director at the Grattan Institute, a well-regarded Melbourne-based think tank—views the high quality of universities as central to Australia's strong performance in the international-student market.[61] Indeed, more and more Australian universities make it to the top of the global rankings. In 2011, only six Australian universities ranked in the top two hundred globally. Today, twelve universities are on the list—the highest number of any country in the Asia-Pacific region (see table 4.3).[62] The influx of international students in turn helps to raise these universities' global rankings given that "international diversity" is a key criterion in rankings' evaluation schemes, leading to a virtuous cycle. It is also important to note another draw of Australian universities for international students: their instruction in English, which many want to learn given its value as a global language.

Besides institutional support and an excellent quality of higher education with English instruction, Australia provides a multiethnic culture that is much more hospitable to international students than the other talent giants included in this study. While international students face social and cultural barriers in Australia too,[63] they still fare much better in interacting with local students than do international students studying in homogeneous societies, such as Japan or Korea.[64] A 2008 City of Melbourne survey finds that 87 percent of international students thought the city was accepting of people from various societies and cultures. This number dropped in 2010 but is still high, at 81 percent.[65] In particular, the major cities of Sydney and Melbourne are

TABLE 4.3. Global ranking of Australian universities by *Times Higher Education*

Year	2011	2021	Rank change from 2011 to 2021
University of Melbourne	36	31	+5
University of Sydney	71	51	+20
Australian National University	43	59	-16
University of Queensland	81	62	+19
Monash University	178	64	+144
University of New South Wales Sydney	152	67	+85
University of Adelaide	73	118	-45
University of Western Australia	N/A	139	N/A
University of Technology Sydney	N/A	160	N/A
University of Canberra	N/A	184	N/A
Queensland University of Technology	N/A	186	N/A
Macquarie University	N/A	195	N/A
Total Australian universities ranked in top 200	6	12	+6

Source: World University Rankings (2021).

cosmopolitan and welcoming—Melbourne, for example, was ranked as the third-best city for international students globally in 2019.[66]

Additionally, Australia continues to cultivate an atmosphere conducive to cultural diversity through initiatives, campaigns, and events. For example, Australia hosts a National Unity Week,[67] organizes Welcoming Cities to support local council efforts,[68] and runs Welcoming Clubs to provide cross-cultural sports and recreation opportunities. Countries looking to emulate Australia's brain gain success may not be able to create a multicultural population out of thin air or may dismiss cultural openness as an inherent Australian trait, but these initiatives suggest otherwise—government rhetoric and action can be marshaled toward inclusion through feasible, concrete steps, as evidenced by the fact that now-multicultural Australia once had a racially exclusive policy. The influx of international students in turn has improved the quality of Australian brain train by bringing cultural diversity to college campuses, creating a synergistic effect.

In addition, the rise of xenophobic, antiforeign, anti-immigration discourse and policy in the two top destinations, the United States and the United Kingdom, has made Australia a more attractive place to international students. For example, various Trump-administration policies on immigration (e.g., restrictions on Muslims and Chinese) are broadly seen by many in US academia as unwelcoming and counterproductive to the cause of recruiting talented students and scholars to American campuses. Phil Honeywood, CEO of the International Education Association of Australia, noted in 2018, "Theresa May in the U.K. and Donald Trump in [the] U.S. have been massive assets for Australia. . . . [Their] negativity towards international students has been to Australia's advantage."[69]

Australia is consistently ranked as the "safest and most welcoming country" for international students. The 2018 International Graduate Outcomes Survey shows that 89 percent of 10,243 respondents who completed their studies in Australian universities between 2013 and 2018 were "satisfied" or "very satisfied" with the education and training that they had received from them. It is in this context that Australia has become a major destination for international students, ranked third in the world, behind only the United States and the United Kingdom,[70] and first in per capita ratio and as a percentage of total higher education.[71] Among 869,185 international students as of November 2018, almost half (46 percent) are enrolled in universities, and more than a quarter (28 percent), in vocational education and training (VET). Four of the top-five countries of origin are Asian, led by China (30 percent) and India (13 percent). The majority majored in management and commerce, and there are more international than domestic students in certain majors, such as IT. They are also an important source of revenue for Australian universities. In 2010, they provided 17.5 percent of total university revenue, and this number continued to increase to 27.3 percent by 2019, only behind government funding at 48.6 percent (see figure 4.4).[72]

HUMAN CAPITAL

Most importantly, international students have become a major source of human capital for Australia, further strengthening the value of brain gain in the country's talent portfolio. Australia encourages both study-work and study-work-migration paths, and employment and migration opportunities down the line offer very attractive incentives to international students. A 2006 study based on interviews with Chinese students (sixty-five who were considering study abroad and thirty currently studying in Australia) reveals that "future migration opportunities" was listed as a top reason for choos-

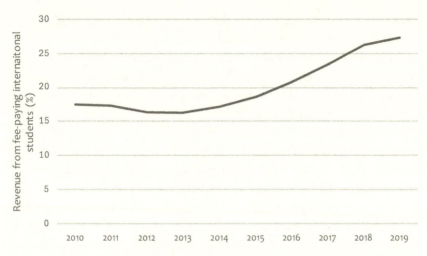

FIGURE 4.4. Percentage of Australian university revenue from fee-paying international students. Source: Ferguson & Spinks (2021).

ing Australia over the United States or United Kingdom.[73] A decade later, a 2018 survey of international students who graduated from an Australian university also finds that the most prominent motivation for their study in Australia is to "progress their career and gain employment." Forty-one percent of respondents say that they applied for a visa to extend their stay.[74] All these figures indicate the major "pull" factor presented by the study-work-migration path.

To utilize international students as human capital, Australia has made it much easier for them to find jobs both during and after study than it is in the United States or the United Kingdom, not to mention in Japan or Korea. Students can work for up to twenty hours a week during the academic year. While the twenty-hour allowance is the international standard, in Australia, the approval process requires significantly less red tape as visas automatically grant international students the right to work, and no further authorization is needed.[75] This ease of working during their studies is another factor that attracts international students to the island. Australian universities and VET institutions stress that students can not only gain work experience while studying but also find plentiful employment opportunities after education and training.[76]

In addition, education within Australia confers an advantage when applying for temporary and permanent residency. Eligible international students who have completed an Australian education can apply for the temporary graduate visa, which allows them to stay to gain work experience for eighteen months to four years, depending on the qualification. There is no restriction on the type of work or number of hours, though students must apply with qualifications that are needed in Australia.[77] In comparison, the optional practical training (OPT) visa in the United States is less generous, as it permits non-STEM students to work for only one year, and the job must be proven relevant to the student's field of study. STEM students can work in the United States for three years after graduation, but they must apply for a two-year extension after their initial OPT year.[78] Moreover, unlike in the United States, Australian graduates also benefit in their permanent migration. If a graduate applies for a permanent visa through the point system, they gain five extra points for having an Australian degree.[79]

International students significantly add to the stock of Australian human capital by providing a crucial source of manpower to the areas of skilled-labor shortage. As figure 4.5 shows, they even outnumber domestic students in certain critical fields, such as management and commerce and information technology, and constitute over 40 percent of students in engineering and related technology as well as food, hospitality, and personal services. Chinese and Indians represent the two largest groups of international students in all levels of degree concentrated in management, IT, and engineering (see table 4.4). According to Hawthorne, international students provide a "productivity premium" as many of them self-fund their education and begin working in Australia at an age fifteen to twenty years younger than that of the average skilled migrant.[80] They seek employment in their skill areas after graduation, and 84 percent of graduates are employed in their preferred fields.[81] The study-work path benefitted from the meticulous oversight by the government, which, following a policy review in 2006, adjusted pathways to lead to increased likelihood of international students working in a relevant occupation after graduation.

The annual International Graduate Outcomes Surveys (IGOS) aptly demonstrate the success of the study-work path for Australia and individual migrants. Its 2018 survey includes 10,243 respondents who completed their studies in Australian universities between 2013 and 2018.[82] Among those in Australia, 87 percent of undergraduates and 86 percent of postgraduates

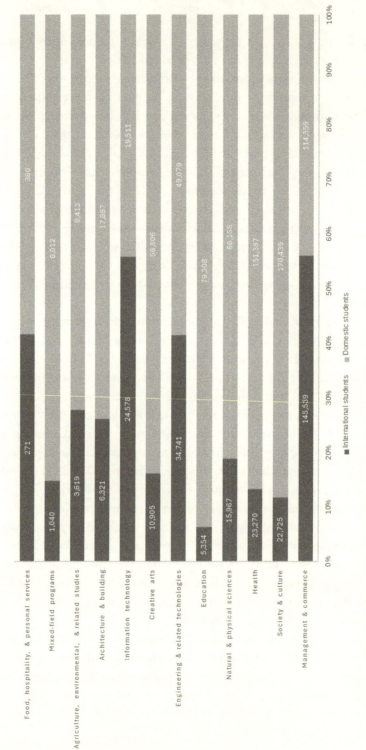

FIGURE 4.5. International students and domestic students by field of education, 2016. *Source:* Tertiary Education Quality and Standards Agency (2018).

TABLE 4.4. Chinese and Indian student enrollment in Australian higher education (2020)

Country	Total enrollments	Level of study	Most popular fields of study
China	131,201	Doctoral degree 4,311 Master's degree (coursework) 59,539 Bachelor's degree 48,388 Bachelor's degree with honors 8,337	Management and commerce 56,864 Information technology 14,417 Engineering 14,366
India	74,363	Doctoral degree 1,366 Master's degree (coursework) 53,006 Bachelor's degree 16,032 Bachelor's degree with honors 1,442	Management and commerce 25,768 Information technology 23,180 Engineering 8,543

Source: Australian Government Department of Education (n.d.).

are employed fulltime, showing little difference in employment outcomes compared to domestic graduates. Of the respondents, 75 percent agree that "their academic units prepared them for the workplace," and 67 percent say that "their Australian degree was worth the financial investment." For them, the average salary from employment in Australia is also consistently higher than elsewhere.

Global Alumni: Tapping into Transnational Social Capital

While brain gain remains the primary component of Australia's talent portfolio, the country has started to experiment with brain linkage to diversify into other Bs. Brain linkage would not replace or diminish the importance of brain gain but can be supplementary and even reinforcing. Interestingly, the main target of Australia's linkage efforts is not its diaspora community, as in China or India (see chapters 5 and 6). Instead, Australia is actively engaged in reaching out to the vast network of international-student alumni, estimated at about 2.5 million, that it has accumulated over the past decades. This group is equivalent in size to 10 percent of the Australian population and more than two times larger than its diaspora community—it is no wonder the country's *2017 Foreign Policy White Paper* hails international alumni as "a significant asset for Australia."[83] To be sure, the United States and United Kingdom have much larger numbers of international alumni, but these alumni usually self-segregate according to the schools they attended and the origins of their country (e.g., Stanford alumni in Korea or India's pan-IIT alumni overseas). While some European nations follow a similar strategy, no other country has such a comprehensive scheme to organize its entire international alumni into one global network. This attention to brain linkage can not only diversify Australia's talent portfolio but also strengthen its brain gain strategy.

A major initiative by the Australian government to promote such transnational linkage is the Global Alumni Engagement Strategy, launched in 2016. It departs from the conventional "drinks-and-networking" method of the past and has evolved into a content-focused program offering professional development and leadership opportunities. The strategy seeks to connect "to other alumni and alumni networks in Australia, the region and globally" by forming an online community paired with in-person programming, supporting partnerships among alumni, the Australian government, and business and research institutions.[84] The network's LinkedIn page boasts over ten thousand followers as of January 2022, and it is exploring additional social media platforms, like WeChat, to engage new graduates from various countries. It takes a tiered approach, with "highly influential alumni" at the core, driving Australia's global alumni engagement as advocates, mentors, and leaders.[85]

Given the program's short history (as well as recent restrictions due to COVID-19), it would be premature to properly assess its efficacy, but this alumni engagement is expected to contribute to brain gain by further strengthening and promoting international education. One of the objectives is for overseas alumni to serve as ambassadors for Australian higher education and inspire more international students to choose the country. Such a strategy has now become much more important given growing competition from other advanced nations in the region, such as Japan and Korea, for transnationally mobile Asian students. Australia's National Strategy for International Education 2025 calls for joint efforts between the government and the education sector to strengthen cross-border partnerships and build community among the alumni.[86] This plan clearly seeks to enhance Australia's brain gain strategy through transnational brain linkage.

This appears to be a sensible approach because most international students cultivate social and professional networks while living in Australia and show interest in staying connected after leaving the country. According to the International Graduate Outcomes Survey of 2018, 58 percent of international graduates say that they had opportunities to make professional connections while studying in Australia, and 79 percent developed ongoing personal friendships, which hold the potential to mature into professional relationships. 78 percent respond that they are likely to develop professional links with Australia, and, even for those currently residing overseas, the figure is high, at 67 percent.[87] This differs vastly from Japan, where most international students end up interacting with each other rather than with local students, which is likely to decrease their chances of staying connected to the host countries after leaving.[88]

Transnational linkage is important for Australia given its geographic isolation and small population, but as critics say, Australia's overseas network has historically been underutilized due to inconsistent and ad hoc efforts.[89] In this context, it is logical and overdue for Australia to tap into its global alumni network using a whole-of-government approach. In fact, global alumni networks are a new trend in the last decade, catering to both national priorities and alumni objectives. In addition to Australia, other nation-led efforts to create global alumni networks, albeit of smaller scale, have started in the Netherlands, Germany, Hungary, France, Denmark, and Sweden. Australia's network has been lauded as a model for planning in other countries, such as Ireland, as it adopts an inclusive approach instead of just catering to a select group of alumni.[90]

Australia's transnational brain linkage efforts go beyond the country's alumni to include outreach to developing countries in the Indo-Pacific region. Aspiring to be a leader in the newly emerging sphere, Australia recognizes the importance of building bridges with countries in the region from which many of its international students and skilled temporary workers come. In the 2018–2019 fiscal year, the government allocated USD 290.5 million in scholarships to 3,154 international students, and the top-five recipient countries were Indonesia, Papua New Guinea, Vietnam, Bangladesh, and the Philippines. The country offers Australia Awards to "support emerging leaders from developing countries to study in Australia or within their region, build people-to-people links and return home to contribute to economic and social development."[91] Australia Award recipients can be valuable as transnational social capital connecting Australia to their homes. Such programs resemble China's efforts to engage students from Belt and Road Initiative countries through scholarships and other support (see chapter 5). Though it is premature to evaluate these policies given their short history, taken together, they clearly demonstrate Australia's appreciation of international students' value as transnational social capital beyond financial and human capital, revealing the continuous efforts to diversify its national talent portfolio. Table 4.5 summarizes the evolution of Australia's talent portfolio.

TABLE 4.5. Australia's talent portfolio

Train	**Strong** Internationalized, high-quality higher education
Gain	**Primary** International students
	Skilled workers
	Permanent migration: family → skilled Temporary migration: supply driven → demand driven
	European immigrants → immigrants from diverse countries of origin, especially China and India
Circulation	**Not noteworthy**
Linkage	**Rebalancing; adding** Engaging with global alumni network
	Engaging with developing countries in the region

Risks for the Land Down Under

Despite the huge success in brain gain and the recent attention to brain linkage, Australia also faces a new set of risks in both the domestic and the geopolitical arenas. In particular, anti-immigration sentiments and geopolitical conflicts present two major unsystematic risks for Australia's talent development. The systematic risk of the COVID-19 pandemic also posed a serious challenge to Australia's brain gain, revealing a danger of investing too heavily in foreign talent, as it restricts talent flow to Australia.

GROWING RESERVATIONS ABOUT MIGRATION

If a brain train–heavy portfolio is vulnerable to the unsystematic risk of demographic crisis, as in Japan, a portfolio that is overreliant on brain gain is susceptible to another unsystematic risk: stoking anti-immigration sentiments. Although Australians largely agree on the value of migration for their country,[92] there are emerging signs that they have become less enthusiastic about taking in more migrants. In a 2019 survey, 47 percent of respondents believe that Australia has too many immigrants, a 10 percent increase when compared to a survey in 2014.[93] This presents a serious risk to Australia's brain gain–heavy talent portfolio.

Growing reservation about immigration largely comes from public complaints that state governments and the Commonwealth have taken the economic windfalls from migration and population growth—such as increased property-stamp duty, payroll, and income taxes—but not spent the money properly to help urban centers deal with the growth, which has led to such problems as crowded commutes and expensive housing.[94] In a February 2018 speech, former prime minister Tony Abbott echoes such public sentiment by saying that he is still proimmigration but that the number of immigrants should be cut in the short-term: "At least until infrastructure, housing stock, and integration have better caught up, we simply have to move the overall numbers substantially down."[95] An Australian National University poll conducted in 2018 reveals that more than two-thirds (69.6 percent) of adults do not support population growth, a significant increase from findings in the 2010 poll (54.2 percent).[96] These "quality-of-life" concerns and complaints have been amplified by a deeper ambivalence about a new wave of non-European immigration, which has been accompanied by renewed politicization of the issue and the rise of populists, such as the right-wing firebrand Pauline Hanson, who has railed against Asian and Muslim migration.[97]

Facing such public complaints, the Australian government responded by reducing the weight of brain gain in its overall talent portfolio, modifying its immigration policy in 2017 to add stricter temporary visa requirements. Echoing Donald Trump's America First policy, then prime minister Malcolm Turnbull says, "We will no longer allow 457 [temporary work] visas to be passports to jobs that could and should go to Australians. We're putting jobs first, and we're putting Australians first."[98] The rules hinder some skilled migrants from working in the country.[99]

Australia has also addressed this risk by making adjustments to its multicultural policy. While most Australians are still supportive of multiculturalism,[100] there exists growing trepidation that if Australia is too open to people from all over the world, the country may risk losing its identity as a nation.[101] In 2017, the Australian Department of Home Affairs released its latest multicultural statement, "Multicultural Australia—United, Strong, Successful," the first since 2011.[102] It reaffirms the principle and value of multiculturalism but also points out terrorism and national-security threats to "Australian values" and, by way of addressing these, stresses "integration" over "inclusion." The statement was met with mixed reactions, revealing visible division in society.[103] Political pundits and experts argue that the statement rests on the presumption that Australia has successfully implemented multiculturalism (it is "the world's most successful multicultural nation," according to the statement), but the country still has quite a way to go.[104] On the other hand, others—including ethnic and community groups themselves—praise the statement for acknowledging current tensions while ultimately striving to create unity among Australians through integration programs as a way of fostering inclusivity amid rising racism.[105]

GEOPOLITICAL CONFLICT

Another unsystematic risk to Australia's talent portfolio is political tension with China, which is not only Australia's top trading partner but also its top source for foreign talent.[106] As such, Australia's gain is particularly vulnerable to a change in Chinese immigrants and international students. Tensions between the two countries began to escalate in 2017 as the Australian media reported on Chinese interference in Australian politics. Australia is one of few advanced democracies that does not bar foreigners from financially contributing to political campaigns, and Australia's major parties (Labor and Liberal) accepted donations from businesses with links to China—these in fact were the largest donors to the parties, giving more than AUD 5.5 million between 2013 and 2015. Some Chinese contributors were reported to have connections to the Chinese Communist Party (CCP), and their donations were alleged to be an effort to influence Australia's policies, especially regarding the South China Sea. This report spurred Prime Minister Turnbull to propose foreign-interference laws in 2017, which led to bans on Chinese telecommunications companies Huawei and ZTE and tightening of foreign-political-donation laws. In 2020, the bilateral relations further deteriorated as Australia pushed for an independent investigation into the alleged origins of COVID-19 from China. The public turned highly negative against China—the 2022 Pew Research Center survey shows that 86 percent of Australians have "unfavorable" views of China, a significant increase from 40 percent in 2008 and 57 percent as recently as 2019.[107] The survey finds 52 percent considering China's involvement in Australian politics to be "very serious."[108]

Following the foreign-interference laws, China strongly responded in kind with a diplomatic freeze and economic retaliation. It reduced the amount of coal imports from Australia, placed tariffs on Australian barley, and banned beef from four major Australian exporters.[109] China's response influenced the talent movement from China to Australia as well. Beijing warned its citizens not to travel to Australia, pointing to a significant increase in racist attacks on Asians.[110] China's education ministry urged students to be cautious when returning to Australia, citing multiple discriminatory incidents against Asians. There have been disputes between Chinese students and Australian professors teaching China-related courses in which students alleged the content taught was false or insulting.[111] Furthermore, concerns have arisen over the extent to which the CCP can exert influence over its diaspora and, by extension, its large diaspora in Australia as well.[112]

Rising political tensions with China stand to exact a heavy price on Australian universities and industry, cutting off one of their biggest suppliers of tuition revenue and skilled workers—severely impacting Australia's brain gain. As of 2020, 191,566 Chinese study in Australia, which account for 28 percent of Australia's international-student population.[113] All seven leading Australian universities reportedly have higher proportions of international and Chinese students than any university in the United States and depend on fee-paying Chinese students more than any other university in the English-speaking world. This dependence, however, represents "a high-risk, high-reward international growth strategy," which amounts to a multi-billion-dollar gamble, according to a report authored by Salvatore Babones, a sociologist at the University of Sydney.[114] Looking at visa applications granted to Chinese migrants, the number of total skill-stream visas was down 14.9 percent from 2015–2016 to 2018–2019 and further down from 2018–2019 by 9.65 percent in 2022–2023. Likewise, the number of temporary resident visas for skilled employment was down 30.4 percent and 15.8 percent, respectively.[115] It is not yet clear if this is the result of political friction with China or something else (e.g., fewer Chinese meet the new English-proficiency standards or COVID-19), but these trends attest to the risk of reliance not just on brain gain but on a particular source.

IMPACT OF COVID-19

Most recently, Australia's talent portfolio has been rocked by a systematic risk: the COVID-19 pandemic. While the pandemic affected all four Bs, the Land Down Under instituted pandemic-control policies that hit its brain gain particularly hard. Like most countries throughout the Asia-Pacific region, Australia took extreme measures to prevent the spread of COVID, closing its borders to all nonresidents as of March 2020 and implementing a stringent "zero-COVID" policy until late 2021.[116] These measures led Australia to have a much lower COVID-infection rate than other nations, such as the United States and United Kingdom, but they meant that many skilled migrants and international students were stuck in their home countries.

As a result—and not surprisingly—Australia's brain gain has been strained, and the country has faced a skills shortage. While only 15 percent of firms reported labor as a significant constraint in October 2019, a repeat survey in April 2022 finds the figure increased to 53 percent. Fields like healthcare, technology, and specialized trade have encountered a "structural shortage of skills" that has been exacerbated by the pandemic's halt in immigration. In the 2020–2021 financial year, Australia had a net outflow of 88,800 people—the highest exodus since World War I. In the mid-2020 to mid-2021 period, the number of temporary residence visas granted dropped to about one-third of the number from a decade earlier, and skilled permanent residency visas also saw a significant decline of about 25 percent from two years earlier.[117] In response, the Australian government shifted to approving more skilled migrants from the onshore talent pool, with about 80 percent of applicants selected onshore as opposed to a previous norm of about half.[118] In June of 2022, the Australian government announced that it would expedite the processing of skilled-labor visas.[119]

The pandemic has also negatively impacted the perception that international students—both prospective and current—have of Australia. The strict border closure led to 27 percent of the 307,038 tertiary students with visas being shut outside of Australia,[120] while many students already in Australia felt unsupported by the government during the pandemic. International students did not receive support from the government's COVID-19 aid programs, JobSeeker and JobKeeper, despite 60 percent of international students having lost their jobs due to the pandemic. Prime Minister Scott Morrison even said that foreign students without the means to support themselves should "return to their home countries"—however, flight prices were much higher due to the pandemic. While the government allocated AUD 7 million for the Red Cross's emergency-relief efforts for temporary visa holders,[121] such programs were far less accommodating than those in the United Kingdom, Canada, and New Zealand, which subsidized the wages of temporary visa holders.[122]

It is no surprise, then, that in 2021, Australia's international-student enrollment decreased by 210,000—a significant drop.[123] This trend has continued into the postpandemic years. While Australia's international-student numbers declined by 7.4 percent from 2019–2020 to 2020–2021, it dropped even further, by 18 percent, in the 2021–2022 school year. This contrasts with peer destination countries, like Canada—which had a decline of nearly 50 percent between 2019–2020 and 2020–2021 but had more than recovered its prepandemic numbers by 2021–2022—and the United Kingdom—which never saw a serious pandemic-era decline in international students.[124]

Furthermore, racial discrimination directed at Asians, the largest group of foreign talent in Australia, reportedly spiked during the pandemic. In a 2020 survey of international students and temporary migrants, 52 percent of Chinese respondents say that they experienced verbal abuse or avoidance due to appearance. Ultimately, 59 percent of respondents in the same survey say that they are less likely to recommend Australia as a place to study or work.[125] The systematic risk caused by COVID-19 has undoubtedly undermined Australia's brain gain strategy, threatening the country's overall talent portfolio.

The Fruits of a Well-Balanced Talent Portfolio

Despite recent risks and challenges, overall, Australia has maintained a well-balanced talent portfolio over the decades. Like Japan, Australia's talent portfolio heavily relies on one particular B: brain gain. However, unlike Japan, Australia has been able to make constant rebalancing of its gain-heavy portfolio, both with new sources of brain gain and outside of brain gain, to maintain the diversification. Australia has reconfigured its brain gain to shift from a White Australia to a multicultural Australia and then from permanent family migration to permanent skilled migration. Australia later emphasized demand-driven temporary migration and the "productivity premium" that international students offer. Both institutional (high quality of higher education and elaborate, skilled-oriented migration policies) and cultural (multiculturalism) factors have made its rebalancing successful.

Outside of brain gain, Australia has been paying more attention to the value of the transnational social capital of its network of global alumni. This is a new trend that Australia leads. These alumni are expected to not only facilitate brain linkage between their home country (or their place of current residence) and Australia but also contribute to brain gain by encouraging more international students to come to the country. On the other hand, brain circulation and linkage with Australia's diaspora community are still limited. Australia does not have talent programs or policies aimed at bringing back its overseas citizens, as China does (chapter 5), or actively engage diaspora communities, as India does (chapter 6). Thus, the importance of these Bs in Australia's talent portfolio remains minor compared to the primacy of brain gain and the strong brain train that has enabled Australia's gain.

While brain gain has been largely driven by market forces, the Australian government has not been a passive observer. It has not been a developmental state, like Japan, but has still played a proactive role as a regulatory state in migration policy and higher education. In this regard, R. Koslowski characterizes the Australian policy of migration as "neo-corporatist," which is based on state selection using a point system with extensive business and labor participation. It differs from both the Canadian "human capital" model based on state selection of permanent immigrants using a point system and the "market-oriented, demand-driven model" based primarily on employer selection of migrants, as practiced by the United States.[126]

Australia's talent portfolio is vulnerable to risks, both systematic and unsystematic, however. Talent portfolio theory illuminates the unsystematic risks of brain gain, such as the decline in support for immigration as well as the impact of geopolitical tensions. To address them, the Australian government has sought to improve conditions of overcrowding and insufficient infrastructure and engage its citizens to ensure that they continue to appreciate the benefits of foreign talent. Faced with growing tensions with China, Australia's universities have been looking for "new markets" outside of Chinese students, particularly in "countries with a growing middle class, such as the subcontinent—India, Nepal, Pakistan—and southeast Asian countries—Vietnam, Indonesia, Philippines, Malaysia."[127]

A brain gain strategy is also vulnerable to systematic risks, best illustrated by the impact of the recent pandemic, which has significantly exacerbated skill shortages and constrained talent flows into the country. The main lesson for Australia is that the country must maintain a robust immigration system—with mechanisms in place to support immigrants when such risks strike. Expanding into brain linkage can also help Australia bolster its talent portfolio during periods when brain gain is necessarily reduced. With TPT, we understand why and how Australia has sought to diversify its talent portfolio, both within (brain gain) and between Bs, to mitigate both systematic and unsystematic risks of its gain-heavy portfolio.

FIVE

China

Returning to Serve the Country

In a 2019 interview with PhocusWire, James Liang stresses that his "experience studying and working in the U.S. was extremely valuable" as he launched his business in China in 1999.[1] That business, Trip.com (formerly Ctrip), would ultimately become the largest travel agency in China and one of the first Chinese companies to be listed on the NASDAQ (National Association of Securities Dealers Automatic Quotation System). After studying at Georgia Tech for his bachelor's and master's degree, he joined the R&D team at Oracle Corporation before cofounding the company at home in China. His case is very different from a typical Japanese talent who goes overseas for training while remaining in the domestic labor market, as discussed in chapter 3. Yet for Chinese talent, Liang is far from alone in this experience: Baidu, the biggest search engine in China, was also cofounded by two Chinese individuals who had studied and worked abroad, Robin Li and Eric Xu. In science and academia as well, Chinese returnees have been instrumental. Chen Zhu, former vice president of the Chinese Academy of Sciences (CAS), minister of health, and president of the Red Cross Society of China, was a returnee,[2] as was Xue Qikun, former vice president of Tsinghua University and 2016 winner of the Chinese Future Science Award, known as "China's Nobel Prize."[3] Both, alongside Trip.com's Liang and Baidu's Li, were named in the 2019 "70 overseas returnees in 70 years"—a list of influential returnees.[4]

These stories exemplify China's talent portfolio driven by brain circulation, which played a crucial role in China's rise to global power. In China, talented returnees are called *haigui* (海归), a homophone for the Chinese word for "sea turtle." The metaphor of sea turtles traveling far overseas is an apt one for these transnationally mobile talents. As China's economy boomed in the last two decades, these "sea turtles" have rushed back ashore, seeing great opportunities to apply their overseas education and work experiences in their homeland. While there are various factors that affect people's decisions to move back to their homelands, the Chinese government has increasingly taken a proactive role in encouraging overseas Chinese to return since the 1990s by building infrastructure and creating recruitment programs to offer perks, such as research funds and housing support.

China's brain circulation has been well covered in the current literature. However, unlike previous works that focus on identifying push-and-pull factors of return migration or evaluating the success/failure of China's talent-recruitment programs,[5] I use talent portfolio theory here to show the role of brain circulation in China's overall talent development and delineate the distinctive features of China's portfolio vis-à-vis other talent giants. TPT is also employed to present the evolution of China's talent portfolio over time. For example, when circulating back talents full-time was difficult, China turned to brain linkage to make use of diasporic talent without permanent return and has been turning inward, facing geopolitical tensions with the United States. TPT thus enables us to see how China's circulation-based portfolio has been rebalanced in the face of various risks and challenges.

One conceptual ambiguity is that in China, as in the academic literature, talents are considered *haigui*/returnees regardless of the nature of their overseas experience. There is no distinction between the types of overseas experiences that I separate into brain train (in which a talent is still embedded in the domestic workforce, as discussed in the Japan chapter) and brain circulation, which entails an initial brain drain. However, it is important to conceptually separate short-term brain train experiences (e.g., visiting scholars) from brain circulation experiences (e.g., overseas PhDs or employment) given that they involve different risks and payoffs. Therefore, in this chapter, I indicate where statistics on returnees represent only brain circulation and where they encompass both overseas brain train and brain circulation. As will be demonstrated below, it is clear that the presence of circulated brains in China is significant and vastly different from the case of Japan, where homegrown talent is valued and the majority of overseas experiences are short-term brain train.

In this chapter, I illustrate the composition and evolution of China's talent portfolio, which features brain circulation, by analyzing government-sponsored talent programs. While there are various factors, both personal and professional, pull and push, that facilitated the return of the Chinese diaspora, these programs are illustrative of China's overall talent strategy. In fact, both Chen and Xue, mentioned above, were awarded by some of China's national-level talent programs.[6] Talent programs, therefore, offer an excellent dataset for empirical analysis via TPT, demonstrating how brain circulation factors into China's overall talent portfolio. Through this analysis, we can also understand how China's talent portfolio has evolved over time to address risks, both systematic and unsystematic. The current literature tends to examine these talent programs narrowly and often highlights their shortcomings, such as their inability to draw top-tier talent or their role in tensions with countries that host Chinese talents.[7] Yet they miss an important insight—that is, how such shortcomings have led to a rebalancing of the talent portfolio, revealing the resilience of China's talent strategy.

From Brain Drain to Brain Circulation

Overseas experience has long been valued in modern China. Tens of thousands of Chinese talents have studied science and engineering in the United States since the turn of the twentieth century, most of whom later returned home after completing their studies. They came back to China for various reasons, including to reunite with family, out of a sense of national responsibility to China, and because the Chinese Exclusion Act (enacted in 1882 and repealed in 1943) made it difficult for them to settle in the United States.[8] When the People's Republic of China (PRC) was founded in 1949, "Who's Who of Chinese Scientists" listed 877 distinguished scientists, of which 71 percent had overseas experience.[9] Scholars who had studied abroad accounted for over 90 percent of the first group of CAS academicians elected in 1955.[10] It would not be an exaggeration to say that scientists who had studied in the West, as well as their students, were the backbone of the modern Chinese research and education system.

However, since then, China became increasingly isolated from the global talent market, culminating during the Cultural Revolution (1966–1976), which failed to develop adequate human capital capacity and resulted in a serious deficit in the brain pool. Children and university students spent years in the countryside doing manual labor instead of learning at school, scholars were denounced, scientists fled China, and entrepreneurship was suppressed. The negative impacts of a "missing generation" of scientists and professionals[11]—particularly in industry, science, and technology—became evident as CCP leader Deng Xiaoping embarked on economic reform and development in the 1980s. Given its population size, China did not have a shortage of unskilled or low-skilled workers, but the decline of talent in science and technology became particularly worrisome as the country lacked the manpower necessary for industrial development and for brain train of future generations.

As early as 1978, Deng began sending thousands and even tens of thousands of students and researchers abroad to improve China's talent pool and capacity, especially in academia and the science sector. Originally, these students were chosen by CAS and the Ministry of Education (MOE) and were required to return to their previous employers in China, resembling the Japanese strategy of brain train. In 1985, however, the process was liberalized, allowing universities and other institutions to directly send students abroad. As a result, self-funded students began to go overseas as well with no requirement to return.[12] China was willing to take this initial risk of brain drain for a future payoff. Then CCP general secretary Zhao Ziyang called this outflow "storing brainpower overseas."[13] Deng expressed an ambitious goal for a return rate of around 90 percent.

The reality, however, fell far short of this aim, and China soon faced serious brain drain.[14] In particular, the tragic incident in Tiananmen Square caused serious concern about China's domestic political situation among overseas Chinese talents and discouraged them from returning home.[15] In 1992, Deng still reaffirmed that China should not be dissuaded by the low return rate from sending students abroad, although his expectation had been significantly lowered from 90 percent. At that point, the Chinese leader believed that if even one-tenth returned, the circulation strategy should be considered a success.[16]

Ultimately, Deng was validated. The return rate began to pick up at the turn of the twenty-first century thanks to growing domestic opportunities, which made China more appealing to overseas Chinese. Rapid growth in the economy—due to China's entry into the World Trade Organization, the decision that Beijing would host the 2008 Olympics, and an increase in foreign investment—offered returnees professional and financial opportunities.[17] Particularly in the sciences, career paths were "wide open" for young and emerging talent due to the Cultural Revolution leaving a big age gap in China's scientific talent.[18] In business, China's Reform and Opening Up policy marked new opportunities,[19] as did financial incentives offered by various levels of government for returnees to start businesses at home.[20] The increase in such opportunities contributed to what Saxenian describes as a "Gold Rush" mentality among US-educated Chinese talents, who increasingly returned home.[21]

There was also a strong sense that returnees could make more of an impact in China than if they remained overseas. Xue Lan, the dean of Schwarzman College at Tsinghua University, returned to China from the United States in 1996 before China's financial opportunities were comparable to those in other advanced host nations. As Xue said in an interview with me, his main motivation for returning was that he felt he would be "able to do something that would be impactful" in China, compared to a relatively straightforward and "routine" career path in the United States. There was, he said, "a huge gap" between China and the United States, meaning that returnees "might be able to do something."[22] Sometimes, such sentiment borders on patriotism. She Zhensu, a returnee mathematician who left his tenured professorship at UCLA to lead an experimental group at Peking University in 1999, says that, despite taking a large salary cut, moving back to China was "an opportunity for me to contribute to higher education and research in my motherland."[23] While survey data find that patriotism is not necessarily a main motivating factor for most returnees[24]—despite the CCP's attempts to appeal to it—there still is a sense of mission or purpose. As molecular biologist Shi Yigong—who resigned from his professorship at Princeton in 2008, turned down a USD 10 million Howard Hughes Medical Institute grant, and returned to China—says, "I felt I owed China something. . . . In the United States, everything is more or less set up. Whatever I do here [in China], the impact is probably tenfold, or a hundredfold."[25]

Other factors further accelerated China's brain circulation. The burst of the dot-com bubble at the turn of the century made it difficult for non-resident foreigners to stay in the United States on a working visa. Xenophobia after the terrorist attacks of September 11, 2001, also led foreigners, including Chinese, to return home.[26] The 2008 financial crisis accelerated this trend, as China's economy remained robust compared to other major economies that struggled with recessions, pulling many Chinese living abroad back home.[27] As H. Wang and Y. Bao note, while the financial crisis led many governments elsewhere to cut back their support for science and technology (S&T) research, China continued to increase its S&T spending.[28] It was not a mere coincidence that, in 2008, the Chinese government initiated its flagship talent program, the Thousand Talents Program (TTP). According to Cong Cao, TTP was established to "further address the 'brain drain' problem" by taking "advantage of the global financial crisis that cost some professionals, including scientists and researchers, their positions."[29] The graph below clearly reveals this trend. While the number of Chinese returnees rather slowly increased between 2000 and 2008, it accelerated from 2009 onward. Since 2013, the return rate has remained stable at over 80 percent (see figure 5.1). A huge brain drain turned into enormous developmental assets through brain circulation. As of 2018, the Chinese government recorded that 5.86 million students had gone abroad since 1978, of whom 3.65 million (62.3 percent) had returned home.[30]

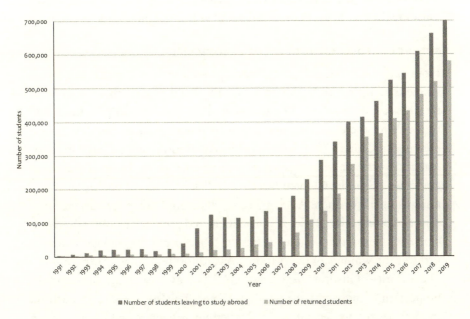

FIGURE 5.1. Number of Chinese students going abroad and returning home, and ratio of returnees to departing students (%).

Source: National Bureau of Statistics (various years), as cited in Cao (2008), p 337.

Note: Numbers of returned students are from the National Bureau of Statistics. As statistics do not differentiate between students who engaged in overseas brain train and those who engaged in brain circulation, this data includes both.

Haigui *Contributions*

China's rise was as impressive as Japan's, but its talent strategy featured brain circulation, differing markedly from Japan's train-centered portfolio. As of 2018, China's share of global science and engineering publications is 21 percent, whereas the United States' is 17 percent.[31] China has increased its number of unicorns—startups with a valuation of more than USD 1 billion each—from twenty-two at the end of 2015 to 312 by the end of 2022.[32] In 2010, according to the Academic Ranking of World Universities, mainland China had no universities in the top one hundred globally and just two in the top two hundred, with twenty-two in the top five hundred. A decade later, China had six in the top one hundred, twenty-two in the top two hundred, and seventy-one in the top five hundred.[33] *Haigui* have played an important role in driving these successes, serving in leadership positions and operating at the forefront of S&T research, academic trends, and high-tech business ventures in China. Their contributions in these sectors illustrate the value that brain circulation has had in China's talent portfolio.

SCIENCE AND TECHNOLOGY DEVELOPMENT

From early on, science and engineering were the most popular majors for Chinese going to study abroad,[34] and these individuals then acted upon return as catalysts in speeding the technology and knowledge transfer and thus closing the developmental gap with more advanced nations. *Haigui* presence in China's S&T is formidable. As of 2004, individuals with overseas brain train or who engaged in brain circulation make up 81 percent of academicians in the Chinese Academy of Sciences and 54 percent of academicians in the Chinese Academy of Engineering.[35] They are 72 percent of directors of key laboratories at the national and provincial levels, two-thirds of the winners of the National Award for Science and Technology, and two-fifths of the winners of the National Award for Technological Invention.[36] The majority of institute directors at CAS have overseas experience, and the proportion of those with overseas experience grew from 60.8 to 72.3 percent from 2002 to 2013 (see table 5.1). While more directors had overseas brain train experience (visiting scholars) than education that is considered brain circulation, the notable percentage of individuals who circulated back to China after receiving overseas PhDs demonstrates the importance of brain circulation to China's science system and differs markedly from Japan.

TABLE 5.1. International experience of institute directors under CAS, 2002 and 2013

Year	Visiting scholars (overseas brain train)	Overseas PhDs (brain circulation)	No overseas experience
2002	41.9%	18.9%	39.2%
2013	45.5%	26.8%	27.7%

Source: Zweig (2017).

Note: This data was collected by Dr. Kang Siqin.

Returnees have helped to raise both the quality and quantity of Chinese research, contributing to the rapid improvement of China's global standing in science and technology. A study of biological publications in *Nature* is illustrative. In 1993, no biological articles had Chinese mainland scholars as first authors, but, in 2013, there were eighteen publications from China, and 64.5 percent of the corresponding authors were cases of brain circulation.[37] Returnees have also facilitated brain linkage through international collaboration—in 2017, 27 percent of China's international papers were authored by returnees, with experiences spanning both overseas brain train and brain circulation.[38] A 2023 study by the Australian Strategic Policy Institute finds that one-fifth of China's high-impact papers are authored by researchers who have postgraduate training in Australia, the United States, Canada, New Zealand, or the United Kingdom.[39]

Haigui scientists have contributed to technological development in China as well. Life sciences, which have been vital to China's biotech boom, serve as a good example. Dan Zhang, the former secretary-general of the Thousand Talents Program and chief executive of Fountain Medical Development, says that returnees have had a "huge impact" on the biotech industry. According to Zhang, returnees are behind most drug approvals in China, prevalent in peer-review committees and as faculty members in the life sciences, and often made university deans at pharmacy and medicine schools. China has been edging out large multinational biopharma firms in attracting top talent by providing large growth prospects, equity offers, and roles with increased responsibility. Chinese companies seek out returnees because they "have worked in countries such as the United States, where the drug industries are more mature and people have had greater experience of overseeing the development of innovative drugs."[40]

Returnees also provide leadership for science and technology, often serving as directors, ministers, and presidents of China's scientific institutes and laboratories. For example, Wan Gang, who was appointed as the minister of science and technology in 2007, is a returnee who received his PhD in Germany and then stayed abroad to serve as manager of Audi's production and planning departments. After fifteen years overseas, Wan returned to China to work on electric automobiles there, earning the nickname of China's Father of Electric Cars. Wan also served as president of Tongji University in Shanghai. During his tenure as minister of science and technology, to boost innovation, Wan introduced various reform measures to Chinese S&T: fostering talent, providing for collaboration between industry and academia, and applying research to improve products. Another example of returnee leadership in reforming China's S&T is Rao Zihe, who received his PhD from the University of Melbourne and worked as a postdoctoral researcher at Oxford before returning to China. Rao became the director of the Institute of Biophysics at CAS and helped lead two programs designed to upgrade China's S&T: the National Frontier Research Program (973 Program) and National High Technology Research and Development Program (863 Program).[41] The impacts of returnees on the S&T sector clearly show the importance of brain circulation in China's talent strategy, contributing to China's economic ascendance.

HIGHER EDUCATION AND BRAIN TRAIN

Haigui scholars have occupied key positions in China's higher education and research institutes as well. Unlike in Japan, advanced degrees from well-known foreign universities, especially those in the United States and United Kingdom, are premiums to professorial careers at Chinese universities. Even for those scholars without foreign degrees, overseas brain train via short-term stays as visiting scholars in foreign universities have become popular as they are important for career development. From 1999 to 2013, the majority of 376 presidents of top Chinese universities had overseas education or experiences, reaching 80 percent by 2007. Among them, about 50 percent had overseas PhDs (circulation), and 30 percent went abroad as visiting scholars (train).[42] As such, upon return, they were able to not only engage in research and reforms but also help with the brain train of China's younger generations of talent and facilitate brain linkage through international collaboration.

A study of over 4,500 university faculty with PhDs in eighty-eight Chinese higher education institutions shows similar findings. As shown in figure 5.2, 28.49 percent of faculty in Project 985 universities—the top universities in China—count as brain circulation, markedly greater than the 18.52 percent of faculty that were brain circulation in the next tier of elite schools, Project 211 universities, and almost three times greater than the percent of circulated faculty in other Chinese universities.[43] Another study finds that from 2011 to 2017, more than 80 percent of newly recruited faculty members at the two leading Chinese universities (Peking University and Tsinghua University) either have overseas degrees or have at least worked full-time abroad.[44] It is quite clear from these findings that overseas Chinese who represent brain circulation are more likely to occupy academic positions at universities with higher prestige and better academic resources.

The role of returnees in the higher education system is indisputable, as China aims to cultivate a massive domestic-talent pool to meet the growing demand for highly skilled labor generated by its transition to a knowledge-

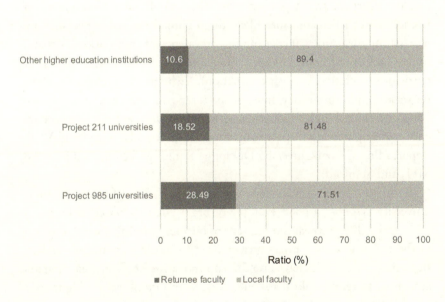

FIGURE 5.2. Ratio of returnee faculty by levels of higher education institutions.

Source: Li, Y. (2020), p. 120.

Note: Project 985 universities represent the top universities in China, while those in Project 211 are also high ranking but not quite as prestigious.

based economy. A 2013 McKinsey report estimates that a third of employers in China struggle to recruit skilled workers, largely due to applicants' lack of skills.[45] To meet this challenge, similar to what the Japanese government did in the 1960s and 1970s, the Chinese government has made huge investments to expand higher education, and the number of universities almost tripled from 2001 to 2014, with a rapid expansion of science and engineering departments.[46] As part of this effort, China seeks to enhance the global competitiveness of its universities. Similar to Japan's Top Global University Project, China's Double First-Class Initiative (the "double" referring to World First-Class University and First-Class Academic Discipline Initiatives), which was launched in 2015, aims at turning forty-two of China's universities and 465 academic disciplines into world-class levels through staff development, funding, and performance assessment.

Given that global rankings are in large part assessed by the number of citations of papers produced in English by faculty members and research collaborations with other universities around the world, the contribution of returnee scholars has been enormous. Compared to domestically trained faculty, returnees are 39 percent more likely to attend international conferences and 71 percent more likely to go abroad for visiting scholar and research opportunities, increasing the prevalence of transnational collaboration—a form of brain linkage.[47] They also lead in internationalizing the curriculum (offering English instruction),[48] which is important for global university rankings. Today, most of the forty-two first-class universities in China are ranked highly globally, and Tsinghua University's Computer Science and Engineering Departments topped the 2020 US News and World Report's Best Global University Discipline Rankings, beating out Harvard, MIT, and Stanford.[49]

Returnees have spearheaded new initiatives and reforms in China's university system—a good example of brain circulation's contribution to brain train. They introduced master's of business administration programs in the 1980s, feeding China's greater need for business managers and entrepreneurs. Returnees have also driven innovative R&D in education and academia, fostering links between academia and industry.[50] In higher education, the difference between returnee talents who represent brain circulation and those who only had short-term overseas brain train experiences becomes clear, with the former making more significant contributions.[51] As a research team led by David Zweig finds, universities with presidents who had an overseas PhD were more likely to attract participants in national-talent programs—that is, top returnees—compared to universities with presidents who only had overseas visiting scholarships. As Zweig says in a 2017 talk at the Wilson Center, these PhDs "will transform that [university's] culture, and the university will do better."[52]

One key example of a returnee-led initiative comes from Professor Andrew Chi-Chih Yao, a leading computer scientist and Turing Award winner who was born in China but completed his undergraduate education in Taiwan and two PhDs in the United States. Upon return to China, Yao set up the famed Yao Class at Tsinghua University in 2005. The program "adopts advanced teaching methods from MIT, Stanford and Princeton" (all institutions at which Yao taught) and has been hailed as a "successful example in China's endeavor to cultivate innovative talents." Yao, who had become a US citizen and held tenure at a prestigious American university, made the remarkable decision to renounce both his citizenship and his secure academic position in 2015. This move underscores his deep commitment to developing China's educational landscape and demonstrates a successful case of brain circulation. Students in the Yao Class have plenty of opportunities for overseas brain train and transnational research collaboration as the course includes exchange programs at leading universities worldwide thanks to Yao's overseas networks.[53]

Other returnees have improved hiring practices and further expanded and internationalized Chinese higher education. Min Weifang, a returnee who received his PhD in the economics of education at Stanford University, served as party secretary of Peking University and led the university in 2004 to launch a groundbreaking educational-reform plan. The reforms were heavily based on the American educational model and were designed to encourage more competitive hiring and promotion processes and the regular evaluation of professors. These new practices would work particularly favorably for returnees.[54] Min was also instrumental to the establishment of the Stanford Center at Peking University, a good example of brain linkage as it seeks to foster international collaboration and "represents a bridge across the Pacific for Stanford."[55] *Haigui* scholars thus contribute to both brain train and linkage, bolstering Chinese universities and stimulating collaboration across borders.

INNOVATION AND ENTREPRENEURSHIP

Haigui, by and large representing brain circulation, have led a new generation of entrepreneurs in a rapidly emerging sphere of China's economy. As of 2011, about 80 percent of the high-tech, NASDAQ-listed Chinese enterprises, including Baidu and Trip.com, were started by those who had returned to China after studying abroad.[56] As of mid-2015, one-third of the total NASDAQ-listed Chinese companies are led by "elite returnees," comprising over 36 percent of members of their management groups.[57] China has made itself a hospitable environment for entrepreneurship and an attractive place for returnees to found startups.[58] As of 2019, there are 367 "pioneer parks" for returnees,[59] hosting more than 23,000 businesses and employing 93,000 personnel.[60] Returnees have also been instrumental in starting up a venture capital arena in China: almost all of the venture capital firms in China were founded by returnees, and almost all international venture capital companies in China are managed or partly owned by returnees.[61] Whereas Silicon Valley has relied heavily on Chinese and Indian immigrants, the development of science and technology hubs in China since the late 1990s has been largely thanks to returnees.[62]

Haigui have led China's innovation in IT and other high-tech areas. A study finds that small and medium-sized enterprises owned by returnees perform better than those owned by local entrepreneurs in the Zhongguancun (known as China's Silicon Valley) cluster. This is in part because returnee entrepreneurs gain a competitive edge by utilizing their knowledge and transnational networks acquired overseas to harness business and development opportunities in China's emerging economy.[63] A study by Zweig et al. also shows that in high-tech zones, foreign PhDs (brain circulation) are more likely than those who have not been overseas to import technology and capital, use that technology to target the domestic market, and establish an international collaborative project.[64] Saxenian calls these entrepreneurs "new Argonauts"—individuals who return home to start new companies while remaining tied to powerful economic and professional communities abroad.[65]

The new Argonauts created a significant knowledge- and technology-spillover effect that promoted innovation in other local high-tech firms, including entrepreneurial firms founded by locals, and collaborated with local firms. For example, graphic-chip technologies developed by returnee-founded company Vimicro Corporation, established in 1999, have impacted the technological landscape of other Chinese companies.[66] Returnees and local talents can often combine their distinct forms of human capital—*haigui*'s management methods learned from overseas and locals' knowledge of local markets—to thrive in Chinese business. A 2012–2013 study by Wang and Bao looks at the core management teams of returnee entrepreneurial firms and finds that the majority of chairmen, general managers, and R&D directors are returnees, while the roles of financial director, human resources manager, and sales or marketing director are more frequently filled by locals.[67] Clearly, brain circulation has played a significant role in boosting China's startup scene.

Returning to Serve the Country

Given the crucial contribution of *haigui* to China's development, previous studies have focused on identifying various factors—both pull and push—that affect their decisions to return since the 1990s.[68] However, in this study, I focus on government policies and initiatives, as they are highly useful in illustrating the overall nature and evolution of China's talent portfolio. This is particularly important in a country, like China, where the developmental state has spearheaded its rise. In fact, under the slogan of "Returning to serve the country" (*hui guo fuwu*; 回国服务), the Chinese government, both central and regional, established countless programs and initiatives to attract overseas Chinese talent. Even for those who did not directly participate in government talent programs, the slogan provides a broader cultural environment in China that is conducive to brain circulation. In this chapter, unlike previous studies that tend to focus on evaluating the efficacy of such talent programs, I use talent portfolio theory to show the role of brain circulation in China's overall talent development and its evolution over time through rebalancing.

The 2006 Five-Year Plan for Overseas Returnees well captures the essence of China's brain circulation strategy.[69] Proclaiming that overseas Chinese are an important source of the national-talent pool and a precious commodity, the plan outlines concrete goals. These include an increase in the number of returnees to between 150,000 and two hundred thousand, the establishment of a total of 150 overseas-scholar pioneer parks, and reaching ten thousand enterprises by overseas returnees in those parks within the plan's five-year period. Those parks offer special perks to returnee entrepreneurs, such as office space and facilities, seed money, discounted rent, and streamlined paperwork procedures.[70] In addition, the plan outlines simplifications for overseas scholars' entry into the country, supporting their settling in. The importance of brain circulation continued to be recognized into the next decade—in 2015, President Xi Jinping called for overseas Chinese students to be one of the three main focus areas of the activities of the powerful United Front Work Department of the CCP.[71] By 2018, brain circulation had become so important that the department took charge of it with the mission of "guiding" overseas Chinese.[72]

In this regard, it is worth noting that brain circulation is necessarily preceded by a certain amount of brain linkage, as diasporic talents must be connected enough to their home from overseas to know about potential opportunities to which they can return. Therefore, as part of its efforts to draw back overseas Chinese, the government has sought to foster a series of networks and organizations to connect with overseas Chinese and encourage them to contribute, and ideally return, to their homeland. The 2006 Five-Year Plan emphasizes the importance of giving "full play to the roles of every type of overseas scholar organization and social group." The best example of this is the Chinese Student and Scholar Associations, of which there are approximately 150 chapters in the United States alone as of 2015.[73] Through these organizations, the Chinese government provides overseas students with guidance on study and travel, connections to Chinese leaders, and information about opportunities in China. The CCP also sent recruitment delegations to meet with overseas Chinese and has built a series of websites and databases where interested talents can obtain information on job openings in China as well as opportunities to participate in talent programs.[74] These efforts represent initial linkage with the diaspora for the purpose of brain circulation—a phenomenon which I will discuss in greater detail below.

The high value placed on brain circulation is nowhere more apparent than in China's multitude of government-sponsored talent programs. This extensive network of programs includes those that have elements of all four Bs, demonstrating China's efforts to maintain a diversified talent portfolio, but brain circulation has been by far the most pervasive. Such brain circulation programs are not unique to China, and in fact, early on, China tried to emulate similar talent strategies from Korea and Taiwan.[75] However, Chinese programs have been far more extensive and aggressive in their recruitment than has been seen anywhere else. Such programs generally may not offer enough of a financial incentive to be the main pull factor drawing back talents, tending to cover only initial setup costs of return or work "more like an added bonus," according to Xue Lan.[76] Still, government-led talent programs have served as extra incentives in addition to market opportunities and have helped to create the sense that returnees are appreciated back home, facilitating China's brain circulation. Furthermore, they offer excellent cases to illustrate China's overall talent strategy, and thus, analyzing these programs helps us to capture the main features and nature of China's talent portfolio and how it has been changed over time.

China's network of programs for the attraction of overseas Chinese talent is vast and run by both central and local governments (such as Beijing and Shanghai). Over 80 percent of talent-recruitment programs are currently run at the subnational level, and these attract as many as seven times more scientists than the national programs.[77] While subnational talent programs thus may have a bigger influence on reverse flow in terms of overall size,[78] I focus on national-level programs because these can be taken as better representative of China's talent-recruitment efforts overall. These programs are aimed at attracting the most highly educated and skilled talents that China desperately needs.[79] Furthermore, local government talent-recruitment initiatives—particularly those aimed at recruiting overseas talents—are often modeled off of national-level programs and take guidance from national policies.[80] Finally, some national-level programs are enacted and recruited into at the local or institutional level. For example, in the national Thousand Talents Program, universities and local governments are tasked with nominating candidates.[81]

One of the earliest circulation-oriented talent programs, the National Natural Sciences Foundation of China's 1994 National Science Fund for Distinguished Young Scholars, is illustrative of China's ambitions for its overseas talents and was, in fact, envisioned by a returnee, Chen Zhangliang. Chen earned his PhD at Washington University in St. Louis before returning to China in 1987 and becoming an associate professor at Peking University at age twenty-seven.[82] Worried about the aging and deteriorating state of China's scientific-research-talent pool, Chen suggested, in a 1994 speech, establishing a fund to annually support young scholars studying abroad to return to China to serve the motherland.[83] The National Science Fund for Distinguished Young Scholars requires awardees to work full-time, nine months per year, in China. The funding amount has been continually increased, and award tenure has been extended from three to four years in 1999 and now to five years.[84] Out of 1,176 recipients awarded by 2004, 98.5 percent had foreign experience encompassing brain circulation (e.g., PhDs, postdocs) or brain train (e.g., visiting scholars), with 32.8 percent having foreign PhDs.[85] As of 2017, the program has funded 3,796 awardees.[86] Among the recipients are former CAS vice president, minister of health, and Red Cross Society president Chen Zhu, and former Tsinghua University vice president Xue Qikun, mentioned earlier.[87]

Although definitive results from many programs are difficult to come by and numbers differ across sources, government reports and scholarly research have collected some notable outcomes from several of the national-level circulation programs.[88] These are listed in table 5.2 below. These programs are run by different agencies of the Chinese government with different focuses from education to science to business, and it is clear from these results that they have been awarded to a significant number of Chinese returnees.

Using talent portfolio theory, I now further examine how brain circulation (vs. other Bs) was featured in China's overall talent portfolio and how this portfolio has evolved over time. I conducted a quantitative analysis of thirty-two top national-level talent programs, which I identified as the major programs aimed at harnessing skilled individuals for China's talent development. The sample set includes programs that provide funding to individuals (and their research projects or their startup ideas) and does not include more generalized programs aimed at upgrading universities or boosting China's technological innovation. In addition, separate tracks within an overarching program are not counted as separate programs (i.e., the Young Chang Jiang Scholars Program was not counted separately from the Chang Jiang Scholars Program). Programs in the sample are run by the Ministry of Human Resources and Social Security, Ministry of Education, National Natural Science Foundation of China (NSFC), Chinese Academy of Sciences, State Administration of Foreign Experts Affairs, Ministry of Science and Technology (MOST), the Organization Department of the CCP, and the Central Leading Group for Coordinating Talent Work. I categorize these programs by the B strategy they have undertaken, based on the following criteria.[89]

"Train programs" are those that award to domestic Chinese talents. Pro-

TABLE 5.2. Select circulation-oriented talent programs and results

Program	Dates	Agency	Sector	Results (most recent)
Financial Support for Outstanding Young Professors	1987–2004	Education Commission (MOE precursor)	Higher ed.	2,218 returning professors by end of 2003, over 90% returnees
Seed Fund for Returned Overseas Scholars	1990–present (suspended in 2015 only)	MOE	Higher ed., S&T	10,926 returnees as of 2009
Hundred Talents Program	1994–present	CAS	S&T	1,122 full-time returnees by 2008
National Science Fund for Distinguished Young Scholars	1994–present	NSFC	S&T	Of 1,176 awardees as of 2004, 98.5% had foreign experience as of 2008
Chang Jiang Scholars Program	1998–present	MOE, Li Ka Shing Foundation	Higher ed.	As of 2017, 2,298 distinguished professors (full-time), 89% of which were returnees
Chunhui Cup	2006–present	MOE, MOST	Business	634 startups established in China by the end of 2018

Sources: Zweig (2006); People's Republic of China Ministry of Education (2009); Hao (2009); Cao (2008); Zhu (2019); Alliance Manchester Business School (2019).

grams that are geared toward circulation generally also award to a small portion of domestic applicants with no foreign experience as well. When this is the case, and when the plan is clearly circulation-focused, train is not counted as a main B of the program. "Gain programs" are those that seek to attract foreign talent to relocate to China permanently. For the purpose of this analysis, I deemed that working in China on a full-time basis (nine months per year) for three years represents a permanent relocation. "Circulation programs" are those that target Chinese diasporic talents to return permanently (again, nine months per year for three years) to China. It can be assumed that most brain train plans also include some returnees among their awardees, so circulation was only counted as a main B of a program if the program description or the secondary literature states that drawing back returnees is a specific goal. "Linkage programs" are those with part-time or short-term (fewer than nine months per year—in most cases two to three months per year) tracks or those that seek to foster collaboration between domestic Chinese and overseas Chinese or foreign talents.

My analysis demonstrates the salience of brain circulation among China's highest-level talent programs in the early years. As shown by figure 5.3, these programs were largely circulation-oriented in the 1990s and 2000s. However, my analysis also shows an important shift in China's talent portfolio since then, which is reflected by the increase in talent programs that are linkage focused—from the mid-2010s, linkage had surpassed circulation. However, as discussed below, this linkage was not to replace circulation but was often supplementary or as a stepping stone to circulation, which continued to be the hallmark of China's talent strategy through the 2010s. The number of brain train programs also remains relatively high since the turn of the century, but it is important to note that this reflects the foundational nature of brain train in any country's talent portfolio. Furthermore, talents participating in these brain train programs generally are not of as high a caliber as those that the circulation and linkage programs seek to attract. Some of these brain train plans in fact involve the train of domestic Chinese talents *by* permanent or temporary returnees who were participants in brain circulation or linkage programs, such as the Chang Jiang Scholars Program or Hundred Talents Program, further illustrating the importance of brain circulation and linkage. Finally, brain gain began to appear from the mid-2010s.

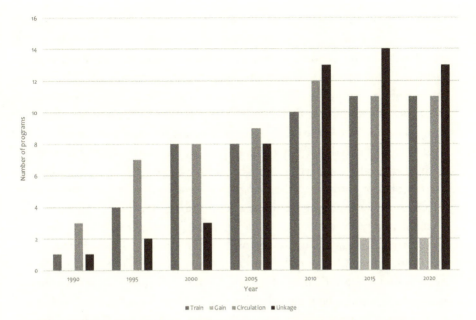

FIGURE 5.3. Four B strategies of China's major talent programs.

Source: Author created.

Note: 1990: N = 4; 1995: N = 9; 2000: N = 14; 2005: N = 17; 2010: N = 23; 2015: N = 24; 2020: N = 24. Numbers in the chart may surpass the total number of programs for that year because one program can pursue multiple B strategies.

Serving the Country

As demonstrated by my analysis, while China continues its efforts toward brain circulation, it has also begun to engage more in brain linkage to diversify its talent portfolio. This shift has especially been important and timely given that China's circulation efforts faced criticism inside the country, as some of the very top-tier overseas Chinese talents that China needs the most were still reluctant to return permanently in spite of proactive recruitment efforts.[90] It is worth noting that China is one of the few countries that has experienced a notable decline in the five-year-stay rate for science and engineering PhDs in the United States (98 to 85 percent from 2001 to 2011),[91] but the rate still remains high. As of 2018, the stay rate of overseas Chinese in the United States with PhDs in artificial intelligence–related disciplines—fields in most strong demand currently—is over 90 percent, which is about the same level as in 2014.[92] Continued lack of institutional autonomy and increasing politicization of universities and companies, along with research conditions that are inhibited by internet censorship and restricted funding, are said to disincentivize globally in-demand Chinese talent from returning.[93]

It was in this context that *People's Daily*, the official newspaper of the Central Committee of the CCP, lamented that China was experiencing "the world's worst brain drain," referring, in 2013, to the statistic that 87 percent of top science and engineering specialists who went to work or study abroad did not plan on returning.[94] Some *haigui* even went back to their previous host country (or to another country) after spending some time in China—a phenomenon referred to as "reverse circulation," or *guihai* (归海).[95] Hongbin Li, an economist and codirector of the Center for the Chinese Economy and Institutions at Stanford University, is one such case of reverse circulation. Li moved from China to Stanford for his PhD in 1995, and when he finished his studies, he joined the Economics Department at the Chinese University of Hong Kong. He then moved back to Beijing to teach at Tsinghua University in 2007 before returning to Stanford in 2016. Describing this reverse circulation in a 2019 interview with me, he said, "My wife and I . . . just made circles."[96]

If top overseas talents were not willing to abandon their current positions abroad, many were still interested in spending short periods in China or working with China, engaging in transnational collaboration. Often, they wanted to both work in China and keep their overseas jobs. In the words of Jun Liu, a Harvard statistician, "If you have a tenured professorship [in the United States], it does not make sense to give up the position."[97] To accommodate such interests in working in both places, the government added part-time tracks to talent programs and even created short-term programs, largely in the hopes that short-term stays in China might ultimately lead talents to permanently relocate.[98] Some talents have indeed relocated after engaging in such brain linkage. Poo Mu-Ming, a neuroscientist who has been a professor at UC Berkeley since 2000, helped create the Institute of Neuroscience in Shanghai in 1999 and served as its founding director. For more than ten years, Poo made frequent trips to Shanghai from Berkeley until, ultimately, this brain linkage led to circulation: in 2017, Poo gave up his US citizenship to return to China full-time.[99]

Even if this goal of permanent return was not reached, such short-term gigs could connect "temporary" returnees—and their social capital and overseas networks—to China, building transnational bridges. The government recognized that overseas talents could play an important role in transferring scientific knowledge and embedding the international research system in Chinese laboratories without making a permanent return. Hongjie Dai, a Chinese American scientist, for example, received his master's of science and PhD in the United States and has served as a professor of chemistry at Stanford since 1997. While staying at Stanford, Dai has also held positions in China: in 2013, he was appointed a member of the International Advisory Board of Suzhou Institute of Biomedical Engineering and Technology at the Chinese Academy of Sciences, and, in 2019, he was named a foreign academician of CAS.[100]

Brain linkage has clearly increased in importance as a feature of China's talent portfolio over time, as illustrated by figure 5.3 above, which shows a rising number of linkage-focused programs. In contrast to the slogan "Returning to serve the country," the phrase "Serving the country" (*wei guo fuwu*; 为国服务)—omitting the "return"—had been in fact used since the late 1990s, providing a rationale for brain linkage.[101] A 2001 policy document titled "A Number of Opinions Regarding the Encouragement of Overseas Scholars to Serve the Country in Various Ways" identifies categories of activities to support linkage with overseas Chinese talent, such as working concurrently in China and the host country, participating in domestic R&D projects from abroad, collaborating with or accepting work from domestic companies, and serving as a bridge between China and foreign countries by establishing intermediary agencies, thereby facilitating cross-border collaboration. Returnees were also encouraged to continue to collaborate with their overseas colleagues, many of whom were "seagulls" (*haiou*; 海鸥), or "new Argonauts"—highly skilled scholars, managers, and investors with internationalized experience, professional networks, and finances who travel back and forth between China and their overseas bases.[102]

The government stepped up its efforts to promote transnational linkage, particularly to engage with the top-tier overseas Chinese talent that was less likely to give up their overseas jobs to return. For instance, the Ministry of Education's Chang Jiang Scholars Program and the Chinese Academy of Science's Hundred Talents Program both initially sought participants who would work full-time—nine months per year—in China. However, when top-tier researchers were reluctant to give up their overseas positions,

MOE quickly created a part-time track (chair professors) within the Chang Jiang Scholars Program for associate professors or higher.[103] Through short-term stays or frequent visits, the diaspora was encouraged to more actively connect with the homeland, facilitating brain linkage.[104] In 2009, the Ministry of Human Resources and Social Security established the Chizi Plan, short for the "Red Sons" Serving the Country Action Plan for Overseas Chinese. Its main objective was to "encourage overseas scholars studying and working abroad who temporarily cannot return to the country to, with their understanding of advanced technology and management knowledge, serve their mother country through various methods as an effective way to fully utilize talent resources both domestically and abroad."[105] Within a decade, the plan attracted more than ten thousand skilled overseas workers "to serve the country," over eighteen thousand collaborative technological projects to participate in implementation in China, over seven thousand signed partnership agreements or established partnership intentions, and over five hundred training lectures held for over ten thousand participating professional technical personnel, with 1,600 on-site.[106] All these efforts capture the rebalancing of China's circulation-focused talent portfolio with increased brain linkage.[107]

Former *haigui* have often continued to engage China after leaving. Li, for example, worked with James Liang (a *haigui*) to establish the Stanford-China Economic Summit and invited many Chinese as visiting scholars to Stanford, fostering brain linkage between the United States and China. Columbia business school professor Dan Wang finds that the returnees who are most successful at transferring knowledge in China are also the most likely to want to ultimately return to the United States. This is because "their network in the United States is very dense and rich—the same thing that provides them with a path to success in their home countries also pulls them back to the United States."[108] It is then only natural that they are well positioned to promote transnational linkage using social capital built in both places even after leaving home again.

China has further diversified its brain linkage efforts, expanding to linkage with non-Chinese foreign talent through initiatives such as the Fellowships and Cooperative Programs for Foreign Talent by CAS. As of 2012, 742 foreign scientists had been brought to China as CAS Visiting Professors for Senior International Scientists, and 240 young researchers from overseas won CAS Fellowships for Young International Scientists. Although these scientists are not generally brain gain for China, as they are not expected to stay in China beyond the scope of their fellowship, they can expand China's brain linkage.[109] One example is the Einstein Professorship, which invites prominent international scholars to China for one or two weeks. During their visit, they tour CAS institutes and give lectures at CAS universities. After returning to their home countries, these professors are encouraged to maintain connections with their Chinese counterparts and often host them or their students for brief periods in their own laboratories. As of 2012, 109 Einstein Professorships were awarded to foreigners in top scientific fields, including sixteen Nobel laureates, three Turing Prize winners, two Wolf Prize winners, and one winner of the Tyler Prize for Environmental Achievement.[110]

Thanks to the increase in brain linkage, China's talent portfolio has become more balanced and diversified in recent years, as figure 5.3 shows: the number of major talent programs with an element of linkage increased more than fourfold from 2000 to 2015 alone. At the same time, the continued prevalence of brain circulation attests that China has not given up its goal of drawing back returnees permanently but that this was increasingly complemented with linkage. In my analysis of major national-level programs, of the fifteen talent programs that had linkage elements, only five of these had linkage itself as a primary goal; the remaining ten utilized linkage either as a means to achieve circulation via "soft landing" or as the second-best option when they struggled to circulate talents back permanently. Thus, while the turn to linkage began to pick up in the mid-2000s, it is important to understand that brain circulation and linkage are not mutually exclusive. Rather, many programs have combined both, and linkage programs with overseas Chinese are often undergirded by the hope that such short-term stays will lead to permanent return. Nonetheless, this trend reveals China's efforts to rebalance its talent portfolio over time—an important insight that TPT illuminates compared to current literature, which focuses on the achievements or shortcomings of brain circulation programs.

Thousand Talents Program

The Thousand Talents Program, launched in 2008 as China's flagship recruitment program, encapsulates the evolution of China's talent portfolio from a circulation-oriented one into a more complex one supplemented by brain linkage and gain. The TTP was a centrally implemented "signature" program of brain circulation aiming to bring leading scientists and other overseas experts to China for innovation, entrepreneurship, and academic research (see table 5.3). The original plan consisted of two tracks, both circulation oriented: the Innovative Talents track and the Entrepreneur track. TTP aimed to utilize top overseas talent to boost China's scientific programs in support of high-tech development, such as the Made in China 2025 plan.[111] It has been key in giving Beijing better access to R&D, strategic intellectual property, and talent pools that took years to develop at US and European institutions.[112] Given its focus on engaging with talent that is already abroad, this strategy departs from Japan's approach toward technological borrowing by sending domestic talents overseas for predetermined periods, as discussed in chapter 3.

TABLE 5.3. Thousand Talents Program tracks: Evolution over time

Track	Date	Term	B
Innovative Talents (long-term)	2008	Full-time (six months per year for three years)	Circulation
Entrepreneur	2008	Full-time	Circulation
Youth TTP	2010	Full-time	Circulation
Innovative Talents (short-term)	2010	Part-time (at least two months per year for three years)	Linkage (foreigners and Chinese)
Foreign Experts	2011	Full-time (nine months per year for three years)	Gain
Topnotch Talents and Teams	2013	Full-time for five years	Gain

Sources: Cao et al. (2020); Cao (2017); Zweig & Kang (2020); Salvina (2015); Communist Party of China Central Organization Department (2020).

Note: The Innovative Talents plan considers six months per year full-time for this track, which was a point of contention when it was first released as those who drafted the plan originally had proposed a true full-time term. It is also worth noting that there apparently were frequent exceptions made to the terms and types of talent (foreign vs. diaspora, e.g.) set out in each of the TTP tracks, such that there could be, for example, nonethnic Chinese individuals in the Innovative Talents long-term track or individuals working part-time when they were supposed to be full-time. See Xin (2009).

Due to interest being lower than anticipated for the reasons identified above, however, two years later, in 2010, a part-time component was introduced (Innovative Talents, short-term), which became immediately popular. As of 2011, the majority of participants are in fact part-time: David Zweig and H. Wang identify 501 cases online and find that only 41.5 percent are full-time.[113] Of these 501 individuals, among scientists and professors that joined the program, only 26.5 percent are full-time.[114] On the other hand, 89 percent of private entrepreneurs recruited are full-time, suggesting that the TTP is more successful at bringing back entrepreneurs full-time, though their number is much smaller than that of scientists and scholars. As Zweig explains, this is partly because entrepreneurs have greater freedom in China, as they do not have to work within the rigid administrative confines of Chinese educational and research institutions. Furthermore, starting and running a business would be difficult to do from overseas and generally necessitates full-time presence in China.[115]

The addition of this short-term track exemplifies a timely rebalancing of China's talent portfolio—a shift from outright brain circulation to a more complex strategy that supplements, rather than replaces, brain circulation with brain linkage, allowing individuals to keep their full-time jobs abroad while participating in the plan. The rebalancing seems to have produced strong results, enabling China to better engage higher-quality talents. As Zweig et al. show, part-time TTP participants are higher quality than full-time TTP awardees.[116] Furthermore, the linkage-focused Innovative Talents short-term track still encourages brain circulation as short-term awardees are given priority in being awarded into the long-term track after the end of their short-term program.[117]

Along with the short-term track, three additional tracks, two of which are aimed at brain gain, were added in 2010, further diversifying the portfolio. The Young TTP is for young ethnic-Chinese talent and includes many returnees among the awardees.[118] Two other tracks introduced in 2011 and 2013, Foreign Experts and Topnotch Talents and Teams,[119] are for nonethnic Chinese, reflecting China's increased interest in brain gain of foreign talent.[120] Still brain circulation prevailed over brain gain: of the 1,500 participants that had been recruited through August 2011, about 90 percent were returnees of overseas Chinese.[121]

It is difficult to fully assess the plan's results as comprehensive data about the TTP are hard to obtain given its political sensitivity, which will be discussed later. However, the available numbers are clearly impressive. As of 2018, the TTP has an estimated over seven thousand participants altogether,[122] including six Nobel Prize winners among the returnees.[123] From its inception through 2018, the Young Thousand Talents Program has supported approximately four thousand young researchers, the majority of which are Chinese returnees.[124] While the Young TTP has been less successful in recruiting the very top overseas scientists (the top 10 percent in terms of research productivity), it has still attracted high-caliber researchers.[125] By 2014, 2,156 talents were recruited through the innovation scheme, and by 2018, there were 1,188 entrepreneurs. As of 2016, there were 313 full-time non-Chinese recipients in the Foreign Talents track.[126] Overall, as H. Wang and L. Miao say, "Compared to other similar programs implemented, the Thousand Talent Plan should be regarded as currently the most successful in attracting international talents."[127] Through the lens of talent portfolio theory, we can observe how timely rebalancing gives TTP access to more talents via brain linkage and brain gain beyond circulation, illustrating the overall trajectory of China's talent portfolio.

Turning Inward with Growing Political Risks

While China has continued to rebalance its talent portfolio, its strategy has encountered unsystematic risks of geopolitical tensions, particularly with the United States. The success of China's brain circulation and linkage created suspicion of illicit technology transfer and a sense of threat to national security in the host countries, contributing to geopolitical tensions. For instance, the Pentagon charged the TTP as an "aggressive, ten-part 'toolkit for foreign technology acquisition,'" and the National Intelligence Council defined the TTP's unadvertised goal as "facilitate[ing] the legal and illicit transfer of U.S. technology, intellectual property and know-how" to China.[128] The Senate Homeland Security Subcommittee on Investigation issued a report of over one hundred pages entitled *Threats to the U.S. Research Enterprise: China's Talent Recruitment Plans*, which reveals that TTP members stole US-funded Department of Energy and National Institutes of Health (NIH) research for Chinese institutions.[129] Geopolitical conflict poses an unsystematic risk to all Bs as they constrain talent flows, both in and out, but more so to circulation and linkage in the case of China. US-China tensions, for example, discourage Chinese from studying in the United States and impede transnational linkages between the two countries.

Furthermore, suspicion of China's talent-recruitment efforts—particularly its talent programs—has mounted, as an increasing number of ethnically Chinese individuals in the United States have been investigated on charges of espionage and theft of intellectual property. This especially has been the case in high-tech fields and US military-tech startups, where there exist concerns over Chinese engagement with US researchers, startups, and companies. Some of these accusations proved false, with devastating consequences for the scientists involved. Anming Hu of the University of Tennessee, Knoxville, National Weather Service's Sherry Chen, Temple University's Xiaoxing Xi, and MIT's Gang Chen are among key examples of ethnically Chinese scientists in the United States who were accused of charges related to economic espionage for China.[130] Gang Chen was a participant in the Thousand Talents Program.[131] All four were acquitted or had their charges dropped but not before they were arrested and terminated or put on leave from their jobs, seriously damaging their careers and impacting their families.

Some accusations, on the other hand, have led to convictions and imprisonment. Hongjin Tan, a Chinese national and American permanent resident, was convicted and sentenced to prison on the charge of stealing more than USD 1 billion worth of trade secrets from a petroleum company. Shan Shi, a Texas-based scientist, was also sentenced to prison on the charge of stealing trade secrets regarding syntactic foam, an important naval technology used in submarines. Both of these Chinese nationals were participants in the TTP. However, such risks are not just confined to individuals of Chinese origin. Charles Lieber, a non-ethnic-Chinese American and the former chair of Harvard University's Chemistry and Chemical Biology Department, was arrested, indicted, and, in 2021, convicted of tax offenses and making false statements to the federal government after failing to disclose funding that he received from China and hiding his participation in the TTP.[132]

Furthermore, while the increasing prevalence of part-time recruitment in the TTP and other talent programs helped China to diversify its circulation-oriented talent portfolio, it also has heightened concerns in the United States over awardees "double-dipping" on research grants and funding. Scientists and academics receiving US-government research funding are often permitted to receive funding from foreign entities as well, but failure to properly disclose this could result in them getting more than their fair share. In May 2019, for example, two scientists at Emory University,

Xiao-Jiang Li and Shihua Li, were fired on the charge that they had received funding from the Thousand Talents Program while simultaneously receiving funding from the NIH.[133] The NIH has launched a broader investigation of its grantees to determine if they had properly disclosed financial ties to foreign governments. Between August 2018 and June 2020, this probe led to the investigation of 189 scientists at eighty-seven institutions, and China was the source of undisclosed support for 93 percent of the cases. According to their investigation, 70 percent of the researchers failed to disclose receipt of foreign grants, and 54 percent failed to disclose awards from a talent program. Fifty-four scientists lost their jobs as a result of the investigation, and seventy-seven were removed from the NIH system. There were an additional 399 "scientists of possible concern," of which investigations into 251 (63 percent) required more scrutiny; 19 percent were exonerated, and the remaining 18 percent are pending.[134]

These investigations were part of the US Department of Justice's China Initiative, launched in 2018 to stop "Chinese economic espionage." However, the initiative faced widespread criticism that it had "veered off course by focusing on academics who had improperly filled in applications" and, in particular, that it was racially profiling Chinese researchers, contributing "to the departure of some leading academic researchers of Chinese descent in the US."[135] The initiative ended in February 2022, but such policies had the consequence of expediting China's brain circulation by stimulating return migration from the United States. In 2021, 1,490 Chinese-origin scientists returned to China amid such tensions—a 22 percent increase from the previous year (see figure 5.4). In fact, 66 percent of respondents to a 2022 survey of academic researchers of Chinese origin cite the "U.S. government's investigations into Chinese-origin researchers" as the reason for not feeling safe as an academic researcher in the United States.[136] As Fei Yan, a professor of sociology at Tsinghua University and himself a *haigui*, said when discussing increasing geopolitical tensions with me, "I think it will have a huge—a *huge*—impact on students' choice" to stay in the United States or return to China.[137] Furthermore, those who return may be less able to engage in collaboration with their former networks in the United States, further stymying the potential for brain linkage.

The unsystematic risks of China's talent programs have grown elsewhere too. As noted in the previous chapter, tensions with Australia have risen in recent years over alleged Chinese interference in Australian politics, as well

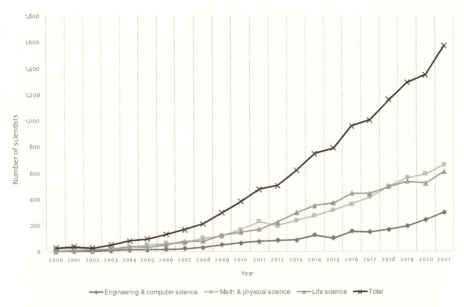

FIGURE 5.4. US-based Chinese scientists who dropped US affiliations for China. *Source:* Data from supplementary information / appendix of Xie et al. (2023), p. 35.

as swirling concerns over growing Chinese influence on Australian universities due to the schools' heavy reliance on revenues from Chinese students. In August 2020, the Australian Strategic Policy Institute (ASPI) released a report titled *Hunting the Phoenix* detailing the CCP's talent-recruitment strategy and highlighting the risks of economic espionage. Like the US counterpart, the Australian government has begun to investigate the issue. In 2020, Australia's Parliamentary Joint Committee on Intelligence and Security launched an "inquiry into national security risks affecting the Australian higher education and research sector."[138] A report submitted to the inquiry by ASPI's Alex Joske, the author of *Hunting the Phoenix*, estimates that CCP talent-recruitment programs in Australia may have resulted in "as much as AU \$280 million [approximately USD 200 million] in grant fraud over the past two decades."[139]

With mounting political risks in main hosts of overseas Chinese talent, the Chinese government has deemphasized some of its talent-recruitment efforts. China stopped promoting the TTP conspicuously and hid the names of participants for their protection. Institutions with TTP awardees were asked to remove references to the plan from their websites, and TTP members themselves were also asked to delete references to the plan on their personal websites.[140] In 2020, search results relating to the TTP were blocked in mainland China on websites, like Baidu, and social networks, like Weibo and WeChat, and Chinese authorities reportedly ordered media outlets to stop reporting on the plan.[141] As of 2019, the program has been repackaged as the National High-End Foreign Experts Recruitment Plan, which absorbed all programs previously under the TTP as well as some additional programs.[142]

China went further in its response to the increased political risks of its brain circulation and linkage by rebalancing its overall talent portfolio, turning inward to focus on the brain train of its domestic talent. As Poo Mu-Ming, the Chinese returnee neuroscientist, says, "the US-China conflict was a wake-up call for China." In 2016, the CCP's highest-ranking body, the Central Committee, proclaimed the adoption of a National Innovation-Driven Development Strategy, noting that "the essence of being innovation-driven is being talent-driven." Reflecting such a new strategy of talent-driven innovation, China's fourteenth Five-Year Plan of 2021–2025 pushes for self-sufficiency in scientific and technological development.[143]

This shift toward brain train has yielded some notable results. China has increased its annual number of STEM PhDs, with domestic universities estimated to produce over seventy-seven thousand per year by 2025. This is double the number in 2010 (about thirty-four thousand) and far more than the United States' projected number of forty thousand in 2025—which includes sixteen thousand international students.[144] Although there is some doubt over the quality of STEM education,[145] the rapid increase in domestically trained doctoral students represents China's effort to rebalance its talent portfolio through more incorporation of brain train. In fact, massive talent pools, vast educational networks, and robust R&D institutions that were created and strengthened through the past few decades of brain circulation and linkage are China's prime strategic assets for creating more homegrown human capital.

With emphasis on "self-sufficiency" in talent development as well as unfavorable geopolitical situations, fewer Chinese talents are headed overseas. As Fei Yan of Tsinghua University says, "In the past two years, the majority of our best students . . . decided to stay" in China for graduate work—a marked change from previous years, when the top students in China went

overseas for PhDs.[146] Ha Wei, a returnee professor of international education at Peking University with a PhD from Harvard, also notes, "In a few
years' time, there will be fewer and fewer Chinese doctoral students coming
back from the USA in the fields of STEM, because they are not getting the
opportunities to study in the USA" due to visa restrictions. Furthermore,
Chinese students have "grown pickier about whether to study abroad at
all, as Chinese universities have risen in global rankings and are viewed
more favorably by some employers, both in China and abroad."[147] China's
two top universities—Peking and Tsinghua—are tied at number sixteen in
the latest *Times Higher Education* global ranking.[148] All these changes are
likely to make a long-term impact on China's talent portfolio, diminishing
circulation and linkage.

On the other hand, China is expanding its linkage with countries that
are part of the Belt and Road Initiative (BRI), a large-scale development and
investment project involving over seventy countries spanning from East Asia
to Europe to Africa. Each year, ten thousand scholarships in Chinese universities are reserved for those from BRI countries. These scholarships entail
free tuition and accommodation with a modest monthly stipend. While the
overall number of international students in China quadrupled from 2004 to
2016, the number from BRI countries grew eightfold.[149] Unlike in Australia
or Japan, where international students are harnessed for brain gain, these
BRI students may not contribute much to China's development as human
capital as most of them return home after their studies.[150] Rather, they have
social-capital value for China as they will look favorably upon China and its
infrastructure projects in their home countries, reinforcing BRI by acting as
transnational bridges in linking their countries to China. As China's conflict with the United States and other advanced democracies intensifies and
with the rise of anti-Chinese sentiment in those places, the BRI students
are increasingly viewed as a valuable strategic asset for China and a way for
the country to diversify its brain linkage into other countries.[151] Table 5.4
summarizes the main features of China's talent portfolio and its evolution
over time.

TABLE 5.4. China's talent portfolio: Past and present

B/Period	1980s~2010	Present
Train	**Growing** Initially weak domestic-training system; improving thanks largely to contributions of returnees Train via short-term overseas experiences (e.g., postdoctoral positions)	**Rebalancing** Increasing focus on domestic training; less emphasis on training via overseas experiences
Gain	**Little to none**	**Rebalancing; adding** Efforts to attract foreign talents (entrepreneurs, scientists, scholars) and students, with particular attention to BRI countries
Circulation	**Strong** Overseas PhDs, overseas postdoctoral fellowships, overseas work experience	**Rebalancing** Increase in talents returning from overseas; decrease in talents going out → will eventually lead to decreased circulation
Linkage	**Growing** With diasporic Chinese (inside out) for the purpose of achieving circulation via "soft landing"	**Rebalancing** Increasing inside-out linkage with BRI countries Decreasing outside-in and inside-out linkage with talents in countries with geopolitical tensions (United States, Australia).

Can China Sustain a Diversified Talent Portfolio?

China has not relied on homegrown talent (as in Japan) or turned to foreign talent (as in Australia) in its ascendance to economic power. Instead, Chinese *haigui* have made crucial contributions to the development of their homeland, helping to lead in various areas from science and technology to innovation and entrepreneurship to education and brain train. While China did well in turning brain drain into circulation, it was not simply a market-driven process, as some scholars argue (e.g., Saxenian). On the contrary, the developmental state of China has been deeply involved in the process, allowing for a large initial outflow of talent and then implementing extensive policies, infrastructure upgrades, and talent programs to draw these overseas talents back home. This circulation model enables the fast upgrading of manpower using external resources, especially those in advanced countries, like the United States. Talented overseas Chinese are well connected to the centers of economic dynamism, making knowledge and technology transfer easier and more effective than reliance on homegrown talent in early stages of development—a marked difference from Japan's technology-borrowing strategy utilizing homegrown talent during its catch-up period.

China has also been able to rebalance its talent portfolio in the face of changing circumstances and new challenges, tapping into broader pools of talent. It has been charged that China's brain circulation programs are limited in effectiveness as they struggle to bring back the top-tier overseas Chinese talent that the country needs the most. In response to this criticism, China has increased the prevalence of linkage in order to better engage overseas talents who are interested in working with China without permanent return. Such efforts have made China's talent portfolio more diversified. Given the CCP's involvement with such programs, however, this portfolio adjustment has backfired to an extent, contributing even more to brewing geopolitical tensions by creating suspicion that Chinese scientists and scholars in the United States were stealing intellectual property or duplicitously receiving double funding from both governments. In the short term, this has accelerated brain circulation by stimulating some overseas Chinese talents, feeling unwelcome abroad, to return to China.[152] In the long term, it may stymie circulation and linkage by discouraging talents from heading abroad in the first place.

China has addressed these circulation- and linkage-associated geopolitical risks with further rebalancing, increasing the importance of brain train in its talent portfolio. Significantly, it was China's brain circulation that enabled the country to improve its brain train, as returnees strengthened the country's academic and research institutions. One could argue that China is ready to shift to a homegrown-talent strategy, largely thanks to decades of circulation and linkage efforts, making brain train the main B in its talent portfolio. The country has been investing heavily in universities and R&D to secure its domestic-talent pool while continuing efforts to bring back talented overseas scholars who can play a critical role in brain train. In fact, Xi Jinping has repeatedly called talent "the primary resource" in China's push for indigenous innovation and development.[153] In his vision, China no longer wants to adopt the Oxbridge or Ivy League model, reversing its earlier effort to emulate these Western schools.[154] During a visit to Peking University, for instance, Xi unequivocally proclaimed that China "should not make Peking University the 'second Harvard or Cambridge,' but the 'first Peking University.'"[155]

However, China's ability to shift to a successful train-centered talent portfolio faces several obstacles. First, it may be hampered by social inequality, as limited opportunities for education and career in rural areas constrain China's domestic-talent pool.[156] A focus on brain train may also undermine China's connection to global centers of knowledge, ultimately leading to a rigid, undiversified portfolio that may not be sufficient to support China's ambition to be a global leader. After all, China was able to rise with success by actively participating in the global labor market through brain circulation and linkage, and this new "inward" turn may only isolate the country from the rest of the world. Fei Yan echoes such concern by saying that in the long term, perhaps seven to ten years, less collaboration with the outside world "would hurt China's overall development because we are living in a globalized world . . . so we have to keep frequent contact, academic exchange, [and] collaboration."[157] There is a danger that China may follow the unfortunate path of Japan, whose labor market became Galápagosized in the post–miracle era. Despite its massive population, China, too, faces a demographic decline as a result of the One-Child Policy that could further undermine a brain train focus and thus stands to learn much from Japan's experience.[158]

SIX

India
Banking on Overseas Talent

During his visit to Silicon Valley in 2015, Indian prime minister Narendra Modi said, "I am often told to do something about brain drain. . . . I say it is not brain drain but 'brain deposit.'" Addressing a crowd of twenty thousand composed largely of Indian expats, he proclaimed that "it is now the time for people who are living outside India to do something for the country."[1] This remark echoes what then prime minister Rajiv Gandhi (1984–1989) said three decades ago when he unequivocally stated that the diaspora was India's "brain bank" to be harnessed when the time came.[2] The large gathering of the Indian expats to welcome Modi's visit showed that the time had indeed come. Modi met with Indian leaders in the tech industry who had pledged to help their homeland, particularly to support his Digital India Initiative—a plan to transform India into a digitally empowered society. IT giants led by Indian expats, Sundar Pichai's Google and Satya Nadella's Microsoft, would provide free Wi-Fi for hundreds of Indian railway stations and help bring wireless internet to five hundred thousand villages, respectively. Another expat leader, Naren Gupta, a founder of the Silicon Valley investment firm Nexus Venture Partners, helped organize Modi's 2015 visit to Silicon Valley, his first ever and the first by an Indian prime minister in more than three decades.[3]

This question of the diaspora as brain drain or brain deposit is particularly pertinent for India as the country is the largest supplier of highly skilled labor in the world.[4] Second only to China in the total number of international students (753,000 worldwide in 2018), India has the highest number of optional practical training (441,400 or 30 percent in 2004–2016) and H-1B visa holders (74 percent in 2021, compared to 12 percent that were Chinese) in the United States.[5] Furthermore, the global weight of Indian talents has increased as China's conflict with countries like the United States and Australia intensifies. The number of Indian students is catching up to that of Chinese in the United States, Australia, and Germany, and since 2019, the number of Indian students has surpassed the number of Chinese students in Canada.

Many Indian students then stay in the host countries after graduation, creating a serious brain drain for their homeland. For instance, the vast majority of Indians who obtain doctorate degrees in science and engineering in the United States remain after graduation, with a five-year-stay rate at 90 percent in 2003, with only a slight dip to 85 percent by 2013.[6] Likewise, among all doctoral recipients with temporary visas in the United States between 2012 and 2022, 86.5 percent of Indians reported their intention to stay—higher than any other group (see table 1.2). According to Fund for Peace, India ranked ninety-ninth out of 179 countries for brain drain in 2022 (ranked from worst [1] to best [179]).[7] From the conventional human capital perspective, the mass exodus of its talent must be a troubling story for India.

Yet, as Indian leaders from Gandhi to Modi have repeatedly stressed, such outflow of talent is not necessarily considered brain drain but rather "brain deposit" in disguise, which can eventually benefit the country. The high transnational mobility of Indian talent is largely owed to the presence of renowned brain train institutions, like the Indian Institutes of Technology (IITs), the Indian Institute of Science (IIS), and the Indian Institute of Management (IIM), which have well prepared young talented Indians for postgraduate paths abroad, conferring high English proficiency upon them. While such strong brain train institutions are formidable, many of these talents would not be fully utilized in India due to a dearth of domestic opportunities. Their graduates have left the country for education or employment, building successful careers overseas that have enabled brain linkage to be a key component of India's talent portfolio. Thus, it is diasporic talent that remains overseas that has made a crucial contribution to Indian development through transnational linkage—making India quite unique compared with the other talent giants of this study.

The story of my colleague at Stanford, Arogyaswami Paulraj, professor of electrical engineering, well captures this process. Paulraj, an alumnus of IIT New Delhi, moved to Stanford at the age of forty-seven after serving in the Indian Navy for twenty-six years, during which he founded three national research centers. As he recounts, "I was a pretty valuable commodity for the country, but it was not easy to change the system. . . . Despite the obvious talent in the country, we've not been able to do a good job [building a flourishing research and development environment]." He recalls, "My leaving was [portrayed as] a great disaster for the country in the press. I myself felt that it was a big blow for the country because I knew I could have done a lot." However, his departure was not a "great disaster" for the country at all as the move enabled him to connect Stanford with India. Paulraj proudly told me in an interview at his Stanford home, "My connection with India began because the Indian universities, like IITs, were constantly trying to make some connections with Stanford. It never work[ed] out, but they're always coming and trying . . . so I became a *bridge* between India and US universities. . . . And then I did three companies here, and all of them had backend engineering in India."[8]

Paulraj and Indian IT leaders in Silicon Valley are exemplary cases of overseas Indians who maintain close ties with and help develop the people and organizations back home. Given India's sizable, active, and well-educated diaspora population, transnational linkage has been instrumental to the country's rise and a key element of its talent portfolio. As part of such brain linkage, overseas Indians frequently make short-term visits to India, and current literature tends to view India's talent flow as a case of brain circulation akin to the situation in China. However, as noted before, such a characterization fails to distinguish between the permanent returns of Chinese talent and the short-term visits of Indian talents who otherwise continue to reside overseas. Thus, I illustrate how India's brain linkage differs from the brain circulation that was a main talent strategy for China (see chapter 5). As Paulraj says, "All my Chinese students, including Taiwanese, have gone back, all my Korean students have gone back, [and] none of my Indian students have gone back. They're all working with companies here or teaching here."[9] And these Indians remain connected with home.

Previous studies indeed find that overseas Indians are more likely to invest in India-based startups than overseas Chinese are to invest in China-based startups,[10] and Indians are more likely to help businesses at home by serving as advisers or arranging contracts.[11] In part, Indian talents tend to stay overseas due to a dearth of domestic opportunities in India for highly skilled workers, limiting the chance for brain circulation in India's talent portfolio. Culturally, too, compared to China, India's more fluid conception of national identity embraces overseas Indians and their achievements, making it easier for these individuals to be considered as still a part of India regardless of whether they return or not. The English proficiency of Indians helps them to be well positioned for success in advanced nations, like the United States, United Kingdom, and Australia. Additionally, where the Chinese developmental state has been able to pour financial resources into building infrastructure and establishing talent programs to ultimately recruit back overseas Chinese talents, the Indian state does not similarly emphasize brain circulation efforts in its talent portfolio, nor is it heavily involved in linkage in its talent portfolio. Transnational talent mobility and linkage have been largely market driven or bottom-up for India. The Indian government plays only a supportive role in brain linkage efforts through providing legal and cultural recognition of Indian expats, like granting them special legal status as nonresident Indians (NRIs) and celebrating their contributions through the annual Pravasi Bharatiya Divas (परवासी भारतीय दिवस; Day of Overseas Indians).

In this chapter, I use TPT again to explain why and how brain linkage has become a main feature of India's talent portfolio and how it has evolved over time. In doing so, I closely examine Indian diasporic organizations, like the Indus Entrepreneurs (TiE), and overseas-alumni networks, such as those of IITs graduates. These groups, rather than the Indian government, have played a leading role in connecting with home via entrepreneurship, education, and philanthropy, as well as maintaining a national identity with Indian culture and immigrants' regional-linguistic communities. Given India's lack of domestic opportunities, poor governance, and low demands for highly skilled talent, brain circulation was not a viable option initially. Still, like other countries in this study, India's talent portfolio has evolved over time with more diversification within and across Bs. In particular, brain circulation has been increasing recently, and there are efforts to emulate the Silicon Valley–linkage model in other regions, such as the Middle East. Brain linkage and circulation are also making a contribution to brain train in the country, further diversifying its talent portfolio.

Indian Emigration

India has a long and rich history of emigration. Prior to British colonization, migration in and out of India was very fluid between the northern and
northeastern parts of the country and Southeast Asia, including southern
China. During colonial rule (1858–1947), emigration reflected a recognizable class division. Lower-class Indians migrated to plantations in British
colonies through an indentured labor scheme resembling enslavement,[12]
while those from the upper class attended British and other foreign universities and often remained abroad.

This pattern of dual-emigration paths has continued well after independence. By the 1990s, a significant diaspora of predominantly unskilled
or low-skilled Indians was built up in the newly developing Gulf region as
well as Southeast Asia. The United Arab Emirates and Saudi Arabia were
top destinations for these lower-skilled Indians.[13] The other emigration path
was to the West, especially to North America as well as the United Kingdom. Following independence from Britain, Indian emigration surged to
the United Kingdom, reflecting the relative ease of Commonwealth immigration policy.[14] Yet later legislations, like the British Commonwealth Immigration Acts of 1962 and 1968,[15] all but paused immigrant streams from
India for the decades to follow.

In contrast, the passage of the US Immigration and Nationality Act
of 1965, which abolished de facto discrimination against Asians and other
groups of would-be immigrants, triggered a new wave of Indian immigration into the country. The Indian immigrants included unskilled laborers
as well as skilled IT workers and nurses, largely motivated to move to the
United States due to a lack of suitable jobs available at home. Kanwal Rekhi,
the first Indian American entrepreneur to take a venture-backed company
public on the NASDAQ (Excelan), is a good example. After attending IIT
Bombay, he came to the United States in 1967 for graduate studies and then
stayed to work. As he explained to me in my Stanford office, "If you [went]
back, there were no jobs to be had in India. When I left college with [an]
IIT [degree], the best you could hope to do is become the sales engineer
for a multinational in India. There were no design jobs, no engineer jobs
to speak of. Engineers were not highly thought of like they are now. If you
wanted a prestigious job, you joined the army, you joined the civil service."[16]
Meanwhile, the United States was hungry for tech talent, given the recent

space race with the Soviet Union. Some Indians wanted to move away from socialism in India and look for new opportunities overseas; Rekhi says that he left for the United States so that "his brain wouldn't go down the drain in socialist India."[17]

The composition of the Indian migrant population in the United States changed significantly after the Immigration Act of 1990, which introduced the H-1B visa, increasing immigration for specialty occupations. As the tech industry took off, India's highly skilled workers, notably graduates of IITs, were attracted to the large number of engineering and tech jobs being created in the United States, in sharp contrast to the dearth of such jobs in India. This group of new immigrants hailed largely from the southern part of India, where software and information industries were taking hold— and therefore where Indians were being educated and trained as engineers, programmers, and computer scientists.[18] For instance, IITs graduates, especially from the upper tier IITs, were very competitive in the US job market due to their training back home. In 2004, IIT Kharagpur, the first IIT, had 4,007 registered alumni in India, 3,480 in the United States, and 739 spread across fifty-nine other countries.[19] As of 2003, about 30 percent of all IIT alumni (about 133,245) were working abroad.[20] At peak out-migration, the IITs sent up to two-thirds of each graduating class to the United States.[21] Even today, a significant proportion work abroad. The outward mobility of these talents set the stage for India's future brain linkage.

The H-1B visa has become a primary work-migration path for Indians to the United States. From 2001 to 2015, Indian workers received the largest share (50.5 percent), far outnumbering Chinese, who were a distant second (9.7 percent). By 2018, nearly three-fourths of H-1B visa holders were Indians. An overwhelming majority (80 percent) are approved for H-1B visa renewal. These rates come as no surprise given that India is the largest supplier of skilled workers in high-demand occupations in the IT industry and at a relatively cheap cost.[22] In addition to the work-migration route, a growing number of Indians study in the United States, second in number only to the Chinese,[23] and many stay after graduation (the study-work path).[24] Ultimately, Indians naturalize more than Chinese, by almost ten thousand more naturalizations per year.[25]

Indian immigrants have been highly successful in the United States over a relatively short period of time, and it is worth recounting the scale of their success in order to demonstrate their immense potential to contribute to India through transnational linkage. Indians are the largest source of immigrant high-tech company founders, and Indian-founded tech startups outnumber those from the next seven groups combined.[26] Indian talent is particularly conspicuous in Silicon Valley. Between 2006 and 2012, 32 percent of immigrant-founded companies started in Silicon Valley had Indian founders. This figure is larger than the next seven groups of immigrant founders combined (China, the United Kingdom, Canada, Germany, Israel, Russia, and Korea). As Ashish Chadha, the author of "Battle for Brand IIT," aptly points out, "A career in Silicon Valley epitomizes the aspirations of the privileged middle-class Indians who form a substantial percentage of the students entering IITs. A degree from Stanford and a job in the Bay Area are what an IIT topper's dreams are made of."[27]

The Indian diaspora's success has not been limited to the IT industry. India has become a major source for medical doctors in the United States too.[28] According to a 2005 study, Indian immigrants represent 4.9 percent of medical doctors in the United States, making India the top source of international medical graduates.[29] By 2017, around sixty-nine thousand India-trained physicians worked in the United States, United Kingdom, Canada, and Australia.[30] Similarly, many Indian academics who moved to the United States for doctoral degrees are now being selected to lead educational institutions after progressing in their careers over several decades. Indians are prevalent among elite business school leaders and have helmed schools like Harvard Business School, Northwestern's Kellogg School of Management, and the University of Chicago Booth School of Business. The newly established School of Sustainability at Stanford is also headed by an India-born scholar, Arun Majumdar. Lately, India-born Americans have also risen in the political realm, reflecting their growing political engagement in the United States and the world. The new head of the World Bank as of 2023, Ajay Banga, was born in India and received his degree from IIM Ahmedabad. In 2023, among the eighteen foreign-born members of the US Congress, three hailed from India. Notably, India was one of only three countries of origin to have multiple representatives in Congress, alongside Korea (with three members) and Mexico (with four members).[31] Certainly, the success of these talents represents a huge brain drain for India but also an incredible opportunity, as these high-positioned overseas Indian talents are better able to engage in brain linkage with their home country.

NRIs and Brain Linkage

Like China, India has a large diaspora while suffering from a serious brain drain. Both were incorporated into the global labor market much later than Japan and Australia. However, the two countries' talent portfolios differ considerably, with brain circulation central to China's portfolio and brain linkage key to India's. Whereas the Chinese government initiated numerous talent programs to bring back their overseas nationals, the Indian government does almost the opposite. It encourages and "handholds" skilled Indians in order to help them find jobs abroad through initiating bilateral agreements with countries facing labor shortages in response to market trends.[32] According to a 2018 study, India will have a skilled-labor surplus in every field, totaling 245.3 million by 2030, and will be the *only* country with an overall skilled-labor surplus.[33] The government set up the India Centre for Migration (ICM) in 2008, an autonomous body that serves as a think tank on international migration for the Ministry of External Affairs. In line with India's national strategy to be globally competitive as a talent supplier, ICM devises and executes medium- to long-term strategies for promoting overseas employment by monitoring international labor markets.[34] These government efforts are relatively new and hope to reproduce the success of Indians in the US IT industry, which occurred absent any major government programs or assistance.

In addition, until lately, India lacked the infrastructure to attract its top-tier researchers, scientists, and engineers back, so the government has instead attempted to engage in brain linkage with its diaspora for India's development and global market connections. To encourage members of the diaspora to connect with home, India grants them a special legal status, though it does not allow dual citizenship. Established in 1961, the title of NRI was ascribed to Indian citizens living abroad (i.e., those who spend over 183 days abroad in a year) and is associated with NRI-tailored social, cultural, legal, and economic institutions, like NRI financial services and bank accounts. The Indian government also introduced a form of permanent residency known as the overseas citizenship of India (OCI) in response to growing diaspora calls for dual citizenship. OCI was enacted as a special lifetime visa for non-Indian citizens who were previously Indian citizens or have parents, grandparents, or great-grandparents who are or were Indian citizens.[35] As of 2020, the Indian Government has identified approximately a total of 13.5 million NRIs and 3.6 million OCI holders.[36]

These measures promote a "culture of migration" with a strong sense of overseas Indian identity.[37] The members of the diaspora are referred to as "Indians"; regardless of their citizenship status, India is always home, and the achievements of the diaspora are the achievements of India. In this spirit, since January 2000, the government has organized an annual celebration, the Pravasi Bharatiya Divas, aimed at making its expatriates feel welcome to return home.[38] The event commemorates Mahatma Gandhi's return to India from South Africa and celebrates overseas Indians for their achievements through the Pravasi Bharatiya Samman (PBS) awards, which implicitly honor NRIs alongside Gandhi and Jawaharlal Nehru—the two representative expats. These are the highest honors conferred by the government on diasporic Indian individuals or organizations. Roughly fifteen awards are made annually, ranging disproportionately across several nations with a prominent Indian diaspora. PBS recipients include Satya Nadella and Kalpana Chawla, the latter being the first Indian woman in space when she first flew on the space shuttle *Columbia* in 1997 as a mission specialist.

This is in sharp contrast to China's appeal to patriotism to induce permanent return of the diaspora. The diasporic subject, then, is not only always seen as Indian at heart but also called upon to repay a debt they implicitly owe to their country—namely, to help it grow either through remittance or knowledge contribution. As Rekhi recalls in his conversation with the president of IIT Bombay during my interview, "[The] Indian freedom movement was led by NRIs—these were the guys who had gone to England and learned the English law and came back and argued. The Indian freedom movement argued against the British government in India. . . . NRIs were doing the same thing now as they were then."[39] A software engineer in N. Dayasindhu's study echoes Rekhi: "I think Indians, at least in the software industry, feel good about transferring the knowledge they possess with others. It gives a sense of pride and satisfaction."[40] Promoting NRI identity seems to have been a very clever strategy for reimagining India "as a potentially powerful country that is culturally (rather than geographically) defined through a trans-nationalized version."[41] It has also been key to clinching brain linkage as the main feature of India's talent portfolio.

The Indian diaspora has in turn responded well. The most prominent monetary contribution is remittance. India receives more remittances than any other country in the world, estimated at USD 83.1 billion in 2020. China, which is the second-highest remittance receiving country, trails far behind at USD 59.5 billion,[42] with the United Arab Emirates (USD 13.8 billion), the United States (USD 11.7 billion), and Saudi Arabia (USD 11.2 billion) as the top-three sources.[43] The Indian government has also raised over USD 10 billion in funds through the India Development Bond, specifically targeting its diasporic community. India and Israel are the only two countries to (successfully) sell bonds specifically to their diaspora communities. Another contribution of the Indian diaspora is real estate investment. The NRI investment in real estate at home was reported to be USD 6 billion in 2013, but by 2017, it had almost doubled, reaching USD 11.5 billion, which amounted to 20 percent of all real estate investment in India.[44]

Indian expats' contributions go far beyond remittance, however. These talents engage their home in a variety of ways, such as recruiting fellow Indians to study and work overseas, helping to transfer technology, outsourcing jobs to Indians, investing in Indian startups, and mentoring young entrepreneurs.[45] Information about the H-1B visa is widely available from peers and through recruitment channels, including the IT companies themselves as well as consultancy firms tasked with recruiting and contracting workers. A sign of the H-1B's regularity in Indian public discourse is the dedicated coverage of the H-1B visa in mainstream newspapers like the *Times of India*,[46] which has a section dedicated to NRI affairs.

NRIs' contributions are also seen in Bengaluru (Bangalore), known as India's Silicon Valley and similar to China's Zhongguancun, where strong networks have been nurtured with US-based entrepreneurs.[47] It is a critical hub of India's economic development, equipped with a rapidly growing startup ecosystem. Ranking among the top-three cities globally for entrepreneurship, Bengaluru houses 25 percent of India's tech startups and over one hundred multinational corporations. Brain linkage with NRIs has been key to Bengaluru's success since early on: as of 2004, it was estimated that "at least half of the IT companies set up in Bangalore since 1999 had some NRI funding."[48] Funds backed by large multinational finance companies may contribute more money to the Indian software industry than do NRIs, but "NRIs have played a crucial role in bringing even these funds into India," via social capital, according to anthropologist Carol Upadhya. These social-capital ties are formed both from the outside in and inside out, as NRI entrepreneurs and venture capitalists have sought to expand into India at the same time as entrepreneurs in Bengaluru have sought to tap into transnational networks. For example, Upadhya writes, "some Indian IT entrepreneurs talk about how they use the 'desi network' in the US, which extends much beyond the tech community."[49]

The result of such leveraging of NRI transnational social capital is that entrepreneurship in Bengaluru—and India more broadly—has boomed. The National Association of Software and Service Companies (NASS-COM) reports an investment increase of USD 2 billion and six thousand tech startups in 2017 to USD 4.3 billion and 7,200 tech startups in 2018.[50] Projections indicate that by 2025, ultra-high-net-worth individuals will invest up to USD 30 billion in Indian tech startups.[51] These figures are astounding when compared with where investments stood just a decade earlier: USD 550 million in 2010.[52] The total number of Indian unicorns more than doubled in 2021 from the previous year (in 2020, there were thirty-eight unicorns), with forty-four new startups added to the list—the highest number in any year to date.[53] At the end of 2022, India had 115 unicorns, becoming the third country to house more than one hundred unicorns (following the United States at 661 and China at 312).[54] Today, one out of every thirteen unicorns worldwide hails from India.[55] The tech-startup ecosystem is becoming more global as Indian startups are expanding to other markets, such as North America, Europe, and the Middle East, and global giants like IBM are gravitating toward India.[56]

Well placed in leading global corporations, such as Google, Microsoft, IBM, General Electric, and American Express, to name a few, Indian expats can influence not only their companies' decision to engage India but also India's policy of development.[57] As Rekhi says, "We're credible, successful people. Many of us are worth hundreds of millions of dollars. We're available to the Indian government."[58] The NRI community's policy influence expanded in the 1990s, facilitated through meetings with politicians traveling overseas and, less frequently, formal access points, like committees and working groups. D. Kapur highlights the government of India's convening of a select group of NRIs, including Rekhi, to formulate "a global strategy for promoting India as a prominent investment destination. The group advised the ministry in formulating IT policies, strengthening telecommunications infrastructure, and providing guidelines on venture capital funds as well as issues related to IT education."[59] The Stanford professor Paulraj chaired the government of India's 5G Steering Committee in 2018, comprising the secretaries of Ministries of Communications, Information Technology, and Science and Technology, along with representatives of industry and academia, which created a roadmap for the 5G wireless technology in India and recommended policy initiatives to actualize the vision.

Saxenian rightly asserts that "Indians in Silicon Valley have become key middlemen linking U.S. businesses to low-cost software expertise in India."[60] She further finds that since the 1990s, Indian professionals in the United States have influenced their employers in the corporate world to establish Indian subsidiaries, invest in startups, and guide government policy.[61] Her study also finds that Indian Americans are more likely than Chinese Americans to help businesses in their home country by serving as advisers or arranging contracts, in agreement with R. Dossani's findings.[62] In Rekhi's words, "We [NRIs] provide a bridge to the United States."[63] Transnational linkage can be also seen through the "social, cultural, political, or ideological dimensions of migrant resource flows."[64]

Diaspora organizations, like TiE, and other social/cultural networks, such as IIT overseas alumni, have led India's brain linkage efforts in a more bottom-up manner, unlike in Northeast Asian countries, where the government has shaped the dynamics of talent development and recruitment through various top-down initiatives and policies. Even when not directly involved in transnational linkage, less formal, culturally focused diaspora organizations can help indirectly by cultivating a strong sense of identity among NRIs, contributing to community organization, whose process merits close examination.

Diasporic Organizations and Social-Capital Formation

In order to comprehend how diaspora organizations have led transnational linkage, it is imperative to closely look into the process by which they build various forms of social capital. I first examine how these organizations contribute to the formation of bonding social capital among NRIs and then look at how they promote local and transnational bridging (concepts explained in chapter 2) by analyzing ninety-seven US-based Indian associations listed in the Ministry of External Affairs' Database of Indian Associations Abroad.[65] While some transnational linkage occurs at the "micro" level, such as personal ties between relatives, friends, and colleagues, this study focuses on "macro" linkages facilitated at the organizational, institutional, and associational levels.[66] The main findings of this analysis shown below confirm prior studies that categorize Indian diasporic organizations' activities.[67] This analysis then extends those studies by evaluating the role of diaspora organizations in brain linkage. Although diaspora organizations contribute extensively to social bonding and local bridging among overseas

Indians, I look most closely at their role in promoting transnational bridging to India to illustrate how brain linkage came to be central to India's talent portfolio.

DIASPORA ORGANIZATIONS AS VEHICLES OF SOCIAL-CAPITAL FORMATION

In my sample, the majority of US-based Indian organizations—sixty-one out of ninety-seven—hold cultural activities, including festivals, language classes, and arts and culture programming.[68] Youth groups are also common, and they focus on instilling community leadership and civic responsibilities. Philanthropic and professional activities are the next most common, with about one-fifth of diaspora organizations participating in activities falling into these categories (see figure 6.1). Professional organizations provide first-generation immigrants, and now second-generation Indian Americans, with professional contacts and networks, labor market information, recruitment channels, and access to successful immigrant entrepreneurs as role models.[69] Historically, the majority of Indian diaspora organizations in the United States have been cultural, although, over time, Indian immigrants have founded new organizations with more expansive missions, as demonstrated by the diversity in my sample (see figure 6.1). Diaspora organizations largely are divided into two groups. The first group consists

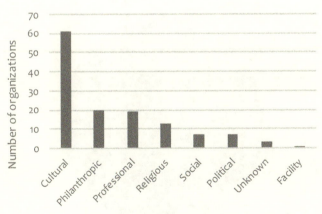

FIGURE 6.1. US-based Indian organizations by type.
Source: Author created.

of those that reinforce a specific identity, whether it be ethnic, religious, or tied to a particular region of origin within India (hereafter "single-identity organizations"). The second group consists of broader organizations that promote a pan-Indian identity. In my sample, as shown in figure 6.2, organizations are split nearly fifty-fifty in whether they are of single- or pan-Indian identity,[70] and pan-Indian-identity organizations tend to be newer than single-identity ones by approximately five years on average.

These diasporic organizations promote various forms of bonding and bridging activities. They include connecting members within their own groups (bonding social capital), linking members of different Indian groups or linking to non-Indians in the same geographic area (local bridging), and connecting members and communities of different countries, especially with home (transnational bridging). Table 6.1 summarizes major activities undertaken to build different forms of social capital among Indian organizations.[71] In my sample, nearly all organizations (97.73 percent) promote bonding social capital among overseas Indians. Local bridging, such as joint community service projects among different Indian organizations and with non-Indian groups, and transnational bridging, such as US-India business delegations, are also common (with 45.5 percent and 42.1 percent, respectively; see table 6.2).

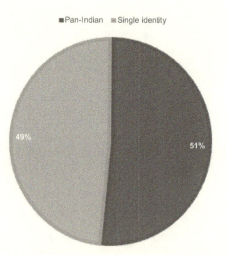

FIGURE 6.2. Identity composition of US-based Indian organizations.
Source: Author created.

TABLE 6.1. Example activities of bonding and bridging

Bonding social capital	Local bridging	Transnational bridging
• Hosting social and religious events to gather members	• Community service to benefit local community and non-co-ethnic neighbors	• Scholarships to low-income students in India
• Professional networking opportunities	• Lobbying US-based policies and creating political connections/ pipelines	• Economic-empowerment and other community programs
• Language and cultural programs		• Food-assistance programs
• Youth groups	• Shared interest groups inviting diverse social groups	• Policy advocacy: immigration, bilateral trade, human rights
• Matrimonial advertisements		• Arts and culture exchanges
• Magazines and publications to share information	• Highly attended India Day parades to showcase history to the surrounding region	• Business delegations, trade missions
• NRI resources and integration support		

TABLE 6.2. Bonding and bridging activities

Bonding social capital	97.73%
Local bridging	45.45%
Transnational bridging	42.05%

The results of my analysis also indicate that organizations often undertake multiple types of activities (67.04 percent), as laid out in table 6.3. The most common combination is bonding social capital and local bridging (27.27 percent), followed by bonding social capital and transnational bridging (21.59 percent). All three types of social capital are promoted by 18.18 percent. On the other hand, organizations may generate social capital among only their members without translating that into linkage, either local or transnational. Approximately 30.68 percent of organizations in my sample only brought about bonding social capital as an outcome of their activities.

Creating bonding social capital was quite natural and important early

TABLE 6.3. Number of bonding and bridging types completed

One	32.95%
Two	48.86%
Three	18.18%

on for the Indian diaspora given its segregation along lines of caste and regional, linguistic, and religious differences, as well as the small number of Indian immigrants during the initial waves to the United States. Standalone organizations exist for various ethnolinguistic groups, like the Bengalis, Punjabis, Tamils, and Gujaratis, and allow for unique cultural and linguistic traditions to be passed on as well as philanthropic initiatives tailored to Indian communities with which they share a connection. The formation of bonding social capital strengthened connections within the Indian diaspora and was the first step toward linkage with India.

Building Bridges to India

Key to this study is the fact that Indian diaspora organizations not only work to build bonding and local bridging capital but also facilitate transnational bridging, or brain linkage, by helping NRIs to connect with home. A good example is the American Association of Physicians of Indian Origin (AAPI), which represents over eighty thousand physicians and forty thousand medical students, residents, and fellows in the United States.[72] Established in 1982, it offers tools for its US-based members to connect among each other (bonding) and then with colleagues and friends from across Indian medical schools. AAPI holds an annual convention, offers continuing medical-education courses, and arranges ongoing social events (travel, interest groups, etc.). Starting in 2007, AAPI has hosted the Global Healthcare Summit in India to address Indian public health issues in conjunction with other diaspora organizations.[73] During India's second coronavirus wave in 2021, the organization sent supplies to hospitals (oxygen concentrators for two hundred units) and held webinars connecting physicians in India with AAPI members from their home states and regions.[74] In addition, AAPI lobbies for US legislation benefiting international medical graduates, operates a charitable foundation establishing clinics and providing disaster relief in India, and offers a clerkship program in India for US medical students. Currently, there are nineteen AAPI clinics in India.

Transnational bridging stands out with Indian diaspora organizations. When compared with a sample of one hundred Chinese diaspora organizations, Indian organizations demonstrate a greater emphasis on transnational bridging (42.05 percent vs. 32.99 percent). This edge in transnational bridging is largely due to the different professional trajectories of the two countries' diasporas. In order to bridge, whether local or transnational, one needs to be well embedded in both places.[75] As noted above, Indians tend to naturalize in the United States more than Chinese by almost ten thousand per year,[76] and English proficiency has helped Indians become well embedded in local society.[77]

The trade and business communities constitute an important subset of Indian transnational linkage within my sample. While several bilateral trade organizations exist, the US India Chamber of Commerce (USICOC) Dallas / Fort Worth illustrates their general purpose and scope of activities, which entails bonding and bridging at the local level as well as transnational bridging. The USICOC supports professional, business, and economic development throughout northern Texas, both encouraging networking among its Texas-based members and connecting them with resources and opportunities in India to facilitate bilateral trade. It has a designated staff that offers business consulting, networking events, seminars and training, and support of exchange programs with India. In doing so, they play a local bridging role by elevating the profile of the Indian American professional community and managing a directory of partners from the wider Dallas / Fort Worth community.

The Indus Entrepreneurs (TiE) is the most prominent example of social capital curried by a diasporic organization extending into transnational bridging.[78] Founded in 1992 by Indians in Silicon Valley with the goal of fostering entrepreneurship among those with South Asian roots, TiE offers mentoring, networking, professional development, incubation, and funding opportunities to its members. With fifteen thousand members as of 2020,[79] it has sixty-one chapters in fourteen different countries with twenty chapters in the United States and twenty-three in India,[80] and it has generated USD 200 billion worth of startup value and engaged ten thousand startups globally.[81] As Rekhi, a cofounder, says, "We set up this group called TiE here in the [Silicon] Valley, and TiE very quickly set up chapters in

Bombay, Bangalore, [and] Chennai, and we would go around and preach the gospel of startups."[82] At that point in time, he explains, "Indians were still not seen as entrepreneurs. They still had trouble getting funding, they still had trouble getting accepted. We decided we should be role models." Through groups such as TiE, older and more established members of the diaspora often act as angel investors to younger members.[83] Investments by Indian entrepreneurs in the United States also confer legitimacy on an Indian company so that it can crack into Silicon Valley's other venture capital funds.

TiE has also sought to "build bridges" to India through "cultivating an entrepreneurial ethos in the homeland."[84] Rekhi says that some of his friends in the United States joke about how they don't need TiE anymore, and that is why he began turning to India—a place he thinks needs a lot more attention now.[85] Not only was TiE's quick success in Silicon Valley a driving factor in its global expansion, but its founders were also closely watching developments in India. As Roy da Silva, the former president of the IIT Foundation and a volunteer in the IIT alumni community, explains in an interview with me, "As the Indian economy liberalized, it was natural for them to say, 'Okay, it looks like the entrepreneur ecosystem is starting to open up in India.' So, they decided to have branches in India. TiE Global, which is part of TiE, had a formal person who was driving the globalization of TiE—a process I would place as starting out around 1995, '96, or '97."[86] In this regard, India departs from China, whose government actively reaches out to the diaspora with the objective of promoting brain circulation, as discussed in the previous chapter.

Transnational linkage is not just business oriented. Arts and cultural programs bringing in artists and performers from India are well represented throughout my sample. Over the past forty years, South India Fine Arts has brought hundreds of well-known artists from India to the Bay Area for performances and workshops, creating ethnic solidarity and providing a space to explore and preserve Indian culture. Here, transnational bridging yields social bonding. There are many other smaller and less formal organizations that complement larger organizations by solidifying ethnic unity and national pride, which in turn prompts individual-level, informal channels of entrepreneurship and philanthropy.[87]

Among the diaspora community, charity has been historically viewed as an individual act toward family and hometown in India,[88] with some particularly well-off individuals establishing foundations. Formalized philanthropy has emerged from the 1990s onward with the establishment of prominent charities like Pratham USA (est. 1999) and the American India Foundation (est. 2001).[89] Advances in Indian philanthropy have often grown out of hardships back home. The 2001 Gujarat earthquake, for example, inspired the formation of the American India Foundation, which has raised over USD 137 million for its Indian NGO partners as of 2021. More recently in 2021, diaspora giving has been particularly visible in efforts to combat India's tragic second wave of COVID-19.[90] Indian American philanthropists have also become "more strategic in several dimensions: geography (from local communities of origin to populations and needs across India), focus (from perceived need to established need), mode (from personal connections to more professional intermediaries and NGOs), and accountability (from subjective milestones to measurable results)."[91] This represents diversification in brain linkage to different regions, populations, and organizations.

The newfound emphasis on philanthropy as a shared diaspora responsibility rather than a private act reflects a broader shift in the role and meaning of the Indian diaspora. D. Naujoks credits institutional configurations—namely, OCI—with providing the diaspora with a sense of being valued and appreciated, ultimately creating a "good-will effect." As one of his interviewees recounts, "When I was growing up in India, Indians leaving India were considered brain drain. We had funded their education and they had gone overseas and they were contributing to the growth and development of a different country. And so they were considered for that reason traitors. . . . Now that the Indian diaspora has gained critical mass, they are for the first time recognizing the value of this diaspora and the Indian diaspora is investing back in the country. . . . [T]he success of our diaspora actually will reinforce success for us and changes the identity."[92] This testimony symbolizes how successfully India's initial brain drain has turned into developmental assets.

IITs: India's Brain Linkage Engine

The most active and exemplary group within the Indian diaspora in leading brain linkage with home has been the overseas alumni of Indian Institutes of Technology (IITs). The IITs are a relatively small but strong bastion of brain train in India's talent portfolio that have fostered many of the well-educated Indian talents that contribute to the country's brain linkage. These alumni maintain a strong sense of community (fostered by bonding social capital) and contribute to educational, business, and social ventures back in India (transnational bridging). Increasingly, IIT alumni and the diaspora organizations in which they participate also serve as local bridges, connecting with local non-Indian populations through professional, advocacy and political, and volunteer activities.

While India is host to several tiers of strong engineering colleges, including National Institutes of Technology and Regional Engineering Colleges, I focus on the IITs as a case to illustrate the nature and process of India's transnational brain linkage, as they are the top schools in India and their alumni have been the most globally visible. The IITs were created in postindependence India, in the words of Jawaharlal Nehru, the first prime minister of India, to "provide scientists and technologists of the highest caliber who would engage in research, design, and development to help build the nation towards self-reliance in her technological needs."[93] In 1946, the Sarkar Committee, composed of leading Indians across science and industry, recommended establishing one government-administered engineering college in each of the four regions of the country. The committee specifically identified MIT as an exemplary model, and the first IIT campus was founded in 1951 at Kharagpur, followed by several others. Soon after, the IITs were designated as "institutes of national importance" by the IIT Act of 1961, which granted them legal status through degree-granting authority, significant autonomy in curriculum development and faculty hiring, and larger funding from the government. The act was particularly key in raising the quality of the IITs domestically,[94] and it also advised the IITs to seek support from foreign industrial powers in order to become world-class engineering colleges.[95] Both in inspiration and implementation, the IITs were global facing from the start—it is perhaps no surprise that the graduates of the institutions have gone overseas for further study and work and have led transnational linkage with home.

For example, more than one-third (37.5 percent) of IIT Bombay graduates left India in the 1980s, and most of them (82 percent of those who left India) stayed abroad, creating a serious brain drain for India before linkage began to emerge later. Similarly, 35 percent of IIT Madras graduates migrated to the United States in 1983–1987, a huge increase from 20 percent in

1968–1972 and 27 percent in 1978–1982.[96] In the mid-1980s, it is estimated that IIT graduates comprised 40 percent of the Indian engineers immigrating to the Western world (the figure is higher in the United States) despite being less than 3 percent of the country's total students, demonstrating their transnational mobility.[97] The reason for such a large outflow is clear: a recent IIT graduate working in the United States could make a salary much higher than one who stays in India, and American corporations carry far more global acclaim.

IIT BONDING SOCIAL CAPITAL

IIT graduates abroad built strong ties or bonding among themselves. Generally, IIT alumni chapters hold one or two events per year, allowing IIT alumni from different graduation cohorts to meet. For example, the IIT Madras Alumni Association of North America oversees local and young alumni chapters and an entrepreneur network in addition to its general alumni network. It offers mixers, web meetings, blogs, and special events to learn from and meet other IIT Madras alumni. It is important to note that alumni connections took off after the creation of the internet. As Roy da Silva recounts in an interview, "After the internet came out, it was possible to create groups with the advent of things like Yahoo! Groups, and the IIT campuses created groups. These were not a formal creation; the groups were informally created by individuals. For instance, I graduated in 1974, and we have a group. In fact, just my class of electrical engineers has a group. And then you have another group, which is called Pre-1993. So little groups formed, and you decided to opt in or out."[98]

Their bonding social capital went beyond a particular IIT to develop a broad "pan-IIT institutional kinship," reflecting a sense of community not just among fellow alumni from the same institutions but from across all IITs, as Harvard anthropologist Ajantha Subramanian describes.[99] This structure differs from the typical alumni organization that focuses on just one university, as well as a nation-led alumni network encompassing an entire country's international alumni, as with Australia. The Pan-IIT Alumni Foundation, charged with networking alumni who graduated from various campuses, is principally responsible for conducting professional events as its larger pool of alumni lends itself well to specialized events that would not achieve a critical mass if solely targeting the alumni base of a particular school. Alongside domain-specific events, the foundation's programming addresses crosscutting topics, like leadership. PanIIT USA's Annual IIT Alumni Summit, the hallmark all-alumni event, has extensive funding and celebrity speakers. As Dinsha Mistree, a research fellow at the Hoover Institution, describes in an interview, "The funding is incredible. They got, a couple of years ago, Bill Clinton at the drop of a hat because one of his friends asked him. They put him on a private plane, brought him down to speak to the group. And I would guess they spend a couple million dollars every year putting these events on."[100] Prime Minister Modi inaugurated the annual event in 2020 with a virtual keynote address, praising the IIT model of alumni engagement and urging its alumni to "set an even higher benchmark on giving back to India."[101]

In promoting a pan-IIT identity, as Subramanian points out, US-based IIT graduates have advanced a narrative of "humble middle-class origins in which the brain is elevated as the sole form of capital" and ensured that "the Indian technical professional is immediately recognizable as a global commodity." According to her, the so-called "Brand IIT" was built in several stages. First, high-profile IIT alumni were called on to highlight their IIT affiliations on their resumes, rather than continuing the status quo of listing a bachelor's degree without mention of an alma mater. Second, IIT attendees worked to cultivate pan-IIT camaraderie: "We realized that if we continued to stay independent, with each campus having its own alumni association, we will not get the level that we would get if we combined them all together and created one common IIT brand."[102] Finally, media coverage played a major role, especially a 2003 feature on CBS's *60 Minutes* about IIT engineers, and was predominantly facilitated by the pan-IIT alumni association. That sense of kinship was formalized in 2004 with the registering of the nonprofit PanIIT USA. Its vision is "for the IIT's [*sic*] to be acknowledged among the world's leading institutions in academics, research excellence and innovation, and for its alumni to be recognized as leaders and innovators in their chosen fields." They have a job board, events, and conferences, seeking to help each other in order to advance the IIT brand.[103]

IIT TRANSNATIONAL LINKAGE

Strong bonding capital among IIT graduates abroad was then developed into transnational-bridging capital, connecting talent from home and abroad. IIT graduates sought to strengthen transnational networks by supporting their alma maters back home. Vinod Gupta and his donations to his alma mater are a prime example. An IIT Kharagpur (IIT KGP) graduate and founder of Infogroup in the United States, a company which essentially digitized the Yellow Pages, Gupta has been very active in alumni affairs, organizing "the first alumni directory" even before the internet era. Roy da Silva recalls, "He would mail it out to people, and they would pass it onto others. And that's how the database got built up."[104] Gupta then made a large donation to his alma mater, establishing the Vinod Gupta School of Management at IIT KGP in 1993. The school offers classes on international business communication and finance as well as a collaborative program with Singapore Management University, which launched in 2019, to give students exposure to international and Asian business leaders.

Similarly, IIT KGP's G. S. Sanyal School of Telecommunications and M. N. Faruqui Innovation Centre were founded with donations from Arjun Malhotra, an IIT KGP alum who grew up in India before moving to the United States to attend Harvard Business School.[105] He funded the travel of IIT KGP representatives across North America to major IIT alumni destinations. Kasturi Chopra, former director of IIT KGP, describes the process by which he and G. S. Sanyal, a professor at IIT KGP, began engaging alumni in the United States. Alumni invited them to stay in their homes and host intimate dinners during which they presented and discussed the IITs' activities. As the alumni reminisced about their experiences, Sanyal would request donations on the spot. The approach was unconventional; as Chopra recollects, "The alumni were somewhat taken aback by this type of fund collection technique. But, they started responding as to how they will go about connecting with the IIT."[106]

IIT KGP went beyond informal networking by establishing its own IIT foundation, a nonprofit registered in the United States by Gupta to connect with and tap into its North America alumni base, which numbers nearly ten thousand. IIT KGP took the lead on these efforts because it not only was the oldest of the IITs but also had the largest number of alumni in the United States at the time. Besides informing them of the progress being made at their beloved institute, the foundation seeks to support further development of IIT KGP by collecting funds for campus development that cannot be covered by government subsidies. Given the alumni's "tremendous love" for the school, the foundation proudly proclaims, it is "our purpose to facilitate and enhance connection and devotion to their alma mater."[107]

The IIT KGP model was replicated at other IITs as their US alumni communities grew, fostering more brain linkage between IITs and their overseas alumni. In 2021, IIT Bombay received a record high in donations from its US alumni, totaling USD 3.6 million. The funds were raised by the IIT Bombay Heritage Foundation, a US nonprofit, and its Go IITB Initiative. Alumni donations play a critical role in supporting IITs at home as they face budget deficits, including IIT Bombay. While PanIIT USA does not directly fundraise, it provides alumni services, like facilitating networking, which helps alumni remain connected to the IITs and helps build school-specific alumni chapters that collect initiative-driven donations.[108] Recognizing their potential, in 2000, the Indian government asked IIT alumni in the United States to raise USD 1 billion for the IITs.[109] Many NRIs even hope their children will attend the IITs so they have yet another personal stake in improving the quality of the IITs.[110]

In addition to connecting overseas alumni to their alma maters back home, the IIT network also plays a key role in bringing its alumni to US educational institutions. As described in *The Caste of Merit*, when an individual identified only as Udhay, a 1992 IIT Madras alumnus, was asked whether he had a good sense about where he wanted to study in the United States, he answered, "Very good. It was all almost written down like a manual for us by our seniors. In fact, the entire application process itself was amazingly coordinated. That was one of the reasons that IITs had a much higher percentage of students going abroad. . . . It was the network." Udhay points to a strict system of determining who among IIT students would apply where in order to maximize admissions. In addition, as IIT graduates took on faculty and leadership positions in American universities, they sought to bring more alumni from their alma maters to their campuses.[111] At Duke, for example, an IIT graduate started a summer internship program targeting IIT undergraduates, with the goal of drawing them to Duke for engineering and computer science PhDs. Through interviews, Subramanian confirms that IIT graduates at Harvard, MIT, and Stanford "are equally explicit about their goal of admitting and hiring their own."[112]

IIT graduates abroad also actively engage in mentoring and supporting their alumni back home. IvyCap Ventures is one example of an IIT/IIM alumni network generating investments and building social capital. IvyCap is a venture capital fund-management company aiming to leverage "global alumni ecosystems" to build technology-driven innovative companies.[113]

The IIT Alumni Trust is among its major investors. Composed of leaders from various fields around the world, IvyCap's IIT/IIM alumni network, IvyCamp, is an "alumni driven engagement platform" that helps "founders enhance their skills, accelerate their business, engage in corporate innovation programs, and connect with investors" and mentors.[114] With more than sixty-five mentors, including founders and business executives, they claim to have direct support from over five thousand IIT and IIM graduates globally. Such a system helps streamline the entire value chain of investment by giving participants an edge in deal sourcing, talent acquisition, exit support, and access to top-quality experts and mentors from both domestic and international networks. IvyCamp has supported and connected over three thousand startups to date. IIT Startups, a nonprofit accelerator based in Silicon Valley, also provides a coaching and mentorship program to IIT alumni, culminating in Demo Day, when IIT entrepreneurs pitch to corporate-development execs and angel and institutional investors.

With these programs and extensive networks in place, it is not surprising to find from my analysis of seventy-one India-based unicorns as of May 2024 that 68 percent of them have at least one cofounder who is an IIT alumnus. Overall, approximately 54 percent of the top-five-hundred companies in India have at least one IIT or IIM graduate on their board.[115] Many of them had foreign experiences or returned home after education or working experiences abroad. IIT alumni have found huge success in both India and the United States, in large part due to linkage that leverages their deep transnational networks.[116] Clearly, the brain linkage, such as activities of IIT graduates, has been a central piece of India's talent portfolio.

Diversification within Linkage and into Circulation

Such linkage-led development then had an impact on diversifying India's talent portfolio with increasing brain circulation. With India's growing economy, improved infrastructure, including higher education, and better governance and with more professional connections with their homeland, in large part thanks to brain linkage, a growing number of Indians are returning home.[117] Whereas circulation has led to linkage for China, linkage has led to circulation for India. This has also contributed to increased diversification within brain linkage. While NRIs led brain linkage from abroad, India now sees expanded linkage through returnees at home.

India does not run government-led talent-recruitment programs, as in China. The Indian government has largely been in the backseat when it comes to brain circulation, except for the introduction of the OCI visa category, which helped facilitate circulation.[118] Studies have shown that in considerations of whether to return home, financial and career reasons carry the most weight among Indian talent overseas.[119] According to Vivek Wadhwa et al., only 10 percent of Indian returnees held senior-management positions in the United States, but after returning, 44 percent occupied such positions, having new opportunities with more impact back home than abroad.[120] Local governments, the private and public sectors, and professionals have coordinated to "woo high-tech professionals, investments, and businesses" through measures like tax breaks, investments in training institutes to develop R&D professionals, and newly constructed residential townships on the city outskirts.[121] With these upscale townships tailored to the tastes of the returnees, described as "a hybrid of India and America," Indians who return face less of a culture shock.[122] They flex their entrepreneurial muscle. My analysis of Indian unicorns reveals that as of May 2024, 66.2 percent have at least one returnee as a cofounder.

It is important to note that brain circulation has not diminished transnational brain linkage, however. Rather, it has facilitated a more reciprocal process of linkage, as many returnees stayed in close touch and collaborated with former colleagues after their return. Wadhwa and his colleagues' study shows that 66 percent of Indian returnees maintain monthly or more frequent contact with former colleagues in the United States (compared to 55 percent of Chinese returnees). They share information about customers, markets, technology, job opportunities, and business funding.[123] Robin Richards Donohoe, founder and cochair of Draper Richards Kaplan Foundation,[124] says, "You could be sitting in Bangalore and hear about 10 great deals in Santa Clara that you could be a venture capital investor in, but you'd hear about them first in Bangalore."[125] This remark not only indicates that India offers great business opportunities for returnees but also illustrates how closely connected the two places are. Returnees maintain numerous links—property, friendships, and work relationships—with the United States and often plan to send their children back to the United States for college, which reinforces and increases the linkages between Silicon Valley and Bengaluru.

Returnee involvement in Indian organizations has spurred global collaboration and trade development, in parallel with diaspora organizations' linkage efforts. A good example is NASSCOM, the trade association for India's tech industry, which has had a tremendous impact on India's IT industry and helped establish an image for India in global software markets. Founded in 1988 by Dewang Mehta and Nandan Nilekani, a returnee and an IIT alum, respectively, the association counts more than 2,800 companies and multinational corporations as members, constituting 90 percent of the IT business-process-management industry in India. It is not strictly a diaspora organization, but NRIs are active members, particularly in its international chapters and Global Trade Development Initiative. Relying on both paid staff and engaged members, including Indians at home and abroad, NASSCOM connects international companies to parts suppliers in India and offers their member companies insight reports on industry trends, opportunities for companies to enhance their visibility, networking opportunities, and mentorship for midsized companies. The NASSCOM Foundation recently joined with Microsoft India to launch the Innovate for Accessible India campaign to help people with disabilities in India through "technology and tools required for better integration into society and access to equal opportunities."[126]

NASSCOM is also increasingly active in supporting cross-border entrepreneurship and business innovation. NASSCOM InnoTrek sends Indian startups to Silicon Valley annually to forge connections, particularly with prominent diaspora members. In 2021, InnoTrek speakers included Abhinav Asthana (CEO and founder of Postman), Priya Rajan (managing director, Silicon Valley Bank), and Neeraj Arora (former global business head, WhatsApp). Of the eight people who form the core organizing team, all are NRIs or returnees. As business and technology has evolved, NASSCOM has been a thought leader around global capability centers (GCCs) in India, which allow global organizations to tap into Indian talent through "large facilities [that] concentrate workers and infrastructure that handle operations . . . and IT support . . . to sustain productivity growth."[127] It hosts an annual GCC conclave with international partners, such as Lowe's, Target, and PayPal. Prime Minister Modi refers to NASSCOM as a "revolution" beyond its time-tested role as an association.[128] Funded by industry and being nongovernmental, NASSCOM signifies India's market-driven, bottom-up approach toward development via transnational brain linkage.

Such interaction between circulation and linkage can be seen in the development of higher education, contributing to brain train and further diversifying India's talent portfolio. NRIs have contributed to improving India's higher education system, whether by staying abroad or ultimately returning home. They have helped Indian institutions to build the necessary infrastructure and resources to make it possible to train globally valuable talent. Additionally, in the past decade, a wave of private liberal arts institutions has emerged in India with US-inspired curricular structures, often with US partnerships via student exchanges and study abroad. The establishment of these schools demonstrates how brain linkage and brain circulation can contribute to brain train, as NRIs and Indian returnees have helped foster connections with foreign scholars and top-tier institutions around the world.

One good example is Ashoka University, founded in 2014. Praised as a pioneer in liberal arts education in India, Ashoka illustrates the virtuous cycle of brain linkage and circulation to strengthen train. Ashok Trivedi, one of Ashoka's founders and a prominent entrepreneur and investor, continues to reside in the United States. After receiving a bachelor's and a master's degree from the University of Delhi, Trivedi moved to the United States in 1973 and received his master's of business administration degree from Ohio University. He cofounded an IT company, IGATE, which expanded to India, other parts of Asia, and North America, before selling it to Capgemini for USD 4 billion. After cofounding Ashoka, Trivedi made several donations to facilitate data sharing with US institutions on politics in India, served on the US-India Security Council, and provided funding for Indian startups. Ashish Dhawan, another cofounder, is a returnee who studied at Yale University and Harvard Business School, worked in investment and private equity, and then returned to India, where he started one of India's leading private equity funds.

Ashoka University is clearly a product of NRI brain linkage and circulation, and it has contributed to India via the brain train of Indian students: the school caters mostly to Indians, and only 6 percent of its student body is international.[129] The education it offers is truly internationalized in nature. As of August 2020, approximately 60 percent of Ashoka's 122 permanent faculty members hold foreign doctorate degrees, representing cases of brain circulation similar to China. Of faculty members with an Indian doctorate degree, nearly all have completed postdoctoral work or taught abroad.[130] Ashoka not only pursues its goal of becoming a top private college in India by hiring foreign-educated faculty but also has made considerable efforts to connect its students with leading global institutions, such as Stanford, Princeton, and Yale. Ashoka and other new colleges adopting similar approaches point to the way in which Indian talents who have circulated back to India or who engage in brain linkage from overseas can enhance India's brain train.

The Limitations of Stratified Linkage

Saxenian observes that "Indians historically are deeply divided and typically segregate themselves by regional and linguistic differences. . . . But in Silicon Valley it seems that the Indian identity has become more powerful than these regional distinctions."[131] The author V. S. Naipaul similarly argues that "in these special circumstances overseas Indians developed something they would have never known in India: a sense of belonging to an Indian community. This feeling of community could override religion and caste."[132]

While Indians are afforded a certain kind of social mobility in the United States, however, social stratification has not disappeared and limits the extent and impact of India's brain linkage. In particular, caste—a three-thousand-year-old social and religious hierarchy that divides Hindus into four classes and has traditionally determined their occupational status—is, to an extent, carried on overseas.

It is estimated that anywhere from 70 to 90 percent of Indians in the United States are from the upper castes, and under 5 percent are Dalit—a group technically considered outside of the caste system as the lowest social category in India's hierarchy.[133] Even in the United States, the opportunity cost for not being part of trusted and deep-rooted upper-caste networks can be high.[134] As one *Washington Post* article puts it, "Networks of engineers from the dominant castes have replicated the patterns of bias within the United States by favoring their peers in hiring, referrals, and performance reviews."[135] Even an IIT degree is not always enough to override caste status in Silicon Valley. This is so much the case that Thenmozhi Soundararajan, the founder and executive director of Equality Labs, a Dalit civil rights organization, explained in an interview with me in the spring of 2021 that Silicon Valley is often referred to as "Agraharam Valley," alluding to the part of an Indian village where Brahmins reside.[136]

In recent years, the question of caste discrimination in Silicon Valley has received more attention, as illustrated by the high-profile 2020 Cisco case, in which California's Department of Fair Employment and Housing, on behalf of an individual of Dalit background, sued the technology company Cisco and two of its employees for caste discrimination. The case alleged that the two employees—both Brahmins—gave the Dalit employee less pay and fewer opportunities due to his caste and then retaliated against him when he filed a human resources complaint.[137] In April 2023, the California Civil Rights Department dismissed the case against the two Indian American engineers (the case against Cisco remains ongoing),[138] but the lawsuit highlights the enduring concern of caste issues in the United States, especially in the tech industry. In the aftermath of the lawsuit's announcement, Soundararajan's Equality Labs reportedly received almost 260 complaints from tech workers in the United States about caste bias, including "caste-based slurs and jokes, bullying, discriminatory hiring practices, bias in peer reviews, and sexual harassment." These claims largely came from employees of global companies, such as Facebook, Cisco, Google, Microsoft, IBM, and Amazon.[139]

Exclusionary upper-caste networks of Indian professionals can constrain brain linkage to mainly the upper caste and thereby reduce its scope and diversification. While it is difficult to measure and determine the amount of social capital possessed by individuals from different castes, Indians with upper-caste backgrounds on the whole clearly have greater proximity to business networks and highly placed individuals in universities and corporations than do those from lower-caste backgrounds, conferring greater social capital to this group overall. That is, Indian migrants from the upper class were able to build the tight social networks (bonding social capital), which in turn would bestow them with stronger bridging capital, both local and transnational. Nevertheless, the upper-class phenomenon has been largely overlooked in previous studies of Indian brain linkage, which tend to emphasize an overarching pan-Indian or NRI identity. Interclass differences in social capital requires a modified model for India's case, as the general transnational-bridging model outlined in the theory chapter (figure 2.1) does not capture such stratified linkage (see figure 6.3 below). Reduced stratification—and greater diversification in terms of social class—in Indian brain linkage could help expand the impact of linkage, not only better harnessing the linkage potential of caste-oppressed talents overseas but also connecting to different segments of Indian society back home. Table 6.4 summarizes the main features of India's talent portfolio and its evolution over time.

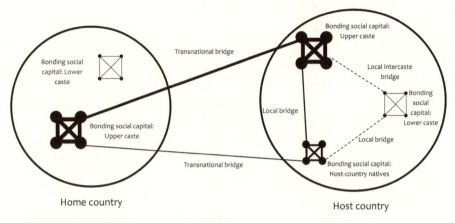

Home country   Host country

FIGURE 6.3. Stratified transnational linkage.
Source: Author created.

TABLE 6.4. India's talent portfolio

Train	Overall weak, with small group of strong universities Indian Institutes of Technology, Indian Institutes of Management
	Diversifying into liberal arts education thanks in part to returnee (brain circulation) and overseas (brain linkage) talents
	Rebalancing Caste-reservation system as a means of diversifying to better train talents from oppressed segments of society
Gain	Little to none
Circulation	Increasing thanks in part to development spurred by brain linkage
Linkage	Strong Overseas Indians bridging to India via philanthropy, business and investment, arts and culture
	Rebalancing Increasing transnational linkage from home: Indian returnees bridging to former host countries
	Diversifying from linkage with US-based diaspora to linkage with diaspora in other regions, like the Middle East

Expanding India's Portfolio beyond Linkage

While India, like China, experienced an extensive outflow of talent, the country has been able to counter this risk of brain drain by utilizing its diaspora as a "brain deposit" via brain linkage. However, unlike China, the Indian government has played a secondary role with legal and symbolic support; while highly organized, loyal diaspora organizations and alumni networks have created strong social bonding and transnational social capital. India's talent portfolio also illustrates the importance of a small but strong component of brain train, which has fostered an excellent and globally competitive talent pool of engineers, entrepreneurs, and doctors with English proficiency, and that has proved critical.

Still, like other talent giants in this study, India's talent portfolio has evolved, becoming more diversified both within and across Bs. Brain linkage has geographically diversified as efforts have increased in other major destinations for Indian talent beyond the United States. For example, top Indian business leaders in the United Arab Emirates—of enterprises such as Lulu International and NMC Healthcare—are not only launching startups across the Gulf region but also expanding their businesses, investments, and philanthropic initiatives in India, closely following the Silicon Valley–linkage model.[140] As Vikram Gupta, founder of IvyCap Ventures, says, "There is more inbound interest from [the] Middle East to invest in India. Earlier, a greater number of investors from that region used to invest in the United States and Europe. Now they are looking at China and India."[141] The United Arab Emirates Business Leaders Forum reports that one hundred expat Indians pooled USD 1 billion to invest in India to address needs spanning healthcare, education, solar power, and infrastructure. Furthermore, India has also turned to places like Bahrain as they share a strong historical link. While Bahrain's population is only one-thousandth of India's, around a third of its residents are Indian. This diasporic linkage has led to the establishment of the Bahrain-India Business Corridor, resulting in over USD 1 billion in annual bilateral trade.[142] In short, the Middle East is looking to build partnerships with India through the diasporic connection to stimulate their own tech-startup ecosystem following the Silicon Valley model. This exemplifies how Indian brain linkage is being expanded from the United States into other parts of the world.

However, it remains unclear whether India's brain linkage can be diversified beyond society's most privileged. The prevailing notion of the Indian diaspora as encompassing a pan-Indian or overarching NRI identity fails to capture the stratified nature of Indian diaspora communities and their linkages with home. Despite their greater awareness (or at least posturing) toward broader identity with references to "India," the "Indian American community," and the "community of Indian heritage" over time,[143] as well as efforts in charity and philanthropy toward the underprivileged at home, India's brain linkage remains largely an upper-class phenomenon and tends to be confined to intracaste linkage.

Rebalancing among Bs has been gradually occurring with the increased weight of brain circulation and brain train in India's talent portfolio. Given India's growing economy and improved infrastructure, including higher education, thanks to the contribution of overseas talent through transnational support, a growing number of Indians are returning home. Brain circulation and linkage also strengthen brain train through supporting higher education, further diversifying India's talent portfolio. India's evolving talent portfolio is an excellent illustration of the interaction effects among the different Bs—a facet of TPT that will be discussed more in the next chapter. A small but strong system of brain train institutions have enabled Indian talents to be transnationally competitive, and the brain linkage they enacted has contributed to India's development, which in turn increased brain circulation and improved brain train, leading to a greater diversification of India's talent portfolio.

This chapter has not addressed any apparent risk to India's linkage-based talent portfolio as no large-scale systematic risks have yet threatened India's brain linkage. At most, it is possible that the COVID-19 pandemic may have somewhat reduced linkage by temporarily constraining the diaspora's ability to travel to India for short-term stays. Furthermore, India's linkage has not faced unsystematic risks, such as the geopolitical tensions that have plagued China's linkage and circulation. Nonetheless, while social capital via brain linkage can be important, ultimately, human capital is fundamental to development, and India will need to better harness other Bs beyond brain linkage in order to sustain development.

SEVEN

Talent Portfolios

No "One-Size-Fits-All" Path

It is clear from the cases of Japan, Australia, China, and India that there is no "one-size-fits-all" path to development via talent strategy. Rather, the "talent giants" have developed their own recipes or formulas leading to distinctive talent portfolios with different emphases on human versus social capital, domestic versus foreign talents, and homegrown versus foreign-educated talents. Their portfolios include all four Bs to an extent, but their compositions significantly differ: each portfolio features one particular B over others, and some portfolios are more diversified than others. Such differences in talent portfolios represent divergent paths to development among the four cases.

However, their portfolios were not formed by historical accident or at random, and we need to explain why each took the particular form that it did. Current scholarship yields insights into specific parts of the talent giants' human resource development (e.g., brain gain or circulation), but there is no study, let alone a theoretical framework, that both offers a holistic picture over time and explains cross-national variation in talent development. As such, this book's novel approach using TPT makes a valuable theoretical contribution to the study of talent development beyond the four cases of this study. TPT provides a holistic picture of a country's talent portfolio, captures changes over time through rebalancing, and offers a framework for cross-national comparison via talent portfolios.

While the previous four chapters detail how each country has developed its talent portfolio and rebalanced it over time, this chapter offers a comparative analysis of the four countries' talent portfolios to draw theoretical insights. More specifically, I explore questions such as, Why does each talent giant feature one B in particular in its talent portfolio? What factors shape a country's talent portfolio, contributing to differences across various countries' portfolios? Why do some countries better diversify their portfolios than others and successfully navigate through risks via rebalancing, while others fall prey to such risks? In tackling these questions, this chapter highlights the key findings from this study to offer theoretical insights that can be applied in studying other countries.

Four Giants, Four Portfolios

Each of the talent giants' portfolios featured one B over the others during its rise, and, therefore, the four cases provide clear illustrations of the benefits and risks of each B. During its catch-up and growth period in the 1960s through 1980s, Japan's portfolio was heavily based on the brain train that supplied a homegrown workforce to the economy. The country stressed robust workplace training for talents that had participated in a national education system that had funneled them into two tracks: K–12 mass education for technical and manufacturing jobs, on the one hand, and higher education in science and engineering, on the other. Even when Japanese went overseas, these experiences were largely part of brain train, as they remained embedded in the domestic labor force. This well-rounded system of brain train enabled Japan to quickly catch up to advanced Western nations, without the risk of a serious brain drain. And yet Japan's brain train ultimately struggled to meet the needs of the new knowledge economy, particularly as the country increasingly became inward-looking and detached from global trends. Japan's demographic crisis posed another major unsystematic risk given the country's overreliance on brain train of domestic labor.

On the other hand, Australia's talent portfolio represents a stark contrast to Japan's, as it relied heavily on brain gain of foreign talent. Thanks to a well-respected and internationalized higher education system as well as government policies to promote multiculturalism targeting skilled migration, Australia effectively used both the "study-work" and "work-migration" paths in attracting foreign talent. This enabled the country to meet its most pressing needs of human capital to sustain economic development. However,

Australia, too, faced risks associated with its brain gain, which has stoked anti-immigrant sentiments at home and also rendered it vulnerable to geopolitical tensions with China—the main supplier of foreign talent to the country. The pandemic hit hard on Australia's brain gain portfolio as it restricted transnational talent mobility as a whole.

China and India developed portfolios that were different not only from Japan and Australia but also from each other—a fact that is not well appreciated in the current literature. Given the countries' comparable economic, demographic, and immigration profiles, it is easy to stress the similarities between their strategies vis-à-vis their skilled diasporas. Indeed, the two most populous nations and suppliers of skilled migrants and international students in the capitalist labor market initially suffered huge brain drains. Both then took advantage of their diasporic talent effectively but differently: China has pursued brain circulation, filling new domestic opportunities with talent that had been trained overseas, while India, still lacking domestic opportunities, has embraced transnational brain linkage without the permanent return of its overseas talent. These strategies have enabled China and India to put to use talents that would have been underutilized or wasted had they stayed in the home country.

The current literature, however, tends to overlook the crucial difference between China and India, largely because it is still centered on the paradigm of return migration. In addition, while both countries have converted brain drain into developmental assets through circulation and/or linkage, China's strategy of circulation through government-led talent-recruitment programs has rendered it vulnerable to geopolitical tensions with host countries, such as the United States and Australia. India has yet to face similar risks to its brain linkage, perhaps due to the lack of proactive government involvement. However, while brain linkage has enabled India to make use of social capital, the country is still losing human capital. Table 7.1 summarizes key features of the talent portfolios of the talent giants during their economic rise.

A key confirmation of this study of the four talent giants is that there is no "one-size-fits-all" portfolio as each features a particular B over others. In order to have the most competitive talent portfolio, a nation will want to fully utilize all four Bs to both maintain diversification and engage the best talent in the world, regardless of whether it is domestic, diasporic, or foreign. In reality, this is hard to achieve for most countries, and each

TABLE 7.1. Key features of four talent portfolios during rise

B/Country	Brain train	Brain gain	Brain circulation	Brain linkage
Japan	National education system: vocational schools, colleges of technology, junior colleges, higher education (small in terms of graduate education) On-the-job training Short-term overseas training: industrial liaison programs, visiting scholars, corporate affiliate programs	Little	Little	Little
Australia	Internationalized, high-quality higher education	International students Skilled workers: permanent migration and temporary migration Talents from diverse countries of origin	Little	Little
China	Mostly weak domestic education system Train via short-term overseas experiences (postdoctoral scholars, visiting scholars)	Little	Chinese talent with overseas PhDs Talents with overseas work experience Talents particularly in three sectors: academia, S&T, entrepreneurship	Use of linkage to encourage "soft-landing" circulation
India	Overall weak, with small group of strong universities (IITs, IIMs)	Little	Little	Overseas Indians bridging to India via philanthropy, business and investment, arts and culture

talent giant has therefore had a strategic focus on a particular B in creating its talent portfolio. To explain why, we must identify the main factors that shape a nation's talent portfolio.

Explaining Diverging Portfolios

To answer the question of *why* each country chose to focus on the B it did, I compare the four talent giants' trajectories to extrapolate factors that explain cross-national variation in talent portfolios. Identifying such factors can yield theoretical insights in understanding the construction of a particular talent portfolio beyond the four cases. While numerous factors can impact talent portfolios, I focus here on the two most important ones— one affecting the *direction* of talent flow, inward or outward, and the other having to do with the *preference* among domestic, foreign, and diasporic layers of talent. These two factors in combination shape the formation of different talent portfolios to focus on different Bs.

WORLD-SYSTEM POSITION

A nation's position in the capitalist world system affects the direction of talent flows. Talent tends to flow from the periphery to the core of the world system, and, thus, a country's world-system position at a given time is crucial in determining whether it will experience a talent inflow or outflow. It also follows that, given the essential role that market forces play in transnational talent flows, TPT supposes a nation's incorporation into the capitalist labor market. Of the four cases in this study, Japan and Australia were well placed in the capitalist world system, having already joined the international division of labor by the mid-twentieth century when they were seeking to formulate a talent portfolio for the modern era. As socialist nations, China and (to a far lesser extent) India, on the other hand, were initially excluded from this integration and therefore were at peripheral positions in the 1980s when they began formulating talent strategy in the world capitalist market.

As a result, neither Japan nor Australia saw extensive outflow of talent. There already existed in Japan plentiful educational and career opportunities to nurture and retain talent at home, explaining why the country did not suffer from any serious brain drain during its postwar "catch-up" period—which, on the other hand, precluded brain circulation and linkage from becoming important parts of Japan's talent portfolio. Some Japanese went abroad for further training, but they remained in the domestic labor market. Australia, too, was already well integrated into the capitalist world system in the post-1945 period and did not witness extensive talent out-flow or brain drain. So, like Japan, brain circulation or linkage had little potential of becoming core elements of Australia's talent portfolio, which instead was suited for retaining and gaining talent. Why Japan and Australia then developed different talent portfolios (brain train–based vs. brain gain–based) despite similar world-system positions is explained in the next section.

In contrast, communist China and socialist-leaning India were largely isolated from the capitalist world system in the post-1945 period. While India saw some students travel overseas to study in the United States or United Kingdom, China engaged in only limited talent exchange within the socialist bloc, which further exacerbated its isolation.[1] There was little transnational talent mobility for both countries. When China and India opened their doors to the world capitalist market to promote their respective economies in the 1980s, they were at the bottom of the international division of labor, and their infrastructure (including higher education) was poor and underdeveloped.[2] With limited educational and career opportunities at home, neither could adequately train or retain their domestic talent, let alone attract foreign talent via brain gain. Therefore, these talents flowed overseas to more advanced nations, leading to a serious brain drain initially but creating the potential for brain circulation or linkage later. Why China and India developed different talent portfolios (brain circulation–based vs. brain linkage–based) despite similar world-system positions is explained in the next section. From these four cases, it is clear that a country's position in the capitalist world system has a significant impact on which Bs it can engage by determining the direction of talent flows.

NATIONAL IDENTITY

The story of the four talent giants also reveals that not every country is equally amenable to all three layers of talent—domestic, foreign, and diasporic—that can be engaged in a talent portfolio. Countries, like Japan and China, that value ethnic and cultural homogeneity are much less hospitable to foreign talent—preferring to utilize domestic or diasporic talent—than those that embrace multiculturalism and diversity, like Australia. This is largely due to different conceptions of national identity, which is another key factor that impacts the composition of a talent portfolio. National identity can be either ethnic or civic, where ethnic nations define themselves by ethnicity and culture and tend to be homogeneous and exclusive, while civic nations are conceptualized as political communities based on values and institutions and tend to be more heterogeneous and inclusive.[3]

The impact of these different conceptions of nation on talent strategy is revealed most clearly in the comparison between Japan and Australia—two countries that did not see extensive outflows of talent due to their similar statuses in the capitalist world system. While Japan had a sufficient supply of domestic talent during its catch-up period and did not need to import talent, its emphasis on ethnic homogeneity and doing things the "Japanese" way further contributed to the absence of brain gain of foreign talent in Japan's talent portfolio, which instead focused on brain train of coethnic domestic talent. Such emphasis also contributed to the lack of value attributed to foreign experience or foreign degrees, further decreasing the chance for brain circulation and linkage. Rather, to gain knowledge and technology from abroad, Japan sent its own coethnic talents overseas for short-term brain train experiences while retaining them in the domestic labor force.

In Australia, in contrast, a civic conception of national identity was conducive to brain gain through import of foreign talent as a key element of its talent portfolio. Even when the country pursued the White Australia Policy, its national identity was still primarily civic and political, hailing its immigrants from various countries of origin in Europe. This helped Australia to better incorporate more ethnically diverse foreign talents—beyond White Europeans—when it embraced broader diversity and multiculturalism in the 1970s. Thus, while both Japan and Australia held similar positions in the world system and did not experience brain drain, Japan's ethnic national identity was not conducive to brain gain, circulation, or linkage in its talent portfolio, while Australia's civic national identity enabled it to successfully do brain gain, which valued foreign talents from different nationalities.

National identity also explains the difference between China and India, which initially witnessed similarly extensive outflows of talent. China's conception of nation is similar to that of Japan, based on "Han nationalism" centered around the Han race as the nation's ethnic core (despite officially acknowledging fifty-five ethnic minorities). As such, China has sought to engage in brain circulation of its coethnic, diasporic talents for the same reasons that Japan made use of its coethnic, domestic talents: an emphasis on ethnic and cultural homogeneity. Indeed, ethnic nationhood may serve as a pull factor for diasporic talents to return as it can often foster a strong sense of belonging and comfort within the home culture as compared to other, more diverse countries. On the other hand, like Japan, China's ethnically defined nation made the country inhospitable to foreign talent, reducing the possibility for brain gain.[4] In comparison, India is a vastly diverse and ethnically heterogeneous nation and has sought to develop a civic national identity that would subsume the apparent ethnic, religious, cultural, and racial differences. While India has not yet developed a civic national or multicultural identity comparable to that of Australia, the country does not emphasize ethnic ties and cultural homogeneity, as does China. There has therefore not been a similar impetus for the Indian diaspora to return, and as a civic nation, India is content to allow these talents to remain overseas.

It is worth noting one related aspect of national identity that also plays a significant role in shaping a nation's talent strategy: that of language. In ethnically conceived nations, such as Japan and China, coethnic talents are more likely to speak the nationally unique, shared language, and, thus, utilizing coethnic rather than foreign talents not only is more practical—as they already speak the same language—but also further contributes to the homogeneity and social harmony that is often prized in ethnic nations. While language does not perfectly align with the ethnic-versus-civic distinction, native language is less important in the latter. Both Australia and India, civically oriented nations, also have high English proficiency due to the British colonial legacy. The emergence of English as the primary global language has further contributed to many civic nations' hospitability to foreign talent, as well as the success of their overseas nationals. For example, English is part of what makes Australia an attractive destination for international students, many of whom want to study in an English-speaking country to hone their language skills.[5] In India, English instruction at institutions such as the IITs and IIMs has conferred fluency on Indian talents, better situating them for global employment opportunities and enabling them to achieve prominence in developed, English-speaking countries, such as the United States.

Taken together, world-system position and national identity combine to shape the construction of a particular national talent portfolio. While most nations wish to utilize all four Bs to engage the best available talent, regardless of whether it is domestic, diasporic, or foreign, my study shows that such efforts are largely constrained by these two factors. Nations that are best positioned to construct the most competitive portfolios fall into the category of both core and civic. Their high level of development not only enables them to foster strong brain train systems and avoid brain drain but also makes them attractive to foreign talent. While, as noted in the theory chapter, all countries regard brain train as the most foundational B and strive to attain strong brain train systems, brain gain becomes increasingly important for core/civic countries because it enables them to attract top global talents, regardless of their ethnic background or country of origin— after all, this is what has made Silicon Valley so successful. On the other hand, as exemplified by Japan, nations that are core and ethnic continue to rely on brain train due to their appreciation of cultural homogeneity, which creates an environment that is inhospitable to foreign talent.

In contrast, peripheral nations are at a disadvantage in constructing a competitive talent portfolio, as they often lose their top talent to core countries due to the lack of a developmental base to foster employment opportunities or a system of strong domestic brain train institutions. Peripheral/ethnic nations may, however, resort to brain circulation after the initial brain drain, as the shared ethnicity, language, and cultural heritage can promote a sense of belonging that serves as a pull factor to draw back diasporic talents. Those returnees can be expected to improve brain train and linkage upon return. This return migration is still limited until the country upgrades its world-system position to create more domestic opportunities, as seen in China. At this point, such opportunities will more likely appeal to coethnic rather than foreign talent due to the nation's ethnic conception. Peripheral nations that are civic, on the other hand, lack both the domestic opportunities and the cultural draw of an ethnic nation to foster brain circulation, rendering brain linkage a more feasible option. Figure 7.1 below gives a visual representation of talent-strategy typology.

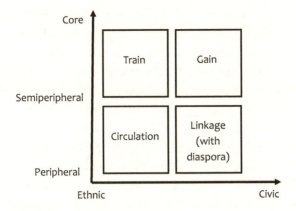

FIGURE 7.1. Typology of talent portfolios.
Source: Author created.

Addressing Risks through Rebalancing

Given that a country's world-system position and national identity shape which Bs it can incorporate into its talent portfolio, these factors also impact the extent to which a country can rebalance its portfolio with new Bs and therefore how well it can mitigate risks. As noted in the theory chapter, it is important here to distinguish between the two types of risk, as systematic risk cannot entirely be addressed with diversification and therefore would not be greatly helped by changing the two factors. Consider the COVID-19 pandemic—a systematic risk faced by all four countries. COVID impacted Japan's and Australia's brain gain efforts, China's brain circulation and brain linkage, and India's brain linkage. Brain train was also affected worldwide, as schools were closed or turned to remote learning. Clearly, since the pandemic affected all four Bs, greater diversification or rebalancing—aided by adjusting the two determining factors—would not have done much to cushion against this systematic risk.

Where unsystematic risks are concerned, the two factors are important in affecting rebalancing options. China was able to address the risk of brain drain by moving up from peripheral to semiperipheral via opening up and investing in its business, S&T, and research sectors, which created opportunities at home for which talents could circulate back. On the other hand, India was able to more easily turn its brain drain into brain linkage by formally expanding its civic nationhood, offering its diaspora special legal status as NRIs and OCI holders. There are also other ongoing efforts to address risks, such as Japan's attempts to move from ethnic to civic nationhood to better engage brain gain to combat a demographic crisis and China's endeavors to develop further in order to be more self-sufficient with brain train in the face of geopolitical tensions with major destination countries for Chinese talents.

Yet world-system position and national identity are deeply rooted in structural and cultural pillars and thus difficult to alter, often requiring long periods of time or sweeping societal reforms. This is clearly illustrated in the difficulty that Japan has faced in attempting to engage in brain gain as the country still struggles to break free of the entrenched ethnic national identity, which serves as a barrier to foreigners. As discussed in chapter 3, Japan's social, cultural, and structural environment makes it difficult for the country to become more civic rather than ethnic—that is, more hospitable to foreign talent.

The four talent giants' newly evolving portfolios, reflecting their recent rebalancing efforts, are shown in table 7.2. The question of how a country can foster changes to its national identity or world-system position is dealt with in the following chapter on policy.

Countries can also rebalance within Bs to mitigate unsystematic risks. Such rebalancing does not necessarily require a structural change in world-system position or a fundamental shift in national identity. Within-B diversification can occur across several dimensions. The first of these is the *sector* in which the talent specializes. A country may invest in training, gaining, circulating, or linking with talents from various sectors, such as STEM talent or business talent, depending on the needs of its economy. In the face of the fourth industrial revolution, for example, countries have a growing need for talent in artificial intelligence, and China has sought to diversify into this sector within all four of its Bs. Australia has attempted to diversify its brain gain by sector with the creation of a global talent visa to draw talent in "future-focused sectors," particularly in science and technology.[6]

The second dimension of diversification within Bs is the *demographics* of talent that a country engages. A country whose labor force has been traditionally male dominated, for example, could choose to engage in more brain train of women. Japan's "womenomics" reflects such efforts. India has a large gender gap in educational attainment and ultimately could re-

TABLE 7.2. Unsystematic risks and rebalancing solutions

Country	Unsystematic risk	Time period	Talent solution (rebalancing)	Catalysts for change
Japan	Demographic crisis	Since 1990s	Add brain gain	Ethnic → civic
	"Inward-lookingness" / detachment from global trends	Present; especially salient during lost decades (1990s–2000s)	Rebalance within brain train (add overseas experiences); add brain gain and brain linkage	Ethnic → civic
Australia	Demographic need	Post–World War II	Rebalance within brain gain (open to migrants from non-White countries of origin)	Racial → multicultural
	Anti-immigration sentiment	Especially since mid-2010s	Temporarily decrease amount of brain gain while improving infrastructure / city overcrowding	N/A
	Geopolitical tensions with China	Present	Rebalance within brain gain (look to other origin countries)	N/A
China	Brain drain	Since 1978	Add brain circulation	Peripheral → semiperipheral
	Geopolitical tensions	Particularly since late 2000s	Increasingly focus on brain train; decrease future brain circulation by discouraging talents from leaving	Semiperipheral → core
	Demographic crisis	Present	None yet (ideally, must increase brain gain)	Ethnic → civic
India	Brain drain	Since 1970s	Add brain linkage	Civic → broader concept of civic to include NRIs
	Human capital drain (while India has gotten social-capital returns by converting its brain drain to linkage, human capital is still desirable)	Since 1970s	Ideally, must increase brain train, gain, or circulation	Semiperipheral → core

balance within brain train by seeking to educate more of its female population. Similarly, a country with an aging population could seek to modify its brain gain or circulation to focus on talents that are from younger-age cohorts. Australia's points system for permanent residency prefers younger immigrants, offering thirty points to individuals aged twenty-five to thirty-two but only fifteen points for those aged forty to forty-four and none for older individuals. China serves as another example of diversifying the demographics of its brain circulation and linkage, as the country has talent programs that aim in particular at younger, up-and-coming overseas Chinese talents, as opposed to drawing back older talents whose career may have already peaked, having made their major contributions to their field.

Third, diversification within each B can occur in terms of *geographic region*. Brain train can be domestic or involve overseas experiences in different countries. A country can do brain gain from different regions or engage in circulation or linkage with talents in different locations. Geographic diversification within brain gain has been particularly salient for Australia, which laid its talent portfolio bare to risk when it became overly reliant on brain gain from China. Now, in the face of geopolitical tensions with China, Australia seeks to rebalance within its brain gain to attract talent from other geographic regions, such as India and Southeast Asia. This demonstrates that, just as overdependence on one B can render a talent portfolio vulnerable to risks, so too can overdependence within one B on a certain sector, demographic group, geographic region, or type of experience.

Finally, the *type of experience* talents have can be diverse within each B. For example, as seen in Japan, brain train includes various levels or dimensions of a country's domestic education system but can also include short-term overseas experiences or on-the-job training during employment. Similarly, brain circulation can involve various overseas education and/or employment before talents return to their home country—experiences that confer on talents different networks and levels of social capital. As was seen in Australia, brain gain can be via the study-work-migration path or the work-migration path.

Within-B diversification is important, as it can, to an extent, make up for a lack of diversification across Bs, as demonstrated by Japan's miracle era. While the country had little brain gain, circulation, or linkage, its brain train was well diversified into a wide variety of types of training and experiences, forming a strong basis for Japan's talent portfolio. It was only when Japan's brain train became highly skewed toward domestic training after its miracle era and when the country began to face a demographic crisis that Japan needed to rebalance by attempting to rediversify its brain train and by increasing the weight of brain gain in its talent portfolio, but that was too little, too late.

The Interrelatedness of the Four Bs

While talent portfolios can be rebalanced exogenously via change to world-system position or national identity, they can also be rebalanced endogenously via interaction effects of the four Bs. Indeed, a final theoretical insight demonstrated by the study of the four talent giants is the extent to which the four Bs are interrelated with each other. In financial portfolios, the success or failure of one type of investment (stocks, bonds, real estate, etc.) does not necessarily affect that of others given that there is low correlation between different asset classes.[7] In talent portfolios, however, the four Bs can supplement and bolster each other, thus leading to alterations in the relative weights of each B in the portfolio and thereby contributing to a natural, endogenous rebalancing.

Brain gain and circulation, for instance, can facilitate linkage. Migrants connect their new home with their old one, and returnees stay connected with those whom they left behind. Accordingly, the amount of brain linkage in a talent portfolio can increase as the amount of gain or circulation does. Likewise, as has been seen in India, a diaspora's brain linkage can lead to improved infrastructure in the homeland, helping to upgrade a country's world-system position and thereby making brain circulation a more attractive option for diasporic talents. Circulation and linkage can also increase train, as demonstrated by China, where diasporic talents contributed to domestic institutions when they returned permanently or for short-term stays. As in Japan, brain gain can also improve train, as the international students that are part of a brain gain strategy interact with domestic students, enhancing their intercultural skills and global-mindedness. While ultimately, world-system position and national identity determine a country's ability to fully incorporate additional Bs into its talent portfolio, interaction effects among the four Bs can also begin or sustain the process of shifting the weight of brain train, gain, circulation, and linkage in a portfolio.

In India, a portfolio adjustment due to interaction effects has occurred as domestic opportunities enhanced by linkage have served to draw more talents back from overseas, increasing the proportion of circulation. Thus far, India's brain circulation has not undermined its linkage. However, if a sending country achieves a sufficient level of infrastructure and development at home, the flow of individuals moving overseas may decline, diminishing the potential for both brain circulation and brain linkage. This phenomenon can be seen in China, where, as returnee talents have boosted domestic brain train systems, more talents are able to stay at home for brain train rather than going overseas and then circulating back.[8] Such a shift leads to a change in the relative weight of brain circulation versus brain train in a talent portfolio. It is therefore important to understand that such an endogenous rebalancing can, in some cases, contribute to diversification, but it also can, in other cases, shrink diversification. Overall, while the Bs' interaction effects can lead to some endogenous rebalancing, an exogenous change to the world-system position or national identity is still needed to fully incorporate new Bs to a talent portfolio. Table 7.3 summarizes adjusted talent portfolios of the four talent giants after both endogenous and exogenous rebalancing.

Finally, it is vital to note that as strategic and effective use of talent contributes to development, brain train, gain, circulation, and linkage, all can help improve a country's world-system position. Accordingly, success in talent-development strategy itself can help to foster an enhanced and more diversified talent portfolio over time. For peripheral countries who need to move up in the world system to add new Bs to their talent portfolios, then, the strategies of brain linkage and brain circulation can foster change both endogenously—by fostering more domestic opportunities that can enhance

TABLE 7.3. Adjusted talent portfolios of four case countries

Country/B	Japan	Australia	China	India
Train	Primary	Strong	Weak (initially)	Partially strong
Gain	Secondary/new	Primary	Marginal	Marginal
Circulation	Marginal	Marginal	Primary	Secondary/new
Linkage	Marginal	Secondary/new	Secondary/new	Primary

Note: As discussed in the chapter 6, India's IIT system, while strong, represents only a very small portion of Indian education.

circulation and train—and exogenously—by contributing to upgrading a country's world-system position. While the four Bs and their interaction effects can contribute to change in world-system position, they may not have the same effect on national identity. For example, a country with a strong brain train system may be more attractive to international students, thereby facilitating brain gain, but this gain will likely be limited until the country's national identity becomes inclusive enough for diverse talent to want to settle there permanently. While this chapter has focused on theoretical implications, the next chapter will delve into specific policy measures that countries can take to formulate well-diversified and resilient talent portfolios, in particular by addressing or preempting risks.

EIGHT

Lessons and Policy Implications for Talent Portfolios

Each talent giant adopted a different but effective portfolio in its rise to economic prominence, reflecting its world-system position and national identity. Each also sought to rebalance its talent portfolio over time with varying degrees of success. While their construction and rebalancing of talent portfolios were shaped by world-system and national identity, their diverse experiences can offer valuable lessons and policy implications for other countries seeking talent strategies for spurring or maintaining development. In particular, it is essential for policymakers to take a portfolio approach to talent development, keeping in mind the importance of diversification and rebalancing. In following the principles of talent portfolio theory, a nation can look for the right recipe for its own talent strategy and continue to make adjustments as new demands and risks arise.

Diversification and rebalancing are not easy tasks, however. Deeply ingrained cultural and institutional factors have proven to be hurdles to achieving stronger, more resilient talent portfolios, even among the talent giants of this study. Bureaucratic inertia is present in both government and the private sector—key players in talent development. Existing legislation or workplace policies, which can be appropriate to initial development needs, can have outsized influence on future policy decisions, resulting in inflexible and outdated approaches later on. Changes to a set course often face budget constraints, status quo bias, and short-term thinking. For example, Y. Godo and Y. Hayami indict the once acclaimed Japanese education system for its failure to supply global talent after catch-up growth was achieved. While the system effectively generated the human capital required for technology borrowing during the catch-up stages, it later became "one of the major factors underlying the descent of the Japanese economy into stagnation, beginning with the 'lost decade' of the 1990s."[1] In addition, social context is often resistant to policy levers—a country may face cemented domestic opinion constraints or firmly established norms around migration.

While it is important not to generalize too much from the specific cases of Japan, Australia, China, and India, the key findings of this study can still offer valuable lessons for many countries that seek to formulate and implement proper talent policies, particularly in how they have strategically tailored their talent portfolios. This chapter illuminates how the diverse and rich experiences of the four talent giants yield concrete insights for how policymakers can diversify and rebalance their portfolios to address risks like brain drain, demographic crisis, "inward-lookingness," geopolitical tensions, and the global pandemic.

For less developed countries (LDCs), a key message is that they should not be afraid of taking an initial risk of brain drain but rather seek to turn it into developmental assets through brain circulation and/or linkage, as China and India, respectively, have done well. For more advanced nations, on the other hand, diversifying into the brain gain of global talent and upgrading brain train as well are crucial to the newly emerging fourth industrial revolution, but, as noted in chapter 7, countries must become more civically than ethnically defined and promote cultural diversity in order to achieve success on this front. Unlike migrant nations that can engage in brain gain with relative ease, for ethnically homogeneous countries that also suffer from a demographic crisis, brain gain through migration is not often feasible. Instead, diversifying into brain linkage and encouraging the study-work-linkage (rather than study-work-migration) path could lend support, taking advantage of the transnational social capital of foreign talent that has studied and worked in the homogeneous country and then left. Finally, nations—including the United States—need to address intensifying geopolitical tensions and politicization of immigration and embrace the new postpandemic era—all of which constrain and change the course and extent of talent mobility, regionally and globally.

No Brain Drain, No Circulation or Linkage

Brain drain is one of the most prominent risks to a country's talent development and has been a long-standing policy concern in both the development-assistance community and LDCs themselves. Several of the negative impacts underscored include a reduced stock of human capital, less consumption and tax revenue, demographic shifts, labor market fluctuations, and diminished capacity to innovate and adopt new technologies.[2] In this regard, it is understandable why LDCs often adopt an overly cautious stance to avoid or address brain drain despite recent works showing some positive returns. A clear example is the continued hesitancy of LDCs to invest in higher education on the premise that highly educated students are likely to move abroad for opportunities, resulting in brain drain and squandering the country's limited educational investments.

Under this assumption, the development-assistance community, such as the World Bank and the official development-assistance members of the OECD, has traditionally focused on supporting K–12 education in LDCs. Yet this community has increasingly recognized the value of higher education in building up a country's human resource capacity and accelerating economic growth.[3] Many LDCs in the Asia-Pacific region have been doing better in improving their brain train thanks to government investment in secondary and higher education. However, these countries can go one step further in benefitting from those investments while addressing brain drain concerns, as China and India have done well.[4]

These LDCs can take two approaches in order to counter brain drain: minimizing the outflow of talent itself and promoting brain circulation and linkage to take advantage of talents that have left the country. They should first seek to ensure, like Japan and Australia, that brain drain rates remain low enough to prevent major talent deficits at home. Empirical work suggests that the acceptable level of brain drain in accumulating human capital is around 10 percent with some fluctuation based on country size, public policies, language, and location.[5] To entice talent to stay, countries must consider offering incentives and creating new opportunities for upward mobility (e.g., seed money for research, housing subsidies, or prestigious professorships) to prevent outflows from occurring in the first place. Another solution is to offer scholarships to young talents who want to study overseas but with return requirements so there is no brain drain. Singapore has done this with great success.[6]

Investing in R&D and infrastructure will not only help retain brain but also enable the logical next step following brain drain, which is the promotion of brain circulation. Indeed, countries need to realize that initial brain drain can reap benefits later through brain circulation, making brain drain only temporary. The sending country can benefit from the human capital improvements gleaned through advanced higher education and work experience abroad. Even without permanent return, furthermore, the diaspora can make contributions to their homeland through brain linkage, utilizing their transnational network or social capital. The prevailing human capital–centered perspective overlooks the value of transnational social capital, which is increasingly important in a globalized economy. My findings from this study show that well-managed brain drain can be a "brain deposit" in disguise, reaping dividends later through conversion to brain linkage and/or brain circulation. It is important to recognize that there is no brain circulation or linkage without taking the risk of an initial drain, as illustrated by the fact that Japan and Australia did not suffer from brain drain but also therefore had little brain circulation or linkage in their talent portfolios.

Let's take as an example several ASEAN countries where brain drain concerns are well founded. The average position of ASEAN countries on the brain drain index is squarely in the middle of the pack, at 4.9 points (on a scale of one to ten, with ten being the worst out of 177 countries), but trails far behind Northeast Asia's average of 3.33.[7] Half of all highly skilled positions in Cambodia, Indonesia, Laos, the Philippines, Thailand, and Vietnam will have to be filled by insufficiently qualified workers by 2025 if current trends hold.[8] These ASEAN countries can certainly learn lessons from China and India in how they can address this inevitable brain drain through recapturing diasporic talent as developmental assets. China's various talent-recruitment programs, as well as investment in infrastructure and R&D to attract back its overseas nationals, are prime examples of policy measures to facilitate brain circulation. Yet where economic opportunities or good governance are lacking, brain linkage might be more feasible in the short to medium term than brain circulation, as in India. That is, these countries should engage their diaspora communities to capitalize on their transnational social capital without permanent return.

Of course, countries outside the Asia-Pacific region also face brain drains and have sought to engage with their diasporas. Latin America's average brain drain is 5.28, and Africa's is even higher, at 6.28, suggesting that many countries in these regions could stand to benefit from brain circulation or linkage.[9] Ethiopia and Ghana are among the African countries that have begun diaspora-outreach programs, with Ethiopia giving its diaspora the same benefits and rights as domestic investors with the issuance of yellow cards and offering duty exemptions and discounted airfare for diasporic entrepreneurs.[10] Such measures have encouraged the Ethiopian diaspora to invest in small businesses in the country. Ghana, like Malaysia and Singapore, has also set up a diaspora unit, called the Diaspora Affairs Bureau, which maintains a website that offers information on job openings and opportunities for diaspora investment in the country.[11] Argentina, meanwhile, has experienced emigration in response to a dearth of domestic opportunities and has seen mixed linkage and circulation outcomes.[12] While the country's RAICES Program (Roots Program)—which has the aim of "developing linkage policies for Argentine researchers abroad" and promoting "the return of researchers residing abroad"[13]—has contributed to the return of 820 scientists since 2003,[14] business linkage appears currently to be minimal—only 23 percent of diaspora members have professional contacts in the country.[15] These countries, too, can learn how to better address brain drain through circulation and linkage, drawing lessons from China and India.

It is important to note that circulation and linkage are not mutually exclusive. They can be simultaneous or sequenced according to the country's capacity and the composition of its emigration flows. In China, circulation was first adopted before linkage as a major strategy. In India, on the other hand, dense linkage networks facilitated the ensuing circulation. In both circumstances, the initial talent approach and outcomes set the groundwork for the subsequent talent strategy, which, rather than replace the initial approach, was layered atop it. China's talent programs gradually diversified into brain linkage based on the limitations of early circulation programs, adding part-time tracks to accommodate top overseas talents' preference for short-term opportunities rather than permanent returns. Such linkage programs were at once a "soft landing" to stimulate circulation and a second-best option to a permanent return. In India, the sequencing was neither a soft landing nor a second-best option. Circulation was only viable later on due to domestic economic growth, legislative changes, and the development and professional success of the Indian diaspora. Then, circulation and linkage became simultaneous and complementary processes.

While India and China present complicated yet optimistic pictures of how brain circulation and linkage can be harnessed by LDCs, a glaring difference between most LDCs and China and India is population size, and one might question the validity of applying either model to other countries. None can build a diaspora of China's or India's size. And indeed, the notion that larger countries fare better in the face of brain drain aligns with previous research. M. Beine et al. demonstrates that more populous countries (with population sizes greater than twenty-five million) are among the "winners" of brain drain, while smaller countries (population size smaller than ten million) tend to experience net losses from brain drain.[16]

Yet despite their smaller diasporas, countries such as Singapore, Korea, and Taiwan have all adopted circulation and linkage strategies with much success. For example, Singapore set up Contact Singapore in 1998—a program that had centers in six cities around the world to promote Singapore to diasporic and foreign talent, helping match talents to employers in Singapore.[17] Singapore went one step further, making specialized efforts to connect with its diaspora and help overseas nationals maintain an "emotional connection" to the country. In 2006, the Overseas Singaporean Unit was established as a new government agency tasked with keeping overseas Singaporeans connected to their home country and facilitating return migration.[18] In both Taiwan and Korea, the government initiated talent-recruitment programs that later became a model for China's circulation strategy. Other countries have followed suit. More recently, Malaysia's Talent Corporation, a national agency that heads the country's talent strategy, established the Returning Expert Programme aimed at circulating back Malaysian talents who have been employed overseas for three years or more.[19] In recent years, Taiwan has taken a unique route through initiatives like the Taiwanese Overseas Pioneers grants, which offer financial support to overseas Taiwanese talents with the condition that they find jobs abroad rather than return to Taiwan. With the goal to "improve the connection between overseas academic communities and Taiwan," such programs actively foster brain linkage over brain circulation.

Migration Is Not the Panacea

While brain drain is a major risk for LDCs, the demographic crisis presents a pressing unsystematic risk for more advanced nations in the Asia-Pacific region, which soon may not have enough talents to fuel their economies. As noted in chapter 1, their populations are aging fast with low birthrates, and their working-age populations (fifteen to sixty-four) are declining as a result, faster than their peers in North America and Western Europe. The experiences in Japan and Australia in tackling demographic changes provide lessons for nations facing similar challenges.

Immigrant-friendly, civically conceived countries, like Australia and Canada, have been able to avoid the demographic bomb through constant streams of brain gain, and some scholars and policymakers in Japan and Korea call for migration as the answer in these countries as well.[20] Yet both Japan and Korea provide a cautionary tale. In Japan, the study-work path has been steadily improving, but the work-migration path has faltered. Due to a long-term emphasis on domestic-talent development and an inhospitable sociocultural environment for foreign talent, skilled workers leave after working for a few years. In Korea, the situation is even worse than in Japan, as neither the study-work nor work-migration path is working. It is estimated, in 2017, that less than 5.8 percent of international students who complete their bachelor's degrees in Korea find full-time employment after graduation.[21] Most international students come to Korea to fill enrollment gaps rather than to provide a new source of human capital for the country.[22] Their struggles with the study-work path, let alone the work-migration one, foretell the difficulties that most countries that are not civically conceived immigrant nations would experience in cultivating the sociocultural environments that are required to facilitate brain gain.

So what can Japan, Korea, and other ethnically homogeneous countries struggling to attract and retain foreign talent do in light of the demographic crisis? In places where migrants are not well accepted due to cultural and institutional barriers, brain linkage can be more effectively enacted than brain gain. Linkage would not solve the demographic crisis itself but can be an important intermediate way for these countries with strong ethnic identities to utilize foreign/global talent until they are culturally and socially ready for mass migration. Such a pivot would entail making use of the social capital of foreign talents—such as international students—that sojourn in the country before returning home. My previous research with Joon Nak Choi uses data on foreign students and professionals in Korea to make a case for the mutual benefits of such study-work-linkage. International students and the country alike can benefit from the student taking on a bridging role between Korea and their home country. After working in Korea for several years, the student can return home to lead local subsidiaries of Korean companies, helped by their knowledge of Korean corporate culture, familiarity with their home markets and potential local partners, and ability to interface between local employees and Korean executives.[23]

A study of international students in Japan supports this idea too. My work with Rennie Moon based on interviews with fifty-five international students who study in Japan finds that even those who only planned to briefly stay after graduation wanted to connect with Japan once they returned home or left for a third country—an ambition that arose during their multinational interactions in Japan. Another finding from the study, one that can be disturbing for Japan though, is that barriers to international students forming home-host ties lead to connections among international (non-Japanese) students themselves and, later, "multinational bridging," or transnational bridging among non-conational international students.[24] Multinational bridging may particularly become relevant to Southeast Asian nations given the growing emphasis in host countries on scholarship programs for Southeast Asian students, as well as the proximity and interdependence of their economies.

Given students' skill sets and demonstrated interest, there has been a new trend to formalize and expand transnational social capital and brain linkage through the development of national-level global alumni networks. In earnestly recognizing that a significant number of international students will leave after graduation—either for their home or for a third country—Japan, Korea, and other similarly situated countries could opt to develop more strategic relationships with their global alumni, learning from the Australian experience. Such networks have been established in over half a dozen countries, mostly in Europe, to enhance alumni relations and public diplomacy.[25] Countries seeking to engage in brain linkage with their global alumni could optimize their alumni networks by facilitating collaboration, soliciting investments and exports, or even encouraging return at a later point.

For example, some global alumni networks offer ways for both the former host country and alumni to benefit via transnational social capital. The British Council's Alumni Awards enable alumni to "access networks and organisations within the UK to maximise and build on their achievements," and the Holland Alumni Network launched an entrepreneurship group open to alumni entrepreneurs, particularly those who are considering starting a business in the Netherlands.[26] In Australia, the global alumni network is aimed at helping recruit more international students to the country, thereby facilitating brain gain. While a linkage-based alumni network falls short of resolving labor-shortage issues, this approach is preferable to the passive hemorrhaging of foreign talent that is currently occurring in countries that are not ready for mass migration. In addition, the study-work-linkage approach can be a useful interim strategy as countries undergo the broader changes to their national identity (i.e., from ethnic to civic) that are needed for long-term talent attraction and retention.

Cultural Diversity Is Key to Competitiveness

The developmental state, which was lauded as a catalyst for economic success in East Asia, spearheaded both Japan's and China's talent strategies. While countries can learn from their developmental policies—such as government investment in higher education, R&D, and talent programs—the developmental state is no "silver bullet." Rather, these countries' past industrial policies urgently need to be supplemented by sociocultural policies to ensure global competitiveness in the new talent market. In particular, countries need to pay more attention to the value of cultural diversity and racial tolerance in the pursuit of upgrading domestic talent and attracting foreign talent. Homogeneity, discipline, and standardization of the labor force were all important values during industrialization, as in Japan, but this is no longer the case in the postindustrial age. Rather, diversity, flexibility, and tolerance have become indispensable to an adaptable and agile talent pool. Yet, despite their economic ascendance, Northeast Asian countries lag behind in these dimensions that are critical to maintaining talent competitiveness when compared to North America and Western Europe.

The 2022 Global Talent Competitiveness Index, an annual benchmarking study that measures national-talent competitiveness, for instance, points to serious deficiencies across the Asia-Pacific region on key measures (figure 8.1). For Japan (twenty-fourth), Korea (twenty-seventh), and China (thirty-sixth), the three economic powers in Northeast Asia, their overall rankings in talent competitiveness conceal drastic underperformance in talent attraction (forty-eighth, fifty-fifth, and eighty-seventh, respectively). The talent-attraction metric includes both external and internal openness.[27] The report notes that "Japan's weakest pillar remains Attract (48th), where there is scope to boost External Openness (56th) towards foreign talent

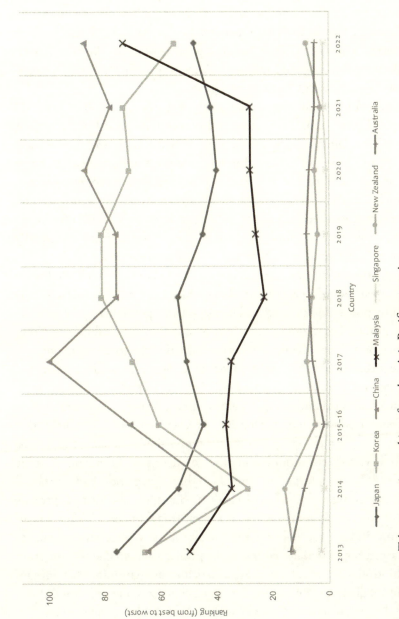

FIGURE 8.1. Talent-attraction rankings for select Asia-Pacific countries.

Sources: Lanvin & Evans (2013–2018); Lanvin & Monteiro (2019–2022).

and more efforts to improve gender equality would increase Internal Openness (46th)." Similarly, "the ability to Attract (55th) talent is also the main challenge facing the Republic of Korea, where a key priority should be to encourage greater External Openness (75th) towards overseas business and talent." Likewise, China's "weakest pillar remains its ability to Attract (87th) talent, which would primarily rise with greater External Openness (102nd) towards foreign business and people."[28]

On the other hand, Singapore presents a sharp contrast in cultural diversity and brain gain. Comparison to Korea is illustrative. On the surface, the two Little Dragons appear to be quite similar, with developmental states that sought to overcome limited natural resources and population size to achieve success. Yet there is a huge gap in global talent competitiveness, in which Singapore ranks second compared to Korea at twenty-seventh. While Korea has been struggling to engage in brain gain (at fifty-ninth) with low tolerance of immigrants (sixty-fifth), Singapore has consistently ranked first or second globally in terms of talent attraction.

Singapore's brain gain can be largely attributed to its multicultural social environment, which it has attained via a history of policies that not only diligently protect minority rights but also actively promote respect for other ethnic groups. For example, as early as 1970, Singapore established a Presidential Council for Minority Rights to ensure that the government does not pass laws that discriminate on the basis of race or religion.[29] In contrast, Korea's National Human Rights Commission, which performs similar work, was not established until 2001.[30] The Singaporean government went further, however, introducing into its Housing Development Board an Ethnic Integration Policy, which sets quotas for the proportion of housing that can be owned by various ethnic groups in order to prevent the formation of ethnic enclaves.[31] This has helped to "promote ethnic integration and harmony" and foster greater respect for diversity, as Singaporeans better appreciate those of other ethnicities or religions as their fellow citizens.[32] While not all governments have the ability to implement such sweeping policies, smaller steps are also appropriate. For example, primary and secondary education could introduce curricular and extracurricular programming that engages various religious and cultural beliefs or teaches the value of cultural diversity and racial tolerance, as Singapore and Australia have done well.

Overall, however, countries with regressive immigration policies must shift their approach from assimilationist to truly multicultural—or risk stunting their brain gain. According to a report by the Asan Institute for

Policy Studies in Seoul, Korea, multicultural policies "refer to the act of respecting different cultures and ethnicities, and helping newcomers adjust to life in a new place without forcing them to assimilate to the new culture."[33] While so-called multiculturalism was introduced to Japan and Korea to accommodate low-skilled labor or foreign brides,[34] its policies turned out to be assimilationist and even discriminatory.

Instead of pushing immigrants to conform to their own cultures, these countries should learn from the experiences of Australia. When the country disbanded the White Australia Policy, it sought to actively foster appreciation for multiculturalism through various programs at all levels of society. Australia has fostered "public endorsement and recognition of cultural diversity" with a "well-ordered immigration program," which has led to public acceptance of multiculturalism, according to Tim Soutphommasane, professor of sociology and political theory as well as Australia's former race discrimination commissioner. Overall, Soutphommasane states, "Australia's multicultural success has been predicated on Australian society accepting immigration as a nation-building project."[35] Countries like Japan and Korea thus must not only improve immigration policies through new legislation but also enact societal programs that promote appreciation of cultural diversity. Doing so will enable the public to better understand why promoting multiculturalism rather than assimilation is crucial for enhancing national economic growth, thereby enabling these countries to better compete in the face of the intensifying global war for talent.

Politics and Geopolitics of Talent Mobility

Even in countries where cultural diversity is appreciated, such as Australia and the United States, the recent politicization of migration issues both poses various risks to brain gain and impacts the brain circulation and linkage of sending countries. While global sentiments toward immigration have dipped slightly—Gallup's Migrant Acceptance Index, a scale of zero to nine, saw a worldwide decline from 5.34 to 5.21 from 2016–2017 to 2019[36]—they have improved in some top-destination countries.[37] Even in the aftermath of the COVID-19 pandemic, it appears that across the European Union and the United States, "immigration attitudes have not systematically become more negative."[38] However, as countries around the world have grown more polarized, migration has clearly become politicized, particularly with the rise of anti-immigrant politicians in many parts of the world.

Indeed, such politicization of migration has been reflected in the rhetorics and policies of anti-immigrant leaders in recent years, with the United States representing a particularly salient case. In the summer of 2020, then president Donald Trump signed an executive order suspending the issuance of new H-1B and other work-related visas and denying employment permits for hundreds of thousands of foreign workers on the grounds that these workers took American jobs and that it was in US interest to close borders to prevent the spread of COVID. This move, combined with extended restrictions on new green cards, is estimated to have significantly decreased the United States' brain gain, barring more than half a million foreign workers from the United States.[39] These were mostly Indian and Chinese nationals, who combined to make up 69 percent of OPT and 85 percent of "highly skilled" H-1B visa holders in 2019.[40] While the United States has by far been the preferred destination for these talents, they were forced to look elsewhere. Even after the Biden administration allowed the Trump-era visa ban to expire in March 2021, there has remained a huge visa backlog in the aftermath of Trump's policies and the COVID-19 pandemic, continuing to stunt the United States' brain gain.[41]

Not surprisingly, tech giants in Silicon Valley—including Apple, Google-parent Alphabet, Amazon, Uber, and Twitter—decried the 2020 executive order, calling it an "unbelievably bad policy" that would undermine America's economic recovery and its competitiveness. Google CEO Sundar Pichai—an immigrant himself from India—tweeted his opposition to the order, saying, "Immigration has contributed immensely to America's economic success, making it a global leader in tech, and also Google the company it is today." Apple CEO Tim Cook also tweeted that he was "deeply disappointed by this proclamation" and noted, "Like Apple, this nation of immigrants has always found strength in diversity and hope in the enduring promise of the American Dream. There is no new prosperity without both."[42]

Indeed, as these tech companies and their leaders espouse, the United States—and other countries—should do *more* rather than *less* to welcome new immigrant talents. For example, the United States has not yet enacted a new visa classification for entrepreneurs, as has been done in two dozen other countries, and the absence of such a visa undermines the retention of startup founders.[43] The employer-based nature of US immigration policy could be revised to allow for worker-initiated requests, as Australia has done. Such steps would lead to outcomes for the broader economy called "multiplier effects," wherein a single skilled job can create additional economic benefits and jobs in both skilled and unskilled industries.[44]

William Kerr, in *The Gift of Global Talent: How Migration Shapes Business, Economy & Society*, suggests some intermediate steps for US talent attraction while acknowledging considerable restraints on reform for partisan reasons. In his view, establishing "a nonpolitical technical group to monitor and adjust immigration policies on a regular basis to optimize talent inflows, much as Australia and Canada attempt to do," would be ideal, but a more realistic starting point would be indexing H-1B admissions to economic conditions: "America should first raise the cap from its present level of eighty-five thousand to reflect the growth over the past decade, and then index future visa increases to population growth or to the national employment growth for skilled workers. When combined with wage ranking and higher minimum salaries for H-1B workers, such indexing would accommodate sector growth in a more secure way."[45] Indeed, one economic analysis conducted in 2013 estimates that an increase in H-1B visas from sixty-five thousand to seventy-five thousand in 2014 and up to 105,000 by 2019 would produce 1.3 million new jobs and add USD 158 billion to the US GDP by 2045.[46] The United States is still behind other countries, such as Canada and Australia, which are enticing top talent through preferential immigration policies.

In addition to domestic politics, geopolitics poses another related unsystematic risk for certain talent portfolios. Ongoing conflict between China and Western and Asia-Pacific nations, such as the United States and Australia, has disrupted global talent flows. US-China tensions have discouraged Chinese students from coming to the United States: in the first half of 2022, the number of student visas issued to Chinese nationals dropped to half of its prepandemic level.[47] Importantly, the growth rate of Chinese students in the United States slowed even before the pandemic, with some experts pointing to bilateral tensions and Trump-era visa restrictions as the reason.[48] Similarly, recent tensions with China have affected Australia, causing the number of Chinese students and workers coming to the country to significantly decline and leading Australia to diversify its brain gain away from Chinese talent and toward talent from India and Southeast Asian nations. Likewise, such geopolitical tensions may redirect Chinese talents away from these main destinations to elsewhere or lead China to invest more resources in domestic brain train, retaining more talent at home.

In particular, tensions over technology and investment have posed threats to the talent portfolios of both China and the United States, increasing the risks of China's strategies of brain circulation and linkage while decreasing the United States' brain gain of Chinese talent. The China Initiative, launched by the US Department of Justice in November 2019, was intended to counter national-security threats from China around economic espionage and trade secret theft. However, the initiative's focus on prosecuting "nontraditional collectors," like researchers in universities or labs, and outreach emphasizing the "threats to academic freedom and open discourse from influence efforts on campus" have led to growing racial profiling, as perceived by Chinese scientists.[49] In a 2021 national survey of 1,949 scientists at top US universities, 42.2 percent of Chinese scientists report that they feel racially profiled by the US government (compared to 8.6 percent of non-Chinese scientists).[50] Of note is that 42.1 percent of the Chinese scientists indicate that the investigations have affected their plans to stay in the United States (compared to 7.1 percent of non-Chinese scientists). Effectively, as discussed in chapter 5, the initiative accelerated China's brain circulation but at the expense of the United States' brain gain.[51] While the initiative ended in February 2022, its effects will continue to be felt and beyond the Chinese. For example, it has contributed to creating hostile campus climates for other minority and migrant groups, especially Asian, posing further risk to the United States' brain gain. Indeed, the 2021 survey finds that about one-third (27.1 percent) of Asian scientists who are not Chinese believe they are racially profiled by the US government.[52]

In terms of geopolitics and tech-talent competition with China in particular, the United States should use caution in adopting overly restrictive measures on tech transfer and export control, which could generate losses for both countries. While being mindful of potential national-security threats, the United States must refrain from politicizing migration issues and resist the urge to implement policies that codify racial profiling in academic and research institutions. Already, the United States' brain gain has lost ground compared to other destinations: Boston Consulting Group finds that the Asia-Pacific is increasingly seen as a top work destination, with two Asian cities (Tokyo and Singapore) outranking New York as a preferred destination for the first time among two hundred thousand workforce respondents from 190 countries.[53]

Accordingly, whereas geopolitical tensions and politicization of migration impair brain gain in countries like the United States, they also may offer a new opportunity for Asia-Pacific nations that were not previously favored destinations for skilled workers. Besides Australia and Singapore, which have appealed to foreign talent, other advanced economies in the region, such as Japan, Korea, and Taiwan, are actively trying to recruit foreign skilled laborers in the face of demographic crises, including talents that are shut out of the United States. Previous research, such as Saxenian's study of Asian skilled workers in Silicon Valley, shows the benefits of brain circulation to the Asia-Pacific region but overlooks emerging geopolitical factors that can impede or redirect this transnational movement. It is worth closely watching how the recent trend of politicizing migration in major receiving countries, as well as shifting geopolitical tensions, will affect the mobility of Chinese and Indian talent. Given these countries' sizes, the consequences will surely affect talent flows around the globe.

Talent Strategies in the Postpandemic World

COVID-19 is the latest systematic risk that has affected the talent portfolios of countries worldwide. Among the four cases, it impacted Japan's and Australia's brain gain efforts, reduced China's future brain circulation and linkage by affecting its outbound flow of talent, and constrained India's brain linkage by reducing short-term visits of NRIs to India.

One important consequence of the pandemic is the increase in virtual forms of interaction, with implications for all four Bs. In particular, virtual forms of brain train continue to be utilized after COVID-19, with online-learning programs enabling the fostering of human capital without the need for talent to leave the country for education.[54] This could expand access to education and reduce brain drain as domestic institutions can use online learning to scale out programs and international schools can provide distance learning and, potentially, reduce costs. Both can help meet the soaring demand for higher education, particularly in developing countries. One benefit of virtual offerings is that they can be more inclusive and accessible compared to traditional on-campus or in-person programs, reaching out to students from faraway locales or who don't have the resources to relocate physically.

However, online education is also detrimental to certain aspects of human capital development, as students are deprived of studying abroad, losing out on new perspectives, experiences, and multicultural skills. In addition, online learning is particularly harmful for social-capital formation, as it significantly impedes the building of social ties and networks. This can especially be the case for developing countries, which stand to benefit greatly from social capital and particularly transnational brain linkage, as India's experiences demonstrate. These countries should therefore continue to allow talents to leave in order to capitalize on brain circulation and linkage potential while taking advantage of virtual-education options to expand brain train at home to underserved populations.

Although this risk has affected all four Bs, it had an outsized effect on brain gain in light of border closures around the world, and, thus, Australia serves as a cautionary tale. Despite the importance of migration to the country, Australia "barred most foreigners" until February 2022, making its policies among the "strictest in the world."[55] Furthermore, the country told international students who could no longer support themselves to "make your way home," damaging its reputation as a friendly and reliable place to study abroad.[56] Given Australia's heavy reliance on brain gain of foreign talents in its talent portfolio, it is no surprise that these policies have caused the Land Down Under to experience a severe skills shortage. As early as 2021, 52 percent of Australian business leaders say it has been more challenging to find qualified employees now than before the pandemic,[57] and by 2022, there were five hundred thousand job vacancies in skilled sectors.[58] These figures illustrate what happens when a country that relies heavily on brain gain sees its talent pipelines shut off.

The pandemic has taught us that risks to talent strategies can be unexpected and sudden. As this study of talent giants through TPT demonstrates, a well-diversified talent portfolio that is rebalanced in a timely manner is key to meeting not only the risk posed by the pandemic but also other risks on the rise in today's world—brain drain, demographic crises, geopolitical challenges, and more. While bearing in mind that a nation's talent portfolio—and the B or Bs it emphasizes—depends on its world-system position and whether it defines itself civically or ethnically, countries can learn from the experiences of the four talent giants in this study. They can be particularly useful in harnessing policy recommendations made above to diversify and rebalance in the face of various risks, recurring and future.

Notes

Chapter 1

1. International Monetary Fund. (2023). *GDP, current prices.*

2. World Bank. (n.d.a). *GDP ranking.*

3. Khanna, P. (2019). *The future is Asian.* Simon & Schuster.

4. Vogel, E. (1991). *The Four Little Dragons: The spread of industrialization in East Asia.* Harvard University Press; Sarel, M. (1996). Growth in East Asia: What we can and what we cannot infer. *International Monetary Fund Economic Issues, 6,* 1–22; Bajpai, A. (2012). The "rise of Asia" thesis: Strategic constraints and theoretical deficits. *World Affairs: The Journal of International Issues, 16*(2), 12–37; Yendamuri, P., & Ingilizian, Z. (2019, December 20). *In 2020 Asia will have the world's largest GDP: Here's what that means.* World Economic Forum.

5. Between 1981 and 2000, the average annual percentage changes in GDP per capita of Singapore, Taiwan, and Korea respectively were 8.52, 9.96, and 11.35. In the next period from 2001 to 2023, Singapore had overtaken Taiwan and Korea, with a 6.18 percent growth rate compared to 4.78 and 3.6, respectively. International Monetary Fund (2023).

6. Woo, J. (2022). *Confronting South Korea's next crisis: Rigidities, polarization, and fear of Japanification.* Oxford University Press.

7. Low, L. (1998). Human resource development in the Asia-Pacific. *Asian-Pacific Economic Literature, 12*(1), 27–40; Litsareva, E. (2017). Success factors of Asia-Pacific fast-developing regions' technological innovation development and economic growth. *International Journal of Innovation Studies, 1*(1), 72–88.

8. Tu, W.-M. (Ed.). (1996). *Confucian traditions in East Asian modernity.* Harvard University Press; Jenco, L. (2013). Revisiting Asian values. *Journal of the History of Ideas, 74*(2), 237–258.

9. Han, S. J. (1999). Asian values: An asset or a liability? In H. S. Joo (Ed.), *Changing values in Asia: Their impact on governance and development* (pp. 3–9). Japan Center for International Exchange.

10. Cumings, B. (1984). The legacy of Japanese colonialism in Korea. In R. Myers & M. Peattie (Eds.), *The Japanese colonial empire, 1895–1945* (pp. 478–496). Princeton University Press; Eckert, C. J. (1991). *Offspring of empire: The Koch'ang Kims and the colonial origins of Korean capitalism, 1876–1945.* University of Washington Press; Kohli, A. (1994). Where do high growth political economies come from? The Japanese lineage of Korea's "developmental state." *World Development, 22*(9), 1269–1293.

11. Rabushka, A. (1979). *Hong Kong: A study in economic freedom* (Vol. 77). University of Chicago, Graduate School of Business.

12. Duara, P. (2018). Nationalism and development in Asia (Working paper no. 2018/95). WIDER.

13. Shin, G. W. (2006). *Ethnic nationalism in Korea: Genealogy, politics, and legacy.* Stanford University Press; Greenfeld, L. (1992). *Nationalism: Five roads to modernity.* Harvard University Press.

14. Wong, J. (2004). The adaptive developmental state in East Asia. *Journal of East Asian Studies, 4*(3), 345–362; Vogel (1991).

15. Kim, E. M. (1997). *Big business, strong state: Collusion and conflict in South Korean development, 1960–1990.* State University of New York Press.

16. Riain, S. Ó. (2000). The flexible developmental state: Globalization, information technology, and the "Celtic tiger." *Politics & Society, 28*(2), 157–193; Asian Development Bank. (2020). The role of markets, the state, and institutions. In *Asia's journey to prosperity: Policy, market, and technology over 50 years* (pp. 29–84). Asian Development Bank.

17. Low (1998); Litsareva (2017).

18. In this study, I focus on skilled and highly skilled labor and use these terms interchangeably with "talent." See the next chapter for its definition.

19. Kirkegaard, J. F. (2008). *Accelerating decline in America's high-skilled workforce: Implications for immigration policy.* Peterson Institute, p. 2.

20. Higher education, also known as "tertiary education" in some countries, refers to all postsecondary education, including both public and private universities, colleges, technical-training institutes, and vocational schools.

21. OECD. (2019a). *Education at a glance 2019: OECD indicators.*

22. World Bank. (2023b). *Tertiary education.*

23. Congressional Research Service. (2022). *Global research and development expenditures: Fact sheet.* US Library of Congress.

24. OECD. (2022c). *Population with tertiary education.*

25. OECD. (2022a). *Gross domestic spending on R&D (indicator).*

26. OECD. (2012). *Education at a glance 2012: Highlights*; UNESCO. (2022). *Higher education: How do we unleash the talent of the next generation?*

27. Altbach, P. G., & Knight, J. (2007). The internationalization of higher education: Motivations and realities. *Journal of Studies in International Education*, *11*(3–4), p. 293.

28. Kiser, G., & Mantha, Y. (2019). *Global AI talent report 2019.*

29. The percentage of top Chinese AI researchers staying home to work rose significantly from 11 percent in 2019 to 28 percent in 2022, influenced by both restrictive US policies toward China and the increasing prestige of Chinese higher education. Ma, Y. (2024). *US security and immigration policies threaten its AI leadership.* Brookings Institution.

30. Population Reference Bureau. (2012, November 27). *South Korea's demographic dividend*; Jiang, Q., Li, S., & Feldman, M. W. (2013). China's population policy at the crossroads: Social impacts and prospects. *Asian Journal of Social Science*, *41*(2), 193–218.

31. E.g., resulting problems could be the fiscal problems due to fewer young workers to subsidize social welfare expenditure, such as pensions, healthcare, and education.

32. Aoki, R. (2013). A demographic perspective on Japan's "lost decades." *Population and Development Review*, *38*(1), 103–112.

33. Regarding Korea's figures, see Korean Statistical Information Service. (n.d.b). 인구동향조사: 출생아수, 합계출산율, 자연증가 등 [Population trend survey: Number of births, total fertility rate, natural increase, etc.]; Korean Statistical Information Service. (n.d.a). 주요 연령계층별 추계인구(생산연령인구, 고령인구 등) / 전국 [Estimated population by major age groups (working-age population, elderly population, etc.) / nationwide]. Regarding the OECD figures, see OECD. (2020a). *Demographic trends.*

34. Lanvin, B., & Monteiro, F. (Eds.). (2022). *The Global Talent Competitiveness Index 2022: The tectonics of talent; Is the world drifting towards increased talent inequalities?* INSEAD.

35. National Science Board. (2020). *2020 science and engineering indicators: The state of U.S. science and engineering* (NSB-2020-1). National Science Foundation.

36. While the actual- and expected-stay rates differ as time since graduation increases, they still tend to remain relatively close. E.g., 76.4 percent of doctoral graduates in the United States from 2001 to 2009 who were temporary visa holders intended to stay in the United States after graduating. As of 2010, 68.5 percent actually remained in the United States. Chang, W.-Y., & Milan, L. M. (2014). *Employment decisions of U.S. and foreign doctoral graduates: A comparative study.* National Science Foundation.

37. Institute for Management Development. (2022). *IMD world talent ranking.* IMD World Competitiveness Center.

38. Yang, P. (2022). China in the global field of international student mobility: An analysis of economic, human and symbolic capitals. *Compare: A Journal of Comparative and International Education, 52*(2), 308–326.

39. Korhonen, V. (2024, July 5). *International students in the U.S., by country of origin 2022/23.* Statista.

40. Efforts to contain COVID-19 reportedly prompted unscheduled school closures across more than one hundred countries worldwide, leaving over one billion learners out of school. Onyema, E. M., Eucheria, N. C., Obafemi, F. A., Sen, S., Atonye, F. G., Sharma, A., & Alsayed, A. O. (2020). Impact of coronavirus pandemic on education. *Journal of Education and Practice, 11*(13), 108–121.

41. Other Asia-Pacific countries, such as Korea, Taiwan, and Singapore, will be referred to where appropriate.

42. Kawada, H., & Levine, S. B. (2014). *Human resources in Japanese industrial development* (Vol. 659). Princeton University Press; Low (1998); Lee, J. W. (1997). *Economic growth and human development in the Republic of Korea, 1945–1992.* United Nations Development Programme.

43. E.g., see Papademetriou, D. G., Somerville, W., & Tanaka, H. (2008). *Talent in the 21st-century economy.* Migration Policy Institute, pp. 215–65.

44. Ho, N. T. T., Seet, P. S., & Jones, J. (2015). Understanding re-expatriation intentions among overseas returnees—an emerging economy perspective. *International Journal of Human Resource Management, 27*(17), 1938–1966; Alberts, H. C., & Hazen, H. D. (2005). "There are always two voices . . .": International students' intentions to stay in the United States or return to their home countries. *International Migration, 43*(3), 131–154.

45. Furthermore, governments outline how businesses and talents engage while paying attention to "the broader societal interests with which governments are entrusted, such as building up their nation's education and training institutions, enforcing rules about employment, etc." Papademetriou et al. (2008), p. 9.

Chapter 2

1. Mincer, J. (1984). Human capital and economic growth. *Economics of Education Review, 3*(3), 195–205; Lucas, R. E., Jr. (1988). On the mechanics of economic development. *Journal of Monetary Economics, 22*(1), 3–42; World Bank. (2019, March 19). *The human capital project: Frequently asked questions.*

2. To be sure, not all economists agree that human capital directly raises productivity. In 1976, for instance, Harvard economist Richard B. Freeman argued that real productivity was derived not from human capital in and of itself but later from training, motivation, and capital equipment. A recent critique by E. Tan also points out that human capital theory is an imperfect, overly simplistic model. Nonetheless, Tan concedes that, despite its shortcomings, the model is still useful.

Here, I do not argue that human capital alone is enough for economic development but rather that it is an important element alongside other factors. Freeman, R. B. (1976). *The overeducated American*. Academic Press; Tan, E. (2014). Human capital theory: A holistic criticism. *Review of Educational Research, 84*(3), 411–445.

3. Becker, G. S. (1993). *Human capital: A theoretical and empirical analysis with special reference to education* (3rd ed.). University of Chicago Press, p. 16.

4. Harbison, F. H., & Myers, C. A. (1965). *Manpower and education: Country studies in economic development*. McGraw-Hill.

5. Vogel (1991).

6. Wong, K. Y., & Yip, C. K. (1999). Education, economic growth, and brain drain. *Journal of Economic Dynamics and Control, 23*(5–6), 699–726; Cervantes, M., & Guellec, D. (2002). The brain drain: Old myths, new realities. *OECD Observer*, (230), p. 40.

7. Beine, M., Docquier, F., & Rapoport, H. (2008). Brain drain and human capital formation in developing countries: Winners and losers. *Economic Journal, 118*(528), 631–652.

8. Cavallini, S., Soldi, R., di Matteo, L., Utma, M. A., & Errico, B. (2018). *Addressing brain drain: The local and regional dimension*. European Committee of the Regions; Grubel, H. G. (1968). The reduction of the brain drain: Problems and policies. *Minerva, 6*, 541–558.

9. Key elements of the framework discussed here can be found in a paper with Haley M. Gordon. See Shin, G.-W., & Gordon, H. M. (2024). Toward a portfolio theory of talent development: Insights from financial theory, illustrations from the Asia-Pacific. *World Development, 184*, 1–14.

10. Hanushek, E. A., & Wößmann, L. (2007). *The role of education quality for economic growth*. World Bank Group.

11. Hayes, A. (2022, December 4). *Skilled Labor: Definition, training, vs. unskilled*. Investopedia.

12. In this book, I define a country's "foreign talents" as those that are born in a foreign country. A country's "diasporic talent" refers to those who were born in the home country and then migrated overseas. Second-generation immigrants, then, would be considered foreign talent to their parents' home country.

13. Shin, G.-W., & Choi, J. N. (2015). *Global talent: Skilled labor as social capital in Korea*. Stanford University Press; Moon, R. J., & Shin, G. W. (2019). International student networks as transnational social capital: Illustrations from Japan. *Comparative Education, 55*(4), 557–574; Shin, G. W., Choi, J. N., & Moon, R. J. (2019). Skilled migrants as human and social capital in Korea. *Asian Survey, 59*(4), 673–692.

14. Putnam, R. D. (2015). Bowling alone: America's declining social capital. In R. T. LeGates & F. Stout (Eds.), *The city reader* (6th ed., pp. 9–14). Routledge.

15. Ployhart, R. E., Weekley, J. A., & Dalzell, J. (2018). *Talent without borders: Global talent acquisition for competitive advantage.* Oxford University Press, p. 71.

16. Su, H. J. J. (2018, March 16). *A healthy circulation of talent mobility boosts quality.* University World News.

17. Gellner, E. (1983). *Nations and nationalism.* Basil Blackwell.

18. Bloom, D. E., Hartley, M., & Rosovsky, H. (2007). Beyond private gain: The public benefits of higher education. In J. J. F. Forest & P. G. Altbach (Eds.), *International handbook of higher education* (pp. 293–308). Springer International Handbooks of Education.

19. Kirkegaard (2008).

20. S. Page demonstrates how various types of diversity can lead to better outcomes for businesses and organizations. Page, S. (2019). *The diversity bonus.* Princeton University Press.

21. Following the collapse of the Soviet Union in the early 1990s, Israel admitted about 850,000 immigrants from there, or 10 percent of its population. More than 40 percent of the new arrivals were college professors, scientists, and engineers, many of whom had abundant experience in research and development. Senor, D., & Singer, S. (2011). *Start-up nation: The story of Israel's economic miracle.* McClelland & Stewart.

22. Generally, this education is done at the tertiary level, but in some cases, foreign talent may move to a country at a younger age for primary or secondary schooling but stay through to employment.

23. Tran, L. T., Rahimi, M., Tan, G., Dang, X. T., & Le, N. (2020). Post-study work for international graduates in Australia: Opportunity to enhance employability, get a return on investment or secure migration? *Globalisation, Societies and Education, 18*(5), 495–510.

24. Matthews, D. (2017, April 21). Why Germany educates international students for free. *Times Higher Education.*

25. Czaika, M., & Parsons, C. R. (2017). The gravity of high-skilled migration policies. *Demography, 54*(2), 603–630.

26. Harrap, B., Hawthorne, L., Holland, M., McDonald, J. T., & Scott, A. (2021). Australia's superior skilled migration outcomes compared with Canada's. *International Migration, 60*(5), p. 103.

27. Canadian Bureau for International Education. (2021). *The student voice: National results of the 2021 CBIE International Student Survey.*

28. Sumption, M., & Brindle, B. (2023, September 29). *Work visas and migrant workers in the UK.* Migration Observatory, University of Oxford.

29. Ho, E., Li, W., Cooper, J., & Holmes, P. (2007). *The experiences of Chinese international students in New Zealand.* Universities NZ–Te Pōkai Tara.

30. Batalova, J., Shymonyak, A., & Sugiyarto, G. (2017). *Firing up regional*

brain networks: The promise of brain circulation in the ASEAN economic community.
Asian Development Bank, p. ix.

31. Some also call this "reverse brain drain."

32. Short-term study or training through student-exchange or corporate-affiliate programs is still considered part of brain train, as talents maintain the affiliation with their home university or corporation and are expected to return.

33. Hazen, H. D., & Alberts, H. C. (2006). Visitors or immigrants? International students in the United States. *Population, Space and Place, 12*(3), 201–216.

34. Talent Corporation Malaysia Berhad. (n.d.). *REP by TalentCorp.*

35. Chen, Y. C. (2008). The limits of brain circulation: Chinese returnees and technological development in Beijing. *Pacific Affairs, 81*(2), 195–215.

36. Tsay, C. (2003). Taiwan: Significance, characteristics and policies on return skilled migration. In R. Iredale, F. Guo, & S. Rozario (Eds.), *Return migration in the Asia Pacific* (pp. 112–135). Edward Elgar.

37. Song, H. (1997). From brain drain to reverse brain drain: Three decades of Korean experience. *Science, Technology and Society, 2*(2), 317–345.

38. Hao, X., Yan, K., Guo, S., & Wang, M. (2017). Chinese returnees' motivation, post-return status and impact of return: A systematic review. *Asian and Pacific Migration Journal, 26*(1), 143–157.

39. Tian, F. (2016). Brain circulation, diaspora and scientific progress: A study of the international migration of Chinese scientists, 1998–2006. *Asian and Pacific Migration Journal, 25*(3), 296–319.

40. Li, W., Bakshi, K., Tan, Y., & Huang, X. (2019). Policies for recruiting talented professionals from the diaspora: India and China compared. *International Migration, 57*(3), p. 376.

41. Shin & Choi (2015).

42. Daugeliene, R., & Marcinkeviciene, R. (2009). Brain circulation: Theoretical considerations. *Engineering Economics, 63*(3), 49–57; Tung, R. L. (2008). Brain circulation, diaspora, and international competitiveness. *European Management Journal, 26*(5), 298–304.

43. Williams, A. M. (2007). Listen to me, learn with me: International migration and knowledge transfer. *British Journal of Industrial Relations, 45*(2), 361–382; Brinkerhoff, J. M. (2012). Creating an enabling environment for diasporas' participation in homeland development. *International Migration, 50*(1), 75–95.

44. Whereas brain circulation does not include the return of second-generation diaspora members who were never embedded in the domestic labor market of their parents' home country (this is brain gain), linkage is broader in scope: it includes activities of second- and third-generation (and so on) diaspora members as well as former international students and short-term workers who then leave the host

country to return home and connect the two. Putnam, R. D. (2000). *Bowling alone: The collapse and revival of American community*. Simon & Schuster.

45. Moon, R. J., & Shin, G. W. (2016). Aid as transnational social capital: Korea's official development assistance in higher education. *Pacific Affairs, 89*(4), 817–837.

46. Gallo, M. (2019). *Ireland global alumni network: Scoping research study*. In addition to linkages between home and host country, internationalization of higher education can also foster linkage between third-party countries, as international students from various places meet in the host country and then maintain ties upon return to their respective home countries. Moon & Shin (2019).

47. Azadi, P., Mirramezani, M., & Mesgaran, M. B. (2020). *Migration and brain drain from Iran*. Stanford Iran 2040 Project, 1–30.

48. Zagade, A., & Desai, S. P. (2017). Brain drain or brain circulation: A study of returnee professionals in India. *Journal of Commerce and Management Thought, 8*(3), 422–435.

49. Shin & Choi (2015).

50. Adeyemi, R. A., Joel, A., Ebenezer, J. T., & Attah, E. Y. (2018). The effect of brain drain on the economic development of developing countries: Evidence from selected African countries. *Journal of Health and Social Issues, 7*(2), 66–76.

51. Saxenian, A. (2005). From brain drain to brain circulation: Transnational communities and regional upgrading in India and China. *Studies in Comparative International Development, 40*(2), 35–61.

52. Zapata-Barrero, R., & Rezaei, S. (2019). Diaspora governance and transnational entrepreneurship: The rise of an emerging social global pattern in migration studies. *Journal of Ethnic and Migration Studies, 46*(10), 1959–1973.

53. Academy of Human Resources Development. (August 2004). *Advances in Developing Human Resources, 6*(3).

54. Heitor, M., Horta, H., & Mendonça, J. (2014). Developing human capital and research capacity: Science policies promoting brain gain. *Technological Forecasting and Social Change, 82*, p. 15. To this, I would add that it is also important to take into account brain train and brain linkage.

55. Shin & Choi (2015), e.g., offers a look at Korea's current talent-development issues but does not take a historical approach.

56. Saxenian, A. (2006). *The new argonauts: Regional advantage in a global economy*. Harvard University Press.

57. Tharenou, P., & Seet, P. S. (2014). China's reverse brain drain: Regaining and retaining talent. *International Studies of Management & Organization, 44*(2), 55–74; Cao, N. T. K. (2022). Determinants of international students' decision to remain in Japan to work after graduation. *Journal of Asian Economics, 82*, 101529; Netierman, E., Harrison, L., Freeman, A., Shoyele, G., Esses, V., & Covell, C.

(2022). Should I stay or should I go? International students' decision-making about staying in Canada. *Journal of International Migration and Integration*, *23*, 43–60; Lee, E. S. (1966). A theory of migration. *Demography*, *3*(1), 47–57.

58. Tzanakou, C., & Henderson, E. F. (2021). Stuck and sticky in mobile academia: Reconfiguring the im/mobility binary. *Higher Education*, *82*(4), 685–693; Cerna, L., & Chou, M. H. (2022). Politics of internationalisation and the migration-higher education nexus. *Globalisation, Societies and Education*, *21*(2), 222–235; Rezaei, S., & Mouritzen, M. R. (2021). Talent flowscapes and circular mobility in a Belt and Road (BRI) perspective—global talent flows revisited. *Asian Journal of Social Science*, *49*(4), 188–197; Kuah, K. E., Rezaei, S., & Zhang, Z. (2021). Negotiating cultural and socio-economic flows in the era of Belt and Road Initiatives: An introductory overview. *Asian Journal of Social Science*, *49*(4), 183–187.

59. Markowitz, H. (1952). Portfolio selection. *Journal of Finance*, *7*(1), 77–91.

60. Here, my unit of analysis is the nation, but talent portfolio theory could also be used to conceptualize how a city, state, or other entity can organize its talent-development strategy.

61. Mangram, M. E. (2013). A simplified perspective of the Markowitz portfolio theory. *Global Journal of Business Research*, *7*(1), p. 66.

62. See, respectively, Markowitz, H. (1991). Foundations of portfolio theory. *Journal of Finance*, *46*(2), p. 470; Mangram (2013), p. 61.

63. Wohlner, R. (2023, July 5). *Why it's important to diversify your investing portfolio*. TIME Stamped.

64. Mangram (2013).

65. Cave, D., & Kwai, I. (2019, April 22). Why has Australia fallen out of love with immigration? *New York Times*.

66. Xie, Y., Lin, X., Li, J., & Huang, J. (2023). Caught in the crossfire: Fears of Chinese-American scientists. *Proceedings of the National Academy of Sciences*, *120*(27), 1–5.

67. Perold, A. F., & Sharpe, W. F. (1995). Dynamic strategies for asset allocation. *Financial Analysts Journal*, *51*(1), 149–160.

Chapter 3

1. The lecture was delivered in Japanese. Maskawa, T. (2008, December 8). *What does CP violation tell us?* [Lecture]. The Nobel Prize.

2. Author's own analysis of the information collected from various sources. This figure is as of 2022. For comparison, only three Chinese nationals have been awarded Nobel Prizes in the natural sciences, and only one, Tu Youyou, a chemist, was educated and conducted research exclusively in China.

3. This figure is as of 2020. Data was combined from multiple sources by the author.

4. Huang, F. (2009). The internationalization of the academic profession in Japan: A quantitative perspective. *Journal of Studies in International Education*, *13*(2), 143–158.

5. Murphy, M., & Contreras, I. (May 12, 2022). Global 2000: World's largest public companies. *Forbes*. [Content no longer available.]

6. Author's own analysis of the information collected from various sources. The rank is according to Murphy & Contreras (2022). For comparison, among the CEOs of the top-thirty Korean companies, fifteen held a foreign degree. The top-thirty Taiwanese companies also had fifteen CEOs with a foreign degree.

7. Nakayama, S. (1989). Independence and choice: Western impacts on Japanese higher education. *Higher Education*, *18*(1), 31–48.

8. In sharp contrast to the University of Tokyo mentioned above, e.g., in Seoul National University's Department of Computer Science and Engineering, only nine of the thirty-four faculty members obtained their PhDs from Korean universities. At National Taiwan University's Department of Computer Science and Information Engineering, only eight of the forty-eight faculty members received PhDs from Taiwanese universities. At Peking University's Department of Computer Science and Technology, sixty-three of the ninety-eight faculty members received PhDs from Chinese universities.

9. Tsuneyoshi, R. (2017). Exceptionalism in Japanese education and its implications. In R. Tsuneyoshi (Ed.), *Globalization and Japanese exceptionalism in education: Insiders' views into a changing system* (pp. 19–42). Taylor & Francis, at p. 20

10. Eight of the twenty-five faculty members at the Computer Science Department of the University of Tokyo had overseas experiences in the form of visiting scholars (six) or postdocs (two).

11. Vogel, E. (1979). *Japan as number one: Lessons for America*. Harvard University Press.

12. Coghlan, A., & Geake, E. (1992, February 15). Industry "does not need research." *New Scientist*.

13. Forester, T. (1993). How Japan became no. 1 in IT. *Policy, Organisation and Society*, *6*(1), 25–32.

14. Cusumano, M. A. (1988, October 15). Manufacturing innovation: Lessons from the Japanese auto industry. *MIT Sloan Management Review*.

15. Lohr, S. (1984, July 8). The Japanese challenge: Can they achieve technological supremacy? *New York Times*.

16. Gerschenkron, A. (1962). *Economic backwardness in historical perspective: A book of essays*. Belknap Press of Harvard University Press, p. 51.

17. Hayami, Y., & Godo, Y. (2005). *Development economics: From the poverty to the wealth of nations*. Oxford University Press; Tilak, J. B. G. (2001). *Building human capital: What others can learn* (Working paper). World Bank Institute; Sti-

glitz, J. E. (1996). Some lessons from the East Asian miracle. *World Bank Research Observer, 11*(2), 151–177.

18. Godo, Y., & Hayami, Y. (2002). Catching up in education in the economic catch-up of Japan with the United States, 1890–1990. *Economic Development and Cultural Change, 50*(4), 961–978.

19. Although elements of Western models (e.g., the German/American model of scientific education) were borrowed in building its modern education system, Japan had the freedom and capacity to develop a system of its own. E.g., Japan's education had traditionally stressed Confucian values, such as unity, conformity, loyalty, seniority, and collectivism, which fostered a work ethic effective for industrial development. Nakayama (1989).

20. With the establishment of technical colleges, daytime junior colleges of engineering were abolished, and evening junior colleges of engineering were retained as junior college divisions of national universities. These junior college divisions offer instruction only in the evening and are three years in duration.

21. Jones, L. D. (1980). *A study of electrical and electronic technical education programs in Japanese technical colleges and junior colleges* [Doctoral dissertation]. Oklahoma State University.

22. Japan had built a modern higher education system anchored on that of the imperial university in the prewar period, and its representatives, such as the Universities of Tokyo and Kyoto, continued to lead Japan's higher education as national universities after 1945. Nakayama (1989).

23. Japan Ministry of Education (1964), as cited in Itoh, A. (2014). Japan's period of high economic growth and science and technology education: The role of higher education institutions. *Japan Labor Review, 11*(3), 35–57.

24. Itoh (2014).

25. Ushiogi, M. (1997). Japanese graduate education and its problems. *Higher Education, 34*(2), p. 238.

26. Cyranoski, D., Gilbert, N., Ledford, H., Nayar, A., & Yahia, M. (2011). Education: The PhD factory. *Nature, 472*(7343), 276–280.

27. Ushiogi (1997).

28. According to the employee who worked at Rakuten for more than five years, in 2017, an MA-degree holder would earn only 10,000 yen more (about seventy US dollars). Rakuten employee (personal communication, February 17, 2023).

29. Nonaka, I., & Takeuchi, H. (1995). *The knowledge-creating company: How Japanese companies create the dynamics of innovation.* Oxford University Press.

30. OECD (1972), as cited in Johnson, C. (1982). *MITI and the Japanese miracle: The growth of industrial policy 1925–1975.* Stanford University Press, p. 14.

31. It should be noted that, while lifelong employment was not universal among Japanese firms, it was adopted by most leading companies.

32. Gilson, R. J., & Roe, M. J. (1999). Lifetime employment: Labor peace and the evolution of Japanese corporate governance. *Columbia Law Review, 99*(508), p. 520.

33. Kim, M. (2016). All or nothing: The employment security laws of Japan and the United States. *Boston University International Law Journal, 34*(2), 415–451.

34. Begin, J. P. (1997). *Dynamic human resource systems: Cross-national comparisons*. Walter de Gruyter.

35. Womack, J. P., Jones, D. T., & Roos, D. (1990). *The machine that changed the world*. Harper Perennial.

36. Koike, K. (1984). Skill formation systems in the U.S. and Japan: A comparative study. In M. Aoki (Ed.), *The economic analysis of the Japanese firms* (pp. 47–75). Elsevier Science.

37. Nonaka & Takeuchi (1995).

38. Domingo, R. (2003). *Management: Japanese style*. RTDOnline.

39. Here, I focus on the large, successful corporations that contributed to Japan's rise. There are, however, some exceptions to such generalizations. In regard to lifetime employment, women were generally considered temporary employees and thus did not receive many of the same benefits as male workers. Despite lifetime employment, Japanese companies were also more easily able to lay off a larger proportion of their workforce during times of business trouble than companies in the West. Drucker, P. F. (March 1971). What we can learn from Japanese management. *Harvard Business Review*.

40. Cummings, W. (1972). *Nihon no Daigaku Kyoju* [University professors in Japan]. Shiseido; Cummings, W. K., & Amano, I. (1977). The changing role of the Japanese professor. *Higher Education, 6*, 209–234.

41. Berelson, B. (1960). *Graduate education in the United States*. McGraw-Hill; Kudo, J. (2007). The historical transition of chair system and its merits and demerits. *Journal of Liberal and General Education Society of Japan, 29*, 119–123; Shimbori, M. (1981). The Japanese academic profession. *Higher Education, 10*, 75–87.

42. Horta, H., Sato, M., & Yonezawa, A. (2011). Academic inbreeding: Exploring its characteristics and rationale in Japanese universities using a qualitative perspective. *Asia Pacific Education Review, 12*, p. 41.

43. This contrasts with brain circulation, to be discussed in depth in chapter 5, which involves an initial brain drain as talents depart from the domestic workforce to move abroad. See also chapter 2.

44. Institute of International Education. (1996). *Open Doors report on international educational exchange*. US Department of State, p. 37.

45. According to one graduate of the University of Tokyo who is working as a scholar in the United States after receiving her PhD from an American university, Japanese scholars overseas may return for personal reasons, such as attachment to

Japanese culture and lifestyle, or "unavoidable reasons," such as lack of funding, issues with visas, language barriers, limited available positions in the United States, and stipulations of domestic scholarships or fellowships. University of Tokyo graduate (personal communication, August 21, 2023).

46. When looking at the overall number of those with nonimmigrant visas, which includes visas for short-term employment or study and temporary visits for tourism or business (visa categories A–L).

47. Japan was in the top three in terms of foreign scholars in the 1960s and 1970s and remained the second-largest foreign-scholar population in the United States (in the 1990s, after China) until the 2001–2002 academic year, when it fell to fourth place. This mirrors the J and L visa data for Japanese in the United States, which began to decline in the early 2000s.

48. Such training entailed seminars, sessions at factory schools, forums, individual-training assignments, observation of work techniques, and practical application of these techniques. The 1960 *Open Doors* report notes that 65 percent of all industrial trainees were in the United States for less than one month, including those that were at corporations for one to three days of technical observation. In 1961, *Open Doors* asked for information on trainees who stayed for a period of one month or more. Japan was the country with the fourth-most trainees (186), behind Germany (278), the United Kingdom (260), and Brazil (235).

49. Institute of International Education. (1960). *Open Doors report on international educational exchange.* US Department of State.

50. Institute of International Education (1996), p. 37.

51. As will be shown in chapter 5, this contrasts with the phenomenon of Chinese scholars, many of whom departed the domestic workforce before heading overseas. Japanese scholars' short-term stays in the United States also differ from Chinese diasporic scholars residing in the United States, who travel to China for short-term stays: the latter case represents efforts on the part of the Chinese government to foster brain linkage with their diaspora, whereas Japanese scholars went overseas for the purpose of refreshing their knowledge, rather than cultivating transnational bridges.

52. Institute of International Education (1960).

53. The program expanded its membership to non-Japanese institutions in 1992 and has since hosted fellows from affiliated Chinese, Korean, and Indian institutions. Still, Japanese are the largest in numbers in the GAP program, while they are the least in formal degree programs, such as PhDs at Stanford. I have personally observed this trend as the director of the Shorenstein APARC since 2005.

54. Florida, R., & Kenney, M. (1994). The globalization of Japanese R&D: The economic geography of Japanese R&D investment in the United States. *Economic Geography, 70*(4), p. 358.

55. After carrying out his Nobel work, Nakamura has since become a brain drain for Japan after he traded his Japanese citizenship for US citizenship in 2005. See Nobel Foundation. (n.d.). *Shuji Nakamura—biographical*. The Nobel Prize.

56. Keys, J. B., & Miller, T. R. (1984). The Japanese management theory jungle. *Academy of Management Review*, 9(2), 342–353.

57. Godo, Y., & Hayami, Y. (2010). The human capital basis of the Japanese miracle: A historical perspective. In K. Otsuka & K. Kalirajan (Eds.), *Community, market and state in development* (pp. 103–120). Palgrave & Macmillan, at pp. 115–116.

58. Lewis, L., & Tabeta, S. (2016, January 11). Japan business leaders urge real globalisation. *Financial Times*.

59. Debroux, P. (2003). *Human resource management in Japan: Changes and uncertainties*. Ashgate; Sakaiya, T. (1991). *The knowledge value revolution or a history of the future*. Kodansha International.

60. Godo & Hayami (2010).

61. Age-dependency ratio is the ratio of dependents—people younger than fifteen and older than sixty-four—to the working-age population—those aged fifteen to sixty-four. Data are shown as the proportion of dependents per one hundred working-age individuals.

62. Japan's Ministry of Economy, Trade and Industry estimated a shortage of 790,000 IT workers by 2030. See Kogure, N. (2019, July 8). Shortage of IT human resources in the digital era. *Nomura Research Institute Journal*. However, the McKinsey estimate is six hundred thousand. See Chokki, S., Odawara, H., Sandler, C., & Tsuda, T. (2020). *A new era for industrial R&D in Japan*. McKinsey.

63. Reuters Graphics. (2019, May 1). *Going gray*. Reuters.

64. This figure is at 28 percent as of 2020, the highest in the world. Elderly citizens accounted for record 28.4% of Japan's population in 2018, data show. (2019, September 15). *Japan Times*.

65. Sharpe, M. O. (2010). When ethnic returnees are *de facto* guestworkers: What does the introduction of Latin American Japanese *Nikkeijin* (Japanese descendants) (LAN) suggest for Japan's definition of nationality, citizenship, and immigration policy? *Policy and Society*, 29(4), 357–369.

66. Japanese cell phones, e.g., led the way in email capabilities, camera phones, 3G networks, and electronic payments—but they became too advanced for the lagging global markets. Tabuchi, H. (2009, July 19). Why Japan's cellphones haven't gone global. *New York Times*.

67. Stewart, D. (2010, June 12). Slowing Japan's Galapagos syndrome. *Huffington Post*.

68. Tsuneyoshi (2017), p. 36. Some Japanese companies have begun to value English-language proficiency—e.g., Panasonic, a Japanese electronics enterprise,

has begun to recruit more graduates educated overseas, while Rakuten in e-commerce and Fast Retailing (which operates UNIQLO) in the fashion industry have changed their official business language to English. See Yonezawa, A., & Shimmi, Y. (2017). Japan's challenge in fostering global human resources: Policy debates and practices. In R. Tsuneyoshi (Ed.), *Globalization and Japanese "exceptionalism" in education: Insiders' views into a changing system* (pp. 43–60). Taylor & Francis, at p. 53. However, these are the exceptions rather than the rule among Japanese corporations—and even with English requirements in place, many Japanese employees continue to use Japanese. As a former Rakuten employee told me in 2023, "Foreign workers who don't speak Japanese often find themselves excluded in various circumstances" as Japanese workers; particularly older ones at the managerial level "find it more difficult and troublesome to communicate in English" and mainly use Japanese. Former Rakuten employee (personal communication, February 17, 2023). See also Tsuneyoshi (2017).

69. Motivations for study abroad tend to change over time depending on the country's level of development. As a country develops, less people may go study abroad, and thus, the decline is not unique to Japan.

70. Yonezawa, A. (2020). Challenges of the Japanese higher education amidst population decline and globalization. *Globalisation, Societies and Education, 18*(1), 43–52.

71. Shirakawa, N., Furukawa, T., Hayashi, K., & Masaroshi, T. (2014). *Double-loop benchmarking methods in the era of data deluge: An empirical scientometric study and assessment of Japan's Galapagos syndrome in scientific research activities* [Conference presentation]. 2014 Portland International Conference on Management of Engineering & Technology (PICMET), Portland, OR, United States.

72. Hammond, C. D. (2019). Dynamics of higher education research collaboration and regional integration in Northeast Asia: A study of the A3 Foresight Program. *Higher Education, 78*(4), 653–668.

73. Shanghai Ranking Consultancy. (2003). *Academic Ranking of World Universities*; Shanghai Ranking Consultancy. (2013). *Academic Ranking of World Universities*.

74. Yonezawa & Shimmi (2017).

75. The project supports universities in two categories: type A, "conducting world-leading education and research," and type B, "leading the globalization of Japanese society." The thirteen type A universities receive 420 million yen (USD 4.2 million) annually from the government, while the twenty-four type B universities receive 170 million yen (USD 1.7 million) annually.

76. Keio University. (n.d.). *Top global university Japan*.

77. University of Tokyo. (n.d.d) *Top Global University Project*.

78. University of Tokyo. (n.d.c). *Strategic partnership project*.

79. Rikkyo participant (personal communication, December 12, 2023).

80. Japan Student Services Organization. (n.d.). *About Tobitate! (leap for tomorrow) study abroad initiative.* Ministry of Education, Culture, Sports, Science and Technology.

81. British Council. (2019, February 7). *Chiba University to make study abroad compulsory for all students from 2020.*

82. Though the data differ, all show increases from 2011 onward. See, e.g., Institute of International Education. (n.d.b). *Infographics and data: Japan*; Nippon. com. (2019, May 13). *Year-round hiring aims to spur more Japanese students to learn overseas*; ICEF Monitor. (2015, November 23). *Signs of strengthening demand for study abroad in Japan.*

83. Japan Association of Overseas Studies. (n.d.). *Number of Japanese studying abroad, including working adults, appears to exceed 200,000.*

84. Japan Association of Overseas Studies. (2019). *Press release.*

85. Such internationalizing efforts have not always been viewed positively in Japan, however. As one student who graduated from the University of Tokyo in 2017 said to me, the university's president Junichi Hamada tried "to push the slogan 'Tough and global Todai-sei/students' and only faced cynical reactions from many students." In her view, this was because "inward-lookingness" meant a "stable 'middle-class Japanese' life" as well as "survival in Japan's shrinking economy." In addition, "after getting through the tough college entrance exams, Hamada's message may have sounded [like] requiring them to make further effort to help address the long-standing 'Galápagos' problem," which, in the students' view, they "were not responsible for creating." University of Tokyo graduate (personal communication, August 21, 2023).

86. It was later renamed the Program for Advancing Strategic International Networks to Accelerate the Circulation of Talented Researchers. Japan Ministry of Education, Culture, Sports, Science and Technology. (n.d.a). *Research with/in Japan.*

87. Japan Society for the Promotion of Science. (n.d.). *Bilateral programs.*

88. Japan Science and Technology Agency. (n.d.). *Strategic international collaborative research program.*

89. Horta et al. (2011).

90. Cutts, R. L. (1997). *An empire of schools: Japan's universities and the molding of a national power elite.* Routledge.

91. Huang, F. (2017). *Who are they and why did they move to Japan? An analysis of international faculty at universities* (Working paper no. 27). Centre for Global Higher Education.

92. Green, D. (2019). Foreign faculty in Japan. *PS: Political Science & Politics*, 52(3), 523–526; Umakoshi, T. (1997). Internationalization of Japanese higher education in the 1980's and early 1990's. *Higher Education*, 34(2), 259–273.

93. For instance, the Japanese Science and Technology Agency created the Japan Research Career Information Network in 2001 to provide information about academic-job openings in both Japanese and English. The government has also made open-faculty searches through the international academic community a requirement to receive funding from programs such as Global Centers of Excellence and World Premier Initiatives. By tying project-based funds to more transparent hiring procedures, the government pressures prestigious universities to expand their recruitment of new faculty members internationally.

94. Asahi Shinbun (2002, 2007, 2013), as cited in Yonezawa, A. (2015). Inbreeding in Japanese higher education: Inching toward openness in a globalized context. In M. Yudkevich, P. G. Altbach, & L. E. Rumbley (Eds.), *Academic inbreeding and mobility in higher education* (pp. 99–129). Palgrave MacMillan.

95. University of Tokyo gives up on plan to start academic year in autumn. (2013, June 20). *Japan Today.*

96. Moon & Shin (2019); Morita, L. (2014). Factors contributing to low levels of intercultural interaction between Japanese and international students in Japan. *Journal of Intercultural Communication, 14*(3), 1–12.

97. This is in contrast to previous years: until the 2000s, international students were largely brought to Japan as part of official development-assistance programs for developing countries or as part of public-diplomacy efforts (i.e., promoting Japanese culture internationally).

98. University of Tokyo. (n.d.a). *PEAK admission statistics.*

99. University of Tokyo. (n.d.b). *PEAK graduates data.*

100. Ritsumeikan Asia Pacific University. (2021). *Job placement and advancement*; University allies with Hello Work to help foreign students find jobs. (2020, November 6). *Japan Times.*

101. Study in Japan. (n.d.). *Chapter 1: Employment environment in Japan.* Japan Student Services Organization; Kyodo, J. (2019, October 23). Number of foreign students seeking jobs in Japan after graduation hits record high. *Japan Times.*

102. Nippon.com. (2018, May 21). *Most international students opt to stay in Japan after graduation.*

103. In 2019, the Ministry of Justice announced a further loosening of rules around residency for international students by allowing graduates to work in any role as long as they earned an annual salary of at least 3 million yen (USD 28,000). The designated activities visa was broadened to include job-hunting activities for graduating international students, allowing them to remain in Japan for up to two years in pursuit of a job. The eligibility requirements for the highly skilled professional visa were also recently adjusted, making it more readily attainable for graduating students, particularly those in postgraduate courses. The Japan Student Services Organization publishes an annual guide entitled *Job Hunting for Interna-*

tional Students featuring practical information not only on job hunting but also regarding visa pathways.

104. Terakura, K. (2009). 我が国における留学生受け入れ政策：これまでの経緯と留学生三十万人計画の策定へ [Japan's past policies of receiving international students: Policy background and the formation of the three hundred thousand international students' plan]. *Refarensu*, (698), 51–72.

105. This is according to 2019 figures found in Japan Student Services Organization. (2021). *Result of an annual survey of international students survey in Japan, 2020.* It is also interesting that there are very few Indian students in Japanese universities. Language, culture, and career prospects seem to be the main reasons. See also D'Costa, A. P. (2008). The barbarians are here. *Asian Population Studies, 4*(3), 311–329.

106. Mazumi, Y. (2021). How are part-time laboring international students incorporated into host labor markets after graduation? The case of South and Southeast Asians in Japan. *Japanese Studies, 41*(2), 201–219.

107. Imahashi, R. (2020, May 10). Japan's foreign students struggle to stay and study amid pandemic. *Nikkei Asia.*

108. Osumi, M. (2022, June 23). Japan aims to up number of international students to 300,000 by 2027. *Japan Times.*

109. Still, they account for only about 2 percent of Japan's labor force, one of the lowest shares in the OECD. Japan Ministry of Health, Labor and Welfare of Japan. (2018). *Gaikokujin koyō jōkyō* [Employment status of foreign nationals].

110. Nippon.com. (2020, March 30). *Record 1.66 million foreign workers in Japan in 2019.*

111. Japan Public Relations Office. (2019). *Points-based system for highly-skilled foreign professionals.* Government of Japan.

112. Prime Minister's Office of Japan. (2018, October 24). 第百九十七回国会における安倍内閣総理大臣所信表明演説 [Prime Minister Abe's policy statement at the 197th Diet session].

113. It still remains to be seen how such initiatives will be implemented, as in the past, actual implementation has not always been successful. In 2010, Japan signed Economic Partnership Agreements with the Philippines and Indonesia for nurses to train in Japan with the ability to gain permanent residence if they pass the national licensing exam. Only 2 percent of Filipino and 1 percent of Indonesian nurses passed in 2010 as compared to 90 percent of Japanese and 80 percent of Chinese nurses. See Hawthorne, L. (2018). Attracting and retaining international students as skilled migrants. In M. Czaika (Ed.), *High-skilled migration: Drivers and policies* (pp. 195–221). Oxford University Press.

114. Burgess, C. (2020). Keeping the door closed: The 2018 revisions to the "Immigration" Control Act as a continuation of Japan's "no-immigration" principle. *Electronic Journal of Contemporary Japanese Studies, 20*(1), 1.

115. These skills include nursing care and building-cleaning management and applicable skills within the fields of the industrial-machinery industry, construction industry, aviation industry, agriculture, food-service industry, and more. The figure is less than 10 percent of the government's projection of 47,550 workers in the first twelve months. The slow growth is partly due to COVID-19-related issues, such as the closing of embassies and testing centers for new visa requirements. Japan Immigration Services Agency. (2020). *Efforts to accept new foreign human resources and realize a symbiotic society.* Ministry of Justice.

116. Kajimoto, T. (2019, May 22). Few Japanese firms plan to hire foreign workers under new immigration law, poll suggests. *Japan Times.*

117. Bloomberg. (2021, December 6). Poll finds 89% in Japan back Kishida's ban on new foreign arrivals. *Japan Times.*

118. Yet Japan still suffered worse outcomes in key metrics, like the earnings gap and percentage of women in leadership roles. See Shambaugh, J., Nunn, R., & Portman, B. (2017). *Lessons from the rise of women's labor force participation in Japan.* Hamilton Project & Brookings Institution.

119. Suzuki, F. (2004). *The diversification of employment patterns in Japan* [Conference presentation]. IIRA Fifth Asian Regional Congress, Seoul, Korea.

120. Kajimoto, T. (2018, December 26). *In Japan, a scramble for new workers disrupts traditional hiring.* Reuters.

121. Sumitomo Corporation. (2020). *Environmental, social, governance communication book 2020* (Vol.1), p. 62.

122. Mitsui. (n.d.). *Human resources development and allocation.*

123. Hof, H., & Tseng, Y. F. (2020). When "global talents" struggle to become local workers: The new face of skilled migration to corporate Japan. *Asian and Pacific Migration Journal, 29*(4), 511–531.

124. Daikin Global. (n.d.). *Fostering human resources.*

125. The human resources practices also discourage women's employment.

126. Hof & Tseng (2020).

Chapter 4

1. Sopheak Tum (Zoom interview, May 28, 2021).

2. This phrase gained popularity following Australian historian Geoffrey Blainey's 1966 book by the same name.

3. In fact, Australia was ranked as having the least brain drain out of more than 170 countries for eight years in the decade between 2013 and 2023. See Fund for Peace. (2022). *Global data.* Fragile States Index.

4. Hugo, G. (2006). An Australian diaspora? *International Migration, 44*(1), 105–133.

5. World Bank. (n.d.b). *World development indicators.*

6. United Nations Development Programme. (2022). *Latest Human Development Index ranking.* Human Development Reports.

7. OECD. (2020c). *Foreign-born population.*

8. Australian Government Department of Foreign Affairs and Trade. (2017, November 21). *2017 foreign policy white paper.*

9. In the same period, net migration was only 40 percent of population growth for the United States. Department of Economic and Social Affairs, Population Division. (2019). *World population prospects: The 2019 revision.* United Nations.

10. Hugo, G. (2001, June). *International migration transforms Australia.* Population Reference Bureau.

11. Australian Bureau of Statistics. (2013, October 4). *Doctors and nurses.* Department of the Treasury; Kaspura, A. (2015). *The engineering profession: A statistical overview, 2014* (11th ed.). Institute of Engineers Australia.

12. Participation rates for temporary residents and recently migrated permanent residents were 69 percent and 72 percent, respectively. Australian Bureau of Statistics. (2019). *Characteristics of recent migrants, November 2019.*

13. Out of twenty-three foreign-born CEOs in the top-fifty publicly listed companies in Australia, nine were from the United Kingdom, four from the United States, three from South Africa, two from New Zealand, and one each from Vietnam, Colombia, India, France, and Ireland.

14. Apollo Communications. (2019). *Australian top 50 CEOs report.*

15. Parr, N., & De Alwis, S. (2019). The birthplaces, languages, ancestries and religions of chief executive officers and managing directors in Australia. *Asia Pacific Journal of Human Resources, 57*(3), 276–298.

16. According to a 2017 report by Startup Muster, 36 percent of Australian startup founders were born overseas. Startup Muster. (2017). *2017 annual report.*

17. OECD. (2020b). *Elderly population.*

18. Migration Council Australia. (2015). *The economic impact of migration,* p. 2.

19. This prediction is benchmarked against Japan's population in 2014, which stood at 127 million.

20. Washington, E. (n.d.). *Chinese on the goldfields.* Museums of History NSW.

21. This included migrants who were deemed undesirable due to their country of origin, criminal record, or moral misalignment with the nation.

22. *The Immigration Restriction Act 1901.* (n.d.). National Archives of Australia.

23. Australian Bureau of Statistics. (1988, January 1). *Year book Australia, 1988.*

24. After World War II, e.g., the United Kingdom discouraged the emigration of British nationals in order to rebuild its own cities and infrastructure.

25. Brain, P. J., Smith, R. L., & Schuyers, G. P. (1979). *Population, immigration, and the Australian economy.* Croom Helm, p. 50.

26. By the late 1970s, the Australian government assisted more than three hundred thousand displaced persons from Eastern Europe to settle in Australia to fill vacant jobs. National Museum of Australia. (2022, June 28). *Postwar immigration drive.*

27. National Museum of Australia. (2021, July 5). *End of the White Australia Policy*. Department of Infrastructure, Transport, Regional Development, Communications and the Arts.

28. Grassby, A. J. (1973). *A multi-cultural society for the future*. Australian Government Publishing Service.

29. Australian Federal Register of Legislation. (n.d.). *Australian Broadcasting Corporation Act 1983*. Australian Government.

30. Australian Government Department of Home Affairs. (2021, January 29). *Australian Multicultural Council*.

31. The Trans-Tasman Travel Agreement between Australia and New Zealand allows for New Zealand citizens to work in Australia under a special category visa that allows them to live, study, and work in Australia for as long as they'd like. If they're not a New Zealand citizen—i.e., a permanent resident—they are not entitled to this visa and must apply for another type of visa, such as through the migration program. The ease in which Australian and New Zealand citizens can migrate to each other's countries stems from shared British colonial heritage. Perhaps most indicative of their close relationship is that New Zealand almost became an Australian state until it opted to be sovereign. See New Zealand Ministry for Culture and Heritage. (n.d.). *New Zealand turns down federation with Australia*. New Zealand History; New Zealand Government. (n.d.). *Passports and visas when you go to Australia*.

32. Arzan Tarapore (interview, April 28, 2021).

33. It is important to note that while the temporary skilled visa only enables talents to stay for a few years, this still represents a brain gain for Australia as these talents are removed from their domestic labor market.

34. In particular, the number of skills that had national shortages skyrocketed to thirty in 1995 from the low of four skills two years prior because of a recession. See Parliament of Australia. (2013, April 14). *Chapter 4—unemployment and the changing labour market*; Australian Government Department of Education. (2019, March 13). *Historical list of skill shortages in Australia*.

35. Harrap et al. (2021), p. 92; Australian Government Department of Home Affairs. (n.d.a). *Australia's migration program—country ranking 2018–19*. Australian Government Department of Home Affairs.

36. This was enacted after a government review in 2006, with a goal of minimizing the risk of the old points system. See Harrap et al. (2021).

37. Harrap et al. (2021), p. 102.

38. In addition, the government takes a more hands-on role in its new Global Talent visa program, which is designed to attract skilled migrants in top future-focused fields, such as agricultural technology, space and advanced manufacturing, fintech, energy and mining technology, medical technology, cyber security,

quantum information, advanced digital communication, data science, and information and communications technology. In 2019–2020, five thousand out of 160,000 places in the permanent migration program were allocated to applicants from the Global Talent Program, and this number grew to fifteen thousand in 2021–2022. However, the visa program has been mostly unsuccessful. In July 2022, the government announced that it would cut back the program, as 77 percent of recipients had already been in Australia, so as to prioritize the normal skilled-migrant streams instead. See BusinessWire. (2020, October 28). *Australia's global talent visa program sees tech CEOs swap Silicon Valley for Sydney*; Coorey, P. (2022, July 19). Permanent skilled workers to be top priority in immigration revamp. *Australian Financial Review.*

39. Australian Government Department of Home Affairs. (2021, July 12b). *Country profile—People's Republic of China*; Australian Government Department of Home Affairs. (2021, July 12a). *Country profile—India*; Australian Government Department of Home Affairs. (2021, July 12c). *Country profile—Philippines*; Australian Government Department of Home Affairs. (2021, July 12d). *Country profile—United Kingdom.*

40. There are various explanations and implications of these occupational trends, both general and country-specific. Overall, international students in Australia gravitate toward courses of studies aligned with the skilled occupation list (SOL). Government officials are hesitant to remove IT/STEM fields from the SOL out of fear that international education will take a hit. In addition, as discussed in the India chapter, a huge draw to Australia is the opportunity for an improved salary and quality of life associated with the IT/STEM occupations. In terms of country-specific factors, the ease of credential transfer is an enabling factor for UK nurses working in Australia.

41. Australian Bureau of Statistics. (2021b). *2021 census: All persons QuickStats.* Department of the Treasury.

42. Australian Bureau of Statistics. (2018). *India-born community information summary.* Department of the Treasury.

43. While this is not as good as a country like Ireland (with 88 percent and 90 percent in medicine and nursing, respectively), it is important to note that licensed medical professionals from other developed Anglosphere countries do not have to take the Australian medical exam. See Medical Board of Australia. (n.d.). *Competent authority pathway.* Ahpra; Hawthorne, L. (2022, July 14–15). [Presentation on Australia's higher education and brain gain.] Presented at a manuscript workshop for this volume, Zoom.

44. Australian Bureau of Statistics (2018).

45. Harrap et al. (2021), p. 103.

46. The adjusted citizenship rate in Australia refines the naturalization rate by accounting for residency requirements, long-term temporary residents, and limited

citizenship pathways for certain groups. Smith, D., Wykes, J., Jayarajah, S., & Fabijanic, T. (2010). *Citizenship in Australia*. Department of Immigration and Citizenship.

47. When compared to Canada—another developed Commonwealth country with a similar skilled-migration system—Australia's system is more successful. Skilled migrants to Australia earn much more than those in Canada. In each field in Australia, fewer than 25 percent of recent arrivals (2009–2016) earn less than a normal income threshold (50 percent of the median wage). In Canada, on the other hand, between 45 percent and 85 percent of recent arrivals earn below the threshold, depending on their field. In 2016, 90 percent of Australian skilled permanent migrants were employed after six months, and 60 percent were in highly skilled positions; in 2018, this number increased to 94 percent and 68 percent, respectively. Harrap et al. (2021), p. 102.

48. Lesleyanne Hawthorne (interview, July 14 2020).

49. Institute of International Education. (2020). *A quick look at global mobility trends*. Project Atlas.

50. This is not only the case in Australia. In about half of the OECD countries, public-education institutions charge different tuition fees for national and foreign students enrolled in the same programs. See Sanchez-Serra, D., & Marconi, G. (2018, February 23). *Foreign students' tuition fees are a double-edged sword*. University World News.

51. Matthews, D., Radloff, A., Doyle, J., & Clarke, L. (2019, July). *International Graduate Outcomes Survey—2018: Final report*. International Education.

52. Australian Government Department of Education. (2021, November 26). *Australian strategy for international education 2021–2030*.

53. Australian Industry Commission. (1991). *Exports of education services, report 12*. Australian Government Publishing Service.

54. Jackson, G. (1984). *Report of the committee to review the Australian overseas aid program* (Vol. 206). Australian Government Publishing Service, p. 87.

55. The United Kingdom began charging tuition fees to cover the full cost of international students in the 1980s, and Australia followed suit.

56. Fraser, S. E. (1984). Australia and international education: The Goldring and Jackson reports—mutual aid or uncommon advantage? *Vestes*, 27(2), 15–29.

57. One good example of such an effort is "the provision of $21 million over four years for a major international marketing campaign to promote Australia's education and training services industry overseas" that the Australian government announced in 1998. This campaign was run by the Australian Education International and "targeted untapped market potential," such as India and China. See Spinks, H. (2016, February 25). *Overseas students: Immigration policy changes 1997–2015*. Parliament of Australia.

58. Its ten-level framework (certificate I to doctoral degree) makes it easy to

230 Notes to Chapter 4

understand requirements for each level. In order, the ten AQF levels are certificate I; certificate II; certificate III; certificate IV; diploma; advanced diploma or associate's degree; bachelor's degree; bachelor's honors degree, vocational graduate certificate, vocational graduate diploma, graduate certificate, or graduate diploma; master's degree; and doctoral degree. The European Commission has a similar qualifications framework.

59. Nyland, C., & Tran, L. T. (2020). The consumer rights of international students in the Australian vocational education and training sector. *Journal of Vocational Education & Training*, 72(1), 71–87. New Zealand also offers TPS through a similar framework. The United Kingdom, too, regulates higher education as a commercial industry, which provides international students with consumer rights. The UK Competition and Markets Authority publishes a guide to consumer rights for higher education students and offers an independent complaint scheme for students. The US Bill of Rights and Responsibilities for International Students and Institutions recognizes fewer rights than Australia's ESOS Act. National qualifications frameworks (NQF) originated in the mid-1980s, particularly in Anglophone and Commonwealth countries. New Zealand, Canada, and the United Kingdom have an NQF. There is no NQF in the United States. See UNESCO-UNEVOC International Centre for Technical and Vocational Education and Training. (2014, May). *World TVET database: United States of America*. US Centre on Education and Training for Employment.

60. Crace, A. (2017, February 10). *International student completion rates remain high in Australia*. PIE News.

61. Redden, E. (2018, August 24). *For international students, shifting choices of where to study*. Inside Higher Ed.

62. For comparison, China and Korea have seven each in the top two hundred. Japan has only two.

63. Pham, L., & Tran, L. (2015). Understanding the symbolic capital of intercultural interactions: A case study of international students in Australia. *International Studies in Sociology of Education*, 25(3), 204–224.

64. Moon & Shin (2019).

65. Community Development Division. (2012, September). *International student strategy discussion paper*. Knowledge Melbourne.

66. Quacquarelli Symonds. (n.d.). *Best student cities 2019*. QS Top Universities.

67. Welcoming Australia. (2021, March 23). *National unity week*.

68. Welcoming Australia. (2019, March 31). *Welcoming cities*.

69. Redden (2018).

70. Australian Government Department of Education. (2019). *International student data 2018—pivot tables*.

71. The number of international students per one hundred thousand of the

population is as follows: Australia (1559), New Zealand (1119), Singapore (945), Austria (847), and United Arab Emirates (824). Institute of International Education (2020).

72. For comparison, in 2015, fees from international students only made up 14 percent of total UK university income.

73. Yang, M. (2007). What attracts mainland Chinese students to Australian higher education. *Studies in Learning, Evaluation, Innovation and Development*, 4(2), 1–12.

74. Matthews et al. (2019).

75. This is the same hours threshold as the United States, Canada (more hours allowed in on-campus roles), Ireland, Germany (180 half days), New Zealand, and the United Kingdom. In Japan, international students can work twenty-eight hours per week.

76. Note that there is a concern about mismatches between what international students study and how they end up contributing to Australia.

77. Australian Government Department of Home Affairs. (n.d.c). *Temporary graduate visa (subclass 485).*

78. US Citizenship and Immigration Services. (n.d.). *Optional practical training extension for STEM students (STEM OPT).* US Department of Homeland Security.

79. Spinks (2016).

80. Hawthorne (2018), p. 199.

81. Matthews et al. (2019). However, Australia also faces an oversupply of international students in certain fields, which leads to worse employment outcomes. While some fields, like medicine, have similar employment rates for domestic and international students, many—including computing and information systems, business, management, and engineering—have drastic differences in their employment rates. E.g., in engineering, there is an 80 percent full-time-employment rate for domestic students but a 45 percent rate for international students. While there are other fields that also have this problem, computing, business, and engineering are also degrees that have high international-student ratios. Social Research Centre. (2021). *2021 International Graduate Outcomes Survey*; Tertiary Education Quality and Standards Agency. (2018). *Statistics report on TEQSA registered higher education providers.* Australian Government.

82. The IGOS was conducted by the Australian Council for Educational Research on behalf of the Australian government's Department of Education and Training to collect data on the outcomes of international graduates from Australian universities who had completed their studies between 2013 and 2018 (*N* = 10,243). Although a large number of Australian universities participated in the IGOS, not all universities chose to participate, and participating universities varied in their response rates. Therefore, these results should not be automatically pre-

sumed to represent all international graduates from all Australian universities. Matthews et al. (2019).

83. Australian Government Department of Foreign Affairs and Trade (2017), p. 112.

84. They involve collaboration between the Department of Foreign Affairs and Trade, Austrade (the Australian trade commission), the Department of Education and Training, and the education sector. Hong, M. (2023). Australia's international alumni engagement strategy: An approach from soft power to knowledge diplomacy. *Studies in Higher Education, 49*(3), p. 467.

85. Australian Government Department of Foreign Affairs and Trade. (n.d.). *Australia global alumni: Connect to a world of possibilities.*

86. Australian Government Department of Education. (2016, April 20). *National Strategy for International Education 2025.*

87. Matthews et al. (2019).

88. Moon & Shin (2019).

89. Of a survey group of 1,039 recently returned and expat Australians (26 percent returnees and 74 percent still overseas), 69 percent of those still residing overseas either see no benefit or aren't yet sure whether there are benefits from engaging with peers back in Australia. When it came to the returnees, 25 percent of respondents say that one of the biggest barriers to maintaining linkage with overseas peers is that Australian colleagues are not interested. See Legal and Constitutional References Committee. (2005). *They still call Australia home: Inquiry into Australian expatriates.* Parliament of Australia. Australia's business sector does not have a strong track record of external collaboration: according to OECD data, only 7.7 percent of Australian businesses collaborate with international firms while innovating products and/or processes (making Australia twenty-seventh among OECD countries). See PricewaterhouseCoopers. (2018). *Out of sight, out of mind? Australia's diaspora as a pathway to innovation.*

90. Gallo (2019).

91. Australian Government Department of Foreign Affairs and Trade. (2021). *Australia's assistance for education.*

92. Markus, A. (2021). *Mapping social cohesion.* Scanlon Foundation Research Institute.

93. Lowy Institute Public Opinion and Foreign Policy Program. (2019). *Lowy Institute poll.* Lowy Institute.

94. Cave & Kwai (2019).

95. Abbott, T. (2018, February 20). *Address to the Sydney Institute, Governor Phillip Tower, Sydney.* The Honourable Tony Abbott.

96. Biddle, N. (2019, January 15). *Big Australia, small Australia, diverse Australia: Australia's views on population.* Australian National University Centre for Social Research & Methods.

97. Cave & Kwai (2019).

98. Williams, J. (2017, April 18). Australian rules would make so-called 457 visa harder for migrants. *New York Times*.

99. In 2017, the government increased restrictions on temporary migration by replacing the 457 visa with the temporary skill shortage (TSS) visa. While the two categories have many similarities, including the requirement that an employer sponsor the migrant, the TSS visa includes a stream without a pathway to permanent residency. As approximately 55 percent of 457 visa holders in the past had transitioned at some point to permanent residency, this was a major change in policy direction. In addition, there are stricter English requirements for the TSS, the visa is significantly costlier depending on the length of stay in the different streams, and it can only be renewed once, so the path to immigration is more difficult. Contrarily, the 475 visa could be renewed for another four years. See Now, Australian PM Turnbull abolishes visa programme popular with Indians. (2017, July 19). *Hindustan Times*.

100. Markus (2021).

101. Oliver, A. (2018, June 20). *2018 Lowy institute poll*. Lowy Institute.

102. Australian Government Department of Home Affairs. (2020, March 17). *Australia's multicultural policy history*.

103. Jakubowicz, A. (2017, March 20). *The government's multicultural statement is bereft of new ideas or policies—why?* The Conversation.

104. Levey, G. B. (2019). The Turnbull government's "post-multiculturalism" multicultural policy. *Australian Journal of Political Science, 54*(4), 456–473.

105. Pearlman, J. (2017, March 21). Australia's new multicultural policy focuses on integration. *Straits Times*.

106. Australian Government Department of Home Affairs (2021, July 12b).

107. Silver, L., Devlin, K., & Huang, C. (2020, October 6). *Unfavorable views of China reach historic highs in many countries*. Pew Research Center.

108. Silver, L., Huang, C., & Clancy, L. (2022, June 29). *Negative views of China tied to critical views of its policies on human rights*. Pew Research Center.

109. Australia was reportedly targeted in part because of its strategic value as a US ally, and its importance is growing in the new Indo-Pacific strategy to balance China's influence in the region. Searight, A. (2020, July 31). *Countering China's influence operations: Lessons from Australia*. Center for Strategic and International Studies.

110. *Coronavirus: China warns students over "risks" of studying in Australia*. (2020, June 9). BBC.

111. Gao, C. (2017, December 15). Australia and China spat over foreign interference escalates. *The Diplomat*.

112. Hamilton, C., & Joske, A. (2018). *Silent invasion: China's influence in Australia*. Hardie Grant Books.

113. Australian Government Department of Education. (2023). *International student numbers by country, by state and territory.*

114. Babones, S. (2019). *The China student boom and the risks it poses to Australian universities.* Center for Independent Studies.

115. In contrast, the number of Indian students and workers exponentially grew: the number of Indian students studying in Australia grew 71 percent between 2014 and 2019 and another 54.5 percent between 2018 and 2019 and 2022 and 2023. Although there were some incidents, such as a string of violent attacks on Indian students by Australian nationals in 2009, India's strategic importance has grown (along with the United States and Japan, both are members of the Quadrilateral Security Dialogue, or Quad, a strategic dialogue in the Indo-Pacific region). Duttagupta, I. (2019, November 22). "Post study work policy" attracting more Indian students, says Australian education minister. *Economic Times.*

116. Tao, Y. (2021). Chinese students abroad in the time of pandemic: An Australian view. In J. Golley, L. Jaivin, & S. Strange (Eds.), *Crisis: China story yearbook* (pp. 290–304). Australian National University Press; Mao, F. (2021, September 3). *Why has Australia switched tack on Covid zero?* BBC.

117. Australian Government Department of Home Affairs. (2021). *Australia's migration trends 2020–21.*

118. Harrap et al. (2021).

119. Kwan, C. (2022, June 27). Why we don't have enough workers to fill jobs (in four graphs). *Australian Financial Review.*

120. Sriram, A., & Lehmann, A. (2020, August 30). *4 out of 5 international students are still in Australia—how we treat them will have consequences.* The Conversation.

121. Roe, I. (2020, August 16). *Most international students would tell others not to come to Australia after coronavirus response.* Australian Broadcasting Corporation News.

122. Florez, C. (2020, August 17). *Australia's international students are going hungry, with 60 per cent now unemployed.* SBS News.

123. *Nearly a third of international students closed to Australia's borders opt to study elsewhere.* (2021, October 21). Australian Broadcasting Corporation News.

124. Institute of International Education. (2021). *Open Doors report on international educational exchange.* US Department of State; Institute of International Education. (2022). *Open Doors report on international educational exchange.* US Department of State.

125. Berg, L., & Farbenblum, B. (2021). *As if we weren't humans: The abandonment of temporary migrants in Australia during COVID-19.* Migrant Justice Institute.

126. Koslowski, R. (2014). Selective migration policy models and changing realities of implementation. *International Migration, 52*(2), p. 27.

127. Packer, H. (2022, April 15). *Slow return of Chinese students could "split" universities*. PIE News.

Chapter 5

1. Sorrells, M. (2019, February 11). *China, part 2: A conversation with Ctrip founder James Liang*. PhocusWire.

2. After obtaining his PhD from the Paris Diderot University (Paris 7) in Paris, France, Chen completed his medical residency and postdoctoral research at the same university and its teaching hospital.

3. After earning his PhD from the Institute of Physics, Chinese Academy of Sciences, Xue worked as a research associate at the Institute for Materials Research, Tohoku University, Japan, and as a visiting assistant professor at the Physics Department of North Carolina State University, United States, from 1994 to 2000.

4. Center for China & Globalization. (2019). *List of 70 influential returnees in 70 years of PRC released*.

5. Mok, K. H., Zhang, Y., & Bao, W. (2022). Brain drain or brain gain: A growing trend of Chinese international students returning home for development. In K. H. Mok (Ed.), *Higher education, innovation and entrepreneurship from comparative perspectives: Reengineering China through the Greater Bay economy and development* (pp. 203–223). Springer; Miao, L., & Wang, H. (2017). *International migration of China: Status, policy and social responses to the globalization of migration*. Springer.

6. Zhang, S. (2006, February 27). 薛其坤：杰青"是个好起点 [Xue Qikun: "Jie Qing" is a good starting point]. National Natural Science Foundation of China.

7. Sharma, Y. (2013, May 25). *"Thousand Talents" academic return scheme under review*. University World News; Zweig, D. (2017, May 19). *Chinese students in America: Who returns, who remains, who benefits?* [Video]. Wilson Center; Cao, C. (2008). China's brain drain at the high end: Why government policies have failed to attract first-rate academics to return. *Asian Population Studies, 4*(3), 331–345.

8. After the Chinese Communist Party took over in 1949, however, most Chinese scientists in the United States decided to stay overseas "while waiting for the political situations in China to settle." Only a few hundred returned to China. Wang, Z. (2010). Transnational science during the Cold War: The case of Chinese/American scientists. *ISIS, 101*(2), p. 370.

9. This likely includes both overseas brain train and brain circulation experiences. Li, C. (2021). *Middle class Shanghai: Reshaping US-China engagement*. Brookings Institution Press.

10. Again, this may include some individuals who engaged in overseas brain train rather than brain circulation. Jonkers, K. (2010). *Mobility, migration and the Chinese scientific research system*. Routledge.

11. According to Cong Cao's estimates, the Cultural Revolution cost China at least one million undergraduates and one hundred thousand graduate students. Cao, C. (2004). *China's scientific elite*. Routledge.

12. Zweig, D. (2006). Competing for talent: China's strategies to reverse the brain drain. *International Labour Review, 145*, p. 65.

13. Zweig, D., & Rosen, S. (2003, August 5). *How China trained a new generation abroad*. SciDev.Net.

14. Cao, C., Baas, J., Wagner, C. S., & Jonkers, K. (2020). Returning scientists and the emergence of China's science system. *Science and Public Policy, 47*(2), 172–183.

15. Further disincentivizing overseas Chinese from returning was the fact that after Tiananmen, Western governments facilitated these individuals staying abroad. In the United States, e.g., the Bush administration issued a 1990 executive order and Congress passed the 1992 Chinese Student Protections Act, which allowed Chinese nationals in the United States to obtain permanent resident status. Cao (2008).

16. Wells, W. A. (2007). The returning tide: How China, the world's most populous country, is building a competitive research base. *Journal of Cell Biology, 176*(4), 376–401.

17. Saxenian (2006).

18. Normile, D. (2000, January 21). New incentives lure Chinese talent back home. *Science, 287*(5452), pp. 417–418.

19. Zhang, G., & Qin, Z. (2008, January 1). *The development of private businesses in China: 1978–2004* [Conference paper]. Asia-Pacific Economic and Business History Conference. University of Melbourne, Melbourne, Victoria, Australia.

20. Chen, Y. C. (2008).

21. Saxenian (2006), p. 198.

22. Xue Lan (interview, February 15, 2023).

23. Normile (2000), p. 417.

24. Wang, H., & Bao, Y. (2015). *Reverse migration in contemporary China: Returnees, entrepreneurship and the Chinese economy*. Springer; Zweig, D., & Changgui, C. (2013). *China's brain drain to the United States*. Routledge.

25. LaFraniere, S. (2010, January 6). Fighting trend, China is luring scientists home. *New York Times*.

26. Chen, Y. C. (2008).

27. Wang, H. (2013). China's return migration and its impact on home development. *UN Chronicle, 50*(3), 34–36.

28. Wang & Bao (2015).

29. Cao, C. (2017). *China's approaches to attract and nurture young biomedical researchers*. National Academies.

30. Zou, S. (2019, March 28). Chinese students studying abroad up 8.83%. *China Daily*.

31. White, K. (2019, December). *Publications output: U.S. trends and international comparisons*. National Science Foundation.

32. In comparison, the United States had thirty-two by the end of 2015 and 661 by the end of 2022. CB Insights. (n.d.). *The complete list of unicorn companies*; Orios Venture Partners. (2022). *The India tech unicorn report*.

33. UniversityRankings.ch. (n.d.). *Shanghai Jiao Tong ranking*.

34. Between 1979 and 1985, 75 percent of Chinese students abroad majored in natural sciences and engineering. In 1992, 75 percent of Chinese citizens studying in US graduate schools were in natural sciences and engineering. Li, C. (Ed.). (2005). *Bridging minds across the Pacific: U.S.-China educational exchanges, 1978–2003*. Lexington Books.

35. *People's Daily* (2004, March 2), p. 11, as cited in Li, C. (2009). China's new think tanks: Where officials, entrepreneurs, and scholars interact. *China Leadership Monitor, 29*, 1–21.

36. Some portion of these returnees may have been visiting scholars still affiliated with Chinese institutions while abroad and thus would not meet my definition of "circulation." However, the numbers are still impressive. See Wang, H. (2013).

37. Including individuals who received brain train overseas and *haiou*, or "seagulls" (working part-time in China while retaining positions abroad), this number is 87 percent. Ma, Y., & Pan, S. (2015). Chinese returnees from overseas study: An understanding of brain gain and brain circulation in the age of globalization. *Frontiers of Education in China, 10*(2), 306–329.

38. Overseas Chinese scientists working in the United States and the European Union were involved in 8 percent and 5 percent, respectively, of China's international copublications, illustrating the value of brain linkage (discussed later in further detail). Cao et al. (2020).

39. Australian Strategic Policy Institute. (2022). *Critical technology tracker*.

40. Ellis, S. (2018, January 17). Biotech booms in China [Supplemental material]. *Nature, 553*, p. S22.

41. Wang & Bao (2015).

42. Kang Siqin's calculation (2020), as cited in National Committee on U.S.-China Relations. (2018, June 6). *Peggy Blumenthal and David Zweig: China's students in the U.S.* [Video]. YouTube. For the original data source, see Zweig, D., Kang, S., & Wang, H. (2020). "The best are yet to come": State programs, domestic resistance and reverse migration of high-level talent to China. *Journal of Contemporary China, 29*(125), p. 786.

43. Project 985 was started in 1998 with the aim of promoting nine universities

to the world-class standard. It ultimately was expanded to include thirty-nine universities, and the original nine, considered the most prestigious universities in China, formed China's C9 League. Project 211 was launched in 1995 and aimed to upgrade 112 universities. The projects have been replaced by the newer Double First-Class Initiative, which began in 2015. Lixu, L. (2004). China's higher education reform 1998–2003: A summary. *Asia Pacific Education Review, 5*(1), 14–22.

44. Li, X., Zuo, Y., & Shen, W. (2018). Who got the academic jobs in the elite universities—a curriculum vitae analysis of new faculty members of Peking University and Tsinghua University in 2011–2017. *China Higher Education Research, 40*(8), p. 47.

45. Chen, L. K., Mourshed, M., & Grant, A. (2013, May). *The $250 billion question: Can China close the skills gap?* McKinsey.

46. The number of science and engineering students at both the undergraduate and the PhD level more than quadrupled between 2000 and 2015, from 360,000 to 1.7 million. In 2016, 77 percent of Chinese doctorates were awarded in science, engineering, agriculture, and medicine. Cao et al. (2020).

47. Returnee faculty in this study are those who "obtained a Ph.D. at a foreign university or have foreign postdoc research experience, and university faculty who only went abroad as a visiting scholar, for advanced study, for joint training, or for international exchange are not included." Li, Y. (2020). Do returnee faculty promote the internationalization of higher education? A study based on the "2014 faculty survey in China." *Chinese Education & Society, 53*(3), p. 120.

48. Chen, Q., & Li, Y. (2019). Mobility, knowledge transfer, and innovation: An empirical study on returned Chinese academics at two research universities. *Sustainability, 11*(22), 6454.

49. Li, Q. (2020, July 21). China's Double First Class programme should open to regional universities. *Times Higher Education.*

50. Wang & Bao (2015).

51. This aligns with the idea that visiting scholars do not get much out of their overseas experience but are merely "looking at flowers from horseback." These individuals can be compared to PhDs, who stay in their host country for many years. Zweig (2017, May 19).

52. Zweig (2017, May 19).

53. Institute for Interdisciplinary Information Sciences. (n.d.). *Yao Class.* Tsinghua University.

54. Some of the measures proved controversial. One that generated the most controversy called for the dismissal of one-third of lecturers and one-fourth of associate professors who were deemed substandard. Other measures included the stipulation that departments would no longer be permitted to hire their own graduates immediately upon their graduation in order to reduce academic inbreeding; new professors in most disciplines were also expected to be able to teach in foreign

languages. Ultimately, the reforms were toned down before implementation, departing significantly from their original design. Yang, R. (2009). Enter the dragon? China's higher education returns to the world community: The case of the Peking University personnel reforms. In J. C. Smart (Ed.), *Higher education: Handbook of theory and research* (Vol. 24, pp. 239–282). Springer; Yang, R. (2010, March 25). Peking University's personnel reforms. *International Higher Education*, (60), 10–11.

55. Stanford Center at Peking University. (n.d.). *About SCPKU*. Stanford University.

56. More students returning from overseas to start business. (2016, July 20). *China Daily USA*.

57. Tsai, K. S. (2017). *Elite returnees in Beijing and Bangalore: Information technology and beyond* (Working paper no. 2017–47). HKUST Institute for Emerging Market Studies.

58. This is in contrast to Japan, where the risk-averse culture, low status associated with entrepreneurship, lifetime employment in companies, and lack of an angel-investment community make for an inhospitable climate for entrepreneurship. Those who have had success tend to be returnees with English proficiency and connections to the United States (and its venture capital networks), or "intrapreneurs," who work in big companies' in-house innovation groups. Karlin, A. (2013, January 2). The entrepreneurship vacuum in Japan: Why it matters and how to address it. *Knowledge at Wharton*.

59. J. Tan defines a "technology park" (also known as a "pioneer park" or "industrial park") as "a property-based activity configured around the following: formal operational links with a university or other higher educational or research institution, the formation and growth of knowledge-based business and other organizations on site, and a management function that is actively engaged in the transfer of technology and business skills to the organizations on site. Typically, it leads to a territorial system of small- and medium-sized firms clustered together, with spatially concentrated networks, often using flexible production technology and characterized by extensive local inter-firm linkages." In China, parks help returnees who are less familiar with working in China to get investments and workspace, and they can even help with returnee paperwork. Tan, J. (2005). Growth of industry clusters and innovation: Lessons from Beijing Zhongguancun Science Park. *Journal of Business Venturing, 21*(6), p. 828. See also Wang, H., Zweig, D., & Lin, X. (2011). Returnee entrepreneurs: Impact on China's globalization process. *Journal of Contemporary China, 20*(70), 413–431.

60. *People's Daily* (2019, July 11) as cited in Lloyd-Damnjanovic, A., & Bowe, A. (2020, October 7). *Overseas Chinese students and scholars in China's drive for innovation*. US-China Economic and Security Review Commission, p. 17.

61. Wang & Bao (2015).

62. Dye, Z. (2017, September 18). Zhongguancun Index 2017. *China Daily*.

63. Dai, O., & Liu, X. (2009). Returnee entrepreneurs and firm performance in Chinese high-technology industries. *International Business Review, 18*(4), 373–386.

64. These findings were based on a sample of 145 with sixty-five returnees and eighty domestically trained researchers working in the zone who had not been overseas. The survey was conducted in Suzhou, Guangzhou, Shanghai, Wuhan, and Hangzhou. Zweig, D., Changgui, C., & Rosen, S. (2004, September 28). Globalization and transnational human capital: Overseas and returnee scholars to China. *China Quarterly, 179*, 735–757.

65. Saxenian (2006), pp. 13–14.

66. Filatotchev, I., Liu, X., Lu, J., & Wright, M. (2011). Knowledge spillovers through human mobility across national borders: Evidence from Zhongguancun Science Park in China. *Research Policy, 40*(3), 453–462.

67. Wang & Bao (2015).

68. Mok et al. (2022); Miao & Wang (2017).

69. People's Republic of China Ministry of Human Resources. (2006, November 15). 关于印发《留学人员回国工作"十一五"规划》的通知 [Notice on printing and distributing the eleventh Five-Year Plan for overseas students returning to China].

70. Rong, X. (2020, January 14). China is winning the race for young entrepreneurs. *Foreign Policy*.

71. The United Front Work Department reports directly to the CCP's Central Committee. It gathers intelligence on, manages relations with, and attempts to influence elite individuals and organizations inside and outside China.

72. Bowe, A. (2018). *China's overseas United Front work: Background and implications for the United States*. US-China Economic and Security Review Commission.

73. Saul, S. (2017, May 4). On campuses far from China, still under Beijing's watchful eye. *New York Times*.

74. Vandenberg, P. (2016). Institutions to attract talent to the People's Republic of China. In K. Kikkawa & K. Hull (Eds.), *Labor migration in Asia: Building effective institutions* (pp. 45–54). Asia Development Bank Institute, International Labour Organization, & Organisation for Economic Co-operation and Development; Hannas, W. C., & Tatlow, D. K. (Eds.). (2020). *China's quest for foreign technology: Beyond espionage*. Routledge.

75. Beijing Zhongguancu (ZGC) is a good example of trying to mimic the success via returnees experienced by Taiwan's Hsinchu. Chen, Y. C. (2008).

76. Xue (interview).

77. Joske, A. (2020). *Hunting the phoenix*. Australian Strategic Policy Institute. Through August 2012, thirty-one Chinese provinces and municipalities and thirty-five industries had established 2,778 local talent plans. Wang & Bao (2015).

78. Center for China & Globalization. (2017). *Attracting skilled international migrants to China: A review and comparison of policies and practices.* International Labour Organization & International Organization for Migration.

79. As David Zweig says in a 2017 talk, "By and large, the state is targeting the very, very best people." Zweig (2017, May 19).

80. Zhu, J. (2019). The composition and evolution of China's high-level talent programs in higher education. *ECNU Review of Education, 2*(1), 104–110.

81. Zweig, D., & Kang, S. (2020, May 5). *America challenges China's national talent programs.* Center for Strategic and International Studies.

82. World Food Prize Foundation. (n.d.). *Dr. Zhangliang Chen.*

83. National Natural Science Foundation. (2004, June 16). 陈章良细说"国家杰出青年科学基金"的设立 [Chen Zhangliang elaborated on the establishment of the "National Science Fund for Outstanding Youth"].

84. Cao (2017).

85. Cao (2008).

86. Zhu (2019).

87. While such talent programs award returnees, these individuals are not always recruited directly from overseas. Chen, e.g., had received his PhD at Paris 7 and then already returned to China before he was awarded by the National Science Fund for Distinguished Young Scholars and the Chang Jiang Scholars Program. Of Chang Jiang Scholars from the years 1998 to 2006, 94 percent of participants had overseas experience. While all the program's 308 part-time (two to three months per year) chair professors were recruited directly from abroad, of the 799 full-time "special professors," only 231, or 29 percent, were recruited directly from overseas or within three years after they had returned from overseas. This means that the vast majority of the returnees in this program had already been in China for more than three years. According to Zweig, this is because such programs are "under pressure to show that they can bring back full-time people." Zweig notes that this differs across programs: while CAS tries to attract talents directly from overseas, for the Thousand Talents Program, "a significant, maybe 20, 30 percent of the people getting the award were already back . . . [because] you gotta fill your quota. It's China." Zweig (2017, May 19). See also Talent Development Office. (2011). "长江学者奖励计划"简介 [Brief introduction of "Changjiang Scholars award scheme"]. People's Republic of China Ministry of Education.

88. It is worth noting that individuals can be awarded by multiple programs, so, in some cases, the same awardee may be counted multiple times across results for different programs.

89. The analysis is coded for primary and secondary strategies and includes all Bs that each program undertook. In most cases, there are no more than two Bs, but in some cases, there are three. E.g., as detailed below, TTP started out as just

circulation in 2008–2009 but transformed into circulation and linkage in 2010 when it added a linkage track. Then in 2011–2019, TTP became circulation/linkage/gain because it had a track for foreigners.

90. Zweig (2017, May 19).

91. This contrasts with other countries: the stay rate for science and engineering PhDs from Korea, e.g., rose from 22 percent in 2001 to 42 percent in 2011. Japan's rate has been more erratic but overall rose from 24 percent to 38 percent in the same period. India experienced a decrease from 89 percent to 82 percent—a drop only about half that of China. See Oak Ridge Institute for Science and Education. (n.d.). *Stay rates of foreign doctorate recipients*.

92. Zwetsloot, R., Dunham, J., Arnold, Z., & Huang, T. (2019). *Keeping top AI talent in the United States*. Center for Security and Emerging Technology.

93. Zweig (2017, May 19).

94. He, D., & Yang, Y. (2013, July 29). China's brain drain may be world's worst. *China Daily*.

95. Wang, D. (2013). *Reversing the brain drain? Skilled return migration and the global movement of expert knowledge* (Research paper no. 15–14) [Dissertation executive summary]. Columbia Business School. Some of the returnees had reportedly faced discrimination upon returning to China as they were viewed as "unfamiliar and even foreign." Columbia Business School. (2013, September 30). Reversing the brain drain. *Chazen Global Insights*.

96. Hongbin Li (interview, July 29, 2019). Nieng Yan, a star structural biologist who received her PhD and postdoctoral training at Princeton, presents an even more complex picture than Li. Yan returned to China in 2007, only to return to Princeton in 2017 after voicing frustrations with China's research system. Yan returned to China again in 2022, where she became the founding dean of Shenzhen Medical Academy of Research and Translation.

97. Hao, X. (2006). Frustrations mount over China's high-priced hunt for trophy professors. *Science, 313*(5794), 1721–1723.

98. This began to happen as early as 1996, when the MOE Foreign Affairs Bureau started to encourage Chinese who remained overseas to take short visits to "serve the country." See Zweig (2006), p. 69.

99. Gruber Foundation. (n.d.). *Mu-Ming Poo*. Yale University; Huang, H. (n.d.). [爱国] 中科院第一位外籍所长蒲慕明恢复中国国籍，"我从来都认为自己是中国人" [[Patriotic] Pu Muming, the first foreign director of the Chinese Academy of Sciences, regained Chinese nationality, "I have always considered myself Chinese"]. Center for Excellence in Brain Science and Intelligent Technology, Chinese Academy of Sciences.

100. Chinese Academy of Sciences. (2013, July 9). *Scientists develop new method for synthesizing high-quality graphene*. Suzhou Institute of Biomedical Engineering

and Technology. [Content no longer available.]; Nankai University. (2019, December 24). *Nankai University researchers develop new method for synthesizing high-quality graphene.*

101. Xiang, B. (2005, January 1). *Promoting knowledge exchange through diaspora networks (the case of People's Republic of China).* Asian Development Bank.

102. Ding, S., & Koslowski, R. (2017). Chinese soft power and immigration reform: Can Beijing's approach to pursuing global talent and maintaining domestic stability succeed? *Journal of Chinese Political Science, 22*(1), 97–116.

103. The chair professor's track was created soon after the Chang Jiang Scholars Program's beginning in 1998, but until 2004, there were only ten or fewer participants recruited into it per year. Starting in 2004, however, the program began to welcome more chair professors, thereby engaging in more linkage. Hao (2006).

104. Saxenian (2005).

105. Xinhua News Agency. (2010, September 16). 我国首次启动实施"海外赤子为国服务行动计划" [China launched and implemented the "Overseas Red Son Service Action Plan for the Country" for the first time]. Central People's Government of the People's Republic of China. Translation by author.

106. People's Daily Overseas Edition. (2019, January 30). "赤子计划"吸引万余留学人才_滚动新闻_中国政府网 ["Chizi Plan" attracts more than ten thousand overseas talents]. State Council of the People's Republic of China. Translated by author.

107. Xiang (2005).

108. Columbia Business School (2013).

109. Such fellowships enable China to make use of foreign talent without importing it long-term given that the fellowship notes that intellectual property rights, such as patents, resulting from the fellowship "shall belong to the host institute if not otherwise specified in a pre-agreed contract." It is worth noting, however, that there are other talent programs—even within CAS—aimed at brain gain: the President's International Fellowship Initiative, e.g., had the goal of increasing the proportion of foreign talent in China's science system.

110. American Association for the Advancement of Science. (2012, August 31). Science in the Chinese Academy of Sciences [Content no longer available]. *Science, 337*(6098), 1123.

111. Made in China 2025 is a strategy that seeks to upgrade China from a producer of cheap low-tech goods by outlining the country's advanced industrial manufacturing and innovation. See Xinhua News Agency. (2017, October 29). 中国迎来留学生"归国潮"背后，存在这个根本性转变 [Behind China's "returning tide" of overseas students, there is a fundamental change]. XinhuaNet.

112. Capri, A. (2020, September 10). US-China techno-nationalism and the decoupling of innovation. *The Diplomat.*

113. Zweig and Wang note that this number may in fact be lower given that there were issues of fabrication with some part-time participants reporting themselves as full-timers. See Zweig, D., & Wang, H. (2013). Can China bring back the best? The Communist Party organizes China's search for talent. *China Quarterly*, *215*, 590–615.

114. Zweig & Kang (2020).

115. Zweig (2017, May 19).

116. However, it is also the case that of overseas Chinese engineers, the very best are found to *not* be participating in China's national-talent programs. These individuals are even stronger than those who participate part-time. See Zweig et al. (2020).

117. The introduction of short-term tracks met with criticism that the program was failing to fulfill its original mission to bring back talents full-time. As Cong Cao points out, "The big question is, how many of them have returned permanently? The government has never released any information about this. It is a flaw in the system." Even when talents are supposed to return to China full-time, there have been instances of individuals maintaining their overseas jobs. Cao explains, "Some are holding two 'permanent' positions, in China and abroad. It's a gain for that person and it's a gain for the [Chinese] university . . . but it is very hard to say if China itself has gained anything." Sharma (2013, May 28). On the other hand, David Zweig explains that talents who are in China part-time can make important contributions—e.g., talents who serve as part-time deans in Chinese universities while keeping their positions overseas, he says, can help transform the culture of their schools, leading to important reforms. See Zweig, D. (2017). Leaders, bureaucrats and institutional culture: The struggle over bringing back China's top overseas talent. In A. Goldstein & J. deLisle (Eds.), *China's global engagement* (pp. 325–358). Brookings Institution Press.

118. Yang, L., & Marini, G. (2019). Research productivity of Chinese Young Thousand Talents. *International Higher Education*, (97), 17–18.

119. These are targeted at exceptional talents—such as winners of prestigious international prizes, including the Nobel, Turing, Fields, etc.—as well as world-famous scholars and other experts who are urgently needed to support innovation and science in China.

120. While the Innovative Talents tracks are supposed to be for Chinese overseas, non-ethnic-Chinese foreigners can also apply to the Innovative Talents short-term track. China Innovation Funding. (n.d.). 千人计划 [Thousand Talents Program].

121. Eighty percent were foreign-passport holders, most of whom were originally from China. See Wang, H. (2012). *Globalizing China: The influence, strategies and successes of Chinese returnee entrepreneurs*. Emerald Group.

122. Jia, H. (2018). China's plan to recruit talented researchers. *Nature, 553*(7688), S8.

123. Mok et al. (2022).

124. Yang & Marini (2019).

125. Shi, D., Liu, W., & Wang, Y. (2023). Has China's Young Thousand Talents Program been successful in recruiting and nurturing top-caliber scientists? *Science, 379*(6627), 62–65.

126. Center for China & Globalization (2017).

127. Miao & Wang (2017). A 2023 study finds that participants in the Young TTP were among the top 15 percent for research productivity in the five years before they returned to China compared to all early-career scientists in the United States but that those who rejected the Young TTP offers and stayed overseas were in the top 10 percent. However, in the period of seven years after Young TTP scholars returned to China, they increased their productivity in comparison to similar researchers who remained in the United States, publishing 27 percent more papers. The study concludes that such research gains are due to the Young TTP participants' greater access to funding and large research teams. See also Shi et al. (2023).

128. Bloomberg. (2018, June 22). China's "Thousand Talents" plan key to seizing US expertise, intelligence officials say. *South China Morning Post.*

129. Committee on Homeland Security and Governmental Affairs. (2019). *Threats to the U.S. research enterprise: China's talent recruitment plans.* US Senate. FBI director Christopher Wray also says that "through its talent recruitment programs, like the so-called Thousand Talents Plan, the Chinese government tries to entice scientists to secretly bring our knowledge and innovation back to China—even if that means stealing proprietary information or violating our export controls and conflict-of-interest rules." Wray, C. (2020, July 7). *The threat posed by the Chinese government and the Chinese Communist Party to the economic and national security of the United States* [Transcript]. Federal Bureau of Investigation.

130. Gilbert, N. (2022, March 7). "I lost two years of my life": US scientist falsely accused of hiding ties to China speaks out. *Nature, 603*(7901), 371–372; Yam, K. (2022, November 15). *After being falsely accused of spying for China, Sherry Chen wins significant settlement.* NBC News; Yam, K. (2023, May 25). *After being wrongly accused of spying for China, professor wins appeal to sue the government.* NBC News.

131. Gerstein, J. (2022, February 18). *Report details collapse of China Initiative case.* Politico.

132. US Attorney's Office District of Massachusetts. (2021, December 21). *Harvard University professor convicted of making false statements and tax offenses* [Press release]. US Department of Justice.

133. The pair had spent more than twenty years at the university researching Huntington's disease and initially denied claims that they failed to report ties to China. Shihua Li protested, "Our work is for humanity. You can't say if I worked in China, I'm not loyal to the U.S." Xiao-Jiang Li ultimately pleaded guilty to underreporting his income on federal tax returns. Kolata, G. (2019, November 4). Vast dragnet targets theft of biomedical secrets for China. *New York Times*. See also Mervis, J. (2020, February 5). Ex-Emory scientist with ties to China charged with fraud. *Science*.

134. Lauer, M. S. (2020, June 12). *ACD working group on foreign influences on research integrity update* [Slides]. National Institute of Health; Mervis, J. (2020, June 12). Fifty-four scientists have lost their jobs as a result of NIH probe. *Science*.

135. Gilbert, N., & Kozlov, M. (2022, March). The controversial China Initiative is ending—researchers are relieved. *Nature, 603*(7900), p. 215; Xie et al. (2023), p. 2.

136. Sixty-five percent cited "anti-Asian hate and violence in the U.S." Xie et al. (2023), p. 3.

137. Fei Yan (Zoom interview, May 14, 2021). Yan has a PhD from Oxford and a postdoctoral fellowship at Stanford.

138. Parliamentary Joint Committee on Intelligence and Security. (2020). *Inquiry into national security risks affecting the Australian higher education and research sector*. Parliament of Australia.

139. Joske, A. (2021, January). *Inquiry into national security risks affecting the Australian higher education and research sector: The Chinese Communist Party's talent recruitment efforts in Australia*. Parliament of Australia, p. 4.

140. Mallapaty, S. (2018, October 24). China hides identities of top scientific recruits amidst growing US scrutiny. *Nature*; Huang, K., & Ho, K. (2019, January 6). As China and US spar over tech, scientists would rather not talk about their talent awards. *South China Morning Post*.

141. Huang, T. T. (2020, May 7). China stops promoting "Thousand Talents plan." *Taiwan News*; *Spy fears prompt China to censor its own recruitment drive*. (2018, October 19). Bloomberg.

142. Barry, E., & Kolata, G. (2020, February 6). China's lavish funds lured U.S. scientists. What did it get in return? *New York Times*.

143. Mallapaty, S. (2021, April 11). China's Five-Year Plan focuses on scientific self-reliance. *Nature, 591*(7850), pp. 353–354.

144. Zwetsloot, R., Corrigan, J., Weinstein, E., Peterson, D., Gehlhaus, D., & Fedasiuk, R. (2021, August). *China is fast outpacing U.S. STEM PhD growth*. Center for Security and Emerging Technology.

145. One study finds that Chinese undergraduates in STEM at nonelite universities had math- and critical-thinking-skill levels decline during their college years.

Loyalka, P., Liu, O. L., Li, G., Kardanova, E., Chirikov, I., Hu, S., Yu, N., Ma, L., Guo, F., Beteille, T., Tognatta, N., Gu, L., Ling, G., Federiakin, D., Wang, H., Khanna, S., Bhuradia, A., Shi, Z., & Li, Y. (2021). Skill levels and gains in university STEM education in China, India, Russia and the United States. *Nature Human Behaviour*, 5(7), 892–904.

146. Fei Yan (Zoom interview, May 14, 2021).

147. Ha Wei (interview, August 31, 2021). In 2020, the Trump administration instituted a presidential proclamation titled "Suspension of Entry as Nonimmigrants of Certain Students and Researchers from the People's Republic of China," which led to the revoking and denial of visas for students and researchers that have or have previously had ties to "an entity in the PRC that implements or supports the PRC's 'military-civil fusion strategy.'" The broad language of the proclamation enables the denial of visas to individuals with ties to certain institutions regardless of their actual research. The Center for Security and Emerging Technology at Georgetown University estimates that the policy will block three thousand to five thousand Chinese graduate students per year. The scope of the policy may be even greater as it may discourage Chinese talents from applying for US visas in the first place. The Biden administration has upheld the proclamation. See Anderson, S. (2021, August 10). Biden keeps costly Trump visa policy denying Chinese grad students. *Forbes*.

148. Hua, S., Hao, K., & Korn, M. (2022, August 11). Chinese student visas to U.S. tumble from prepandemic levels. *Wall Street Journal*.

149. Why China is lavishing money on foreign students. (2019, January 26). *The Economist*.

150. Breeze, V., & Moore, N. (2017, June 29). *China more popular than US with African students*. CNN.

151. It is also worth noting that such geopolitical tensions have not halted China's brain gain efforts, which persist. In 2021, Xi Jinping announced that China would "exhaust all means" to attract top international talent. In May 2022, e.g., the Chinese coastal city Wuxi announced that it would offer Nobel Prize winners the equivalent of almost USD 1.5 million in housing subsidies to relocate to the city. While such brain gain efforts still have not achieved much notable success, the country is certainly trying to rebalance in order to make gain a more prominent part of its talent portfolio. Sun, L. (2021, December 16). Xi Jinping says China will exhaust all means to lure global talent. *South China Morning Post*; *Chinese city offers Nobel Prize winners $15 mln housing subsidies*. (2022, May 12). Reuters.

152. Of the Chinese scientists, 42.1 percent indicate that the FBI investigations and/or the China Initiative have affected their plans to stay in the United States (compared to 7.1 percent of non-Chinese scientists). Effectively, the China Initiative is accelerating China's brain circulation. Lee, J., & Li, X. (2021). *Racial profil-*

ing among scientists of Chinese descent and consequences for the U.S. scientific community. Committee of 100 & University of Arizona.

153. CGTN. (2018, March 7). *Xi Jinping: Talents are primary resources for China's development* [Video]. YouTube.

154. For a recent trend in China to contain Western influence, including the prevalence of English, see Li, Y. (2021, September 9). "Reversing gears": China increasingly rejects English, and the world. *New York Times.*

155. Liu, Q., Turner, D., & Jing, X. (2019). The "Double First-Class Initiative" in China: Background, implementation, and potential problems. *Beijing International Review of Education, 1*(1), 92–108.

156. Rozelle, S., & Hell, N. (2021). *Invisible China: How the urban-rural divide threatens China's rise.* Chicago University Press.

157. Fei Yan (Zoom interview, May 14, 2021).

158. One recent study shows that China's population could decline by nearly 50 percent by 2050. As Beijing seeks to move national industries up the value chain in manufacturing, technology, and services, demand for highly skilled labor is outpacing supply. China thus faces an acute skills shortage. Qi, L., & Li, M. (2024, July 11). The One-Child Policy supercharged China's economic miracle: Now it's paying the price. *Wall Street Journal*; Boland, B., Dong, K., Blanchette, J., Hass, R., & Ye, E. (2024, June 17). *How China's human capital impacts its national competitiveness.* Center for Strategic and International Studies.

Chapter 6

1. Banerjee, S. (2015, September 28). 10 things from Narendra Modi's speech at San Jose. *Business Standard.*

2. Gandhi, S. (2007, October 1). *Address by Smt. Sonia Gandhi chairperson of the UPA to Indian Overseas Congress and other Indian organisations, New York* [Transcript]. Embassy of India.

3. Goel, V. (2015, September 27). Narendra Modi, Indian premier, courts Silicon Valley to try to ease nation's poverty. *New York Times.*

4. ICEF Monitor. (2019, November 6). *More than 750,000 Indian students abroad in 2018.*

5. Ruiz, N. G., & Budiman, A. (2018, May 10). *Number of foreign college students staying and working in U.S. after graduation surges.* Global Attitudes Project, Pew Research Center; Migration Policy Institute. (2017, May 15). *Chinese immigrants in the United States.*

6. Khan, B., Robbins, C., & Okrent, A. (2020, January). *The state of U.S. science and engineering 2020.* National Science Foundation.

7. Fund for Peace (2022).

8. Arogyaswami Paulraj (interview, August 26, 2019). Emphasis added.

9. Paulraj (interview).

10. Dossani, R. (2002). *Chinese and Indian engineers and their networks in Silicon Valley*. Asia-Pacific Research Center, Stanford University; Dossani, R., & Kenney, M. (2002). Creating an environment for venture capital in India. *World Development, 30*(2), 227–253.

11. Saxenian, A. (2002). Brain circulation: How high-skill immigration makes everyone better off. *Brookings Review, 20*(1), 28–31.

12. Kale, M. (1996). "Capital spectacles in British frames": Capital, empire and Indian indentured migration to the British Caribbean. *International Review of Social History, 41*(S4), 109–133.

13. Khadria, B. (2014). The dichotomy of the skilled and unskilled among nonresident Indians and persons of Indian origin: Bane or boon for development in India? In G. Tejada, U. Bhattacharya, B. Khadria, & C. Kuptsch (Eds.), *Indian skilled migration and development: To Europe and back* (pp. 29–45). Springer.

14. Naujoks, D. (2009, October 15). *Emigration, immigration, and diaspora relations in India*. Migration Policy Institute.

15. Taken together, the acts significantly restricted entry into Britain by Commonwealth citizens, fueled by opposition to immigration among the Conservative Party and other political groups.

16. Kanwal Rekhi (interview, October 2, 2019).

17. Dugger, C. W. (2000, February 29). Return passage to India: Emigres pay back. *New York Times*; Rekhi (interview).

18. Li, W., & Lo, L. (2009). *Highly-skilled Indian migrations in Canada and the US: The tale of two immigration systems* (Working paper no. 4). International Migration and Diaspora Studies Working Paper Series.

19. Kapur, D. (2010). *Diaspora, development, and democracy: The domestic impact of international migration from India*. Princeton University Press. The author notes that due to selection bias in who becomes a member of the alumni association, overseas numbers are likely overrepresented.

20. Altbach, P. G., & Salmi, J. (Eds.). (2011). *The road to academic excellence: The making of world-class research universities*. World Bank.

21. Subramanian, A. (2015). Making merit: The Indian institutes of technology and the social life of caste. *Comparative Studies in Society and History, 57*(2), 291–322.

22. Among the top-twenty companies whose employees were awarded H-1B visas in 2018, six are either headquartered in India or are subsidiaries of companies headquartered in India, with Tata Group and Infosys ranked as the second and third, respectively. Associated Press analysis of H-1B and Bureau of Labor statistics find that foreign workers in computer science–related careers generally make less than their American counterparts, and other estimates claim that Tata and

Infosys—two leading Indian multinational corporations—save over USD 20,000 per H-1B hire per year despite nominal wage safeguards in place at the federal level. Zhou, Y. (2017, April 18). *Most H-1B workers are paid less, but it depends on the type of job.* AP News; Hira, R. (2015, February 19). *New data show how firms like Infosys and Tata abuse the H-1B program.* Working Economics Blog.

23. ICEF Monitor (2019); Indians form 2nd largest group of international students in US. (2017, November 13). *Economic Times.*

24. One caveat to the Indian share of H-1Bs is that due to difficulties getting employment-based green cards, Indians stay on OPT to remain in the United States, whereas other nationalities take on permanent residency. Bier, D. J. (2020, May 20). *The facts about optional practical training (OPT) for foreign students.* CATO at Liberty.

25. Office of Homeland Security Statistics. (n.d.). *Profiles on naturalized citizens.* US Department of Homeland Security.

26. In order, the next seven are China, the United Kingdom, Canada, Germany, Israel, Russia, and Korea. Wadhwa, V., Saxenian, A., & Siciliano, F. D. (2012, October 1). *Then and now: America's new immigrant entrepreneurs, part VII* (Working paper no. 215987). Stanford Public Law; Wadhwa, V., Saxenian, A., Rissing, B. A., & Gereffi, G. (2007, January 4). *America's new immigrant entrepreneurs: Part I* (Working paper no. 23). Duke Science, Technology & Innovation.

27. Chadha, A. (2006, June 25). Battle for brand IIT. *The Hindu.*

28. Dutt, E. (2018, December 6). Immigrants, including Indians and Indian-Americans, crucial to health care services. *News India Times.*

29. Mullan, F. (2005). The metrics of the physician brain drain. *New England Journal of Medicine, 353*(17), 1810–1818.

30. Walton-Roberts, M., & Rajan, S. I. (2020, January 23). *Global demand for medical professionals drives Indians abroad despite acute domestic health-care worker shortages.* Migration Policy Institute.

31. Chavda, J. (2023). *Immigrants and children of immigrants make up at least 15% of the 118th Congress.* Pew Research Center.

32. Duttagupta, I. (2007, September 20). Govt to handhold skilled Indians to land jobs abroad. *Economic Times.*

33. Korn Ferry. (2018). *Future of work: The global talent crunch.*

34. India Ministry of External Affairs. (n.d.a). *India Centre for Migration (ICM).*

35. OCI is also available to those who have been married to an Indian citizen or OCI for two years. An OCI holder has lifelong multiple entries to India and does not need special visas for work or study. OCI entails most of the social, economic, and financial perks of NRI status, such as special bank accounts and local fees for tourist sites, with similar limitations (e.g., restrictions on investing in agricultural property). However, OCI holders are ineligible to vote. Once the OCI status was

introduced, many NRIs acquired citizenship in their settled nations, enjoying their original legal benefits alongside the security and status of a relatively powerful passport.

36. India Ministry of External Affairs. (n.d.c). *Population of overseas Indians*; India Ministry of External Affairs. (n.d.b). *Nationality wise OCI card issued.*

37. As stated in a 2014 interview with a twenty-seven-year-old highly skilled Indian migrant to the United Kingdom, "I think amongst the high dreams of life by the urban Indian definition, going abroad and studying or working . . . and eventually getting settled there is one of the most common, had always been." Kōu, A., & Bailey, A. (2014). "Movement is a constant feature in my life": Contextualising migration processes of highly skilled Indians. *Geoforum, 52,* 113–122.

38. Tharoor, S. (2013, January 15). *The global Indian.* Project Syndicate.

39. Rekhi (interview).

40. Dayasindhu, N. (2002). Embeddedness, knowledge transfer, industry clusters and global competitiveness: A case study of the Indian software industry. *Technovation, 22*(9), p. 557.

41. Upadhya, C. (2013). Return of the global Indian: Software professionals and the worlding of Bangalore. In B. Xiang, B. S. A. Yeoh, & M. Toyota (Eds.), *Return: Nationalizing transnational mobility in Asia* (pp. 141–161). Duke University Press, at p. 145.

42. KNOMAD. (n.d.). *Remittances.*

43. Ketkar, S. L., & Ratha, D. (2004). *Development finance via diaspora bonds track record and potential* (Working paper no. 4311). World Bank.

44. Agarwal, V., Singla, H., Kashyap, P., & Mohan, R. (n.d.). *The global Indian fraternity: New locomotive of Indian real estate.* Square Yards.

45. Siar, S. (2014). Diaspora knowledge transfer as a development strategy for capturing the gains of skilled migration. *Asian and Pacific Migration Journal, 23*(3), 299–323.

46. As of March 14, 2022, a search for "H-1B" brought up nearly as many results in the *Times of India*'s search bar as a search for "coronavirus" (7,647 compared to 9,043). Kably, L. (2022, January 13). H-1B denial rates for new application drops to 4% in fiscal 2021. *Times of India.*

47. While Bengaluru was the earliest IT cluster, additional clusters have emerged in Hyderabad, Pune, and Delhi, among others, thanks to India's role and integration in the global IT market. Kapur (2010), p. 92.

48. Additionally, Software Technology Parks of India–Bangalore estimated that 70 percent of the foreign enterprises in Bengaluru were supported by NRIs. Upadhya, C. (2004). A new transnational capitalist class? Capital flows, business networks and entrepreneurs in the Indian software industry. *Economic and Political Weekly, 39*(48), p. 5143.

49. Upadhya (2004), p. 5147.

50. NASSCOM. (2018). *Indian tech start-up ecosystem: Approaching escape velocity*. NASSCOM-Zinnov.

51. HNIs to invest $30 billion in Indian tech startups by 2025: Report. (2021, June 17). *Economic Times*.

52. Arakali, H. (2020, January 10). Indian tech startups raise $14.5 billion in 2019, up 25x from 2010. *Forbes India*.

53. Orios Venture Partners (2022).

54. China's unicorn growth slowed a lot in 2022. Before 2022, the United States had 487 and China had 301, but in 2022, the United States added 174, and China only added eleven. India added twenty-four.

55. Orios Venture Partners. (2019). *The future of work: How startups are disrupting the way we work*.

56. NASSCOM (2018); Goel, V. (2017, October 8). IBM shifts center of gravity half a world away, to India. *Seattle Times*.

57. Pandey, A., Aggarwal, A., Devane, R., & Kuznetsov, Y. (2006). The Indian diaspora: A unique case? In Y. Kuznetsov (Ed.), *Diaspora networks and the international migration of skills: How countries can draw on their talent abroad* (pp. 71–98). World Bank.

58. Rekhi (interview).

59. Kapur (2010), p. 154.

60. Saxenian (2002), p. 30.

61. Saxenian (2005).

62. Dossani (2002); Dossani & Kenney (2002).

63. Rekhi (interview).

64. Upadhya, C., & Rutten, M. (2012). Migration, transnational flows, and development in India: A regional perspective. *Economic and Political Weekly*, 47(19), 54–62.

65. I supplement the database with founding dates, number of members, activities, types of linkage activities, and government affiliation, if any. Organizations can complete multiple categories of activities (e.g., an organization can be both cultural and social). Only sustained activities are counted in the dataset—e.g., a one-off charity event is not sufficient for an organization to be categorized as philanthropic. There are three shortcomings of the sample. First, organizations with multiple chapters, such as TiE, are only counted as one organization, which can be slightly misleading when doing aggregate-level analysis. Second, the organizations are predominantly those located near Indian embassy and consulate locations, which collected the information (Houston, Chicago, San Francisco, and Atlanta). While the location of Indian embassies may reflect the general spread of the Indian diaspora, it is unclear whether the findings are generalizable to other locations. It

is also worth noting that diaspora organizations often include not just first-generation migrants from India but also their children and other Indian Americans who do not fall within my definition of the diaspora. Finally, eight organizations in the original list have insufficient information available online to determine their linkage activities. Any inaccuracies or organizational changes in the Ministry of External Affairs dataset, such as misspelled names or groups that have merged, are corrected.

66. Sahoo, A. K. (2006). Issues of identity in the Indian diaspora: A transnational perspective. *Perspectives on Global Development and Technology*, 5(1–2), 81–98.

67. For those studies, see Chakravorty, S., Kapur, D., & Singh, N. (2016). *The other one percent: Indians in America*. Oxford University Press; Migration Policy Institute. (2014). *The Indian diaspora in the United States*.

68. My breakdown is consistent with the findings of the Rockefeller Foundation-Aspen Institute Diaspora Program that show, as of 2014, the majority of 224 US-based Indian groups surveyed are cultural organizations (51 percent), "many of which focused on teaching the languages and artistic traditions of India to the next generation. Charities made up 26 percent of the organizations in this analysis, and 14 percent of the groups were business or professional groups." Migration Policy Institute (2014).

69. Saxenian, A. (2000). *Silicon Valley's new immigrant entrepreneurs* (Working paper no. 15). Center for Comparative Immigration Studies, University of California, San Diego.

70. E.g., umbrella organizations like the India Association of Phoenix or the National Federation of Indian American Associations have a pan-Indian identity, seeking to unify and integrate the diverse Indian American community. Their activities tend to focus on facilitating bonding and coordination around shared interests and history, like celebrating Indian Independence Day and advancing Indian business and policy positions. Examples of single subethnic, religious, or regional groups include the Gujarati Society of Southern California, Maharashtra Mandal Bay Area, and Kerala Hindus of Arizona.

71. This analysis was conducted for eighty-eight out of the ninety-seven groups in my sample, excluding those with insufficient information.

72. While these numbers include second-generation Indian Americans, the organization was established by first-generation Indian diaspora members.

73. E.g., the 2012 Indo-US Healthcare Summit was hosted in conjunction with the Federation of Andhra Pradesh Medical Graduates in USA.

74. Parikh Worldwide Media. (2021, April 27). Indian-American physicians launch campaign to help India combat COVID-19. *News India Times*.

75. Shin & Choi (2015).

76. Office of Homeland Security Statistics (n.d.).

77. Of the Indian population in the United States who are aged five or older, 82 percent are proficient in English. This figure is among the highest English-proficiency levels of Asian-origin groups. Budiman, A., & Ruiz, N. G. (2021, April 29). *Key facts about Asian origin groups in the U.S.* Pew Research Center.

78. According to Saxenian, "Indus" in "Indus Entrepreneurs" was used to be inclusive toward Pakistanis, Bangladeshis, and Nepalese. Saxenian (2000), p. 15.

79. TiE Global. (n.d.a). *Annual report 2020.*

80. TiE Global. (n.d.b). *TiE regions and chapters.*

81. TiE Global. (n.d.a).

82. Rekhi (interview, October 2, 2019).

83. Saxenian (2000).

84. Subramanian, A. (2019). *The caste of merit: Engineering education in India.* Harvard University Press, p. 300.

85. Warner, M. (2000, May 15). The Indians of Silicon Valley: The hidden geniuses of the tech revolution are Indian engineers. *Fortune.*

86. Roy da Silva (interview, July 16, 2021).

87. Asha Jadeja and the Motwani Jadeja Foundation illustrate the role of individual-led transnational linkage, propelled by her "own desperate need to be connected back home." Despite her success in venture capital, Asha said in an interview in my office at Stanford, "I was missing India a lot. But I started to sense that there was a huge gap between men and women, and women had to deal with the social climate in India." So she chose to stay in the United States, and in 2015, she launched the foundation, a nonprofit global venture fund supporting South Asian entrepreneurs and US-India entrepreneurship, building off her decades of experience coinvesting with her husband, Rajeev Motwani, the founding advisor to Google and investor in over one hundred startups in Silicon Valley. Her foundation runs the Rajeev Circle Fellowship, which mentors budding entrepreneurs and links them to Silicon Valley. She believes that "95 percent of their confidence comes from knowing they have a network, and I have given them a permanent home." In just five years, the foundation supported over one hundred fellows. Asha hopes that "more entrepreneurs get empowered and realize they can bypass Indian bureaucracy and come here to get funded, . . . and it will make a huge impact on poverty in India." Asha Jadeja (interview, August 23, 2019).

88. Khandelwal, M. S. (2002). *Becoming American, being Indian: An immigrant community in New York City.* Cornell University Press; Menezes, R., Pike, D., & Patel, S. M. (2015, November 9). Giving back to India. *Stanford Social Innovation Review.*

89. Niumai, A. (2011). Indian diaspora philanthropy: A sociological perspective. *Man in India, 91*(1), 93–114.

90. Li, S., & Ansari, T. (2021, May 6). India's diaspora aids families caught in COVID-19 "medical war zone." *Wall Street Journal*.

91. Menezes et al. (2015), p. 17.

92. Naujoks, D. (2013). *Migration, citizenship, and development: Diasporic membership policies and overseas Indians in the United States*. Oxford University Press, p. 298.

93. Council of Indian Institute of Technology. (n.d.). *History*.

94. As Rafiq Dossani—former director of the RAND Center for Asia Pacific Policy, a senior economist at the RAND Corporation, and a professor of policy analysis at the Pardee RAND Graduate School—told me in an email exchange, "The average quality of Indian engineering education is poor relative to the US and China. Somewhat similar to China, but with much less money, the state concentrated funding in a few schools, classified as 'Institutions of National Importance' (INI). These consist primarily of the IITs, IIMs and other designated high-quality national institutions." According to Dossani, "INIs, which number only 167 out of the over 2,500 institutions that offer engineering education in India, received approximately 68 percent of the federal higher education budget in 2022. This is down from 85 percent in 2010 but shows that the direction of higher education policy is still to create a limited number of centers of excellence that will attract the best students. The result is a neglect of the funding requirements for educating the average student." Rafiq Dossani (personal communication, January 29, 2023).

95. Yokoi, K. (2014). The Colombo Plan and industrialization in India: Technical cooperation for the Indian institutes of technology. In S. Akita, G. Krozewski, & S. Watanabe (Eds.), *The transformation of the international order of Asia: Decolonization, the Cold War, and the Colombo Plan* (pp. 74–95). Routledge.

96. Mahadevan, I., & Sukhatme, S. P. (1987). *Pilot study on magnitude and nature of the brain drain of graduates of the IIT, Bombay*. Department of Humanities and Social Sciences, IIT Bombay.

97. Singh, J., & Krishna, V. V. (2015). Trends in brain drain, gain and circulation: Indian experience of knowledge workers. *Science, Technology and Society*, *20*(3), 300–321; Sharma, K. (2018, July 30). *IITs, IIMs, NITs have just 3% of total students but get 50% of government funds*. ThePrint.

98. Roy da Silva (interview, September 7, 2021).

99. Subramanian (2019), p. 295.

100. Dinsha Mistree (interview, May 17, 2021).

101. Education Desk. (2020, December 5). Responsibility of post COVID world is huge but your shoulders capable, PM to IIT alumni. *Indian Express*.

102. Subramanian (2019), pp. 260, 296.

103. PanIIT USA. (n.d.). *About PanIIT USA*.

104. Da Silva (interview, September 7, 2021).

105. Kapoor, U., & Fairbairn, D. (2018, November 15). *Oral history of Arjun Malhotra.* Computer History Museum.

106. Chopra, K. L. (n.d.). *Professor GS Sanyal: A tribute.* Maulana Abul Kalam Azad University of Technology, West Bengal.

107. IIT Kharagpur Foundation. (n.d.). *The mission and vision of the IITKGP Foundation.*

108. PanIIT USA (n.d.).

109. Dugger (2000).

110. Ramya, M. (2014, December 24). IITs continue to be NRIs' first choice. *Times of India.*

111. Subramanian (2019), pp. 281–285.

112. Subramanian (2015), p. 315.

113. IvyCap Ventures Advisors. (2018). *Who we are.* IvyCap Ventures. The IIMs are top public business schools in India.

114. IvyCap Ventures. (n.d.). *IvyCamp—alumni-driven startup engagement platform.* IvyCamp.

115. IvyCap Ventures Advisors (2018).

116. IvyCap Ventures Advisors (2018).

117. Lalwani, A. (2019, October 2). *This is how India can become the next Silicon Valley.* World Economic Forum.

118. Ironically, C. Upadhya argues, "A decision to apply for a U.S. (or other foreign) passport is linked to a definite plan to return [to India], because it provides assurance that one can always go back to the United States if things do not work out in India. . . . What is usually regarded as the final step in the assimilation of immigrants—attainment of citizenship—ironically has become the mechanism that allows them to return to the home country." Upadhya (2013), p. 147. Thus, while, on the surface, the OCI status increases the number of Indian nationals relinquishing their Indian citizenship, in reality, it was a strategic move by the government to make it easier for even NRIs to return, thereby strengthening their linkage and circulation efforts.

119. Zagade & Desai (2017).

120. Wadhwa, V., Jain, S., Saxenian, A., Gereffi, G., & Wang, H. (2011, April 8). *The grass is indeed greener in India and China for returnee entrepreneurs: America's new immigrant entrepreneurs—part VI.*

121. Chacko, E. (2007). From brain drain to brain gain: Reverse migration to Bangalore and Hyderabad, India's globalizing high tech cities. *GeoJournal, 68*(2), 131–140.

122. Jones, L. (2015, March 13). *More Indians who moved to the U.S. decide to return home.* NPR.

123. Wadhwa et al. (2011).

124. According to their website, "The Draper International India Fund was the first western Venture Fund to go into India. The Fund (1994 to 2000) gave a 15 times return to its investors." Draper Richards Kaplan Foundation. (n.d.). *Team— Robin Richards Donohoe.* In my analysis of the twenty-five India-based unicorns as of 2020, 95.94 percent of lead investors are foreign, suggesting the importance of overseas Indians tapping into international networks.

125. Saxenian (2006), p. 303.

126. Microsoft News Center India. (2020, March 17). *Innovate for Accessible India launched to harness the power of technology to empower people with disabilities.* Microsoft Stories India.

127. Banerjee, I., Chanakya, A., Das, A. C., & Lal, A. (2020, August 4). *Global capability centers in the next normal.* McKinsey Digital.

128. NASSCOM. (2021). *About us.*

129. Ashoka University. (2023). *Admissions brochure.*

130. This is in sharp contrast to the old private university Birla Institute of Technology and Science, Pilani (est. 1901), where the faculty of the computer science department has exclusively Indian PhD holders.

131. Saxenian (2000), p. 17.

132. Naipaul, V. S. (1990). *India: A million mutinies now.* Heinemann, p. 15.

133. Kapur (2010); Ray, T. (2019, March 8). *The US isn't safe from the trauma of caste bias.* The World.

134. A 2016 survey by Equality Labs of over 1,500 South Asian descendants in the United States finds that one-fourth of Dalits who responded say they have faced verbal or physical assault based on their caste, one-third of Dalit students are discriminated against during their education, two-thirds of Dalits are treated unfairly at their workplace, and half of all Dalit respondents live in fear of their caste being "outed." An anonymous Silicon Valley employee shares, "Many companies fill vacant positions with internal referrals. Upper-caste Indians have the first-mover advantage and misuse the system of internal referrals to fill posts with people from their caste." Mukherji, A. (2020, July 8). The Cisco case could expose rampant prejudice against Dalits in Silicon Valley. *The Wire.*

135. Tiku, N. (2020, October 27). India's engineers have thrived in Silicon Valley: So has its caste system. *Washington Post.*

136. Thenmozhi Soundararajan (Zoom interview, May 28, 2021). It is therefore no surprise that battles over caste discrimination are playing out in California, where the topic remains contentious. A 2023 bill would have made California the first US state to explicitly ban caste-based discrimination, adding caste as a protected category alongside race, color, religion, ancestry, and others. Ultimately, in October of that year, Governor Gavin Newsom vetoed the bill on the grounds that caste-based discrimination is already banned under such existing categories. Some,

however, have suggested that Newsom may have been wary that supporting the bill would have alienated its opponents—many of whom are upper-caste members and have high social capital as powerful, wealthy, and politically significant Silicon Valley players. Clayton, A. (2023, October 8). Ban on caste discrimination deemed "unnecessary" by California governor. *The Guardian*; Koseff, A. (2023, October 16). *Bashing Republicans for "rights regression," Newsom sidesteps protections for marginalized Californians.* Cal Matters.

137. Mukherji (2020).

138. Associated Press. (2023, April 12). *California scraps caste bias case against Cisco engineers: Company still being sued.* NBC News.

139. Tiku (2020).

140. FrontAd Media. (2020, February 11). *The NRI's contribution to the Indian economy.* CompareRemit.

141. Poojary, T., & Bakshi, S. R. (2019, July 28). *Arabian nights and Indian startup dreams: Middle East investors eager to fund tech businesses.* YourStory.

142. India Ministry of External Affairs. (2023). *India-Bahrain bilateral relations.*

143. The Kerala Hindus of Arizona, e.g., promotes "unity and cooperation among Hindus without having any cast [*sic*] barriers." See Kerala Hindus of Arizona. (n.d.). *About Us.*

Chapter 7

1. Between 1950 and 1965, China sent just 10,689 students to twenty-nine countries, with about 80 percent heading to the Soviet Union. China suspended its overseas study program during the Cultural Revolution, with no students studying abroad between 1966 and 1972. See Miao, D. (2010). 出国留学六十年 [Sixty years of overseas study]. Central Party Literature Press.

2. India's IIT system stands as an exception, as discussed in chapter 6.

3. Smith, A. D. (1991). *National identity.* University of Nevada Press.

4. China's authoritarian political system also serves to deter foreigners from settling there. However, even if the PRC were to democratize, its ethnic national identity would still be a major barrier to successful brain gain.

5. It is worth noting the increasing relevance of Chinese as a second global language. As one international student at National Taiwan University told me in the summer of 2023, "I came to Taiwan to receive a Mandarin-language education." National Taiwan University student (interview, June 1, 2023). Certainly, this will be a trend to watch in the coming years.

6. Australian Government Department of Home Affairs. (n.d.b). *Global Talent Program.*

7. Greer, R. J. (1997). What is an asset class, anyway? *Journal of Portfolio Management, 23*(2), p. 86.

8. It is important to note that in China, this inward turn is due partly to geo-political tensions and not entirely the natural course of the Bs' interaction effects.

Chapter 8

1. Godo & Hayami (2010), p. 104.

2. Cavallini et al. (2018).

3. Official development assistance from Development Assistance Committee countries toward higher education amounted to USD 3.73 billion in 2014 but jumped to USD 6.67 billion in 2021—an almost twofold increase. OECD. (2007). *Cross-border tertiary education: A way towards capacity development.* International Bank for Reconstruction and Development & World Bank.

4. BRINK. (2017, February 21). *The brain as a commodity: Migration of labor in ASEAN.*

5. Docquier, F. (2014, May). *The brain drain from developing countries—the brain drain produces many more losers than winners in developing countries.* IZA World of Labor.

6. Since 2001, Singapore's Agency for Science, Technology and Research has offered scholarships that support students for overseas study at the undergraduate and graduate levels with the stipulation that they return and work for the agency's research institutes for a set number of years—a measure intended to prevent brain drain. Yarbrough, C. (2015). Singapore's talent strategy. *International Educator, 24*(4), p. 16.

7. The global average is 5.21. Global Economy. (2022). *Human flight and brain drain—country rankings.*

8. Susantono, B. (2015, September 29). Stopping ASEAN's brain drain. *Phnom Penh Post.*

9. Global Economy (2022).

10. While Ethiopia does not permit dual citizenship, foreign nationals of Ethiopian origin may receive a yellow card, which allots them certain privileges, such as exemption from residency or work permits.

11. Wolff, V., Opoku-Owusu, S., & Bloe, D. (2016). *Diaspora engagement on country entrepreneurship and investment: Policy trends and notable practices in the Rabat Process region.* International Centre for Migration Policy Development & African Foundation for Development.

12. Kuznetsov, Y., Nemirovsky, A., & Yoguel, G. (2006). Argentina: Burgeoning networks of talent abroad, weak institutions at home. In Y. Kuznetsov (Ed.), *Diaspora networks and the international migration of skills: How countries can draw on their talent abroad* (pp. 153–170). World Bank.

13. Ministerio de Ciencia, Tecnología e Innovación Argentina. (n.d.). *RAICES Program.* Red de Argentinos/as Investigadores/as, Científicos/as y Tecnólogos/as

en el Exterior, p. 1.

14. Margheritis, A. (2021). Diaspora engagement policies in Argentina: The unfolding of a still lukewarm approach. In V. Bravo & M. De Moya (Eds.), *Latin American diasporas in public diplomacy* (pp. 63–78). Palgrave Macmillan.

15. Kuznetsov et al. (2006).

16. This same paper finds that the smallest countries, with populations lower than one million, had substantial losses. Beine et al. (2008).

17. Fong, P. E. (2006). Foreign talent and development in Singapore. In C. Kuptsch and P. E. Fong (Eds.), *Competing for global talent* (pp. 155–168). International Institute for Labour Studies.

18. Ziguras, C., & Gribble, C. (2015). Policy responses to address student "brain drain": An assessment of measures intended to reduce the emigration of Singaporean international students. *Journal of Studies in International Education, 19*(3), 246–264.

19. Talent Corporation Malaysia Berhad (n.d.).

20. Mo Jongrin. (2013). 이민 강국: 인재 전쟁 시대 의 이민 정책 [Immigration powerhouse: Immigration policy in the era of talent wars]. Korean Studies Information Service System.

21. OECD. (2019b). *Recruiting immigrant workers: Korea 2019.*

22. Study International. (2018, April 10). *South Korea drops entry requirements, offers scholarships to international students.*

23. Shin & Choi (2015).

24. Moon & Shin (2019).

25. Gallo (2019).

26. Gallo (2019), p. 29.

27. These include eleven variables. Those variables related to external openness include foreign direct investment and technology transfer, prevalence of foreign ownership, migrant stock, international students, and brain gain. Those variables related to internal openness include tolerance of minorities, tolerance of immigrants, social mobility, women in tertiary education, women in highly skilled jobs, and business-leadership opportunities for women.

28. Lanvin & Monteiro (2022), p. 37.

29. SG101. (n.d.). *Building a multicultural Singapore.* Singaporean Government.

30. National Human Rights Commission of the Republic of Korea. (n.d.). *History.*

31. SG101 (n.d.).

32. Singaporean Housing & Development Board. (n.d.). *Ethnic integration policy (EIP) and Singapore permanent resident (SPR) quota.* Government of Singapore.

33. Lee, C. (2014, July 30). Koreans not ready for multiculturalism. *Korea Herald.*

34. Parreñas, R. S., & Kim, J. K. (2011). Multicultural East Asia: An introduction. *Journal of Ethnic and Migration Studies, 37*(10), 1555–1561.

35. Klein, M. (2016). Managing diversity: Is Australia bucking the post-multiculturalist trend or on its way to embrace interculturalism? *Australia and New Zealand Journal of European Studies, 8*(2), p. 66.

36. Esipova, N., Ray, J., & Pugliese, A. (2020, September 23). *World grows less accepting of migrants.* Gallup.

37. In 2016–2017, the United States' acceptance score was 7.86, and Australia's was 7.98, and in 2019, these rose to 7.95 and 8.28, respectively. Among seven European countries, three had significantly negative changes from 2014 to 2018, and three had significantly positive changes. See Gonzalez-Barrera, A., & Connor, P. (2019, March 14). *Around the world, more say immigrants are a strength than a burden.* Pew Research Center; Esipova, N., Ray, J., & Pugliese, A. (2018, April 26). *Migrant acceptance in Canada, U.S. follows political lines.* Gallup.

38. Dennison, J., Kustov, A., & Geddes, A. (2023). Public attitudes to immigration in the aftermath of Covid-19: Little change in policy preferences, big drops in issue salience. *International Migration Review, 57*(2), p. 567.

39. Shear, M. D., & Jordan, M. (2020, June 22). Trump suspends visas allowing hundreds of thousands of foreigners to work in the U.S. *New York Times.*

40. Institute of International Education. (n.d.a). *Academic level and places of origin.* Open Doors.

41. Immigration Advice Service. (n.d.). *Combination of Trump policy & COVID causes massive US work visa backlog.*

42. Sonnemaker, T., & Zaveri, P. (2020, June 22). *Amazon, Google, Apple, and other tech companies are speaking out against Trump's freeze on immigrant work visas.* Business Insider.

43. Kreighbaum, A. (2022, March 21). *Startup backers eye China competition bill to add new visa (1).* Bloomberg Law.

44. Muro, M. (2012, August 23). *Multiplier effects: Connecting the innovation and opportunity agendas.* Brookings Institution.

45. Kerr, W. R. (2018). *The gift of global talent: How migration shapes business, economy & society.* Stanford University Press, p. 176.

46. Treyz, F. R., Stottlemyer, C., & Motamedi, R. (2013, July 17). *Key components of immigration reform: An analysis of the economic effects of creating a pathway to legal status, expanding high-skilled visas, & reforming lesser-skilled visas.* Regional Economic Models.

47. Hua et al. (2022).

48. Silver, L. (2021, December 6). *Amid pandemic, international student enrollment at U.S. universities fell 15% in the 2020–21 school year.* Pew Research Center.

49. National Security Division. (2021, November 19). *Information about the De-*

partment of Justice's China Initiative and a compilation of China-related prosecutions since 2018. US Department of Justice.

50. Notably, comparatively few Chinese scientists feel that they are profiled by their university (12.2 percent) or by their colleagues (10.9 percent). Committee of 100 & University of Arizona. (2021). *Racial profiling among scientists of Chinese descent and consequences for the U.S. scientific community* [White paper].

51. Xie et al. (2023).

52. Committee of 100 & University of Arizona (2021).

53. Melbourne (thirteenth), Seoul (fifteenth, new to top thirty), Kuala Lumpur (eighteenth, new to top thirty), Hong Kong (twenty-first), and Beijing (twenty-third, new to top thirty) also rank in the top thirty. Singapore, New Zealand, Australia, and Japan all rank in the top-ten countries for global talent. Kovács-Ondrejkovic, O., Strack, R., Baier, J., Antebi, P., Kavanagh, K., & López Gobernado, A. (2021). *Decoding global talent, onsite and virtual.* Boston Consulting Group.

54. In higher education, in the aftermath of the pandemic, a majority of students still prefer at least some virtual learning, according to a 2023 McKinsey survey of seven thousand students in seventeen countries. The survey finds that while higher education students are still hesitant to enroll in fully online programs, 65 percent of them say "they want aspects of their learning experience to remain virtual" because they "appreciate the flexibility and convenience." Chad, F., Frank, M., Law, J., & Sarakatsannis, J. (2023, June 7). *What do higher education students want from online learning?* McKinsey.

55. Mao, F. (2021, May 26). *"Fortress Australia": Why calls to open up borders are meeting resistance.* BBC.

56. Ross, J. (2020, April 3). "Time to go home," Australian PM tells foreign students. *Times Higher Education.* See also Abrams, J. (2020, October 6). *Why international students are choosing the UK—despite coronavirus.* The Conversation.

57. Bavin, E. (2021, October 28). *"Global war for talent": Australia's great skills shortage.* Yahoo! Finance.

58. Parliament of Australia. (2021, March). *Interim report of the inquiry into Australia's skilled migration program: Foreword.*

Bibliography

Abbott, T. (2018, February 20). *Address to the Sydney Institute, Governor Phillip Tower, Sydney*. The Honourable Tony Abbott. Retrieved from http://tonyabbott.com.au/2018/02/address-sydney-institute-governor-phillip-tower-sydney/.

Abrams, J. (2020, October 6). *Why international students are choosing the UK—despite coronavirus*. The Conversation. Retrieved from https://theconversation.com/why-international-students-are-choosing-the-uk-despite-coronavirus-147064.

Academy of Human Resources Development. (August 2004). *Advances in Developing Human Resources, 6*(3).

Adeyemi, R. A., Joel, A., Ebenezer, J. T., & Attah, E. Y. (2018). The effect of brain drain on the economic development of developing countries: Evidence from selected African countries. *Journal of Health and Social Issues, 7*(2), 66–76. Retrieved from https://www.researchgate.net/publication/329814545_The_Effect_of_Brain_Drain_on_the_Economic_Development_of_Developing_Countries_Evidence_from_Selected_African_Countries.

Agarwal, V., Singla, H., Kashyap, P., & Mohan, R. (n.d.). *The global Indian fraternity: New locomotive of Indian real estate*. Square Yards. Retrieved November 14, 2022, from https://www.squareyards.com/blog/wp-content/uploads/2017/01/report-update-1-2.pdf.

Alberts, H. C., & Hazen, H. D. (2005). "There are always two voices . . .": International students' intentions to stay in the United States or return to their home countries. *International Migration, 43*(3), 131–154. Retrieved from https://doi.org/10.1111/j.1468-2435.2005.00328.x.

Alliance Manchester Business School. (2019, June 4). *The "Chunhui Cup" oversea students innovation and entrepreneurship competition*. University of Manchester.

Retrieved from https://www.alliancembs.manchester.ac.uk/news/the-chunhui-cu
p-oversea-students-innovation-and-entrepreneurship-competition/.

Altbach, P. G., & Knight, J. (2007). The internationalization of higher education: Motivations and realities. *Journal of Studies in International Education, 11*(3–
4), 290–305. Retrieved from https://doi.org/10.1177/1028315307303542.

Altbach, P. G., & Salmi, J. (Eds.). (2011). *The road to academic excellence: The
making of world-class research universities.* World Bank.

American Association for the Advancement of Science. (2012). Science in the
Chinese Academy of Sciences. *Science, 337*(6098), 1123. Retrieved from https://scie
nce.sciencemag.org/content/337/6098/1123.3. [Content no longer available.]

Anderson, S. (2021, August 10). Biden keeps costly Trump visa policy denying
Chinese grad students. *Forbes.* Retrieved from https://www.forbes.com/sites/stuar
tanderson/2021/08/10/biden-keeps-costly-trump-visa-policy-denying-chinese-gra
d-students/?sh=1a8998903641.

Aoki, R. (2013). A demographic perspective on Japan's "lost decades." *Population and Development Review, 38*(1), 103–112. Retrieved from https://doi.org/10.1111
/j.1728–4457.2013.00554.x.

Apollo Communications. (2019). *Australian top 50 CEOs report.* Retrieved from
https://apollocommunications.com.au/ceo-report/.

Arakali, H. (2020, January 10). Indian tech startups raise $14.5 billion in 2019,
up 25x from 2010. *Forbes India.* Retrieved from https://www.forbesindia.com/artic
le/special/indian-tech-startups-raise-145-billion-in-2019-up-25x-from-2010/57077/1
#:~:text=Funding%20over%20the%20last%20decade,acquisitions%20and%20817
%20active%20investors.

Ashoka University. (2023). *Admissions brochure.* Retrieved from https://www.as
hoka.edu.in/wp-content/uploads/2023/03/Ashoka-Brochure-2023.pdf_compresse
d.pdf.

Asian Development Bank. (2020). The role of markets, the state, and institutions. In *Asia's journey to prosperity: Policy, market, and technology over 50 years* (pp.
29–84). Asian Development Bank. Retrieved from https://www.adb.org/sites/defa
ult/files/publication/549191/asias-journey-prosperity.pdf.

Associated Press. (2023, April 12). *California scraps caste bias case against Cisco
engineers: Company still being sued.* NBC News. Retrieved from https://www.nbcn
ews.com/news/asian-america/calif-scraps-caste-bias-case-cisco-engineers-compan
y-still-sued-rcna79434.

Australian Bureau of Statistics. (1961). *1961 census: Birthplaces of the population
of Australia by states and territories.* Retrieved from https://www.ausstats.abs.gov.a
u/ausstats/free.nsf/0/E2E226D8C98EF964CA2578EA00207AE0/$File/1961%20C
ensus%20-%20Bulletin%20No%2030.pdf.

Australian Bureau of Statistics. (1988, January 1). *Year book Australia, 1988.* Re-

trieved from https://www.abs.gov.au/AusStats/ABS@.nsf/Previousproducts/1301.0
Feature%20Article161988?opendocument&tabname=Summary&prodno=1301.0&
issue=1988&num=&view=#:~:text=After%20World%20War%20II%20Australia,in
flow%20all%20contributed%20to%20growth.

Australian Bureau of Statistics. (2001). *2001 census community profiles*. Retrieved
from https://www.abs.gov.au/census/find-census-data/community-profiles/2001/0.

Australian Bureau of Statistics. (2013, October 4). *Doctors and nurses*. Department of the Treasury. Retrieved from https://www.abs.gov.au/ausstats/abs@.nsf/lo
okup/4102.0main+features20april+2013#:~:text=were%20much%20higher.-,WER
E%20MANY%20DOCTORS%20AND%20NURSES%20BORN%20OVERSE
AS%3F,and%2037%25%20respectively%20in%202001.

Australian Bureau of Statistics. (2016). *2016 census community profiles*. Retrieved
from https://www.abs.gov.au/census/find-census-data/community-profiles/2016/0.

Australian Bureau of Statistics. (2018). *India-born community information summary*. Department of the Treasury. Retrieved from https://www.homeaffairs.gov.a
u/mca/files/2016-cis-india.PDF.

Australian Bureau of Statistics. (2019). *Characteristics of recent migrants, November 2019*. Retrieved from https://www.abs.gov.au/statistics/people/people-and-
communities/characteristics-recent-migrants/latest-release#labour-market-outco
mes.

Australian Bureau of Statistics. (2021a). *Migration, Australia*. Department of
the Treasury. Retrieved from https://www.abs.gov.au/statistics/people/population/
migration-australia/latest-release.

Australian Bureau of Statistics. (2021b). *2021 census: All persons QuickStats*. Department of the Treasury. Retrieved from https://www.abs.gov.au/census/find-cen
sus-data/quickstats/2021/AUS.

Australian Federal Register of Legislation. (n.d.). *Australian Broadcasting Corporation Act 1983*. Australian Government. Retrieved July 13, 2021, from https://w
ww.legislation.gov.au/C2004A02723/2018-03-14/text.

Australian Government Department of Education. (n.d.). *Where do international students come from and what do they study?* International Education. Retrieved September 30, 2021, from https://internationaleducation.gov.au/research/
DataVisualisations/Pages/nationalitySummary.aspx.

Australian Government Department of Education. (2016, April 20). *National
Strategy for International Education 2025*. Retrieved from https://nsie.education.go
v.au/.

Australian Government Department of Education. (2019, March 13). *Historical
list of skill shortages in Australia*. Retrieved from https://www.dese.gov.au/labour-m
arket-information-portal/resources/historical-list-skill-shortages-australia.

Australian Government Department of Education. (2019). *International student*

data 2018—pivot tables. Retrieved from https://www.education.gov.au/higher-edu
cation-statistics/resources/student-enrolments-pivot-table.

Australian Government Department of Education. (2021, November 26). *Australian strategy for international education 2021–2030*. Retrieved from https://www.
education.gov.au/australian-strategy-international-education-2021–2030.

Australian Government Department of Education. (2023). *International student numbers by country, by state and territory*. Retrieved from https://www.educat
ion.gov.au/international-education-data-and-research/international-student-num
bers-country-state-and-territory.

Australian Government Department of Foreign Affairs and Trade. (n.d.). *Australia global alumni: Connect to a world of possibilities*. Retrieved June 20, 2021,
from https://www.dfat.gov.au/sites/default/files/global-alumni-brochure.pdf.

Australian Government Department of Foreign Affairs and Trade. (2017, November 21). *2017 foreign policy white paper*. Retrieved from https://www.dfat.gov.a
u/publications/minisite/2017-foreign-policy-white-paper/fpwhitepaper/foreign-pol
icy-white-paper.html.

Australian Government Department of Foreign Affairs and Trade. (2021). *Australia's assistance for education*. Retrieved from https://www.dfat.gov.au/aid/topics/
investment-priorities/education-health/education/Pages/education.

Australian Government Department of Home Affairs. (n.d.a). *Australia's migration program—country ranking 2018–19*. Australian Government Department of
Home Affairs. Retrieved July 20, 2022, from https://www.homeaffairs.gov.au/rese
arch-and-stats/files/country-position-2018–19.pdf.

Australian Government Department of Home Affairs. (n.d.b). *Global Talent
Program*. Retrieved July 20, 2022, from https://immi.homeaffairs.gov.au/visas/wo
rking-in-australia/visas-for-innovation/global-talent-independent-program.

Australian Government Department of Home Affairs. (n.d.c). *Temporary graduate visa (subclass 485)*. Retrieved January 13, 2022, from https://immi.homeaffairs
.gov.au/visas/getting-a-visa/visa-listing/temporary-graduate-485.

Australian Government Department of Home Affairs. (2020, March 17). *Australia's multicultural policy history*. Retrieved from https://www.homeaffairs.gov.au
/about-us/our-portfolios/multicultural-affairs/about-multicultural-affairs/our-poli
cy-history.

Australian Government Department of Home Affairs. (2021, January 29). *Australian Multicultural Council*. Retrieved from https://www.homeaffairs.gov.au/mc
a/Pages/australian-multicultural-council.aspx.

Australian Government Department of Home Affairs. (2021). *Australia's migration trends 2020–21*. Retrieved from https://www.homeaffairs.gov.au/research-a
nd-stats/files/migration-trends-highlights-2020–21.PDF.

Australian Government Department of Home Affairs. (2021, July 12a). *Country*

profile—India. Retrieved from https://www.homeaffairs.gov.au/research-and-stati
stics/statistics/country-profiles/profiles/india.

Australian Government Department of Home Affairs. (2021, July 12b). *Country profile—People's Republic of China.* Retrieved from https://www.homeaffairs.gov.au/ research-and-statistics/statistics/country-profiles/profiles/peoples-republic-of-china.

Australian Government Department of Home Affairs. (2021, July 12c). *Country profile—Philippines.* Retrieved from https://www.homeaffairs.gov.au/research-and -statistics/statistics//country-profiles/profiles/philippines.

Australian Government Department of Home Affairs. (2021, July 12d). *Country profile—United Kingdom.* Retrieved from https://www.homeaffairs.gov.au/rese arch-and-statistics/statistics/country-profiles/profiles/united-kingdom.

Australian Government Department of Home Affairs. (2023). *Historical migration statistics.* Retrieved from https://data.gov.au/data/dataset/historical-migration -statistics/resource/b59a15df-86ea-4c4c-95be-4dd9fc9f8ac4.

Australian Industry Commission. (1991). *Exports of education services, report 12.* Australian Government Publishing Service. Retrieved from https://www.pc.gov.a u/inquiries/completed/export-education-services/12educationservices.pdf.

Australian Strategic Policy Institute. (2022). *Critical technology tracker.* Re-trieved from https://aspi.org.au/report/critical-technology-tracker.

Azadi, P., Mirramezani, M., & Mesgaran, M. B. (2020). *Migration and brain drain from Iran.* Stanford Iran 2040 Project, 1–30. Retrieved from https://iranian-studies.st anford.edu/iran-2040-project/publications/migration-and-brain-drain-iran.

Babones, S. (2019). *The China student boom and the risks it poses to Australian universities.* Center for Independent Studies. Retrieved from https://www.cis.org.a u/wp-content/uploads/2019/08/ap5.pdf.

Bajpai, A. (2012). The "rise of Asia" thesis: Strategic constraints and theoretical deficits. *World Affairs: The Journal of International Issues, 16*(2), 12–37. Retrieved from https://www.jstor.org/stable/48504921.

Banerjee, I., Chanakya, A., Das, A. C., & Lal, A. (2020, August 4). *Global capability centers in the next normal.* McKinsey Digital. Retrieved from https://www .mckinsey.com/business-functions/mckinsey-digital/our-insights/global-capabilit y-centers-in-the-next-normal.

Banerjee, S. (2015, September 28). 10 things from Narendra Modi's speech at San Jose. *Business Standard.* Retrieved from https://www.business-standard.com/a rticle/current-affairs/10-things-from-narendra-modi-s-speech-at-san-jose-11509280 0795_1.html.

Barry, E., & Kolata, G. (2020, February 6). China's lavish funds lured U.S. scientists. What did it get in return? *New York Times.* Retrieved from https://www .nytimes.com/2020/02/06/us/chinas-lavish-funds-lured-us-scientists-what-did-it-g et-in-return.html.

Batalova, J., Shymonyak, A., & Sugiyarto, G. (2017). *Firing up regional brain networks: The promise of brain circulation in the ASEAN economic community.* Asian Development Bank. Retrieved from https://www.migrationpolicy.org/research/firing-regional-brain-networks-promise-brain-circulation-asean-economic-community.

Bavin, E. (2021, October 28). *"Global war for talent": Australia's great skills shortage.* Yahoo! Finance. Retrieved from https://au.finance.yahoo.com/news/australias-great-skills-shortage-235914173.html.

Becker, G. S. (1993). *Human capital: A theoretical and empirical analysis with special reference to education* (3rd ed.). University of Chicago Press.

Begin, J. P. (1997). *Dynamic human resource systems: Cross-national comparisons.* Walter de Gruyter.

Beine, M., Docquier, F., & Rapoport, H. (2008). Brain drain and human capital formation in developing countries: Winners and losers. *Economic Journal, 118*(528), 631–652. Retrieved from https://doi.org/10.1111/j.1468-0297.2008.02135.x.

Berelson, B. (1960). *Graduate education in the United States.* McGraw-Hill.

Berg, L., & Farbenblum, B. (2021). *As if we weren't humans: The abandonment of temporary migrants in Australia during COVID-19.* Migrant Justice Institute. Retrieved from https://static1.squarespace.com/static/593f6d9fe4fcb5c458624206/t/5f6056e68758b84c79540c5c/1600149242800/As+if+we+weren%E2%80%99t+humans+Report.pdf%20-.

Biddle, N. (2019, January 15). *Big Australia, small Australia, diverse Australia: Australia's views on population.* Australian National University Centre for Social Research & Methods. Retrieved from https://csrm.cass.anu.edu.au/research/publications/big-australia-small-australia-diverse-australia-australia-s-views-population.

Bier, D. J. (2020, May 20). *The facts about optional practical training (OPT) for foreign students.* CATO at Liberty. Retrieved from https://www.cato.org/blog/facts-about-optional-practical-training-opt-foreign-students.

Bloom, D. E., Hartley, M., & Rosovsky, H. (2007). Beyond private gain: The public benefits of higher education. In J. J. F. Forest & P. G. Altbach (Eds.), *International handbook of higher education* (pp. 293–308). Springer International Handbooks of Education. Retrieved from https://doi.org/10.1007/978-1-4020-4012-2_15.

Bloomberg. (2018, June 22). China's "Thousand Talents" plan key to seizing US expertise, intelligence officials say. *South China Morning Post.* Retrieved from https://www.scmp.com/news/china/policies-politics/article/2152005/chinas-thousand-talents-plan-key-seizing-us-expertise.

Bloomberg. (2021, December 6). Poll finds 89% in Japan back Kishida's ban on new foreign arrivals. *Japan Times.* Retrieved from https://www.japantimes.co.jp/news/2021/12/06/national/kishida-arrivals-ban-support/.

Boland, B., Dong, K., Blanchette, J., Hass, R., & Ye, E. (2024, June 17). *How*

China's human capital impacts its national competitiveness. Center for Strategic and International Studies. Retrieved from https://www.csis.org/analysis/how-chinas-h uman-capital-impacts-its-national-competitiveness.

Bowe, A. (2018). *China's overseas United Front work: Background and implications for the United States*. US-China Economic and Security Review Commission. Retrieved from https://www.uscc.gov/research/chinas-overseas-united-front-work -background-and-implications-united-states.

Brain, P. J., Smith, R. L., & Schuyers, G. P. (1979). *Population, immigration, and the Australian economy*. Croom Helm.

Breeze, V., & Moore, N. (2017, June 29). *China more popular than US with African students*. CNN. Retrieved from https://edition.cnn.com/2017/06/29/africa/af rican-students-china-us/index.html.

BRINK. (2017, February 21). *The brain as a commodity: Migration of labor in ASEAN*. Retrieved from https://www.brinknews.com/the-brain-as-a-commodity- migration-of-labor-in-asean/.

Brinkerhoff, J. M. (2012). Creating an enabling environment for diasporas' participation in homeland development. *International Migration, 50*(1), 75–95. Retrieved from https://doi.org/10.1111/j.1468–2435.2009.00542.x.

British Council. (2019, February 7). *Chiba University to make study abroad compulsory for all students from 2020*. Retrieved from https://opportunities-insight.briti shcouncil.org/news/market-news/chiba-university-make-study-abroad-compulsor y-all-students-2020.

Budiman, A., & Ruiz, N. G. (2021, April 29). *Key facts about Asian origin groups in the U.S.* Pew Research Center. Retrieved from https://www.pewresearch.org/fa ct-tank/2021/04/29/key-facts-about-asian-origin-groups-in-the-u-s/.

Burgess, C. (2020). Keeping the door closed: The 2018 revisions to the "Immigration" Control Act as a continuation of Japan's "no-immigration" principle. *Electronic Journal of Contemporary Japanese Studies, 20*(1), 1. Retrieved from https://ww w.japanesestudies.org.uk/ejcjs/vol20/iss1/burgess.html.

BusinessWire. (2020, October 28). *Australia's global talent visa program sees tech CEOs swap Silicon Valley for Sydney*. Retrieved from https://www.businesswire.co m/news/home/20201028005616/en/Australia%E2%80%99s-Global-Talent-Visa-Pr ogram-Sees-Tech-CEOs-Swap-Silicon-Valley-for-Sydney.

Canadian Bureau for International Education. (2021). *The student voice: National results of the 2021 CBIE International Student Survey*. Retrieved from https:// cbie.ca/student-surveys/.

Cao, C. (2004). *China's scientific elite*. Routledge.

Cao, C. (2008). China's brain drain at the high end: Why government policies have failed to attract first-rate academics to return. *Asian Population Studies, 4*(3), 331–345. Retrieved from https://doi.org/10.1080/17441730802496532.

Cao, C. (2017). *China's approaches to attract and nurture young biomedical researchers.* National Academies. Retrieved from https://sites.nationalacademies.org/cs/groups/pgasite/documents/webpage/pga_184821.pdf.

Cao, C., Baas, J., Wagner, C. S., & Jonkers, K. (2020). Returning scientists and the emergence of China's science system. *Science and Public Policy, 47*(2), 172–183. Retrieved from https://doi.org/10.1093/scipol/scz056.

Cao, N. T. K. (2022). Determinants of international students' decision to remain in Japan to work after graduation. *Journal of Asian Economics, 82*, 101529. Retrieved from https://doi.org/10.1016/j.asieco.2022.101529.

Capri, A. (2020, September 10). US-China techno-nationalism and the decoupling of innovation. *The Diplomat.* Retrieved from https://thediplomat.com/2020/09/us-china-techno-nationalism-and-the-decoupling-of-innovation/.

Cavallini, S., Soldi, R., di Matteo, L., Utma, M. A., & Errico, B. (2018). *Addressing brain drain: The local and regional dimension.* European Committee of the Regions. Retrieved from https://cor.europa.eu/en/engage/studies/Documents/addressing-brain-drain/addressing-brain-drain.pdf.

Cave, D., & Kwai, I. (2019, April 22). Why has Australia fallen out of love with immigration? *New York Times.* Retrieved from https://www.nytimes.com/2019/04/22/world/australia/immigration.html.

CB Insights. (n.d.). *The complete list of unicorn companies.* Retrieved August 27, 2021, from https://www.cbinsights.com/research-unicorn-companies.

Center for China & Globalization. (2017). *Attracting skilled international migrants to China: A review and comparison of policies and practices.* International Labour Organization & International Organization for Migration. Retrieved from https://www.ilo.org/sites/default/files/wcmsp5/groups/public/@asia/@ro-bangkok/@ilo-beijing/documents/publication/wcms_565474.pdf.

Center for China & Globalization. (2019). *List of 70 influential returnees in 70 years of PRC released.* Retrieved from http://en.ccg.org.cn/archives/59303.

Cerna, L., & Chou, M. H. (2022). Politics of internationalisation and the migration-higher education nexus. *Globalisation, Societies and Education, 21*(2), 222–235. Retrieved from https://doi.org/10.1080/14767724.2022.2073975.

Cervantes, M., & Guellec, D. (2002). The brain drain: Old myths, new realities. *OECD Observer,* (230), 40–42. Retrieved from https://www.proquest.com/docview/217470347?sourcetype=Scholarly%20Journals.

CGTN. (2018, March 7). *Xi Jinping: Talents are primary resources for China's development* [Video]. YouTube. https://www.youtube.com/watch?v=xMTJrComfIw.

Chacko, E. (2007). From brain drain to brain gain: Reverse migration to Bangalore and Hyderabad, India's globalizing high tech cities. *GeoJournal, 68*(2), 131–140. Retrieved from https://www.jstor.org/stable/41148150.

Chad, F., Frank, M., Law, J., & Sarakatsannis, J. (2023, June 7). *What do higher education students want from online learning?* McKinsey. Retrieved from https://w ww.mckinsey.com/industries/public-sector/our-insights/what-do-higher-educatio n-students-want-from-online-learning.

Chadha, A. (2006, June 25). Battle for brand IIT. *The Hindu*. Retrieved from http://www.thehindu.com/todays-paper/tp-features/tp-sundaymagazine/battle-fo r-brand-iit/article3232237.ece.

Chakravorty, S., Kapur, D., & Singh, N. (2016). *The other one percent: Indians in America*. Oxford University Press.

Chang, W.-Y., & Milan, L. M. (2014). *Employment decisions of U.S. and foreign doctoral graduates: A comparative study*. National Science Foundation. Retrieved from https://www.nsf.gov/statistics/infbrief/nsf15302/nsf15302.pdf.

Chavda, J. (2023). *Immigrants and children of immigrants make up at least 15% of the 118th Congress*. Pew Research Center. Retrieved from https://www.pewresearch .org/short-reads/2023/02/28/immigrants-and-children-of-immigrants-make-up-at -least-15-of-the-118th-congress/.

Chen, L. K., Mourshed, M., & Grant, A. (2013, May). *The $250 billion question: Can China close the skills gap?* McKinsey. Retrieved from https://www.mckinsey .com/~/media/mckinsey/industries/public%20and%20social%20sector/our%20ins ights/the%20250%20billion%20question%20can%20china%20close%20the%20sk ills%20gap/the%20dollar%20250%20billion%20question%20can%20china%20clo se%20the%20skills%20gap.pdf.

Chen, Q., & Li, Y. (2019). Mobility, knowledge transfer, and innovation: An empirical study on returned Chinese academics at two research universities. *Sustainability*, *11*(22), 6454. Retrieved from https://doi.org/10.3390/su11226454.

Chen, Y. C. (2008). The limits of brain circulation: Chinese returnees and technological development in Beijing. *Pacific Affairs*, *81*(2), 195–215. Retrieved from https://doi.org/10.5509/2008812195.

China Innovation Funding. (n.d.). 千人计划 [Thousand Talents Program]. Retrieved September 20, 2021, from https://storage.googleapis.com/public-talent-sou rces/talent_039/Source%202.pdf.

Chinese Academy of Sciences. (2013, July 9). *Scientists develop new method for synthesizing high-quality graphene*. Suzhou Institute of Biomedical Engineering and Technology. [Content no longer available.]

Chinese city offers Nobel Prize winners $15 mln housing subsidies. (2022, May 12). Reuters. Retrieved from https://www.reuters.com/world/asia-pacific/chinese-city- offers-nobel-prize-winners-15-mln-housing-subsidies-2022-05-12/.

Chokki, S., Odawara, H., Sandler, C., & Tsuda, T. (2020). *A new era for industrial R&D in Japan*. McKinsey. Retrieved from https://www.mckinsey.com/busin ess-functions/operations/our-insights/a-new-era-for-industrial-rnd-in-japan.

Chopra, K. L. (n.d.). *Professor GS Sanyal: A tribute*. Maulana Abul Kalam Azad

University of Technology, West Bengal. Retrieved August 16, 2021, from https://m
akautwb.ac.in/datas/users/0-gs_sanyal.pdf.

Clayton, A. (2023, October 8). Ban on caste discrimination deemed "unnecessary" by California governor. *The Guardian*. Retrieved from https://www.theguar
dian.com/us-news/2023/oct/07/california-caste-discrimination-ban-vetoed-gavin-
newsom.

Coghlan, A., & Geake, E. (1992, February 15). Industry "does not need research." *New Scientist*. Retrieved from https://www.newscientist.com/article/mg13
318080-800-industry-does-not-need-research/.

Columbia Business School. (2013, September 30). Reversing the brain drain.
Chazen Global Insights. https://business.columbia.edu/cgi-leadership/chazen-globa
l-insights/reversing-brain-drain.

Committee of 100 & University of Arizona. (2021). Racial profiling among
scientists of Chinese descent and consequences for the U.S. scientific community
[White paper]. Retrieved from https://www.committee100.org/projects/white-pap
er-2/.

Committee on Homeland Security and Governmental Affairs. (2019). *Threats
to the U.S. research enterprise: China's talent recruitment plans*. US Senate. Retrieved
from https://www.hsgac.senate.gov/imo/media/doc/2019-11-18%20PSI%20Staff%2
0Report%20-%20China's%20Talent%20Recruitment%20Plans.pdf.

Communist Party of China Central Organization Department. (2020, July). "
千人计划"高层次外国专家项目工作细则 [Detailed rules for the "Thousand
Talents Program" high-level foreign expert project]. CSET. Retrieved from https://
/cset.georgetown.edu/publication/detailed-rules-for-the-thousand-talents-progra
m-high-level-foreign-expert-project/.

Community Development Division. (2012, September). *International student
strategy discussion paper*. Knowledge Melbourne. Retrieved from https://s3-ap-sout
heast-2.amazonaws.com/ehq-production-australia/846168e28515e9b02d5f09acffc4
df291a770823/documents/attachments/000/000/356/original/International_Stude
nt_Strategy_Discussion_Paper_September_2012.pdf?1380867359.

Congressional Research Service. (2022). *Global research and development expenditures: Fact sheet*. US Library of Congress. Retrieved from https://sgp.fas.org/crs/
misc/R44283.pdf.

Coorey, P. (2022, July 19). Permanent skilled workers to be top priority in immigration revamp. *Australian Financial Review*. Retrieved from https://www.afr
.com/politics/federal/permanent-skilled-workers-to-be-top-priority-in-immigratio
n-revamp-20220719-p5b20i.

Coronavirus: China warns students over "risks" of studying in Australia. (2020,
June 9). BBC. Retrieved from https://www.bbc.com/news/world-asia-china-52980
637.

Council of Indian Institute of Technology. (n.d.). *History*. Retrieved October 25, 2024, from https://www.iitsystem.ac.in/history.

Crace, A. (2017, February 10). *International student completion rates remain high in Australia*. PIE News. Retrieved from https://thepienews.com/news/internationa l-student-completion-australia/.

Cumings, B. (1984). The legacy of Japanese colonialism in Korea. In R. Myers & M. Peattie (Eds.), *The Japanese colonial empire, 1895–1945* (pp. 478–496). Princeton University Press.

Cummings, W. (1972). *Nihon no Daigaku Kyoju* [University professors in Japan]. Shiseido.

Cummings, W. K., & Amano, I. (1977). The changing role of the Japanese professor. *Higher Education, 6*, 209–234. Retrieved from https://doi.org/10.1007/BF0014 1879.

Cusumano, M. A. (1988, October 15). Manufacturing innovation: Lessons from the Japanese auto industry. *MIT Sloan Management Review*. Retrieved from https: //sloanreview.mit.edu/article/manufacturing-innovation-lessons-from-the-japanes e-auto-industry/.

Cutts, R. L. (1997). *An empire of schools: Japan's universities and the molding of a national power elite*. Routledge.

Cyranoski, D., Gilbert, N., Ledford, H., Nayar, A., & Yahia, M. (2011). Education: The PhD factory. *Nature, 472*(7343), 276–280. Retrieved from https://doi.org /10.1038/472276a.

Czaika, M., & Parsons, C. R. (2017). The gravity of high-skilled migration policies. *Demography, 54*(2), 603–630. Retrieved from https://doi.org/10.1007/s1352 4-017-0559-1.

Dai, O., & Liu, X. (2009). Returnee entrepreneurs and firm performance in Chinese high-technology industries. *International Business Review, 18*(4), 373–386. Retrieved from https://doi.org/10.1016/j.ibusrev.2009.03.004.

Daikin Global. (n.d.). *Fostering human resources*. Retrieved January 5, 2022, from https://www.daikin.com/csr/employee/development.html.

Daugeliene, R., & Marcinkeviciene, R. (2009). Brain circulation: Theoretical considerations. *Engineering economics, 63*(3), 49–57. Retrieved from https://www.re searchgate.net/publication/228931144_Brain_circulation_Theoretical_considerati ons.

Dayasindhu, N. (2002). Embeddedness, knowledge transfer, industry clusters and global competitiveness: A case study of the Indian software industry. *Technovation, 22*(9), 551–560. Retrieved from https://doi.org/10.1016/S0166–4972(01)0009 8–0.

D'Costa, A. P. (2008). The barbarians are here. *Asian Population Studies, 4*(3), 311–329. Retrieved from https://doi.org/10.1080/17441730802496524.

Debroux, P. (2003). *Human resource management in Japan: Changes and uncertainties.* Ashgate.

Dennison, J., Kustov, A., & Geddes, A. (2023). Public attitudes to immigration in the aftermath of Covid-19: Little change in policy preferences, big drops in issue salience. *International Migration Review, 57*(2), 557–577. Retrieved from https://doi.org/10.1177/01979183221134272.

Department of Economic and Social Affairs, Population Division. (2019). *World population prospects: The 2019 revision.* United Nations. Retrieved from http s://population.un.org/wpp2019/Download/Standard/Interpolated/.

Ding, S., & Koslowski, R. (2017). Chinese soft power and immigration reform: Can Beijing's approach to pursuing global talent and maintaining domestic stability succeed? *Journal of Chinese Political Science, 22*(1), 97–116. Retrieved from http s://doi.org/10.1007/s11366-016-9417-z.

Docquier, F. (2014, May). *The brain drain from developing countries—the brain drain produces many more losers than winners in developing countries.* IZA World of Labor. Retrieved from https://wol.iza.org/uploads/articles/31/pdfs/brain-drain-fro m-developing-countries.pdf?v=1.

Domingo, R. (2003). *Management: Japanese style.* RTDOnline. Retrieved from http://www.rtdonline.com/BMA/ABM/3.html.

Dossani, R. (2002). *Chinese and Indian engineers and their networks in Silicon Valley.* Asia-Pacific Research Center, Stanford University. Retrieved from https://a parc.fsi.stanford.edu/publications/chinese_and_indian_engineers_and_their_net works_in_silicon_valley.

Dossani, R., & Kenney, M. (2002). Creating an environment for venture capital in India. *World Development, 30*(2), 227–253. Retrieved from https://doi.org/10. 1016/S0305–750X(01)00110–3.

Draper Richards Kaplan Foundation. (n.d.). *Team—Robin Richards Donohoe.* Retrieved November 13, 2024, from https://www.drkfoundation.org/team-membe r/robin-richards-donohoe/#:~:text=The%20Draper%20International%20India%20 fund,acquisitions%2C%20including%20Hotmail%20and%20Skype.

Drucker, P. F. (March 1971). What we can learn from Japanese management. *Harvard Business Review.* Retrieved from https://hbr.org/1971/03/what-we-can-lear n-from-japanese-management.

Duara, P. (2018). *Nationalism and development in Asia* (Working paper no. 2018/95). WIDER. Retrieved from https://www.wider.unu.edu/sites/default/files/P ublications/Working-paper/PDF/wp2018–95.pdf.

Dugger, C. W. (2000, February 29). Return passage to India: Emigres pay back. *New York Times.* Retrieved from https://www.nytimes.com/2000/02/29/wor ld/return-passage-to-india-emigres-pay-back.html.

Dutt, E. (2018, December 6). Immigrants, including Indians and Indian-

Americans, crucial to health care services. *News India Times*. Retrieved from http s://www.newsindiatimes.com/immigrants-including-indians-and-indian-america ns-crucial-to-health-care-services/.

Duttagupta, I. (2007, September 20). Govt to handhold skilled Indians to land jobs abroad. *Economic Times*. Retrieved from https://economictimes.indiatimes .com/the-global-indian-takeover/govt-to-handhold-skilled-indians-to-land-jobs-a broad/articleshow/2384640.cms?from=mdr.

Duttagupta, I. (2019, November 22). "Post study work policy" attracting more Indian students, says Australian education minister. *Economic Times*. Retrieved from https://economictimes.indiatimes.com/nri/visa-and-immigration/post-study -work-policy-attracting-more-indian-students-says-australian-education-minister/ articleshow/72183211.cms?from=mdr#:~:text=Synopsis,year%2C%20according%20 to%20an%20official.

Dye, Z. (2017, September 18). Zhongguancun Index 2017. *China Daily*. Re-trieved from http://www.chinadaily.com.cn/m/beijing/zhongguancun/2017–09/18 /content_32162437_2.htm.

Eckert, C. J. (1991). *Offspring of empire: The Koch'ang Kims and the colonial ori-gins of Korean capitalism, 1876–1945*. University of Washington Press.

Education Desk. (2020, December 5). Responsibility of post COVID world is huge but your shoulders capable, PM to IIT alumni. *Indian Express*. Retrieved from https://indianexpress.com/article/education/pm-modi-to-address-iit-global-s ummit-today-7091296/.

Elderly citizens accounted for record 28.4% of Japan's population in 2018, data show. (2019, September 15). *Japan Times*. Retrieved from https://www.japantimes. co.jp/news/2019/09/15/national/elderly-citizens-accounted-record-28–4-japans-po pulation-2018-data-show/.

Ellis, S. (2018, January 17). Biotech booms in China [Supplemental material]. *Nature, 553*, S19–S22. Retrieved from https://doi.org/10.1038/d41586-018-00542-3.

Esipova, N., Ray, J., & Pugliese, A. (2018, April 26). *Migrant acceptance in Canada, U.S. follows political lines*. Gallup. Retrieved from https://news.gallup.com/ poll/233147/migrant-acceptance-canada-follows-political-lines.aspx.

Esipova, N., Ray, J., & Pugliese, A. (2020, September 23). *World grows less ac-cepting of migrants*. Gallup. Retrieved from https://news.gallup.com/poll/320678/w orld-grows-less-accepting-migrants.aspx.

Ferguson, H., & Spinks, H. (2021, April 23). *Overseas students in Australian higher education: A quick guide*. Parliament of Australia. Retrieved from https://w ww.aph.gov.au/About_Parliament/Parliamentary_Departments/Parliamentary_L ibrary/pubs/rp/rp2021/Quick_Guides/OverseasStudents.

Filatotchev, I., Liu, X., Lu, J., & Wright, M. (2011). Knowledge spillovers through human mobility across national borders: Evidence from Zhongguancun

Science Park in China. *Research Policy, 40*(3), 453–462. Retrieved from https://doi.org/10.1016/j.respol.2011.01.003.

Finn, M. G. (1996). The stay rate of foreign doctoral students in science and engineering. In T. M. Davis (Ed.), *Open Doors 1995–1996: Report on international educational exchange* (pp. 121–122). Institute of International Education. Retrieved from https://files.eric.ed.gov/fulltext/ED404959.pdf.

Finn, M. G., & Pennington, L. A. (2018). *Stay rates of foreign doctorate recipients from U.S. universities, 2013.* Office of Scientific and Technical Information, US Department of Energy. Retrieved from https://www.osti.gov/servlets/purl/1425458/.

Florez, C. (2020, August 17). *Australia's international students are going hungry, with 60 per cent now unemployed.* SBS News. Retrieved from https://www.sbs.com.au/news/article/australias-international-students-are-going-hungry-with-60-per-cent-now-unemployed/ocb102066.

Florida, R., & Kenney, M. (1994). The globalization of Japanese R&D: The economic geography of Japanese R&D investment in the United States. *Economic Geography, 70*(4), 344–369. Retrieved from https://doi.org/10.2307/143728.

Fong, P. E. (2006). Foreign talent and development in Singapore. In C. Kuptsch and P. E. Fong (Eds.), *Competing for global talent* (pp. 155–168). International Institute for Labour Studies. Retrieved from https://www.ilo.org/publications/competing-global-talent.

Forester, T. (1993). How Japan became no. 1 in IT. *Policy, Organisation and Society, 6*(1), 25–32. Retrieved from https://doi.org/10.1080/10349952.1993.11876784.

Fraser, S. E. (1984). Australia and international education: The Goldring and Jackson reports—mutual aid or uncommon advantage? *Vestes, 27*(2), 15–29. Retrieved from https://files.eric.ed.gov/fulltext/EJ321245.pdf.

Freeman, R. B. (1976). *The overeducated American.* Academic Press.

FrontAd Media. (2020, February 11). *The NRI's contribution to the Indian economy.* CompareRemit. Retrieved from https://www.compareremit.com/money-transfer-guide/the-nris-contribution-to-the-indian-economy/.

Fund for Peace. (2022). *Global data.* Fragile States Index. Retrieved from https://fragilestatesindex.org/global-data/.

Gallo, M. (2019). *Ireland global alumni network: Scoping research study.* Retrieved from https://static1.squarespace.com/static/58b0a415d482e9ff05247c85/t/5ff9bed4346f08773289a0f5/1610202838707/Ireland+Global+Alumni+Scoping+Study+Final+Nov+2019.pdf.

Gandhi, S. (2007, October 1). *Address by Smt. Sonia Gandhi chairperson of the UPA to Indian Overseas Congress and other Indian organisations, New York* [Transcript]. Embassy of India. Retrieved from https://www.indianembassyusa.gov.in/ArchivesDetails?id=836.

Gao, C. (2017, December 15). Australia and China spat over foreign interference escalates. *The Diplomat*. Retrieved from https://thediplomat.com/2017/12/australia-and-china-spat-over-foreign-interference-escalates/.

Gellner, E. (1983). *Nations and nationalism*. Basil Blackwell.

Gerschenkron, A. (1962). *Economic backwardness in historical perspective: A book of essays*. Belknap Press of Harvard University Press.

Gerstein, J. (2022, February 18). *Report details collapse of China Initiative case*. Politico. Retrieved from https://www.politico.com/news/2022/02/18/china-initiative-case-00010281.

Gilbert, N. (2022, March 7). "I lost two years of my life": US scientist falsely accused of hiding ties to China speaks out. *Nature, 603*(7901), 371–372. Retrieved from https://doi.org/10.1038/d41586-022-00528-2.

Gilbert, N., & Kozlov, M. (2022, March). The controversial China Initiative is ending—researchers are relieved. *Nature, 603*(7900), 214–215. Retrieved from https://doi.org/10.1038/d41586-022-00555-z.

Gilson, R. J., & Roe, M. J. (1999). Lifetime employment: Labor peace and the evolution of Japanese corporate governance. *Columbia Law Review, 99*(508), 508–541. Retrieved from https://scholarship.law.columbia.edu/cgi/viewcontent.cgi?article=1056&context=faculty_scholarship.

Global Economy. (2022). *Human flight and brain drain—country rankings*. Retrieved from https://www.theglobaleconomy.com/rankings/human_flight_brain_drain_index/Asia/#:~:text=The%20average%20for%202022%20based,available%20from%202007%20to%202022.

Godo, Y., & Hayami, Y. (2010). The human capital basis of the Japanese miracle: A historical perspective. In K. Otsuka & K. Kalirajan (Eds.), *Community, market and state in development* (pp. 103–120). Palgrave & Macmillan.

Godo, Y., & Hayami, Y. (2002). Catching up in education in the economic catch-up of Japan with the United States, 1890–1990. *Economic Development and Cultural Change, 50*(4), 961–978. Retrieved from https://doi.org/10.1086/342762.

Goel, V. (2015, September 27). Narendra Modi, Indian premier, courts Silicon Valley to try to ease nation's poverty. *New York Times*. Retrieved from https://www.nytimes.com/2015/09/28/technology/narendra-modi-prime-minister-of-india-visits-silicon-valley.html.

Goel, V. (2017, October 8). IBM shifts center of gravity half a world away, to India. *Seattle Times*. Retrieved from https://www.seattletimes.com/business/ibm-shifts-center-of-gravity-half-a-world-away-to-india/.

Gonzalez-Barrera, A., & Connor, P. (2019, March 14). *Around the world, more say immigrants are a strength than a burden*. Pew Research Center. Retrieved from https://www.pewresearch.org/global/2019/03/14/around-the-world-more-say-immigrants-are-a-strength-than-a-burden/.

Grassby, A. J. (1973). *A multi-cultural society for the future*. Australian Government Publishing Service. Retrieved from https://www.multiculturalaustralia.edu.au/doc/grassby_1.pdf.

Green, D. (2019). Foreign faculty in Japan. *PS: Political Science & Politics*, *52*(3), 523–526. Retrieved from https://doi.org/10.1017/S104909651900043X.

Greenfeld, L. (1992). *Nationalism: Five roads to modernity.* Harvard University Press.

Greer, R. J. (1997). What is an asset class, anyway? *Journal of Portfolio Management*, *23*(2), 86–91. Retrieved from https://doi.org/10.3905/jpm.23.2.86.

Grubel, H. G. (1968). The reduction of the brain drain: Problems and policies. *Minerva*, *6*, 541–558. Retrieved from https://doi.org/10.1007/BF01096547.

Gruber Foundation. (n.d.). *Mu-Ming Poo.* Yale University. Retrieved October 4, 2024, from https://gruber.yale.edu/recipient/mu-ming-poo.

Hamilton, C., & Joske, A. (2018). *Silent invasion: China's influence in Australia.* Hardie Grant Books.

Hammond, C. D. (2019). Dynamics of higher education research collaboration and regional integration in Northeast Asia: A study of the A3 Foresight Program. *Higher Education*, *78*(4), 653–668. Retrieved from https://doi.org/10.1007/s10734-019-00363-x.

Han, S. J. (1999). Asian values: An asset or a liability? In H. S. Joo (Ed.), *Changing values in Asia: Their impact on governance and development* (pp. 3–9). Japan Center for International Exchange.

Hannas, W. C., & Tatlow, D. K. (Eds.). (2020). *China's quest for foreign technology: Beyond espionage.* Routledge.

Hanushek, E. A., & Wößmann, L. (2007). *The role of education quality for economic growth.* World Bank Group. Retrieved from http://documents.worldbank.org/curated/en/260461468324885735/The-role-of-education-quality-for-economic-growth.

Hao, X. (2006). Frustrations mount over China's high-priced hunt for trophy professors. *Science*, *313*(5794), 1721–1723. Retrieved from https://doi.org/10.1126/science.313.5794.1721.

Hao, X., Yan, K., Guo, S., & Wang, M. (2017). Chinese returnees' motivation, post-return status and impact of return: A systematic review. *Asian and Pacific Migration Journal*, *26*(1), 143–157. Retrieved from https://doi.org/10.1177/0117196817690294.

Harbison, F. H., & Myers, C. A. (1965). *Manpower and education: Country studies in economic development.* McGraw-Hill.

Harrap, B., Hawthorne, L., Holland, M., McDonald, J. T., & Scott, A. (2021). Australia's superior skilled migration outcomes compared with Canada's. *International Migration*, *60*(5), 91–107. Retrieved from https://doi.org/10.1111/imig.12940.

Hawthorne, L. (2018). Attracting and retaining international students as skilled migrants. In M. Czaika (Ed.), *High-skilled migration: Drivers and policies* (pp. 195–221). Oxford University Press. Retrieved from https://doi.org/10.1093/oso/9780198815273.003.0010.

Hawthorne, L. (2022, July 14–15). [Presentation on Australia's higher education and brain gain.] Presented at a manuscript workshop for this volume, Zoom.

Hayami, Y., & Godo, Y. (2005). *Development economics: From the poverty to the wealth of nations*. Oxford University Press.

Hayes, A. (2022, December 4). *Skilled Labor: Definition, training, vs. unskilled*. Investopedia. Retrieved from https://www.investopedia.com/terms/s/skilled-labor.asp.

Hazen, H. D., & Alberts, H. C. (2006). Visitors or immigrants? International students in the United States. *Population, Space and Place, 12*(3), 201–216. Retrieved from https://doi.org/10.1002/psp.409.

He, D., & Yang, Y. (2013, July 29). China's brain drain may be world's worst. *China Daily*. Retrieved from http://www.chinadaily.com.cn/china/2013–07/29/content_16845100.htm.

Heitor, M., Horta, H., & Mendonça, J. (2014). Developing human capital and research capacity: Science policies promoting brain gain. *Technological Forecasting and Social Change, 82*, 6–22. Retrieved from https://doi.org/10.1016/j.techfore.2013.07.008.

Hira, R. (2015, February 19). *New data show how firms like Infosys and Tata abuse the H-1B program*. Working Economics Blog. Retrieved from https://www.epi.org/blog/new-data-infosys-tata-abuse-h-1b-program/.

HNIs to invest $30 billion in Indian tech startups by 2025: Report. (2021, June 17). *Economic Times*. Retrieved from https://economictimes.indiatimes.com/tech/startups/hnis-to-invest-30-billion-in-indian-tech-startups-by-2025-report/articleshow/83607846.cms?from=mdr.

Ho, E., Li, W., Cooper, J., & Holmes, P. (2007). *The experiences of Chinese international students in New Zealand*. Universities NZ–Te Pōkai Tara. Retrieved from https://www.universitiesnz.ac.nz/latest-news-and-publications/what-happens-international-students-who-remain-new-zealand-after.

Ho, N. T. T., Seet, P. S., & Jones, J. (2015). Understanding re-expatriation intentions among overseas returnees—an emerging economy perspective. *International Journal of Human Resource Management, 27*(17), 1938–1966. Retrieved from https://doi.org/10.1080/09585192.2015.1088884.

Hof, H., & Tseng, Y. F. (2020). When "global talents" struggle to become local workers: The new face of skilled migration to corporate Japan. *Asian and Pacific Migration Journal, 29*(4), 511–531. Retrieved from https://doi.org/10.1177/0117196820984088.

Hong, M. (2023). Australia's international alumni engagement strategy: An approach from soft power to knowledge diplomacy. *Studies in Higher Education*, *49*(3), 460–475. https://doi.org/10.1080/03075079.2023.2238763.

Horta, H., Sato, M., & Yonezawa, A. (2011). Academic inbreeding: Exploring its characteristics and rationale in Japanese universities using a qualitative perspective. *Asia Pacific Education Review*, *12*, 35–44. Retrieved from https://doi.org/10.1007/s12564-010-9126-9.

Hua, S., Hao, K., & Korn, M. (2022, August 11). Chinese student visas to U.S. tumble from prepandemic levels. *Wall Street Journal*. Retrieved from https://www.wsj.com/articles/chinese-student-visas-to-u-s-tumble-from-prepandemic-levels-11660210202.

Huang, F. (2009). The internationalization of the academic profession in Japan: A quantitative perspective. *Journal of Studies in International Education*, *13*(2), 143–158. Retrieved from https://doi.org/10.1177/1028315308331101.

Huang, F. (2017). *Who are they and why did they move to Japan? An analysis of international faculty at universities* (Working paper no. 27). Centre for Global Higher Education. Retrieved from https://www.researchcghe.org/wp-content/uploads/migrate/publications/wp27.pdf.

Huang, H. (n.d.). [爱国] 中科院第一位外籍所长蒲慕明恢复中国国籍，"我从来都认为自己是中国人" [[Patriotic] Pu Muming, the first foreign director of the Chinese Academy of Sciences, regained Chinese nationality, "I have always considered myself Chinese"]. Center for Excellence in Brain Science and Intelligent Technology, Chinese Academy of Sciences. Retrieved January 11, 2022, from http://www.cebsit.cas.cn/zt/hykxjjs/jxdt/202011/t20201125_5779688.html.

Huang, K., & Ho, K. (2019, January 6). As China and US spar over tech, scientists would rather not talk about their talent awards. *South China Morning Post*. Retrieved from https://www.scmp.com/news/china/diplomacy/article/2180752/china-and-us-spar-over-tech-scientists-would-rather-not-talk.

Huang, T. T. (2020, May 7). China stops promoting "Thousand Talents plan." *Taiwan News*. Retrieved from https://www.taiwannews.com.tw/en/news/3929496.

Hugo, G. (2001, June). *International migration transforms Australia*. Population Reference Bureau. Retrieved from https://www.prb.org/resources/international-migration-transforms-australia/.

Hugo, G. (2006). An Australian diaspora? *International Migration*, *44*(1), 105–133. Retrieved from https://doi.org/10.1111/j.1468-2435.2006.00357.x.

ICEF Monitor. (2015, November 23). *Signs of strengthening demand for study abroad in Japan*. Retrieved from https://monitor.icef.com/2015/11/signs-of-strengthening-demand-for-study-abroad-in-japan/.

ICEF Monitor. (2019, November 6). *More than 750,000 Indian students abroad in 2018*. Retrieved from https://monitor.icef.com/2019/11/more-than-750000-indian-students-abroad-in-2018/.

IIT Kharagpur Foundation. (n.d.). *The mission and vision of the IITKGP Foundation*. Retrieved August 2, 2021, from https://www.iitkgpfoundation.org/mission.html.

Imahashi, R. (2020, May 10). Japan's foreign students struggle to stay and study amid pandemic. *Nikkei Asia*. Retrieved from https://asia.nikkei.com/Business/Education/Japan-s-foreign-students-struggle-to-stay-and-study-amid-pandemic2.

Immigration Advice Service. (n.d.). *Combination of Trump policy & COVID causes massive US work visa backlog*. Retrieved October 28, 2024, from https://us.iasservices.org.uk/us-work-visa-backlog/.

The Immigration Restriction Act 1901. (n.d.). National Archives of Australia. Retrieved June 20, 2022, from https://www.naa.gov.au/explore-collection/immigration-and-citizenship/immigration-restriction-act-1901.

India Ministry of External Affairs. (n.d.a). *India Centre for Migration (ICM)*. Retrieved August 2, 2021, from https://mea.gov.in/icm.htm.

India Ministry of External Affairs. (n.d.b). *Nationality wise OCI card issued*. Retrieved August 1, 2021, from https://www.mha.gov.in/MHA1/Par2017/pdfs/par2020-pdfs/ls-17032020/3695.pdf.

India Ministry of External Affairs. (n.d.c). *Population of overseas Indians*. Retrieved July 30, 2021, from https://www.mea.gov.in/images/attach/NRIs-and-PIOs_1.pdf.

India Ministry of External Affairs. (2023). *India-Bahrain bilateral relations*. Retrieved from https://www.mea.gov.in/Portal/ForeignRelation/India_Bahrain.pdf.

Indians form 2nd largest group of international students in US. (2017, November 13). *Economic Times*. Retrieved from https://economictimes.indiatimes.com/nri/visa-and-immigration/indians-form-2nd-largest-group-of-international-students-in-us/articleshow/61624993.cms?from=mdr.

Institute for Interdisciplinary Information Sciences. (n.d.). *Yao Class*. Tsinghua University. Retrieved December 13, 2021, from https://iiis.tsinghua.edu.cn/en/yaoclass/.

Institute for Management Development. (2022). *IMD world talent ranking*. IMD World Competitiveness Center. Retrieved from https://www.imd.org/wp-content/uploads/2023/03/2022-imd-world-talent-ranking-1.pdf.

Institute of International Education. (n.d.a). *Academic level and places of origin*. Open Doors. Retrieved October 27, 2020, from https://opendoorsdata.org/data/international-students/academic-level-and-places-of-origin/.

Institute of International Education. (n.d.b). *Infographics and data: Japan*. Retrieved October 27, 2020, from https://www.iie.org/en/Research-and-Insights/Project-Atlas/Explore-Data/Japan.

Institute of International Education. (1960). *Open Doors report on international educational exchange*. US Department of State.

Institute of International Education. (1970). *Open Doors report on international educational exchange*. US Department of State.

Institute of International Education. (1996). *Open Doors report on international educational exchange*. US Department of State.

Institute of International Education. (2020). *A quick look at global mobility trends*. Project Atlas. Retrieved from https://iie.widen.net/s/g2bqxwkwqv/project-atlas-infographics-2020.

Institute of International Education. (2021). *Open Doors report on international educational exchange*. US Department of State.

Institute of International Education. (2022). *Open Doors report on international educational exchange*. US Department of State.

International Monetary Fund. (2023). *GDP, current prices*. Retrieved from https://www.imf.org/external/datamapper/NGDPD@WEO/KOR/SGP/AUS/IDN/BGD.

Itoh, A. (2014). Japan's period of high economic growth and science and technology education: The role of higher education institutions. *Japan Labor Review*, *11*(3), 35–57. Retrieved from https://www.jil.go.jp/english/JLR/documents/2014/JLR43_itoh.pdf.

IvyCap Ventures. (n.d.). *IvyCamp—alumni-driven startup engagement platform*. IvyCamp. https://ivycamp.in/.

IvyCap Ventures Advisors. (2018). *Who we are*. IvyCap Ventures. Retrieved from http://www.ivycapventures.com/who-we-are.php.

Jackson, G. (1984). *Report of the committee to review the Australian overseas aid program* (Vol. 206). Australian Government Publishing Service.

Jakubowicz, A. (2017, March 20). *The government's multicultural statement is bereft of new ideas or policies—why?* The Conversation. Retrieved from https://theconversation.com/the-governments-multicultural-statement-is-bereft-of-new-ideas-or-policies-why-74838.

Japan Association of Overseas Studies. (n.d.). *Number of Japanese studying abroad, including working adults, appears to exceed 200,000*. Retrieved January 5, 2023, from https://www.jaos.or.jp/wp-content/uploads/2018/01/JAOS-Survey-2017_Number-of-Japanese-studying-abroad180124.pdf.

Japan Association of Overseas Studies. (2019). *Press release*. Retrieved from https://www.jaos.or.jp/wp-content/uploads/2020/03/JAOS-Survey-2019_-JapaneseStudent191219.pdf.

Japan Immigration Services Agency. (2020). *Efforts to accept new foreign human resources and realize a symbiotic society*. Ministry of Justice. Retrieved from https://www.moj.go.jp/content/001293198.pdf.

Japan Ministry of Education, Culture, Sports, Science and Technology. (n.d.a). *Research with/in Japan*. Retrieved June 20, 2022, from https://www.mext.go.jp/en/policy/science_technology/policy/title01/detail01/1304788.htm.

Japan Ministry of Education, Culture, Sports, Science and Technology. (n.d.b). *Statistics on enrollment and advancement rate.* Retrieved July 7, 2022, from https://www.mext.go.jp/en/publication/statistics/title01/detail01/1373636.htm#06.

Japan Ministry of Health, Labor and Welfare of Japan. (2018). *Gaikokujin koyō jōkyō* [Employment status of foreign nationals]. Retrieved from https://www.mhlw.go.jp/content/11655000/000472892.pdf.

Japan Public Relations Office. (2019). *Points-based system for highly-skilled foreign professionals.* Government of Japan. Retrieved from https://www.japan.go.jp/tomodachi/2017/summer2017/points_system_aims_to_attract.html#:~:text=%E2%80%9CHighly%20skilled%20foreign%20professionals%E2%80%9D%20are,development%20of%20specialized%2Ftechnical%20labor.

Japan Science and Technology Agency. (n.d.). *Strategic international collaborative research program.* Retrieved October 28, 2024, from https://www.jst.go.jp/inter/english/program_e/structure_e/general.html.

Japan Society for the Promotion of Science. (n.d.). *Bilateral programs.* Retrieved October 28, 2024, from https://www.jsps.go.jp/english/e-bilat/index.html.

Japan Student Services Organization. (n.d.). *About Tobitate! (leap for tomorrow) study abroad initiative.* Ministry of Education, Culture, Sports, Science and Technology. Retrieved January 7, 2021, from https://tobitate-mext.jasso.go.jp/about/english.html.

Japan Student Services Organization. (2021). *Result of an annual survey of international students survey in Japan, 2020.* Retrieved from https://www.studyinjapan.go.jp/en/_mt/2021/03/date2020z_e.pdf.

Jenco, L. (2013). Revisiting Asian values. *Journal of the History of Ideas, 74*(2), 237–258.

Jia, H. (2018). China's plan to recruit talented researchers. *Nature, 553*(7688), S8. Retrieved from https://doi.org/10.1038/d41586-018-00538-z.

Jiang, Q., Li, S., & Feldman, M. W. (2013). China's population policy at the crossroads: Social impacts and prospects. *Asian Journal of Social Science, 41*(2), 193–218. Retrieved from https://www.jstor.org/stable/43291300.

Johnson, C. (1982). *MITI and the Japanese miracle: The growth of industrial policy 1925–1975.* Stanford University Press.

Jones, L. (2015, March 13). *More Indians who moved to the U.S. decide to return home.* NPR. Retrieved from https://www.npr.org/2015/03/13/392718538/growing-number-of-indians-who-moved-to-u-s-decide-to-return-home.

Jones, L. D. (1980). *A study of electrical and electronic technical education programs in Japanese technical colleges and junior colleges* [Doctoral dissertation]. Oklahoma State University. Retrieved from https://shareok.org/bitstream/handle/11244/21612/Thesis-1980D-J77s.pdf?sequence=1&isAllowed=y.

Jonkers, K. (2010). *Mobility, migration and the Chinese scientific research system.* Routledge.

Joske, A. (2020). *Hunting the phoenix.* Australian Strategic Policy Institute. Retrieved from https://www.aspi.org.au/report/hunting-phoenix.

Joske, A. (2021, January). *Inquiry into national security risks affecting the Australian higher education and research sector: The Chinese Communist Party's talent recruitment efforts in Australia.* Parliament of Australia. Retrieved from https://www.aph.gov.au/DocumentStore.ashx?id=2e06f477-b466–440c-9286-ce7bab77a7e4&subId=700059.

Kably, L. (2022, January 13). H-1B denial rates for new application drops to 4% in fiscal 2021. *Times of India.* Retrieved from https://timesofindia.indiatimes.com/world/us/h-1b-denial-rates-for-new-application-drops-to-4-in-fiscal-2021/articleshow/88873539.cms.

Kajimoto, T. (2018, December 26). *In Japan, a scramble for new workers disrupts traditional hiring.* Reuters. Retrieved from https://www.reuters.com/article/us-japan-economy-newgraduates/in-japan-a-scramble-for-new-workers-disrupts-traditional-hiring-idUSKCN1OP1DD.

Kajimoto, T. (2019, May 22). Few Japanese firms plan to hire foreign workers under new immigration law, poll suggests. *Japan Times.* Retrieved from https://www.japantimes.co.jp/news/2019/05/23/business/corporate-business/japanese-firms-plan-hire-foreign-workers-new-immigration-law-poll-suggests/.

Kale, M. (1996). "Capital spectacles in British frames": Capital, empire and Indian indentured migration to the British Caribbean. *International Review of Social History, 41*(S4), 109–133. Retrieved from https://doi.org/10.1017/S0020859000114294.

Kapoor, U., & Fairbairn, D. (2018, November 15). *Oral history of Arjun Malhotra.* Computer History Museum. Retrieved from https://archive.computerhistory.org/resources/access/text/2019/01/102740453-05-01-acc.pdf.

Kapur, D. (2010). *Diaspora, development, and democracy: The domestic impact of international migration from India.* Princeton University Press.

Karlin, A. (2013, January 2). The entrepreneurship vacuum in Japan: Why it matters and how to address it. *Knowledge at Wharton.* https://knowledge.wharton.upenn.edu/article/the-entrepreneurship-vacuum-in-japan-why-it-matters-and-how-to-address-it/.

Kaspura, A. (2015). *The engineering profession: A statistical overview, 2014* (11th ed.). Institute of Engineers Australia. Retrieved from https://www.engineersaustralia.org.au/sites/default/files/content-files/2016–12/statistical_overview_2015.pdf.

Kawada, H., & Levine, S. B. (2014). *Human resources in Japanese industrial development* (Vol. 659). Princeton University Press.

Keio University. (n.d.). *Top Global University Japan.* Retrieved October 7, 2020, from https://tgu.mext.go.jp/en/universities/keio/index.html.

Kerala Hindus of Arizona. (n.d.). *About Us.* Retrieved October 25, 2024, from https://www.khaaz.org/aboutkha.htm.

Kerr, W. R. (2018). *The gift of global talent: How migration shapes business, economy & society.* Stanford University Press.

Ketkar, S. L., & Ratha, D. (2004). *Development finance via diaspora bonds track record and potential* (Working paper no. 4311). World Bank. Retrieved from https://documents1.worldbank.org/curated/en/867801468165874505/pdf/wps4311.pdf.

Keys, J. B., & Miller, T. R. (1984). The Japanese management theory jungle. *Academy of Management Review, 9*(2), 342–353. Retrieved from https://doi.org/10.2307/258447.

Khadria, B. (2014). The dichotomy of the skilled and unskilled among non-resident Indians and persons of Indian origin: Bane or boon for development in India? In G. Tejada, U. Bhattacharya, B. Khadria, & C. Kuptsch (Eds.), *Indian skilled migration and development: To Europe and back* (pp. 29–45). Springer.

Khan, B., Robbins, C., & Okrent, A. (2020, January). *The state of U.S. science and engineering 2020.* National Science Foundation. Retrieved from https://ncses.nsf.gov/pubs/nsb20201/global-science-and-technology-capabilities.

Khandelwal, M. S. (2002). *Becoming American, being Indian: An immigrant community in New York City.* Cornell University Press.

Khanna, P. (2019). *The future is Asian.* Simon & Schuster.

Kim, E. M. (1997). *Big business, strong state: Collusion and conflict in South Korean development, 1960–1990.* State University of New York Press.

Kim, M. (2016). All or nothing: The employment security laws of Japan and the United States. *Boston University International Law Journal, 34*(2), 415–451. Retrieved from https://www.bu.edu/ilj/files/2016/06/BIN207.pdf.

Kirkegaard, J. F. (2008). *Accelerating decline in America's high-skilled workforce: Implications for immigration policy.* Peterson Institute.

Kiser, G., & Mantha, Y. (2019). *Global AI talent report 2019.* Retrieved from https://jfgagne.com/talent-2019/.

Klein, M. (2016). Managing diversity: Is Australia bucking the post-multiculturalist trend or on its way to embrace interculturalism? *Australia and New Zealand Journal of European Studies, 8*(2), 64–79. https://doi.org/10.30722/anzjes.vol8.iss2.15166.

KNOMAD. (n.d.). *Remittances.* Retrieved October 31, 2021, from https://www.knomad.org/data/remittances.

Kogure, N. (2019, July 8). Shortage of IT human resources in the digital era. *Nomura Research Institute Journal.* Retrieved from https://www.nri.com/en/journal/2019/0708.

Kohli, A. (1994). Where do high growth political economies come from? The Japanese lineage of Korea's "developmental state." *World Development, 22*(9), 1269–1293. Retrieved from https://doi.org/10.1016/0305–750X(94)90004–3.

Koike, K. (1984). Skill formation systems in the U.S. and Japan: A comparative study. In M. Aoki (Ed.), *The economic analysis of the Japanese firms* (pp. 47–75). Elsevier Science.

Kolata, G. (2019, November 4). Vast dragnet targets theft of biomedical secrets for China. *New York Times*. Retrieved from https://www.nytimes.com/2019/11/04 /health/china-nih-scientists.html.

Korean Statistical Information Service. (n.d.a). 주요 연령계층별 추계인구(생 산연령인구, 고령인구 등) / 전국 [Estimated population by major age groups (working-age population, elderly population, etc.) / nationwide]. Retrieved November 14, 2024, from https://kosis.kr/statHtml/statHtml.do?orgId=101&tblId=D T_1BPA003&conn_path=I2.

Korean Statistical Information Service. (n.d.b). 인구동향조사: 출생아수, 합 계출산율, 자연증가 등 [Population trend survey: Number of births, total fertility rate, natural increase, etc.]. Retrieved November 14, 2024, from https://kosis.kr/st atHtml/statHtml.do?orgId=101&tblId=INH_1B8000F_01&conn_path=I2.

Korhonen, V. (2024, July 5). *International students in the U.S., by country of origin 2022/23*. Statista. Retrieved November 14, 2024, from https://www.statista .com/statistics/233880/international-students-in-the-us-by-country-of-origin/.

Korn Ferry. (2018). *Future of work: The global talent crunch*. Retrieved from htt ps://www.kornferry.com/content/dam/kornferry/docs/pdfs/KF-Future-of-Work-T alent-Crunch-Report.pdf.

Koseff, A. (2023, October 16). *Bashing Republicans for "rights regression," Newsom sidesteps protections for marginalized Californians*. Cal Matters. Retrieved from htt ps://calmatters.org/politics/2023/10/gavin-newsom-vetoes-rights/.

Koslowski, R. (2014). Selective migration policy models and changing realities of implementation. *International Migration, 52*(2), 26–39. Retrieved from https://d oi.org/10.1111/imig.12136.

Kôu, A., & Bailey, A. (2014). "Movement is a constant feature in my life": Contextualising migration processes of highly skilled Indians. *Geoforum, 52*, 113–122. Retrieved from https://doi.org/10.1016/j.geoforum.2014.01.002.

Kovács-Ondrejkovic, O., Strack, R., Baier, J., Antebi, P., Kavanagh, K., & López Gobernado, A. (2021). *Decoding global talent, onsite and virtual*. Boston Consulting Group.

Kreighbaum, A. (2022, March 21). *Startup backers eye China competition bill to add new visa (1)*. Bloomberg Law. Retrieved from https://news.bloomberglaw.com /daily-labor-report/startup-backers-eye-china-competition-bill-as-path-to-a-new-visa.

Kuah, K. E., Rezaei, S., & Zhang, Z. (2021). Negotiating cultural and socio-economic flows in the era of Belt and Road Initiatives: An introductory overview. *Asian Journal of Social Science, 49*(4), 183–187. Retrieved from https://doi.org/10.101 6/j.ajss.2021.09.010.

Kudo, J. (2007). The historical transition of chair system and its merits and demerits. *Journal of Liberal and General Education Society of Japan, 29,* 119–123. Retrieved from https://papers.ssrn.com/sol3/papers.cfm?abstract_id=2550694.

Kuznetsov, Y., Nemirovsky, A., & Yoguel, G. (2006). Argentina: Burgeoning networks of talent abroad, weak institutions at home. In Y. Kuznetsov (Ed.), *Diaspora networks and the international migration of skills: How countries can draw on their talent abroad* (pp. 153–170). World Bank.

Kwan, C. (2022, June 27). Why we don't have enough workers to fill jobs (in four graphs). *Australian Financial Review.* Retrieved from https://www.afr.com/policy/economy/why-we-don-t-have-enough-workers-to-fill-jobs-in-4-graphs-20220621-p5avcc.

Kyodo, J. (2019, October 23). Number of foreign students seeking jobs in Japan after graduation hits record high. *Japan Times.* Retrieved from https://www.japantimes.co.jp/news/2019/10/23/national/foreign-students-seeking-jobs-after-graduation-japan/.

LaFraniere, S. (2010, January 6). Fighting trend, China is luring scientists home. *New York Times.* Retrieved from https://www.nytimes.com/2010/01/07/world/asia/07scholar.html.

Lalwani, A. (2019, October 2). *This is how India can become the next Silicon Valley.* World Economic Forum. Retrieved from https://www.weforum.org/agenda/2019/10/india-technology-development-silicon-valley/.

Lanvin, B., & Evans, P. (Eds.). (2013). *The Global Talent Competitiveness Index 2013.* INSEAD. Retrieved from https://www.insead.edu/sites/default/files/assets/dept/globalindices/docs/GTCI-2013-report.pdf.

Lanvin, B., & Evans, P. (Eds.). (2014). *The Global Talent Competitiveness Index 2014: Growing talent for today and tomorrow.* INSEAD. Retrieved from https://www.insead.edu/sites/default/files/assets/dept/globalindices/docs/GTCI-2014-report.pdf.

Lanvin, B., & Evans, P. (Eds.). (2016). *The Global Talent Competitiveness Index 2015–16: Talent attraction and international mobility.* INSEAD. Retrieved from https://www.insead.edu/sites/default/files/assets/dept/globalindices/docs/GTCI-2015–2016-report.pdf.

Lanvin, B., & Evans, P. (Eds.). (2017). *The Global Talent Competitiveness Index 2017: Talent and technology.* INSEAD. Retrieved from https://www.insead.edu/sites/default/files/assets/dept/globalindices/docs/GTCI-2017-report.pdf.

Lanvin, B., & Evans, P. (Eds.). (2018). *The Global Talent Competitiveness Index 2018: Diversity for competitiveness.* INSEAD. Retrieved from https://www.insead.edu/sites/default/files/assets/dept/globalindices/docs/GTCI-2018-report.pdf.

Lanvin, B., & Monteiro, F. (Eds.). (2019). *The Global Talent Competitiveness Index 2019: Entrepreneurial talent and global competitiveness.* INSEAD. Retrieved from https://www.insead.edu/sites/default/files/assets/dept/globalindices/docs/GT CI-2019-Report.pdf.

Lanvin, B., & Monteiro, F. (Eds.). (2020). *The Global Talent Competitiveness Index 2020: Global talent in the age of artificial intelligence.* INSEAD. Retrieved from https://www.insead.edu/sites/default/files/assets/dept/globalindices/docs/GT CI-2020-report.pdf.

Lanvin, B., & Monteiro, F. (Eds.). (2021). *The Global Talent Competitiveness Index 2021: Talent competitiveness in times of COVID.* INSEAD. Retrieved from https://www.insead.edu/sites/default/files/assets/dept/fr/gtci/GTCI-2021-Report.pdf.

Lanvin, B., & Monteiro, F. (Eds.). (2022). *The Global Talent Competitiveness Index 2022: The tectonics of talent; Is the world drifting towards increased talent inequalities?* INSEAD. Retrieved from https://www.insead.edu/sites/default/files/assets/dept/fr/gtci/GTCI-2022-report.pdf.

Lauer, M. S. (2020, June 12). *ACD working group on foreign influences on research integrity update* [Slides]. National Institute of Health. Retrieved from https://acd.od.nih.gov/documents/presentations/06122020ForeignInfluences.pdf.

Lee, C. (2014, July 30). Koreans not ready for multiculturalism. *Korea Herald.* Retrieved from http://www.koreaherald.com/view.php?ud=20140730000857.

Lee, E. S. (1966). A theory of migration. *Demography, 3*(1), 47–57. Retrieved from https://doi.org/10.2307/2060063.

Lee, J., & Li, X. (2021). *Racial profiling among scientists of Chinese descent and consequences for the U.S. scientific community.* Committee of 100 & University of Arizona. Retrieved from https://www.committee100.org/wp-content/uploads/2021/10/C100-Lee-Li-White-Paper-FINAL-FINAL-10.28.pdf.

Lee, J. W. (1997). *Economic growth and human development in the Republic of Korea, 1945–1992.* United Nations Development Programme. Retrieved from https://hdr.undp.org/content/economic-growth-and-human-development-republic-korea-1945–1992.

Legal and Constitutional References Committee. (2005). *They still call Australia home: Inquiry into Australian expatriates.* Parliament of Australia. Retrieved from https://www.aph.gov.au/~/media/wopapub/senate/committee/legcon_ctte/completed_inquiries/2004_07/expats03/report/report_pdf.ashx.

Levey, G. B. (2019). The Turnbull government's "post-multiculturalism" multicultural policy. *Australian Journal of Political Science, 54*(4), 456–473. Retrieved from https://doi.org/10.1080/10361146.2019.1634675.

Lewis, L., & Tabeta, S. (2016, January 11). Japan business leaders urge real globalisation. *Financial Times.* Retrieved from https://www.ft.com/content/80bb0344-78d6-11e5-a95a-27d368e1ddf7.

Li, C. (Ed.). (2005). *Bridging minds across the Pacific: U.S.-China educational exchanges, 1978–2003.* Lexington Books.

Li, C. (2009). China's new think tanks: Where officials, entrepreneurs, and scholars interact. *China Leadership Monitor, 29*, 1–21.

Li, C. (2021). *Middle class Shanghai: Reshaping US-China engagement.* Brookings Institution Press.

Li, Q. (2020, July 21). China's Double First Class programme should open to regional universities. *Times Higher Education*. Retrieved from https://www.timeshighereducation.com/blog/chinas-double-first-class-programme-should-open-regional-universities#survey-answer.

Li, S., & Ansari, T. (2021, May 6). India's diaspora aids families caught in COVID-19 "medical war zone." *Wall Street Journal*. Retrieved from https://www.wsj.com/articles/indias-diaspora-aids-families-caught-in-covid-19-medical-war-zone-11620317233.

Li, W., Bakshi, K., Tan, Y., & Huang, X. (2019). Policies for recruiting talented professionals from the diaspora: India and China compared. *International Migration, 57*(3), 373–391. Retrieved from https://doi.org/10.1111/imig.12456.

Li, W., & Lo, L. (2009). *Highly-skilled Indian migrations in Canada and the US: The tale of two immigration systems* (Working paper no. 4). International Migration and Diaspora Studies Working Paper Series. Retrieved from http://lib.jnu.ac.in/sites/default/files/pdf/imds_p/IMDS_Mar_2009_WP_4.pdf.

Li, X., Zuo, Y., & Shen, W. (2018). Who got the academic jobs in the elite universities—a curriculum vitae analysis of new faculty members of Peking University and Tsinghua University in 2011–2017. *China Higher Education Research, 40*(8), 47–52. Retrieved from https://doi.org/10.16298/j.cnki.1004-3667.2018.08.09.

Li, Y. (2020). Do returnee faculty promote the internationalization of higher education? A study based on the "2014 faculty survey in China." *Chinese Education & Society, 53*(3), 115–133. Retrieved from https://doi.org/10.1080/10611932.2020.1791543.

Li, Y. (2021, September 9). "Reversing gears": China increasingly rejects English, and the world. *New York Times*. Retrieved from https://www.nytimes.com/2021/09/09/business/china-english.html.

Litsareva, E. (2017). Success factors of Asia-Pacific fast-developing regions' technological innovation development and economic growth. *International Journal of Innovation Studies, 1*(1), 72–88. Retrieved from https://doi.org/10.3724/SP.J.1440.101006.

Liu, Q., Turner, D., & Jing, X. (2019). The "Double First-Class Initiative" in China: Background, implementation, and potential problems. *Beijing International Review of Education, 1*(1), 92–108. Retrieved from https://brill.com/view/journals/bire/1/1/article-p92_92.xml.

Lixu, L. (2004). China's higher education reform 1998–2003: A summary. *Asia Pacific Education Review, 5*(1), 14–22. Retrieved from https://doi.org/10.1007/BF03026275.

Lloyd-Damnjanovic, A., & Bowe, A. (2020, October 7). *Overseas Chinese students and scholars in China's drive for innovation.* US-China Economic and Security Review Commission. https://www.uscc.gov/sites/default/files/2020-10/Overse as_Chinese_Students_and_Scholars_in_Chinas_Drive_for_Innovation.pdf.

Lohr, S. (1984, July 8). The Japanese challenge: Can they achieve technological supremacy? *New York Times.* Retrieved from https://www.nytimes.com/1984/07/0 8/magazine/the-japanese-challenge.html.

Low, L. (1998). Human resource development in the Asia-Pacific. *Asian-Pacific Economic Literature, 12*(1), 27–40. Retrieved from https://doi.org/10.1111/1467–8411 .00027.

Lowy Institute Public Opinion and Foreign Policy Program. (2019). *Lowy Institute poll.* Lowy Institute. Retrieved from https://poll.lowyinstitute.org/charts/imm igration-rate.

Loyalka, P., Liu, O. L., Li, G., Kardanova, E., Chirikov, I., Hu, S., Yu, N., Ma, L., Guo, F., Beteille, T., Tognatta, N., Gu, L., Ling, G., Federiakin, D., Wang, H., Khanna, S., Bhuradia, A., Shi, Z., & Li, Y. (2021). Skill levels and gains in university STEM education in China, India, Russia and the United States. *Nature Human Behaviour, 5*(7), 892–904. Retrieved from https://doi.org/10.1038/s41562-02 1-01062-3.

Lucas, R. E., Jr. (1988). On the mechanics of economic development. *Journal of Monetary Economics, 22*(1), 3–42. Retrieved from https://doi.org/10.1016/0304–3932 (88)90168–7.

Ma, Y. (2024). *US Security and immigration policies threaten its AI leadership.* Brookings Institution. Retrieved from https://www.brookings.edu/articles/us-sec urity-and-immigration-policies-threaten-its-ai-leadership/.

Ma, Y., & Pan, S. (2015). Chinese returnees from overseas study: An understanding of brain gain and brain circulation in the age of globalization. *Frontiers of Education in China, 10*(2), 306–329. Retrieved from https://doi.org/10.1007/BF0 3397067.

Mahadevan, I., & Sukhatme, S. P. (1987). *Pilot study on magnitude and nature of the brain drain of graduates of the IIT, Bombay.* Department of Humanities and Social Sciences, IIT Bombay. Retrieved from http://www.nstmis-dst.org/pdfs/Pilo tStudy.pdf.

Mallapaty, S. (2018, October 24). China hides identities of top scientific recruits amidst growing US scrutiny. *Nature.* Retrieved from https://doi.org/10.1038 /d41586-018-07167-6.

Mallapaty, S. (2021, April 11). China's Five-Year Plan focuses on scientific self-reliance. *Nature, 591*(7850), 353–354. Retrieved from https://doi.org/10.1038/d41586 -021-00638-3.

Mangram, M. E. (2013). A simplified perspective of the Markowitz portfolio theory. *Global Journal of Business Research, 7*(1), 59–70. Retrieved from https://pap ers.ssrn.com/sol3/papers.cfm?abstract_id=2147880.

Mao, F. (2021, May 26). *"Fortress Australia": Why calls to open up borders are meeting resistance.* BBC. Retrieved from https://www.bbc.com/news/world-austral ia-57224635.

Mao, F. (2021, September 3). *Why has Australia switched tack on Covid zero?* BBC. Retrieved from https://www.bbc.com/news/world-australia-58406526.

Margheritis, A. (2021). Diaspora engagement policies in Argentina: The unfolding of a still lukewarm approach. In V. Bravo & M. De Moya (Eds.), *Latin American diasporas in public diplomacy* (pp. 63–78). Palgrave Macmillan. Retrieved from https://doi.org/10.1007/978-3-030-74564-6_4.

Markowitz, H. (1952). Portfolio selection. *Journal of Finance, 7*(1), 77–91. Retrieved from https://doi.org/10.2307/2975974.

Markowitz, H. (1991). Foundations of portfolio theory. *Journal of Finance, 46*(2), 469–477. Retrieved from https://doi.org/10.2307/2328831.

Markus, A. (2021). *Mapping social cohesion.* Scanlon Foundation Research Institute. Retrieved from https://scanloninstitute.org.au/sites/default/files/2021–11/ Mapping_Social_Cohesion_2021_Report_0.pdf.

Maskawa, T. (2008, December 8). *What does CP violation tell us?* [Lecture]. The Nobel Prize. Retrieved from https://www.nobelprize.org/prizes/physics/2008/mas kawa/lecture/.

Matthews, D. (2017, April 21). Why Germany educates international students for free. *Times Higher Education.* Retrieved from https://www.timeshighereducati on.com/news/why-germany-educates-international-students-for-free.

Matthews, D., Radloff, A., Doyle, J., & Clarke, L. (2019, July). *International Graduate Outcomes Survey—2018: Final report.* International Education. Retrieved from https://research.acer.edu.au/higher_education/65/.

Mazumi, Y. (2021). How are part-time laboring international students incorporated into host labor markets after graduation? The case of South and Southeast Asians in Japan. *Japanese Studies, 41*(2), 201–219. Retrieved from https://doi.org/10 .1080/10371397.2021.1941824.

Medical Board of Australia. (n.d.). *Competent authority pathway.* Ahpra. Retrieved August 1, 2022, from https://www.medicalboard.gov.au/registration/intern ational-medical-graduates/competent-authority-pathway.aspx.

Menezes, R., Pike, D., & Patel, S. M. (2015, November 9). Giving back to India. *Stanford Social Innovation Review.* Retrieved from https://ssir.org/articles/en try/giving_back_to_india.

Mervis, J. (2020, February 5). Ex-Emory scientist with ties to China charged with fraud. *Science.* Retrieved from https://www.sciencemag.org/news/2020/02/ex -emory-scientist-ties-china-charged-fraud.

Mervis, J. (2020, June 12). Fifty-four scientists have lost their jobs as a result of NIH probe. *Science*. Retrieved from https://www.sciencemag.org/news/2020/06/fifty-four-scientists-have-lost-their-jobs-result-nih-probe-foreign-ties.

Miao, D. (2010). 出国留学六十年 [Sixty years of overseas study]. Central Party Literature Press.

Miao, L., & Wang, H. (2017). *International migration of China: Status, policy and social responses to the globalization of migration*. Springer.

Microsoft News Center India. (2020, March 17). *Innovate for Accessible India launched to harness the power of technology to empower people with disabilities*. Microsoft Stories India. Retrieved from https://news.microsoft.com/en-in/innovate-accessible-india-empower-people-with-disabilities/.

Migration Council Australia. (2015). *The economic impact of migration*. Retrieved from https://www.aph.gov.au/DocumentStore.ashx?id=cd4721e9–17e8–4352-b5c7–15b646a0382f&subId=350950.

Migration Policy Institute. (2014). *The Indian diaspora in the United States*. Retrieved from https://www.migrationpolicy.org/sites/default/files/publications/RAD-IndiaII-FINAL.pdf.

Migration Policy Institute. (2017, May 15). *Chinese immigrants in the United States*. Retrieved from https://www.migrationpolicy.org/article/chinese-immigrants-united-states.

Mincer, J. (1984). Human capital and economic growth. *Economics of Education Review, 3*(3), 195–205. Retrieved from https://doi.org/10.1016/0272–7757(84)90032–3.

Ministerio de Ciencia, Tecnología e Innovación Argentina. (n.d.). *RAICES Program*. Red de Argentinos/as Investigadores/as, Científicos/as y Tecnólogos/as en el Exterior. Retrieved October 28, 2024, from https://www.argentina.gob.ar/sites/default/files/eng_-_bases_y_condiciones_premios_raices_y_leloir_0.pdf.

Mitsui. (n.d.). *Human resources development and allocation*. Retrieved June 20, 2022, from https://www.mitsui.com/jp/en/sustainability/social/resources/rearing/index.html.

Mo Jongrin. (2013). 이민 강국: 인재 전쟁 시대 의 이민 정책 [Immigration powerhouse: Immigration policy in the era of talent wars]. Korean Studies Information Service System.

Mok, K. H., Zhang, Y., & Bao, W. (2022). Brain drain or brain gain: A growing trend of Chinese international students returning home for development. In K. H. Mok (Ed.), *Higher education, innovation and entrepreneurship from comparative perspectives: Reengineering China through the Greater Bay economy and development* (pp. 203–223). Springer. Retrieved from https://doi.org/10.1007/978-981-16-8870-6_11.

Moon, R. J., & Shin, G. W. (2016). Aid as transnational social capital: Korea's official development assistance in higher education. *Pacific Affairs, 89*(4), 817–837. Retrieved from https://doi.org/10.5509/2016894817.

Moon, R. J., & Shin, G. W. (2019). International student networks as transnational social capital: Illustrations from Japan. *Comparative Education, 55*(4), 557–574. Retrieved from https://doi.org/10.1080/03050068.2019.1601919.

More students returning from overseas to start business. (2016, July 20). *China Daily USA*. Retrieved from https://usa.chinadaily.com.cn/china/2016-07/20/content_26159729.htm.

Morita, L. (2014). Factors contributing to low levels of intercultural interaction between Japanese and international students in Japan. *Journal of Intercultural Communication, 14*(3), 1–12. Retrieved from https://doi.org/10.36923/jicc.v14i3.681.

Mukherji, A. (2020, July 8). The Cisco case could expose rampant prejudice against Dalits in Silicon Valley. *The Wire*. Retrieved from https://thewire.in/caste/cisco-caste-discrimination-silicon-valley-dalit-prejudice.

Mullan, F. (2005). The metrics of the physician brain drain. *New England Journal of Medicine, 353*(17), 1810–1818. Retrieved from https://doi.org/10.1056/NEJMsa050004.

Muro, M. (2012, August 23). *Multiplier effects: Connecting the innovation and opportunity agendas*. Brookings Institution. Retrieved from https://www.brookings.edu/articles/multiplier-effects-connecting-the-innovation-and-opportunity-agendas/.

Murphy, M., & Contreras, I. (May 12, 2022). Global 2000: World's largest public companies. *Forbes*. Retrieved from https://www.forbes.com/lists/global2000/. [Content no longer available.]

Naipaul, V. S. (1990). *India: A million mutinies now*. Heinemann.

Nakayama, S. (1989). Independence and choice: Western impacts on Japanese higher education. *Higher Education, 18*(1), 31–48. Retrieved from https://www.jstor.org/stable/3447442.

Nankai University. (2019, December 24). *Nankai University researchers develop new method for synthesizing high-quality graphene*. Retrieved from https://en.nankai.edu.cn/2019/1224/c22794a325364/page.htm.

NASSCOM. (2018). *Indian tech start-up ecosystem: Approaching escape velocity*. NASSCOM-Zinnov. Retrieved from https://nasscom.in/product/94#.

NASSCOM. (2021). *About us*. Retrieved from https://nasscom.in/about-us.

National Committee on U.S.-China Relations. (2018, June 6). *Peggy Blumenthal and David Zweig: China's students in the U.S.* [Video]. YouTube. Retrieved from https://www.youtube.com/watch?v=fcSWwbwO-Cg.

National Human Rights Commission of the Republic of Korea. (n.d.). *History*. Retrieved June 14, 2023, from https://www.humanrights.go.kr/eng/contents/view?contentsNo=125&menuLevel=3&menuNo=124.

National Museum of Australia. (2021, July 5). *End of the White Australia Policy*. Department of Infrastructure, Transport, Regional Development, Communications and the Arts. Retrieved from https://www.nma.gov.au/defining-moments/re sources/end-of-white-australia-policy.

National Museum of Australia. (2022, June 28). *Postwar immigration drive*. Retrieved from https://www.nma.gov.au/defining-moments/resources/postwar-im migration-drive.

National Natural Science Foundation. (2004, June 16). 陈章良细说"国家杰出青年科学基金"的设立 [Chen Zhangliang elaborated on the establishment of the "National Science Fund for Outstanding Youth"]. Retrieved from http://自然科学基金会.cn/publish/portal0/tab440/info60004.htm.

National Science Board. (2020). *2020 science and engineering indicators: The state of U.S. science and engineering* (NSB-2020-1). National Science Foundation. https://ncses.nsf.gov/pubs/nsb20201.

National Science Foundation. (2019). *Doctorate recipients with temporary visas intending to stay in the United States after doctorate receipt, by country of citizenship: 2012–18*. Retrieved from https://ncses.nsf.gov/pubs/nsf20301/data-tables/.

National Science Foundation. (2022). *Research doctorate recipients with temporary visas intending to stay in the United States after doctorate receipt, by country or economy of citizenship: 2016–22*. Retrieved from https://ncses.nsf.gov/pubs/nsf24300/table/2-8.

National Security Division. (2021, November 19). *Information about the Department of Justice's China Initiative and a compilation of China-related prosecutions since 2018*. US Department of Justice. Retrieved from https://www.justice.gov/nsd/infor mation-about-department-justice-s-china-initiative-and-compilation-china-relate d.

Naujoks, D. (2009, October 15). *Emigration, immigration, and diaspora relations in India*. Migration Policy Institute. Retrieved from https://www.migrationp olicy.org/article/emigration-immigration-and-diaspora-relations-india/.

Naujoks, D. (2013). *Migration, citizenship, and development: Diasporic membership policies and overseas Indians in the United States*. Oxford University Press.

Nearly a third of international students closed to Australia's borders opt to study elsewhere. (2021, October 21). Australian Broadcasting Corporation News. Retrieved from https://www.abc.net.au/news/2021-10-22/nearly-a-third-of-internatio nal-students-closed-to/13598876.

Netierman, E., Harrison, L., Freeman, A., Shoyele, G., Esses, V., & Covell, C. (2022). Should I stay or should I go? International students' decision-making about staying in Canada. *Journal of International Migration and Integration*, *23*, 43–60. Retrieved from https://doi.org/10.1007/s12134-021-00835-0.

New Zealand Government. (n.d.). *Passports and visas when you go to Australia*.

Retrieved September 27, 2021, from https://www.govt.nz/browse/leaving-nz/trave l-or-move-to-australia/passports-and-visas-when-you-go-to-australia/.

New Zealand Ministry for Culture and Heritage. (n.d.). *New Zealand turns down federation with Australia*. New Zealand History. Retrieved September 27, 2021, from https://nzhistory.govt.nz/page/nz-says-no-aussie-federation.

Nippon.com. (2018, May 21). *Most international students opt to stay in Japan after graduation*. Retrieved from https://www.nippon.com/en/features/h00197/.

Nippon.com. (2019, May 13). *Year-round hiring aims to spur more Japanese students to learn overseas*. Retrieved from https://www.nippon.com/en/japan-data/h00446/ye ar-round-hiring-aims-to-spur-more-japanese-students-to-learn-overseas.html.

Nippon.com. (2020, March 30). *Record 1.66 million foreign workers in Japan in 2019*. Retrieved from https://www.nippon.com/en/japan-data/h00676/record-1–6 6-million-foreign-workers-in-japan-in-2019.html.

Niumai, A. (2011). Indian diaspora philanthropy: A sociological perspective. *Man in India*, *91*(1), 93–114. Retrieved from https://doi.org/10.13140/2.1.1297.7443.

Nobel Foundation. (n.d.). *Shuji Nakamura—biographical*. The Nobel Prize. Retrieved November 8, 2022, from https://www.nobelprize.org/prizes/physics/201 4/nakamura/biographical/.

Nonaka, I., & Takeuchi, H. (1995). *The knowledge-creating company: How Japanese companies create the dynamics of innovation*. Oxford University Press.

Normile, D. (2000, January 21). New incentives lure Chinese talent back home. *Science*, *287*(5452), 417–418. Retrieved from https://science.sciencemag.org/content /287/5452/417.full.

Now, Australian PM Turnbull abolishes visa programme popular with Indians. (2017, July 19). *Hindustan Times*. Retrieved from https://www.hindustantimes.com /business-news/australia-toughens-visa-rules-says-australian-jobs-for-australians/s tory-mtk88ciHHV8FVwf2hA1REI.html.

Nyland, C., & Tran, L. T. (2020). The consumer rights of international students in the Australian vocational education and training sector. *Journal of Vocational Education & Training*, *72*(1), 71–87. Retrieved from https://doi.org/10.1080/1 3636820.2019.1597758.

Oak Ridge Institute for Science and Education. (n.d.). *Stay rates of foreign doctorate recipients*. Retrieved August 24, 2021, from https://orise.orau.gov/stem/work force-studies/stay-rates-of-foreign-doctorate-recipients.html.

OECD. (n.d.). *Working-age population*. Retrieved January 14, 2022, from https ://www.oecd.org/en/data/indicators/working-age-population.html.

OECD. (2007). *Cross-border tertiary education: A way towards capacity development*. International Bank for Reconstruction and Development & World Bank. Retrieved from https://www.worldbank.org/en/topic/education/publication/cross-border-tertiary-education-a-way-towards-capacity-development.

OECD. (2012). *Education at a glance 2012: Highlights*. Retrieved from https://doi.org/10.1787/eag_highlights-2012-9-en.

OECD. (2019a). *Education at a glance 2019: OECD indicators*. Retrieved from https://doi.org/10.1787/f8d7880d-en.

OECD. (2019b). *Recruiting immigrant workers: Korea 2019*. Retrieved from https://doi.org/10.1787/9789264307872-en.

OECD. (2020a). *Demographic trends*. Retrieved from https://www.oecd-ilibrary.org/sites/c05578aa-en/index.html?itemId=/content/component/c05578aa-en.

OECD. (2020b). *Elderly population*. Retrieved from https://data.oecd.org/pop/elderly-population.htm.

OECD. (2020c). *Foreign-born population*. Retrieved from https://data.oecd.org/migration/foreign-born-population.htm.

OECD. (2022a). *Gross domestic spending on R&D (indicator)*. Retrieved from https://doi.org/10.1787/d8b068b4-en.

OECD. (2022b). *Labour force participation rate (indicator)*. Retrieved from https://doi.org/10.1787/8a801325-en.

OECD. (2022c). *Population with tertiary education*. Retrieved from https://data.oecd.org/eduatt/population-with-tertiary-education.htm.

Office of Homeland Security Statistics. (n.d.). *Profiles on naturalized citizens*. US Department of Homeland Security. Retrieved March 14, 2022, from https://www.dhs.gov/profiles-naturalized-citizens.

Oliver, A. (2018, June 20). *2018 Lowy Institute poll*. Lowy Institute. Retrieved from https://www.lowyinstitute.org/publications/2018-lowy-institute-poll.

Onyema, E. M., Eucheria, N. C., Obafemi, F. A., Sen, S., Atonye, F. G., Sharma, A., & Alsayed, A. O. (2020). Impact of coronavirus pandemic on education. *Journal of Education and Practice, 11*(13), 108–121. Retrieved from https://doi.org/10.7176/JEP/11-13-12.

Orios Venture Partners. (2019). *The future of work: How startups are disrupting the way we work*. Retrieved from https://www.oriosvp.com/_files/ugd/060e74_c38c7b13f38f4890a732e03b4bab48ff.pdf.

Orios Venture Partners. (2022). *The India tech unicorn report*. Retrieved from https://www.oriosvp.com/the-india-tech-unicorn-report.

Osumi, M. (2022, June 23). Japan aims to up number of international students to 300,000 by 2027. *Japan Times*. Retrieved from https://www.japantimes.co.jp/news/2022/06/23/national/international-students-increase-plan/.

Packer, H. (2022, April 15). *Slow return of Chinese students could "split" universities*. PIE News. Retrieved from https://thepienews.com/news/australia-chinese-split-universities/.

Page, S. (2019). *The diversity bonus*. Princeton University Press.

Pandey, A., Aggarwal, A., Devane, R., & Kuznetsov, Y. (2006). The Indian diaspora: A unique case? In Y. Kuznetsov (Ed.), *Diaspora networks and the international migration of skills: How countries can draw on their talent abroad* (pp. 71–98). World Bank.

PanIIT USA. (n.d.). *About PanIIT USA*. Retrieved October 21, 2021, from https://www.iit.org/page/about-paniit-usa.

Papademetriou, D. G., Somerville, W., & Tanaka, H. (2008). *Talent in the 21st-century economy*. Migration Policy Institute. Retrieved from https://www.migrationpolicy.org/sites/default/files/publications/Talent.pdf.

Parikh Worldwide Media. (2021, April 27). Indian-American physicians launch campaign to help India combat COVID-19. *News India Times*. Retrieved from https://www.newsindiatimes.com/indian-american-physicians-launch-campaign-to-help-india-combat-covid-19/.

Parliamentary Joint Committee on Intelligence and Security. (2020). *Inquiry into national security risks affecting the Australian higher education and research sector*. Parliament of Australia. Retrieved from https://www.aph.gov.au/Parliamentary_Business/Committees/Joint/Intelligence_and_Security/NationalSecurityRisks.

Parliament of Australia. (2013, April 14). *Chapter 4—unemployment and the changing labour market*. Retrieved from https://www.aph.gov.au/parliamentary_business/committees/senate/community_affairs/completed_inquiries/2002-04/poverty/report/c04.

Parliament of Australia. (2021, March). *Interim report of the inquiry into Australia's skilled migration program: Foreword*. Retrieved from https://www.aph.gov.au/Parliamentary_Business/Committees/Joint/Migration/SkilledMigrationProgram/Report/section?id=committees%2Freportjnt%2F024650%2F76420.

Parr, N., & De Alwis, S. (2019). The birthplaces, languages, ancestries and religions of chief executive officers and managing directors in Australia. *Asia Pacific Journal of Human Resources, 57*(3), 276–298. Retrieved from https://doi.org/10.1111/1744-7941.12210.

Parreñas, R. S., & Kim, J. K. (2011). Multicultural East Asia: An introduction. *Journal of Ethnic and Migration Studies, 37*(10), 1555–1561. Retrieved from https://doi.org/10.1080/1369183X.2011.613331.

Pearlman, J. (2017, March 21). Australia's new multicultural policy focuses on integration. *Straits Times*. Retrieved from https://www.straitstimes.com/asia/australianz/australias-new-multicultural-policy-focuses-on-integration.

People's Daily Overseas Edition. (2019, January 30). "赤子计划"吸引万余留学人才_滚动新闻_中国政府网 ["Chizi Plan" attracts more than ten thousand overseas talents]. State Council of the People's Republic of China. Retrieved from http://www.gov.cn/xinwen/2019-01/30/content_5362147.htm.

People's Republic of China Ministry of Education. (2009, September 16). *Co-*

operation & exchanges. Retrieved from http://en.moe.gov.cn/cooperation_exchang es/201506/t20150626_191376.html.

People's Republic of China Ministry of Human Resources. (2006, November 15). 关于印发《留学人员回国工作"十一五"规划》的通知 [Notice on printing and distributing the eleventh Five-Year Plan for overseas students returning to China]. Retrieved from http://www.mohrss.gov.cn/xxgk2020/fdzdgknr/ghtj/fzgh/ 202011/t20201102_394328.html.

Perold, A. F., & Sharpe, W. F. (1995). Dynamic strategies for asset allocation. *Financial Analysts Journal*, *51*(1), 149–160. Retrieved from https://doi.org/10.2469/f aj.v51.n1.1871.

Pham, L., & Tran, L. (2015). Understanding the symbolic capital of intercultural interactions: A case study of international students in Australia. *International Studies in Sociology of Education*, *25*(3), 204–224. Retrieved from https://doi.org/10 .1080/09620214.2015.1069720.

Ployhart, R. E., Weekley, J. A., & Dalzell, J. (2018). *Talent without borders: Global talent acquisition for competitive advantage*. Oxford University Press.

Poojary, T., & Bakshi, S. R. (2019, July 28). *Arabian nights and Indian startup dreams: Middle East investors eager to fund tech businesses*. YourStory. Retrieved from https://yourstory.com/2019/07/india-startups-middle-east-investors-funding.

Population Reference Bureau. (2012, November 27). *South Korea's demographic dividend*. Retrieved from https://www.prb.org/resources/south-koreas-demograph ic-dividend/.

PricewaterhouseCoopers. (2018). *Out of sight, out of mind? Australia's diaspora as a pathway to innovation*. Retrieved from https://www.pwc.com.au/publications/pd f/the-australian-diaspora.pdf.

Prime Minister's Office of Japan. (2018, October 24). 第百九十七回国会にお ける安倍内閣総理大臣所信表明演説 [Prime Minister Abe's policy statement at the 197th Diet session]. Retrieved from https://www.kantei.go.jp/jp/98_abe/stat ement2/20181024shoshinhyomei.html.

Putnam, R. D. (2000). *Bowling alone: The collapse and revival of American community*. Simon & Schuster.

Putnam, R. D. (2015). Bowling alone: America's declining social capital. In R. T. LeGates & F. Stout (Eds.), *The city reader* (6th ed., pp. 9–14). Routledge. Retrieved from https://doi.org/10.4324/9781315748504.

Qi, L., & Li, M. (2024, July 11). The One-Child Policy supercharged China's economic miracle: Now it's paying the price. *Wall Street Journal*. https://www.wsj .com/world/china/china-population-slowing-economy-7ff938e5.

Quacquarelli Symonds. (n.d.). *Best student cities 2019*. QS Top Universities. Retrieved September 28, 2021, from https://www.topuniversities.com/city-rankings/2 019.

Rabushka, A. (1979). *Hong Kong: A study in economic freedom* (Vol. 77). University of Chicago, Graduate School of Business.

Ramya, M. (2014, December 24). IITs continue to be NRIs' first choice. *Times of India*. Retrieved from https://timesofindia.indiatimes.com/home/education/ne ws/IITs-continue-to-be-NRIs-first-choice/articleshow/45623660.cms.

Ray, T. (2019, March 8). *The US isn't safe from the trauma of caste bias*. The World. Retrieved from https://www.pri.org/stories/2019-03-08/us-isn-t-safe-traum a-caste-bias.

Redden, E. (2018, August 24). *For international students, shifting choices of where to study*. Inside Higher Ed. Retrieved from https://www.insidehighered.com/news /2018/08/24/international-enrollments-slowing-or-declining-some-top-destinatio n-countries-look.

Reuters Graphics. (2019, May 1). *Going gray*. Reuters. Retrieved from https://w ww.reuters.com/graphics/JAPAN-AGING/010091PB2LH/index.html.

Rezaei, S., & Mouritzen, M. R. (2021). Talent flowscapes and circular mobility in a Belt and Road (BRI) perspective—global talent flows revisited. *Asian Journal of Social Science, 49*(4), 188–197. Retrieved from https://doi.org/10.1016/j.ajss.2021.0 9.005.

Riain, S. Ó. (2000). The flexible developmental state: Globalization, information technology, and the "Celtic tiger." *Politics & Society, 28*(2), 157–193. Retrieved from https://doi.org/10.1177/00323292000280020.

Ritsumeikan Asia Pacific University. (2021). *Job placement and advancement*. Retrieved from https://en.apu.ac.jp/home/career/content9/.

Roe, I. (2020, August 16). *Most international students would tell others not to come to Australia after coronavirus response*. Australian Broadcasting Corporation News. Retrieved from https://www.abc.net.au/news/2020-08-17/international-stu dents-would-tell-others-not-to-come-australia/12558882.

Rong, X. (2020, January 14). China is winning the race for young entrepreneurs. *Foreign Policy*. Retrieved from https://foreignpolicy.com/2020/01/14/china-i s-winning-the-race-for-young-entrepreneurs/.

Ross, J. (2020, April 3). "Time to go home," Australian PM tells foreign students. *Times Higher Education*. Retrieved from https://www.timeshighereducation .com/news/time-go-home-australian-pm-tells-foreign-students.

Rozelle, S., & Hell, N. (2021). *Invisible China: How the urban-rural divide threatens China's rise*. Chicago University Press.

Ruiz, N. G., & Budiman, A. (2018, May 10). *Number of foreign college students staying and working in U.S. after graduation surges*. Global Attitudes Project, Pew Research Center. Retrieved from https://www.pewresearch.org/global/2018/05/10/ number-of-foreign-college-students-staying-and-working-in-u-s-after-graduation- surges/.

Sahoo, A. K. (2006). Issues of identity in the Indian diaspora: A transnational perspective. *Perspectives on Global Development and Technology, 5*(1–2), 81–98. Retrieved from https://doi.org/10.1163/156915006777354482.

Sakaiya, T. (1991). *The knowledge value revolution or a history of the future.* Kodansha International.

Salvino, L. (2015). *China's talent recruitment programs: The road to a Nobel Prize and world hegemony in science?* Study of Innovation and Technology in China. Retrieved from https://apps.dtic.mil/sti/pdfs/ADA625270.pdf.

Sanchez-Serra, D., & Marconi, G. (2018, February 23). *Foreign students' tuition fees are a double-edged sword.* University World News. Retrieved from https://www.universityworldnews.com/post.php?story=20180220142151532.

Sarel, M. (1996). Growth in East Asia: What we can and what we cannot infer. *International Monetary Fund Economic Issues, 6,* 1–22. Retrieved from https://www.imf.org/external/pubs/ft/issues1/issue1.pdf.

Saul, S. (2017, May 4). On campuses far from China, still under Beijing's watchful eye. *New York Times.* Retrieved from https://www.nytimes.com/2017/05/04/us/chinese-students-western-campuses-china-influence.html.

Saxenian, A. (2000). *Silicon Valley's new immigrant entrepreneurs* (Working paper no. 15). Center for Comparative Immigration Studies, University of California, San Diego. Retrieved from https://ccis.ucsd.edu/_files/wp15.pdf.

Saxenian, A. (2002). Brain circulation: How high-skill immigration makes everyone better off. *Brookings Review, 20*(1), 28–31. Retrieved from https://doi.org/10.2307/20081018.

Saxenian, A. (2005). From brain drain to brain circulation: Transnational communities and regional upgrading in India and China. *Studies in Comparative International Development, 40*(2), 35–61. Retrieved from https://doi.org/10.1007/BF02686293.

Saxenian, A. (2006). *The new argonauts: Regional advantage in a global economy.* Harvard University Press.

Searight, A. (2020, July 31). *Countering China's influence operations: Lessons from Australia.* Center for Strategic and International Studies. Retrieved from https://www.csis.org/analysis/countering-chinas-influence-operations-lessons-australia.

Senor, D., & Singer, S. (2011). *Start-up nation: The story of Israel's economic miracle.* McClelland & Stewart.

SG101. (n.d.). *Building a multicultural Singapore.* Singaporean Government. Retrieved June 13, 2021, from https://www.sg101.gov.sg/social-national-identity/multicultural/.

Shambaugh, J., Nunn, R., & Portman, B. (2017). *Lessons from the rise of women's labor force participation in Japan.* Hamilton Project & Brookings Institution. Retrieved from https://www.brookings.edu/wp-content/uploads/2017/10/es_11011

7_lessons_from_rise_womens_labor_force_participation_japan_economic_anal
ysis.pdf.

Shanghai Ranking Consultancy. (2003). *Academic Ranking of World Universities*. Retrieved from https://www.shanghairanking.com/rankings/arwu/2003.

Shanghai Ranking Consultancy. (2013). *Academic Ranking of World Universities*. Retrieved from https://www.shanghairanking.com/rankings/arwu/2013.

Sharma, K. (2018, July 30). *IITs, IIMs, NITs have just 3% of total students but get 50% of government funds*. ThePrint. Retrieved from https://theprint.in/india/gover
nance/iits-iims-nits-have-just-3-of-total-students-but-get-50-of-government-funds
/89976/.

Sharma, Y. (2013, May 25). *"Thousand Talents" academic return scheme under review*. University World News. Retrieved from https://www.universityworldnews
.com/post.php?story=20130524153852829.

Sharma, Y. (2013, May 28). China's effort to recruit top academic talent faces hurdles. *Chronicle of Higher Education*. https://www.chronicle.com/article/chinas
-effort-to-recruit-top-academic-talent-faces-hurdles/.

Sharpe, M. O. (2010). When ethnic returnees are *de facto* guestworkers: What does the introduction of Latin American Japanese *Nikkeijin* (Japanese descendants) (LAN) suggest for Japan's definition of nationality, citizenship, and immigration policy? *Policy and Society, 29*(4), 357–369. Retrieved from https://doi.org/10
.1016/j.polsoc.2010.09.009.

Shear, M. D., & Jordan, M. (2020, June 22). Trump suspends visas allowing hundreds of thousands of foreigners to work in the U.S. *New York Times*. Retrieved from https://www.nytimes.com/2020/06/22/us/politics/trump-h1b-work-v
isas.html.

Shi, D., Liu, W., & Wang, Y. (2023). Has China's Young Thousand Talents Program been successful in recruiting and nurturing top-caliber scientists? *Science, 379*(6627), 62–65. Retrieved from https://doi.org/10.1126/science.abq1218.

Shimbori, M. (1981). The Japanese academic profession. *Higher Education, 10*(1), 75–87. Retrieved from https://doi.org/10.1007/BF00154894.

Shin, G. W. (2006). *Ethnic nationalism in Korea: Genealogy, politics, and legacy*. Stanford University Press.

Shin, G.-W., & Choi, J. N. (2015). *Global talent: Skilled labor as social capital in Korea*. Stanford University Press.

Shin, G. W., Choi, J. N., & Moon, R. J. (2019). Skilled migrants as human and social capital in Korea. *Asian Survey, 59*(4), 673–692. Retrieved from https://doi.or
g/10.1525/as.2019.59.4.673.

Shin, G.-W., & Gordon, H. M. (2024). Toward a portfolio theory of talent development: Insights from financial theory, illustrations from the Asia-Pacific. *World Development, 184*, 1–14.

Shirakawa, N., Furukawa, T., Hayashi, K., & Masaroshi, T. (2014). *Double-loop benchmarking methods in the era of data deluge: An empirical scientometric study and assessment of Japan's Galapagos syndrome in scientific research activities* [Conference presentation]. 2014 Portland International Conference on Management of Engineering & Technology (PICMET), Portland, OR, United States.

Siar, S. (2014). Diaspora knowledge transfer as a development strategy for capturing the gains of skilled migration. *Asian and Pacific Migration Journal, 23*(3), 299–323. Retrieved from https://doi.org/10.1177/011719681402300303.

Silver, L. (2021, December 6). *Amid pandemic, international student enrollment at U.S. universities fell 15% in the 2020–21 school year.* Pew Research Center. Retrieved from https://www.pewresearch.org/fact-tank/2021/12/06/amid-pandemic-international-student-enrollment-at-u-s-universities-fell-15-in-the-2020–21-school-year/.

Silver, L., Devlin, K., & Huang, C. (2020, October 6). *Unfavorable views of China reach historic highs in many countries.* Pew Research Center. Retrieved from https://www.pewresearch.org/global/2020/10/06/unfavorable-views-of-china-reach-historic-highs-in-many-countries/pg_2020-10-06_global-views-china_0–05/.

Silver, L., Huang, C., & Clancy, L. (2022, June 29). *Negative views of China tied to critical views of its policies on human rights.* Pew Research Center. Retrieved from https://www.pewresearch.org/global/2022/06/29/negative-views-of-china-tied-to-critical-views-of-its-policies-on-human-rights/.

Singaporean Housing & Development Board. (n.d.). *Ethnic integration policy (EIP) and Singapore permanent resident (SPR) quota.* Government of Singapore. Retrieved June 15, 2023, from https://www.hdb.gov.sg/cs/infoweb/residential/buying-a-flat/buying-procedure-for-resale-flats/plan-source-and-contract/planning-considerations/eip-spr-quota.

Singh, J., & Krishna, V. V. (2015). Trends in brain drain, gain and circulation: Indian experience of knowledge workers. *Science, Technology and Society, 20*(3), 300–321. Retrieved from https://doi.org/10.1177/0971721815597132.

Smith, A. D. (1991). *National identity.* University of Nevada Press.

Smith, D., Wykes, J., Jayarajah, S., & Fabijanic, T. (2010). *Citizenship in Australia.* Department of Immigration and Citizenship. Retrieved from https://www.homeaffairs.gov.au/research-and-stats/files/citizenship-in-australia-2011.pdf.

Social Research Centre. (2021). *2021 International Graduate Outcomes Survey.* Retrieved from https://www.qilt.edu.au/docs/default-source/default-document-library/2021-gos-international-reportb5ff0a7af7a54ca2a1ebc620f2570151.pdf?sfvrsn=845a4689_0.

Song, H. (1997). From brain drain to reverse brain drain: Three decades of Korean experience. *Science, Technology and Society, 2*(2), 317–345. Retrieved from https://doi.org/10.1177/097172189700020020.

Sonnemaker, T., & Zaveri, P. (2020, June 22). *Amazon, Google, Apple, and other tech companies are speaking out against Trump's freeze on immigrant work visas*. Business Insider. Retrieved from https://www.businessinsider.com/amazon-google-twi tter-speak-out-against-trump-h1b-visa-freeze-2020–6.

Sorrells, M. (2019, February 11). *China, Part 2: A conversation with Ctrip founder James Liang*. PhocusWire. Retrieved from https://www.phocuswire.com/China-se ries-part-2-Ctrip-James-Liang.

Spinks, H. (2016, February 25). *Overseas students: Immigration policy changes 1997–2015*. Parliament of Australia. Retrieved from https://www.aph.gov.au/About _Parliament/Parliamentary_Departments/Parliamentary_Library/pubs/rp/rp1516/ OverseasStudents.

Spy fears prompt China to censor its own recruitment drive. (2018, October 19). Bloomberg. Retrieved from https://www.bloomberg.com/news/articles/2018-09-19 /china-censors-mentions-of-thousand-talents-as-spy-fears-grow.

Sriram, A., & Lehmann, A. (2020, August 30). *4 out of 5 international students are still in Australia—how we treat them will have consequences*. The Conversation. Retrieved from https://theconversation.com/4-out-of-5-international-students-are -still-in-australia-how-we-treat-them-will-have-consequences-145099.

Stanford Center at Peking University. (n.d.). *About SCPKU*. Stanford University. Retrieved November 1, 2022, from https://scpku.fsi.stanford.edu/.

Startup Muster. (2017). *2017 annual report*. Retrieved from https://www.startu pmuster.com/reports.

Stewart, D. (2010, June 12). Slowing Japan's Galapagos syndrome. *Huffington Post*. Retrieved from https://www.huffpost.com/entry/slowing-japans-galapagos_ b_557446.

Stiglitz, J. E. (1996). Some lessons from the East Asian miracle. *World Bank Research Observer, 11*(2), 151–177. Retrieved from https://www.jstor.org/stable/3986429.

Study in Japan. (n.d.). *Chapter 1: Employment environment in Japan*. Japan Student Services Organization. Retrieved January 3, 2021, from https://www.studyin japan.go.jp/en/job/employment/general-info/injapan.html.

Study International. (2018, April 10). *South Korea drops entry requirements, offers scholarships to international students*. Retrieved from https://www.studyinternation al.com/news/south-korea-drops-entry-requirements-offers-scholarships-internatio nal-students/.

Su, H. J. J. (2018, March 16). *A healthy circulation of talent mobility boosts quality*. University World News. Retrieved from https://www.universityworldnews .com/post.php?story=20180306120646729.

Subramanian, A. (2015). Making merit: The Indian institutes of technology and the social life of caste. *Comparative Studies in Society and History, 57*(2), 291–322. Retrieved from https://doi.org/10.1017/S0010417515000043.

Subramanian, A. (2019). *The caste of merit: Engineering education in India*. Harvard University Press.

Sumitomo Corporation. (2020). *Environmental, social, governance communication book 2020* (Vol.1). Retrieved from https://www.sumitomocorp.com/jp/-/media/Files/hq/sustainability/report/esg/esg-2020v1.pdf?la=en.

Sumption, M., & Brindle, B. (2023, September 29). *Work visas and migrant workers in the UK*. Migration Observatory, University of Oxford. Retrieved from https://migrationobservatory.ox.ac.uk/resources/briefings/work-visas-and-migrant-workers-in-the-uk/.

Sun, L. (2021, December 16). Xi Jinping says China will exhaust all means to lure global talent. *South China Morning Post*. Retrieved from https://www.scmp.com/economy/china-economy/article/3159975/xi-jinping-says-china-will-exhaust-all-means-lure-global.

Susantono, B. (2015, September 29). Stopping ASEAN's brain drain. *Phnom Penh Post*. Retrieved from https://www.phnompenhpost.com/columns/stopping-a-seans-brain-drain.

Suzuki, F. (2004). *The diversification of employment patterns in Japan* [Conference presentation]. IIRA Fifth Asian Regional Congress, Seoul, Korea. Retrieved from https://library.fes.de/pdf-files/gurn/00194.pdf.

Tabuchi, H. (2009, July 19). Why Japan's cellphones haven't gone global. *New York Times*. Retrieved from https://www.nytimes.com/2009/07/20/technology/20cell.html.

Talent Corporation Malaysia Berhad. (n.d.). *REP by TalentCorp*. Retrieved October 29, 2024, from https://rep.talentcorp.com.my/.

Talent Development Office. (2011). "长江学者奖励计划"简介 [Brief introduction of "Changjiang Scholars award scheme"]. People's Republic of China Ministry of Education. Retrieved from https://web.archive.org/web/20111211220313mp_/http://www.cksp.edu.cn/news/16/16-20070319-136.htm.

Tan, E. (2014). Human capital theory: A holistic criticism. *Review of Educational Research*, *84*(3), 411–445. Retrieved from https://doi.org/10.3102/0034654314533269.

Tan, J. (2005). Growth of industry clusters and innovation: Lessons from Beijing Zhongguancun Science Park. *Journal of Business Venturing*, *21*(6), 827–850. Retrieved from https://doi.org/10.1016/j.jbusvent.2005.06.006.

Tao, Y. (2021). Chinese students abroad in the time of pandemic: An Australian view. In J. Golley, L. Jaivin, & S. Strange (Eds.), *Crisis: China story yearbook* (pp. 290–304). Australian National University Press. Retrieved from https://doi.org/10.2307/j.ctv1m9x316.30.

Teichler, U. (1997). Higher education in Japan: A view from outside. *Higher Education*, *34*(2), 275–298. Retrieved from https://doi.org/10.1023/A:1003032909075.

Terakura, K. (2009). 我が国における留学生受け入れ政策：これまでの経緯と留学生三十万人計画の策定へ [Japan's past policies of receiving international students: Policy background and the formation of the three hundred thousand international students' plan]. *Refarensu*, (698), 51–72. Retrieved from http://www.ndl.go.jp/jp/datalpublication/refer/200903_698/069803.pdf.

Tertiary Education Quality and Standards Agency. (2018). *Statistics report on TEQSA registered higher education providers*. Australian Government. Retrieved from https://files.eric.ed.gov/fulltext/ED592405.pdf.

Tharenou, P., & Seet, P. S. (2014). China's reverse brain drain: Regaining and retaining talent. *International Studies of Management & Organization*, 44(2), 55–74. Retrieved from https://doi.org/10.2753/IMO0020–8825440203.

Tharoor, S. (2013, January 15). *The global Indian*. Project Syndicate. Retrieved from https://www.project-syndicate.org/commentary/india-s-diaspora-at-home-by-shashi-tharoor.

Tian, F. (2016). Brain circulation, diaspora and scientific progress: A study of the international migration of Chinese scientists, 1998–2006. *Asian and Pacific Migration Journal*, 25(3), 296–319. Retrieved from https://doi.org/10.1177/011719681 66566.

TiE Global. (n.d.a). *Annual report 2020*. Retrieved October 28, 2024, from https://tie.org/wp-content/uploads/2022/05/2020-Annual-Report.pdf.

TiE Global. (n.d.b). *TiE regions and chapters*. Retrieved September 14, 2021, from https://tie.org/tie-regions-chapters/.

Tiku, N. (2020, October 27). India's engineers have thrived in Silicon Valley: So has its caste system. *Washington Post*. Retrieved from https://www.washingtonpost.com/technology/2020/10/27/indian-caste-bias-silicon-valley/.

Tilak, J. B. G. (2001). *Building human capital: What others can learn* (Working paper). World Bank Institute. Retrieved from https://documents1.worldbank.org/curated/en/412751468770664542/pdf/multiopage.pdf.

Tran, L. T., Rahimi, M., Tan, G., Dang, X. T., & Le, N. (2020). Post-study work for international graduates in Australia: Opportunity to enhance employability, get a return on investment or secure migration? *Globalisation, Societies and Education*, 18(5), 495–510. Retrieved from https://doi.org/10.1080/14767724.2020.1 789449.

Treyz, F. R., Stottlemyer, C., & Motamedi, R. (2013, July 17). *Key components of immigration reform: An analysis of the economic effects of creating a pathway to legal status, expanding high-skilled visas, & reforming lesser-skilled visas*. Regional Economic Models. Retrieved from http://www.remi.com/wp-content/uploads/2017/10/50-Key-Components-of-Immigration-Reform.pdf.

Tsai, K. S. (2017). *Elite returnees in Beijing and Bangalore: Information technology and beyond* (Working paper no. 2017–47). HKUST Institute for Emerging

Market Studies. Retrieved from https://iems.ust.hk/publications/iems-working-pa pers/tsai-elite-returnees-beijing-bangalore.

Tsay, C. (2003). Taiwan: Significance, characteristics and policies on return skilled migration. In R. Iredale, F. Guo, & S. Rozario (Eds.), *Return migration in the Asia Pacific* (pp. 112–135). Edward Elgar.

Tsuneyoshi, R. (2017). Exceptionalism in Japanese education and its implications. In R. Tsuneyoshi (Ed.), *Globalization and Japanese exceptionalism in education: Insiders' views into a changing system* (pp. 19–42). Taylor & Francis.

Tu, W.-M. (Ed.). (1996). *Confucian traditions in East Asian modernity*. Harvard University Press.

Tung, R. L. (2008). Brain circulation, diaspora, and international competitiveness. *European Management Journal, 26*(5), 298–304. Retrieved from https://doi.or g/10.1016/j.emj.2008.03.005.

Tzanakou, C., & Henderson, E. F. (2021). Stuck and sticky in mobile academia: Reconfiguring the im/mobility binary. *Higher Education, 82*(4), 685–693. Retrieved from https://doi.org/10.1007/s10734-021-00710-x.

Umakoshi, T. (1997). Internationalization of Japanese higher education in the 1980's and early 1990's. *Higher Education, 34*(2), 259–273. Retrieved from https://d oi.org/10.1023/A:1003049301267.

UNESCO. (2022). *Higher education: How do we unleash the talent of the next generation?* Retrieved from https://www.unesco.org/en/articles/higher-education-h ow-do-we-unleash-talent-next-generation.

UNESCO Institute for Statistics. (n.d.). *Other policy relevant indicators: Inbound mobility rate*. Retrieved September 28, 2021, from http://data.uis.unesco.org /#.

UNESCO-UNEVOC International Centre for Technical and Vocational Education and Training. (2014, May). *World TVET database: United States of America*. US Centre on Education and Training for Employment. Retrieved from https ://unevoc.unesco.org/wtdb/worldtvetdatabase_usa_en.pdf.

United Nations Development Programme. (2022). *Latest Human Development Index ranking*. Human Development Reports. Retrieved from http://hdr.undp.org /en/content/latest-human-development-index-ranking.

University allies with Hello Work to help foreign students find jobs. (2020, November 6). *Japan Times*. Retrieved from https://www.japantimes.co.jp/news/20 20/11/06/national/university-job-office-help-foreign-students-find-employment-ja pan/.

University of Tokyo. (n.d.a). *PEAK admission statistics*. Retrieved April 3, 2023, from https://peak.c.u-tokyo.ac.jp/whypeak/documents/index.html.

University of Tokyo. (n.d.b). *PEAK graduates data*. Retrieved April 3, 2023, from https://peak.c.u-tokyo.ac.jp/courses/careers-information/l4/peakgraduates.html.

University of Tokyo. (n.d.c). *Strategic partnership project.* Retrieved June 20, 2022, from https://www.u-tokyo.ac.jp/en/academics/sp-uni.html.

University of Tokyo. (n.d.d). *Top Global University Project.* Retrieved June 15, 2020, from https://www.u-tokyo.ac.jp/en/academics/sgu.html.

University of Tokyo gives up on plan to start academic year in autumn. (2013, June 20). *Japan Today.* Retrieved from https://japantoday.com/category/national/university-of-tokyo-gives-up-on-plan-to-start-academic-year-in-autumn.

UniversityRankings.ch. (n.d.). *Shanghai Jiao Tong ranking.* Retrieved August 24, 2021, from https://www.universityrankings.ch/.

Upadhya, C. (2004). A new transnational capitalist class? Capital flows, business networks and entrepreneurs in the Indian software industry. *Economic and Political Weekly, 39*(48), 5141–5151. Retrieved from http://www.jstor.org/stable/4415838.

Upadhya, C. (2013). Return of the global Indian: Software professionals and the worlding of Bangalore. In B. Xiang, B. S. A. Yeoh, & M. Toyota (Eds.), *Return: Nationalizing transnational mobility in Asia* (pp.141–161). Duke University Press.

Upadhya, C., & Rutten, M. (2012). Migration, transnational flows, and development in India: A regional perspective. *Economic and Political Weekly, 47*(19), 54–62. Retrieved from http://www.jstor.org/stable/23214977.

US Attorney's Office District of Massachusetts. (2021, December 21). *Harvard University professor convicted of making false statements and tax offenses* [Press release]. US Department of Justice. Retrieved from https://www.justice.gov/usao-ma/pr/harvard-university-professor-convicted-making-false-statements-and-tax-offenses.

US Bureau of Consular Affairs. (1966–2020). *Report of the Visa Office.* US Department of State. Retrieved from https://travel.state.gov/content/travel/en/legal/visa-law0/visa-statistics/annual-reports.html.

US Citizenship and Immigration Services. (n.d.). *Optional practical training extension for STEM students (STEM OPT).* US Department of Homeland Security. Retrieved September 28, 2021, from https://www.uscis.gov/working-in-the-united-states/students-and-exchange-visitors/optional-practical-training-extension-for-stem-students-stem-opt.

Ushiogi, M. (1997). Japanese graduate education and its problems. *Higher Education, 34*(2), 237–244. Retrieved from https://www.jstor.org/stable/3448179.

Vandenberg, P. (2016). Institutions to attract talent to the People's Republic of China. In K. Kikkawa & K. Hull (Eds.), *Labor migration in Asia: Building effective institutions* (pp. 45–54). Asia Development Bank Institute, International Labour Organization, & Organisation for Economic Co-operation and Development.

Vogel, E. (1979). *Japan as number one: Lessons for America.* Harvard University Press.

Vogel, E. (1991). *The Four Little Dragons: The spread of industrialization in East Asia.* Harvard University Press.

Wadhwa, V., Jain, S., Saxenian, A., Gereffi, G., & Wang, H. (2011, April 8). *The grass is indeed greener in India and China for returnee entrepreneurs: America's new immigrant entrepreneurs—Part VI.* Retrieved from http://dx.doi.org/10.2139/ssrn.1 824670.

Wadhwa, V., Saxenian, A., Rissing, B. A., & Gereffi, G. (2007, January 4). *America's new immigrant entrepreneurs: Part I* (Working paper no. 23). Duke Science, Technology & Innovation. Retrieved from http://dx.doi.org/10.2139/ssrn.990 152.

Wadhwa, V., Saxenian, A., & Siciliano, F. D. (2012, October 1). *Then and now: America's new immigrant entrepreneurs, part VII* (Working paper no. 215987). Stanford Public Law. Retrieved from http://dx.doi.org/10.2139/ssrn.2159875.

Walton-Roberts, M., & Rajan, S. I. (2020, January 23). *Global demand for medical professionals drives Indians abroad despite acute domestic health-care worker shortages.* Migration Policy Institute. Retrieved from https://www.migrationpolicy .org/article/global-demand-medical-professionals-drives-indians-abroad.

Wang, D. (2013). *Reversing the brain drain? Skilled return migration and the global movement of expert knowledge* (Research paper no. 15–14) [Dissertation executive summary]. Columbia Business School. Retrieved from http://dx.doi.org/10.2 139/ssrn.2549315.

Wang, H. (2012). *Globalizing China: The influence, strategies and successes of Chinese returnee entrepreneurs.* Emerald Group.

Wang, H. (2013). China's return migration and its impact on home development. *UN Chronicle, 50*(3), 34–36. Retrieved from https://www.un.org/en/chronicl e/article/chinas-return-migration-and-its-impact-home-development.

Wang, H., & Bao, Y. (2015). *Reverse migration in contemporary China: Returnees, entrepreneurship and the Chinese economy.* Springer.

Wang, H., Zweig, D., & Lin, X. (2011). Returnee entrepreneurs: Impact on China's globalization process. *Journal of Contemporary China, 20*(70), 413–431. Retrieved from https://doi.org/10.1080/10670564.2011.565174.

Wang, Z. (2010). Transnational science during the Cold War: The case of Chinese/American scientists. *ISIS, 101*(2), 367–377. Retrieved from https://doi.org/10.1 086/653098.

Warner, M. (2000, May 15). The Indians of Silicon Valley: The hidden geniuses of the tech revolution are Indian engineers. *Fortune.* Retrieved from https://mone y.cnn.com/magazines/fortune/fortune_archive/2000/05/15/279748/index.htm.

Washington, E. (n.d.). *Chinese on the goldfields.* Museums of History NSW. Retrieved September 27, 2021, from https://sydneylivingmuseums.com.au/stories/ chinese-goldfields.

Welcoming Australia. (2019, March 31). *Welcoming cities*. Retrieved from https ://welcoming.org.au/initiatives/welcoming-cities/#:~:text=Welcoming%20Cities% 20is%20a%20national,cultural%2C%20economic%20and%20civic%20life.

Welcoming Australia. (2021, March 23). *National unity week*. Retrieved from h ttps://welcoming.org.au/initiatives/national-unity-week/.

Wells, W. A. (2007). The returning tide: How China, the world's most populous country, is building a competitive research base. *Journal of Cell Biology*, *176*(4), 376–401. Retrieved from https://doi.org/10.1083/jcb.200701150.

White, K. (2019, December). *Publications output: U.S. trends and international comparisons*. National Science Foundation. Retrieved from https://ncses.nsf.gov/p ubs/nsb20206.

Why China is lavishing money on foreign students. (2019, January 26). *The Economist*. Retrieved from https://www.economist.com/china/2019/01/26/why-chi na-is-lavishing-money-on-foreign-students.

Williams, A. M. (2007). Listen to me, learn with me: International migration and knowledge transfer. *British Journal of Industrial Relations*, *45*(2), 361–382 Retrieved from https://doi.org/10.1111/j.1467–8543.2007.00618.x.

Williams, J. (2017, April 18). Australian rules would make so-called 457 visa harder for migrants. *New York Times*. Retrieved from https://www.nytimes.com/2 017/04/18/world/australia/malcolm-turnbull-australia-457-visas.html.

Wohlner, R. (2023, July 5). *Why it's important to diversify your investing portfolio*. TIME Stamped. Retrieved from https://time.com/personal-finance/article/import ance-of-diversification/.

Wolff, V., Opoku-Owusu, S., & Bloe, D. (2016). *Diaspora engagement on country entrepreneurship and investment: Policy trends and notable practices in the Rabat Process region*. International Centre for Migration Policy Development & African Foundation for Development. Retrieved from https://www.rabat-process.org/ima ges/RabatProcess/Documents/background-paper-thematic-meeting-bamako-201 6-diaspora-engagement-rabat-process.pdf.

Womack, J. P., Jones, D. T., & Roos, D. (1990). *The machine that changed the world*. Harper Perennial.

Wong, J. (2004). The adaptive developmental state in East Asia. *Journal of East Asian Studies*, *4*(3), 345–362. Retrieved from https://www.jstor.org/stable/23417946.

Wong, K. Y., & Yip, C. K. (1999). Education, economic growth, and brain drain. *Journal of Economic Dynamics and Control*, *23*(5–6), 699–726. Retrieved from http://dx.doi.org/10.1016/S0165–1889(98)00040–2.

Woo, J. (2022). *Confronting South Korea's next crisis: Rigidities, polarization, and fear of Japanification*. Oxford University Press.

World Bank. (n.d.a). *GDP ranking*. Retrieved January 3, 2022, from https://da tacatalog.worldbank.org/dataset/gdp-ranking.

World Bank. (n.d.b). *World development indicators.* Retrieved October 28, 2024, from https://datacatalog.worldbank.org/dataset/world-development-indicators.

World Bank. (2019, March 19). *The human capital project: Frequently asked questions.* Retrieved from https://www.worldbank.org/en/publication/human-capital/brief/the-human-capital-project-frequently-asked-questions#HCP2.

World Bank. (2023a). *Labor force participation rate (% of population).* World Bank Group Gender Data Portal. Retrieved from https://genderdata.worldbank.org/indicators/sl-tlf-acti-zs/?gender=female&geos=&view=trend.

World Bank. (2023b). *Tertiary education.* Retrieved from https://www.worldbank.org/en/topic/tertiaryeducation.

World Food Prize Foundation. (n.d.). *Dr. Zhangliang Chen.* Retrieved November 15, 2024, from https://www.worldfoodprize.org/en/about_the_foundation/council_of_advisors_old/dr_zhangliang_chen/?nodeID=87773&audienceID=1.

World university rankings. (2021). *Times Higher Education.* Retrieved from https://www.timeshighereducation.com/world-university-rankings/2021/world-ranking#!/page/0/length/25/sort_by/rank/sort_order/asc/cols/stats.

Wray, C. (2020, July 7). *The threat posed by the Chinese government and the Chinese Communist Party to the economic and national security of the United States* [Transcript]. Federal Bureau of Investigation. Retrieved from https://www.fbi.gov/news/speeches/the-threat-posed-by-the-chinese-government-and-the-chinese-communist-party-to-the-economic-and-national-security-of-the-united-states.

Xiang, B. (2005, January 1). *Promoting knowledge exchange through diaspora networks (the case of People's Republic of China).* Asian Development Bank. Retrieved from https://www.compas.ox.ac.uk/publication/er-2005-knowledge_exchange_diaspora_china_adb.

Xie, Y., Lin, X., Li, J., & Huang, J. (2023). Caught in the crossfire: Fears of Chinese-American scientists. *Proceedings of the National Academy of Sciences,* *120*(27), 1–5. Retrieved from https://doi.org/10.1073/pnas.2216248120.

Xinhua News Agency. (2010, September 16). 我国首次启动实施"海外赤子为国服务行动计划" [China launched and implemented the "Overseas Red Son Service Action Plan for the Country" for the first time]. Central People's Government of the People's Republic of China. Retrieved from http://www.gov.cn/jrzg/2010–09/16/content_1704114.htm.

Xinhua News Agency. (2017, October 29). 中国迎来留学生"归国潮"背后，存在这个根本性转变 [Behind China's "returning tide" of overseas students, there is a fundamental change]. XinhuaNet. Retrieved from http://www.xinhuanet.com//politics/2017–10/29/c_1121871668.htm.

Yam, K. (2022, November 15). *After being falsely accused of spying for China, Sherry Chen wins significant settlement.* NBC News. Retrieved from https://www.n

bcnews.com/news/asian-america/falsely-accused-spying-china-sherry-chen-wins-s
ignificant-settlement-rcna56847.

Yam, K. (2023, May 25). *After being wrongly accused of spying for China, professor wins appeal to sue the government.* NBC News. Retrieved from https://www.nbcne
ws.com/news/asian-america/wrongfully-accused-spying-china-professor-wins-app
eal-sue-government-rcna86109.

Yang, L., & Marini, G. (2019). Research productivity of Chinese Young Thou-sand Talents. *International Higher Education*, (97), 17–18. Retrieved from https://d
oi.org/10.6017/ihe.2019.97.10944.

Yang, M. (2007). What attracts mainland Chinese students to Australian higher education. *Studies in Learning, Evaluation, Innovation and Development*, 4(2), 1–12. Retrieved from https://hdl.handle.net/10018/5964.

Yang, P. (2022). China in the global field of international student mobility: An analysis of economic, human and symbolic capitals. *Compare: A Journal of Comparative and International Education*, 52(2), 308–326. Retrieved from https://doi.or
g/10.1080/03057925.2020.1764334.

Yang, R. (2009). Enter the dragon? China's higher education returns to the world community: The case of the Peking University personnel reforms. In J. C. Smart (Ed.), *Higher education: Handbook of theory and research* (Vol. 24, pp. 239–282). Springer. Retrieved from https://doi.org/10.1007/978-1-4020-9628-0_11.

Yang, R. (2010, March 25). Peking University's personnel reforms. *International Higher Education*, (60), 10–11. Retrieved from https://doi.org/10.6017/ihe.2010.60.8
500.

Yarbrough, C. (2015). Singapore's talent strategy. *International Educator*, 24(4), 16–19.

Yendamuri, P., & Ingilizian, Z. (2019, December 20). *In 2020 Asia will have the world's largest GDP: Here's what that means.* World Economic Forum. Retrieved from https://www.weforum.org/agenda/2019/12/asia-economic-growth/.

Yokoi, K. (2014). The Colombo Plan and industrialization in India: Technical cooperation for the Indian Institutes of Technology. In S. Akita, G. Krozewski, & S. Watanabe (Eds.), *The transformation of the international order of Asia: Decolonization, the Cold War, and the Colombo Plan* (pp. 74–95). Routledge.

Yonezawa, A. (2015). Inbreeding in Japanese higher education: Inching toward openness in a globalized context. In M. Yudkevich, P. G. Altbach, & L. E. Rum-bley (Eds.), *Academic inbreeding and mobility in higher education* (pp. 99–129). Pal-grave MacMillan.

Yonezawa, A. (2020). Challenges of the Japanese higher education amidst population decline and globalization. *Globalisation, Societies and Education*, 18(1), 43–52. Retrieved from https://doi.org/10.1080/14767724.2019.1690085.

Yonezawa, A., & Shimmi, Y. (2017). Japan's challenge in fostering global human resources: Policy debates and practices. In R. Tsuneyoshi (Ed.), *Globalization and Japanese "exceptionalism" in education: Insiders' views into a changing system* (pp. 43–60). Taylor & Francis.

Zagade, A., & Desai, S. P. (2017). Brain drain or brain circulation: A study of returnee professionals in India. *Journal of Commerce and Management Thought, 8*(3), 422–435. Retrieved from https://doi.org/10.5958/0976–478X.2017.00025.8.

Zapata-Barrero, R., & Rezaei, S. (2019). Diaspora governance and transnational entrepreneurship: The rise of an emerging social global pattern in migration studies. *Journal of Ethnic and Migration Studies, 46*(10), 1959–1973. Retrieved from https://doi.org/10.1080/1369183X.2018.1559990.

Zhang, G., & Qin, Z. (2008, January 1). *The development of private businesses in China: 1978–2004* [Conference paper]. Asia-Pacific Economic and Business History Conference. University of Melbourne, Melbourne, Victoria, Australia. Retrieved from https://ro.uow.edu.au/commpapers/1872.

Zhang, S. (2006, February 27). 薛其坤："杰青"是个好起点 [Xue Qikun: "Jie Qing" is a good starting point]. National Natural Science Foundation of China. Retrieved from http://www.nsfc.gov.cn/publish/portal0/tab440/info59503.htm.

Zhou, Y. (2017, April 18). *Most H-1B workers are paid less, but it depends on the type of job.* AP News. Retrieved from https://apnews.com/article/archive-immigration-h-1b-visa-politics-873580003.

Zhu, J. (2019). The composition and evolution of China's high-level talent programs in higher education. *ECNU Review of Education, 2*(1), 104–110. Retrieved from https://doi.org/10.1177/2096531119840869.

Ziguras, C., & Gribble, C. (2015). Policy responses to address student "brain drain": An assessment of measures intended to reduce the emigration of Singaporean international students. *Journal of Studies in International Education, 19*(3), 246–264. Retrieved from https://doi.org/10.1177/1028315314561121.

Zou, S. (2019, March 28). Chinese students studying abroad up 8.83%. *China Daily.* Retrieved from http://www.chinadaily.com.cn/a/201903/28/WS5c9c355da31 0484226ob30eb.html.

Zweig, D. (2006). Competing for talent: China's strategies to reverse the brain drain. *International Labour Review, 145,* 65–90. Retrieved from https://doi.org/10.1 111/j.1564–913X.2006.tb00010.x.

Zweig, D. (2017, May 19). *Chinese students in America: Who returns, who remains, who benefits?* [Video]. Wilson Center. Retrieved from https://www.wilsoncenter.org/event/chinese-students-america-who-returns-who-remains-who-benefits.

Zweig, D. (2017). Leaders, bureaucrats and institutional culture: The struggle over bringing back China's top overseas talent. In A. Goldstein & J. deLisle (Eds.), *China's global engagement* (pp. 325–358). Brookings Institution Press.

Zweig, D., & Changgui, C. (2013). *China's brain drain to the United States.* Routledge.

Zweig, D., Changgui, C., & Rosen, S. (2004, September 28). Globalization and transnational human capital: Overseas and returnee scholars to China. *China Quarterly, 179*, 735–757. Retrieved from https://doi.org/10.1017/S0305741004000566.

Zweig, D., & Kang, S. (2020, May 5). *America challenges China's national talent programs*. Center for Strategic and International Studies. Retrieved from https://www.csis.org/analysis/america-challenges-chinas-national-talent-programs.

Zweig, D., Kang, S., & Wang, H. (2020). "The best are yet to come": State programs, domestic resistance and reverse migration of high-level talent to China. *Journal of Contemporary China, 29*(125), 776–791. Retrieved from https://doi.org/10.1080/10670564.2019.1705003.

Zweig, D., & Rosen, S. (2003, August 5). *How China trained a new generation abroad*. SciDev.Net. Retrieved from https://www.scidev.net/global/features/how-china-trained-a-new-generation-abroad/.

Zweig, D., & Wang, H. (2013). Can China bring back the best? The Communist Party organizes China's search for talent. *China Quarterly, 215*, 590–615. Retrieved from https://www.jstor.org/stable/23510804.

Zwetsloot, R., Corrigan, J., Weinstein, E., Peterson, D., Gehlhaus, D., & Fedasiuk, R. (2021, August). *China is fast outpacing U.S. STEM PhD growth*. Center for Security and Emerging Technology. Retrieved from https://doi.org/10.51593/20210018.

Zwetsloot, R., Dunham, J., Arnold, Z., & Huang, T. (2019). *Keeping top AI talent in the United States*. Center for Security and Emerging Technology. Retrieved from https://cset.georgetown.edu/publication/keeping-top-ai-talent-in-the-united-states/.

Index

Page numbers in *italics* refer to tables and figures.

The New Great Game: China and South and
Central Asia in the Era of Reform
Edited by Thomas Fingar (2016)

The Colonial Origins of Ethnic Violence in India
Ajay Verghese (2016)

Rebranding Islam: Piety, Prosperity, and a Self-Help Guru
James Bourk Hoesterey (2015)

Global Talent: Skilled Labor as Social Capital in Korea
Gi-Wook Shin and Joon Nak Choi (2015)

Failed Democratization in Prewar Japan:
Breakdown of a Hybrid Regime
Harukata Takenaka (2014)

New Challenges for Maturing Democracies in Korea and Taiwan
Edited by Larry Diamond and Gi-Wook Shin (2014)

Spending Without Taxation: FILP and the Politics of Public Finance in Japan
Gene Park (2011)

The Institutional Imperative: The Politics of
Equitable Development in Southeast Asia
Erik Martinez Kuhonta (2011)

One Alliance, Two Lenses: U.S.-Korea Relations in a New Era
Gi-Wook Shin (2010)

Collective Resistance in China: Why Popular Protests Succeed or Fail
Yongshun Cai (2010)

For a complete listing of titles in this series, visit the
Stanford University Press website, www.sup.org.

www.ingramcontent.com/pod-product-compliance
Lightning Source LLC
Jackson TN
JSHW080726070525
83937JS00002B/3